Black Women in America

T0375120

Black Women in America

SOCIAL SCIENCE PERSPECTIVES

Edited by

Micheline R. Malson

Elisabeth Mudimbe-Boyi

Jean F. O'Barr

and Mary Wyer

THE UNIVERSITY OF CHICAGO PRESS □ *Chicago and London*

The essays in this volume originally appeared in various issues of
SIGNS: JOURNAL OF WOMEN IN CULTURE AND SOCIETY.
Acknowledgment of the original publication data can be found on the
first page of each essay.

The University of Chicago Press, Chicago 60637
The University of Chicago Press, Ltd., London
© 1977, 1979, 1984, 1986, 1988, 1989 and 1990 by The University
of Chicago
All rights reserved. Published 1990
Printed in the United States of America
94 93 92 91   5 4 3 2

Library of Congress Cataloging-in-Publication Data
Black women in America : social science perspectives / Micheline R.
    Malson . . . [et al.].
        p.   cm.
    Includes bibliographical references.
    ISBN 0-226-50295-3 (alk. paper) : $30.00 (est.). — ISBN
0-226-50296-1 (pbk. : alk. paper) : $15.00 (est.)
    1. Afro-American women.   I. Malson, Micheline R.
    E185.86.C29   1990
    305.48'896073—dc20
                                                            89-49110
                                                            CIP

CONTENTS

Inventing Selves and Constituting Community

ACKNOWLEDGMENTS

Essay collections by definition are products of the work of many and this volume is no exception. We thank Cheryl Townsend Gilkes and Deborah McDowell for providing intellectual support and encouragement at a critical point. We thank Jill Petty, Connie Pearcy, and Alice Poffinberger for the energy and commitment they contributed throughout the production process. Finally, we thank the Duke-UNC Center for Research on Women for its contribution to a climate of good will and encouragement for research on black women.

INTRODUCTION

This is a book for the classroom. It is a collection of essays from a diverse group of scholars (some black, some white, some women, some men) who share in common an interest in correcting the record. The record, in scholarly terms, is that official body to which we look for relevant, accurate, complete information about women. The task of teaching this information about black American women is just beginning.[1] This is not to say that research on black women is new, only that there is still much to do, much to learn. Indeed, there is a long tradition of scholarship on the black family, women's work roles and labor force participation, and black women's literature and history.[2] Yet with a few notable exceptions (in historically black schools and colleges and as a result of the pioneering efforts of a few scholars), American institutions of higher education only recently have begun to include materials about black women in the curriculum.

This is a book based on the premise that the task is more than teaching and learning something new. There is unlearning and relearning to be done as well. These articles (all of them published in *Signs* between 1977 and 1989) are based in the social sciences—that is to say that the authors were trained within the conventions of sociology, anthropology, history, public

[1]Authors' decisions about terminology—whether to use "African-American," "Afro-American," "Black," "Black American," and with or without hyphens, with capital letters or lowercase—are complicated ones, and there are good arguments for each choice. All of these choices are evident in these essays. We have tried to honor the choices made for each essay in our discussion of that work.

[2]For a sample of this work, consult any of the following bibliographies: Lenwood G. Davis, *The Black Woman in American Society: A Selected Annotated Bibliography* (Boston: Hall, 1975); Arlene B. Enabulele, *A Resource Guide on Black Women in the United States* (Washington, D.C.: Institute for Urban Affairs and Research, Howard University, 1978); Gloria T. Hull, Patricia Bell Scott, and Barbara Smith, *All the Women Are White, and All the Blacks Are Men, but Some of Us Are Brave: Black Women's Studies* (Old Westbury, N.Y.: Feminist Press, 1982); Phyllis R. Klotman and Wilmer H. Baatz, comps., *The Black Family and the Black Woman: A Bibliography* (New York: Arno Press, 1978); Marilyn Richardson, *Black Women and Religion: A Bibliography* (Boston: Hall, 1980); J. C. Roberts, comp., *Black Lesbians: An Annotated Bibliography* (Weatherby Lake, Missouri: Naiad Press, 1981); Janet Sims, "The Afro-American Woman: Researching Her History," *Reference Service Review* 11, no. 1 (Spring 1980): 9–30; Janet Sims, *The Progress of Afro-American Women: A Selected Bibliography and Resource Guide* (Westport, Conn.: Greenwood Press, 1980); Rosemary M. Stevenson, "Black

policy research, economics, and political science. We have collected together this particular group of readings from *Signs* because their disciplinary diversity complements our intention to represent the social, economic, and individual diversity of black women in America. Moreover, the variety of authors' perspectives, methodologies, and interpretations is good provocation for discussion about the qualities and meanings of cultural diversity in American higher education.

The earliest of the articles, Diane Lewis's "A Response to Inequality: Black Women, Racism, and Sexism" and Bonnie Thornton Dill's "The Dialectics of Black Womanhood," are familiar classics and are reprinted here as benchmarks in the development of black feminist thought. Deborah King, as she wrote "Multiple Jeopardy, Multiple Consciousness: The Context of a Black Feminist Ideology" (included herein) some ten years later, referred to both articles for key points in her argument even while her argument extends and refines the earlier work of Dill and Lewis. So, too, Patricia Hill Collins builds her theoretical exploration of the constructing forces behind black feminist thought in part on the essays by Lewis, Dill, and King as well as that of Cheryl Townsend Gilkes ("Together and in Harness: Women's Traditions in the Sanctified Church"), also reprinted here.

This is not to say that black feminist thought is homogenous. These essays disagree with one another on key assumptions. For instance, Bonnie Thornton Dill's essay emphasizes the importance of recognizing the contradictions that confront women: "Black women must be studied within a dynamic and contradictory framework to understand the complexities of their relations to all aspects of society" (74). Deborah King takes another tack altogether: "Ideological and political choices cannot be assumed to be determined solely by the historical dynamics of racism, sexism, and classism" (295). Her conclusions emphasize the dynamics of the *individual's* negotiation of conflicting social influences. Patricia Hill Collins, in yet another reading, says that African-American women experience a convergence of Afrocentric and feminist values.

Women in the United States: A Bibliographical Essay," *Sage Race Relations Abstracts* 8, no. 4 (November 1983): 1–19; Rosemary M. Stevenson, "Black Women in the United States: A Bibliography of Recent Works," *Black Scholar* 16, no. 2 (March/April 1985): 45–49; Pauline T. Stone, *The Black American Woman in the Social Science Literature* (Ann Arbor, Mich.: Women's Studies Program, University of Michigan, 1978); Sarah M. Washington, "An Annotated Bibliography of Black Women Biographies and Autobiographies for Secondary School Students" (Ph.D. diss., University of Illinois, 1980); Ora Williams, *American Black Women in the Arts and Social Sciences: A Bibliography* (Metuchen, N.J.: Scarecrow Press, 1978). There is also a rapidly growing body of literature on women of color in general. See, e.g., Bernice Redfern, *Women of Color in the United States: A Guide to the Literature* (New York: Garland, 1989); and Andrea Timberlake et al., *Women of Color and Southern Women: A Bibliography of Social Science Research, 1975–1988* (Memphis, Tenn.: Center for Research on Women, Memphis State University, 1988).

   Three articles challenge specific methodological issues and ask questions not about how it is black women view the world but, rather, how the scholarly record views black women. Walter Allen's "Family Roles, Occupational Statuses, and Achievement Orientation among Black Women in the United States" argues that research on achievement orientation must take into account the forces (social and institutional) that systematically deny black women equal opportunity to achieve at levels commensurate with their abilities. Research that fails to do so simply perpetuates stereotypes about black women as underachievers. Similarly, Mary Corcoran, Greg J. Duncan, and Martha S. Hill confront the myth that the earnings gap between women and men can be accounted for fully by the "human capital" explanation—that is, by work-force participation patterns, choices of occupations, education, and acquisition of job skills. Corcoran, Duncan, and Hill maintain that when public policymakers assume that women are earning less than men because of choices the women themselves have made, the policymakers lend weight to the social and institutional forces that have promoted the earnings gap between women and men and between blacks and whites—an earnings gap that continues to threaten the well-being of black children. James Geschwender and Rita Carroll-Seguin, in "Exploding the Myth of African-American Progress," contend that much of contemporary scholarship documenting the closing of the earnings gap between African-American and European-American households overestimates improvements in African-American income because it fails to look comparatively at trends within households. In particular, they warn that the ability of two-earner African-American middle-class households to maintain their incomes is eroding in comparison to two-earner European-American households in the same income brackets. All three articles confront the social science research paradigm that neatly divides work and family, and they support the theoretical insights of Dill and Lewis in formulating research that focuses on the intersection of these two areas.

   Two of the articles, Susan Mann's study of the transition from slavery to sharecropping and Sh'aron Harley's article on the black community in Washington, D.C., at the turn of the century, confront a tension between recognizing that black women in America have never lived within the confines of nineteenth-century notions of protected domesticity and recognizing that this fact has not necessarily meant their relations with black men were free of patriarchal constraint. Both authors argue that racism in American culture has been a more salient force in women's lives than sexism. Yet each sees a different reason why this is so. Harley maintains that the black community honored a sex-based division of labor in part because it protected the rights of women to work in selected jobs. Though Mann focuses on another historical period, she too notes a sex-based division of labor in the Black household. Her argument, however, is that, in the context of Black/white power relations, the division of labor in the sharecropping household served the interests of white landowners, not Black women sharecroppers.

The notion that in order to overcome racism, black women must also confront sexism has a long life in the history of black women in America. Maggie Lena Walker was one of those who most clearly articulated this with what we now call a "womanist consciousness."[3] Elsa Barkley Brown's biographical study of Walker's work expands our understanding of the economic spheres in which black women worked and nuances the family labor/paid labor dichotomy by adding a third dimension, community labor.

It is in the context of her community work that Walker combined her efforts to confront the forces of racism and sexism. Walker's civil rights activities were a part of the Richmond, Virginia, late nineteenth-century black community's efforts to respond to a battery of regressive, racist governmental initiatives. She argued that the economic viability and cohesion of the community depended on the abilities of all of its citizens: that black men could best protect and defend black womanhood by supporting women's rights. Walker's life story, as Barkley Brown recounts it, both challenges and enriches the insights of Lewis's essay. Lewis maintains that black women historically have tended to see racism as the dominant reason for their subordinate position: "Their interests as blacks have taken precedence over their interests as women" (45). She argues that growing numbers of black women became more receptive to the feminist movement when civil rights leaders in the 1950s and 1960s failed to address sexism within the movement and the black community. Her essay concludes that "whether black women develop a sense of common interests that is manifested more in opposition to sexism or to racism will depend upon the structural relationship between the sexes and between the races" (62). By presenting us with a detailed account of Walker's life and her community, then, Barkley Brown has suggested that historically many black women did not accept this either/or choice, challenging us to take up the concept of "womanist" as a more holistic political perspective than that of feminism. Yet Walker's story might also suggest that in fundamental structural ways, the relationships between the races and the sexes have not changed in the last hundred years—a dismal thought.

Maxine Baca Zinn's review of two contemporary research models lends support to Lewis's emphasis on structural approaches. Baca Zinn finds the

[3]"Womanist" is articulated and defined by Alice Walker in *In Search of Our Mothers' Gardens: Womanist Prose* (New York: Harcourt, Brace, Jovanovich, 1983), xi–xiii: "Womanist, 1. . . . Responsible. In Charge. *Serious.* 2. . . . Appreciates . . . women's strength. . . . Committed to survival and wholeness of entire people, male *and* female. Not separatist, except periodically, for health. Traditionally universalist. . . . Traditionally capable. . . . 3. . . . Loves struggle. *Loves* the Folk. Loves herself. *Regardless.* 4. Womanist is to feminist as purple is to lavender."

cultural model too willing to endorse deficiency theories, theories that locate the reasons for poverty outside racist and sexist privileging systems,
theories that locate the reasons for poverty within the culture, family, and
economics of the underclass itself. She argues that the structural approach,
one that recognizes macrostructural forces that shape family trends and demographic patterns, is less likely to "blame the victim" and more likely to
see the ways in which opportunity, marriage, and housing patterns influence an economic community. She critiques those structural approaches,
however, for their failure to address gender as an important analytic category. Class, race, *and* gender must be taken by policymakers as interlocking systems, she maintains, if we are to generate constructive social change
through social policy.

Baca Zinn is concerned about how the scholarly record defines and analyzes influences that are experienced by Black and Hispanic women in general. Diane Sadoff's article, "Black Matrilineage: The Case of Alice Walker
and Zora Neale Hurston," and Patricia Williams's essay, "On Being the Object of Property," examine how individual black women have interpreted
their own particular cross-generational and life course experiences. Sadoff's study of matriliny and literary influences outlines how a womanist consciousness helps to regenerate lost, loving relationships between
generations of black women. Williams's first-person narrative describes the
life course trajectory of a black woman lawyer whose life is a paradox. She
teaches a course on property law, a body of knowledge that has historically
both defined and defiled her. Yet teaching property is how she claims and
transforms a part of herself that society despises, in this case the legacy of
slavery, into a source of strength and self-confidence. Both essays are richly
suggestive about the power of language and discourse in the representation
of black women's experience as these create a space for that experience in
the public record.

In the opening sentence of the opening essay in this collection, Elsa
Barkley Brown ("African-American Women's Quilting: A Framework for
Conceptualizing and Teaching African-American Women's History") points
out that "one of the central problems that confronts those of us who attempt
to teach or write about nonwhite, non-middle-class, non-Western persons
is how to center our work, our teaching, in the lives of the people about
whom we are teaching and writing" (9). Information about black American
women can be collected, corrected, interpreted, challenged, and revised
in the classroom, but this is not enough. Perhaps more important than re-
vising existing concepts and theoretical frameworks is work that frees our
imaginations and allows us to conceive new theories, new language, and
new questions. How can we describe and name an existence that consists of
multiple realities and many different situations of oppression? How do we
teach the psychological responses to multiple social relationships and multiple relationships of oppression? Is there a black women's voice and per-

spective that is distinct and recognizable? What are the ways in which black women's experiences converge and diverge from those of other women?

We offer this collection of essays as our contribution toward recentering our work, our teaching—toward pondering these questions. It is a beginning.

PART I

PATTERNS AND RESISTANCES
PERSPECTIVES ON PROCESS
AND PROGRESS

AFRICAN-AMERICAN WOMEN'S QUILTING: A FRAMEWORK FOR CONCEPTUALIZING AND TEACHING AFRICAN-AMERICAN WOMEN'S HISTORY

ELSA BARKLEY BROWN

One of the central problems that confronts those of us who attempt to teach or write about nonwhite, non-middle-class, non-Western persons is how to center our work, our teaching, in the lives of the people about whom we are teaching and writing. As researchers, this is a persistent problem, but as teachers, it is perhaps an even more enormous problem. No matter how much prior preparation they have had, in large measure our students come to us having learned a particular perspective on the world, having been taught to see and analyze the world in particular ways, and having been

Many of the ideas in this essay were refined through numerous lengthy conversations with Lillian Jones. I have also benefited greatly from my students' frank and detailed evaluations of our efforts as we explored "Black Women in Historical Perspective" at Emory University, 1985–87, and Memphis State University, 1987–88. My ideas have been developed through the practice of teaching, research, and writing. Transferring these ideas to paper rather than practice was difficult; Stephanie Shaw, Dianne Pinderhughes, and Deborah K. King offered the encouragement I needed to be able to do this. Jacquelyn Dowd Hall and my daughter, Nataki H Goodall, read a draft and offered important advice. My thanks for their support.

taught that there are normative experiences and that they are those of white, middle-class, Western men and women.

Thus, the most important and most difficult questions in African-American women's history ask how to center the experiences of African-American women and how to foster in our students the ability to center those experiences. How do our students overcome years of notions of what is normative? While trying to think about these issues in my teaching, I have come to understand that this is not merely an intellectual process. It is not merely a question of whether or not we have learned to analyze in particular kinds of ways, or whether people are able to intellectualize about a variety of experiences. It is also about coming to believe in the possibility of a variety of experiences, a variety of ways of understanding the world, a variety of frameworks of operation, without imposing consciously or unconsciously a notion of the norm. What I have tried to do in my own teaching is to address both the conscious level, through the material, and the unconscious level, through the very structure of the course, thus, perhaps, allowing my students, in Bettina Aptheker's words, to "pivot the center," to center in another experience.[1]

I do not mean that white or male students can learn to feel what it is like to be a Black woman. Rather, I believe that all people can learn to center in another experience, validate it, and judge it by its own standards without need of comparison or need to adopt that framework as their own. Thus, one has no need to "decenter" anyone in order to center someone else;[2] one has only to constantly, appropriately, "pivot the center."[3]

---

[1] Bettina Aptheker, *Tapestries of Life: Women's Work, Women's Consciousness and the Meaning of Daily Life* (Amherst: University of Massachusetts Press, 1989), chap. 1. Aptheker's paradigm avoids the dualistic opposition of center/margin and allows everyone constantly to be at the center of their own experience. She requires herself, as a historian, to look out from numerous centers and thus to maintain the reality that all these centers exist simultaneously. This nonlinear, polyrhythmic way of understanding history highlights the necessary *gumbo ya ya* of an inclusive history. My understanding of Aptheker's framework is based on her presentation in the "Roundtable Discussion: Direction of Scholarship in the Field" at the "Afro-American Women and the Vote: 1837–1965" conference, University of Massachusetts at Amherst, November 1987, our subsequent conversation and communications, and my reading of chapters 1 and 5 of her manuscript. I wish to express my appreciation to her for sharing her book manuscript with me.

[2] I refer here to the presumed need to decenter (and thus invalidate) the experiences of men in order to center women or the experiences of Euro-Americans in order to center African-Americans. Jacquelyn Hall has pointed out to me that such a framework also makes it unnecessary for students and scholars to decenter themselves in order to center the experiences of the people they are studying.

[3] Jacquelyn Dowd Hall's "Partial Truths" urges us to avoid the recreation of monologic histories and emphasizes the importance of creating "a historical practice

African-American women's quilting, I have increasingly come to understand, provides us with a framework to be able to do this. In their discussion of the "Aesthetic Principles of Afro-American Quilts," Maude Southwell Wahlman and John Scully argue that African-American female quiltmakers operate from a different aesthetic sense than Euro-American quiltmakers.

> When the colors of the strips are different from the colors in the row of blocks or designs, two distinct movements can be seen: one along the strips and the other within the designs. . . . This represents a textile aesthetic which has been passed down for generations among Afro-American women who were descendants of Africans. . . . Afro-American quilters do not seem interested in a uniform color scheme. They use several methods of playing with colors to create unpredictability and movement. A strong color may be juxtaposed with another strong color, or with a weak one; light colors can be used next to dark ones, or put together once and never again. Comparisons are made between similar and opposing colors at the same time in the same quilt. . . . Contrast is used to structure or organize.[4]

Wahlman and Scully argue that African-American quilters prefer the sporadic use of the same material in several squares when this material could have been used uniformly because they prefer variation to regularity. " 'Off-beat patterning' serves to . . . describe how Afro-American quilters control their improvisations" and the term "multiple rhythms" describes how the quilters multiply the off-beat patterns and "carry them to complex aesthetic solutions," thus creating the impression of several patterns moving in different directions or multiple rhythms within the context of a controlled design (see figs. 1 and 2, e.g.).[5] In other words, the symmetry in African-American quilts does not come from unifor-

---

that turns on partiality, that is self-conscious about perspective," and "that releases multiple voices rather than competing orthodoxies." I hope the approach I describe herein is a step in that direction (Jacquelyn Dowd Hall, "Partial Truths," in this issue).

[4] Maude Southwell Wahlman and John Scully, "Aesthetic Principles of Afro-American Quilts," in *Afro-American Folk Art and Crafts*, ed. William Ferris (Boston: G. K. Hall, 1983), 79–97.

[5] Ibid.

FIG. I. Rosie Lee Baker, strip quilt made of old pants, 1967, 84″ × 58½″.
© 1988 by Roland L. Freeman.

mity as it does in Euro-American quilts; rather, the symmetry comes through the diversity.[6]

Wahlman and Scully use musical terminology in their description of this aesthetic because the notion of polyrhythms is characteristic of African-American dance and music as well. It is also characteristic of African-American language. Luisah Teish, in *Jambalaya: The Natural Woman's Book of Personal Charms and*

---

[6] John Michael Vlach, in a direct comparison of the two quilting traditions, asserts that the strip quilts of African-Americans would never be mistaken for those of Euro-Americans. "Euro-American quilters tend to draw their designs into a tight and ordered symmetry. When strip designs are used they are the same size and are pieced together in an orderly manner." Euro-American quilts are rigid, uniform, repetitious, and predictable. "By contrast, Afro-American strip quilts are random and wild, seemingly out of control. . . . A concept more important than order . . . is improvisation, the basis of Afro-American creativity" (John Michael Vlach, *The Afro-American Tradition in Decorative Arts* [Cleveland: Cleveland Museum of Art, 1978], 44–75, esp. 67, 74). For examples of nineteenth- and early twentieth-century African-American women's strip quilting, see *Broken Star: Post-Civil War Quilts Made by Black Women* (Dallas: Museum of African-American Life and Culture, 1986); for contemporary examples, see *Something to Keep You Warm: The Roland Freeman Collection of Black American Quilts from the Mississippi Heartland* (Jackson: Mississippi Department of Archives and History, 1981).

FIG. 2. Malissa Banks, strip quilt, variation on a log cabin pattern, 1973, 86″ × 72″. © 1988 by Roland L. Freeman.

Practical Rituals, describes the practice of *gumbo ya ya*, which has been passed down among the women in her family. When she goes home to New Orleans to visit and is met by her family at the airport, she writes, "Before I can get a good look in my mother's face, people begin arranging themselves in the car. They begin to talk gumbo ya ya, and it goes on for 12 days. . . . Gumbo ya ya is a creole term that means 'Everybody talks at once.' " It is through *gumbo ya ya* that Teish learns everything that has happened in her family and community and she conveys the essential information about herself to the group. To an outsider, *gumbo ya ya* can only sound like chaos. How can anyone be listening to everyone else at once while they are also themselves speaking? But, as Teish describes it, this indeed is possible. In fact, the only time the conversation stops is when someone has asked a member of the group a question to which they do not respond—in other words everyone is hearing themselves and everyone else at once.[7]

[7] Luisah Teish, *Jambalaya: The Natural Woman's Book of Personal Charms and Practical Rituals* (San Francisco: Harper & Row, 1985), 139–40. Teish acknowledges her own difficulty in reentering the world of *gumbo ya ya* after years in a more Westernized environment.

Gumbo ya ya is the essence of the Black musical tradition where "the various voices in a piece of music may go their own ways but still be held together by their relationship to each other."[8] In jazz, for example, each musician has to listen to what the other is doing and know how to respond while each is, at the same time, intent upon her/his own improvisation. It is in this context that the jazz pianist Ojeda Penn has called jazz an expression of true democracy, for each person is allowed, in fact required, to be an individual, to go his/her own way, and yet to do so in concert with the group—to be an individual in the context of the community.[9] "The great . . . blending capacity" of African-American cultural forms and African-American consciousness "derives primarily from a rhythmic substructure that can incorporate with ease the most diverse melodic and harmonic resources."[10]

The implications of this aesthetic for African-American women's economic, political, and social history are enormous. Culture in the largest sense is, after all, a resource that provides the context in which people perceive their social world. Perceptions of alternatives in the social structure take place only within a framework defined by the patterns and rhythms of that particular culture.[11] Developments within specific elements of African-American culture provide clues to economic and political developments. A people's cultural aesthetic is not different from their economic or political aesthetic; it is just visible to us in different form. Elements of material culture, such as quilting, are in fact illustrative of a particular way of seeing, of ordering the world.[12]

This should be important not merely to the analytical frameworks we imagine but to the structures we create as well. In fact, through both political and academic experience, I have come to learn that the whole process by which we teach the material quite often invalidates the very concepts we wish to convey. If in fact

---

[8] Lawrence Levine, *Black Culture and Black Consciousness: Afro-American Folk Thought from Slavery to Freedom* (New York: Oxford University Press, 1977), 133.

[9] Ojeda Penn, "Jazz: American Classical Music as a Philosophic and Symbolic Entity" (faculty lecture series, Fifteenth Anniversary of African and African-American Studies Program, Emory University, Atlanta, March 1986).

[10] Charles Keil, *Urban Blues* (Chicago: University of Chicago Press, 1966), 33–34, makes this argument solely in relation to African-American musical forms.

[11] Sidney Mintz, "Foreword," in *Afro-American Anthropology: Contemporary Perspectives*, ed. Norman E. Whitten, Jr., and John F. Szwed (New York: Free Press, 1970), 8–11.

[12] Leroi Jones, *Blues People: Negro Music in White America* (New York: Morrow, 1963), 153, made this same point: "Negro music can be seen to be the result of . . . certain specific ways of thinking about the world."

African-American women's history is based upon nonlinear, poly-rhythmic, and what white Western traditions term "nonsymmetrical" notions of the world in which individual and community are not competing identities, then one cannot adequately teach this history employing the pedagogical assumptions that come out of linear, Western, symmetrical notions of the world. Such assumptions emphasize objectivity, equate fairness with uniformity and sameness, and thus create and bolster individualistic competitive enterprise. To structure a course in African-American women's history by these pedagogical assumptions would, in fact, invalidate the experiences of African-American women.

In my course on African-American women's history, I seek to create a polyrhythmic, "nonsymmetrical," nonlinear structure in which individual and community are not competing entities. I do that by challenging the most basic notions of the academy. Just as I attempt in content to challenge the notion that people who are trained to investigate other people's lives can better understand those lives than the people who live those lives, I attempt in structure to challenge the notion that people who are trained to teach can better understand what and how students need to learn than the students themselves. I, therefore, do not attempt to adopt a feminist pedagogy in which the instructor uses her power to empower the previously disempowered. Rather, with great difficulty, I attempt, sometimes better than others, to disempower myself and therefore give students the opportunity to empower themselves, thus allowing them to become the voices of authority in their own education. How do we come to understand, not just intellectually but unconsciously as well, that African-American women have indeed created their own lives, shaped their own meanings, and are the voices of authority on their own experience? We do this by learning that we can be our own voices of authority. We fear we cannot because we have been taught we cannot. We learn we can, and we thus empower ourselves. Experiencing their own authority better enables my students to hear authority in the various voices of the African-American women we study.

These ideas become clearer as we explore the structure of my course, particularly as we look at the class time itself, the evaluation process, and the nature of written assignments. I choose the reading material for the course and the schedule of when it will be read. Having done that, I have no other authority. Students are responsible for preparing and conducting each class, but no one is responsible by herself, so that each student is required to do something each week to assist another student in their preparation for the course. Each person has the right to expect others to be as concerned about her understanding in the class as their own. The instructor never has the right to overrule the students' decisions about how best to approach the week's class time. Students always have the right actively to prevent any effort on the part of the instructor to guide the class along "more appropriate" lines.

Each member of the class evaluates herself and each other member weekly. The instructor also does an evaluation of each. No one's evaluation (including the instructor's) counts more than anyone else's. Students begin with a very normative, linear, uniform notion of what is equitable and fair, establish in their own minds a standard, and judge all persons by it. They come to learn the impossibility—in this framework—of that, for this class is not a linear, unirhythmic experience. Who, for example, is the greatest contributor to a class discussion: someone who speaks only once but raises a central and profound point which makes it possible for everyone else to see in new ways; someone who is constantly speaking, thus keeping the conversation going; someone who never opens her mouth in class, but always comes with a most appropriate tape or poem that, by its use in the class, really leads people to see the material differently; or someone who can always be counted on to have read all the material and thus is prepared to keep us grounded?

Written assignments are handed out without reference to how they should be achieved. Students begin, based on their previous training, to try to fulfill the assignments individually. They soon discover that this is impossible, and, one hopes, not only that they must approach the project collectively but also that it takes a variety of skills, resources, and emphases to achieve this goal. All are important to the process.

The manner in which we distribute responsibility and what represents a fair share is dependent on us each being responsible for our own effort and for others'. If I, in fact, believed you were not contributing to your potential, and I did nothing to help you do so, then I can only legitimately devalue your contribution by acknowledging my responsibility as well and devaluing my own contribution. Thus, only in the context of the whole can each individual contribution be understood and valued. One can stand alone only by remaining part of the group. Ultimately, it is the resources of the whole which determine the fate of the individual. Yet it is in fact their individuality which makes them part of the community.

The structure I create is, by Western norms, a disorganized, chaotic, sporadic, and very unworkable class. What in fact we get by the end of the semester is a serious improvisation, a *gumbo ya ya* in which people are empowered by their own authority and their right to expect things from others. Like urban blues, it precisely allows each individual "greater voice for their individuality" while keeping them "still members of the group, still on familiar ground," still in touch with the community.[13] They stand alone, like the contrasting strips of the quilt, and at the same time remain part of the group.

The class is a quilt. It is precisely the contrast which organizes the whole and holds it together. The class is *gumbo ya ya*. It is only when each individual contributes her talents at the same time as all the others that the collective can work, and only through the collective that each individual talent takes meaning.

The implications for understanding the complexity of African-American women's lives and thought are enormous. One example will have to suffice: it is from personal history.[14] Some years ago when I was married and had two small daughters and a husband who was in graduate school, I wrote a series of letters to my mother expressing my desire to go to graduate school as well. I wanted to get on with my own career. In return, I received from my mother a lengthy letter reminding me of my responsibilities as a Black woman/wife/mother, reminding me that my central concern should be the care of my home, my husband, and my children and that graduate school and career should not be my focus. I should, therefore, give up these ideas and be happy being a proper wife and mother, a responsible Black woman. The letter continued in this vein for three or four pages and ended with the usual, "Love, Mama." In the same envelope with that letter was a check in the amount of tuition for graduate school. By these actions, my mother demonstrated her understanding of the need to teach me to live my life one way and, at the same time, to provide me with all the tools I would need to live it quite differently.

What my mother teaches me are the essential lessons of the quilt: that people and actions do move in multiple directions at once.[15] If we analyze those people and actions by linear models, we

[13] Levine, 238.
[14] A fuller telling of this can be found in Elsa Barkley Brown, "Mothers of Mind," which is most appropriately subtitled, "how my mother taught me to be a historian in spite of my academic training" (faculty lecture series, Fifteenth Anniversary of African-American and African Studies, Emory University, Atlanta, April 1986).
[15] It is not just that African-American women did different, seemingly contradictory, things at different times, which they did, but that they did different, seemingly contradictory things, simultaneously. It is the simultaneity of their seemingly contradictory actions and beings for which we must account in our historical analyses. I have elsewhere (ibid.) suggested that the simultaneous promotion of two seemingly contradictory sets of values (some of which may be quite conscious, some of which may be unconscious but understood as necessary) is essential to the

will create dichotomies, ambiguities, cognitive dissonance, disorientation, and confusion in places where none exist. If, however, we follow the cultural guides which African-American women have left us, we can allow the way in which they saw and constructed their own lives to provide the analytical framework by which we attempt to understand their experiences and their world and to provide the structural framework by which we attempt to teach this to others.[16] In the final analysis, how we teach is a reflection of how we think.

Elsa Barkley Brown
State University of New York at Binghamton

---

survival of individual African-Americans and of the African-American community as a whole.

[16] Darlene Clark Hine, in "Rape and the Inner Lives of Black Women in the Middle West: Preliminary Thoughts on the Culture of Dissemblance" (in this issue), provides us with an example of a nonlinear framework which highlights the fact that, even stopped for a moment in time, African-American women's lives and thought would still be polyrhythmic.

ON BEING THE OBJECT
OF PROPERTY

PATRICIA J. WILLIAMS

On being invisible
Reflections

For some time I have been writing about my great-great-grandmother.
I have considered the significance of her history and that of slavery
from a variety of viewpoints on a variety of occasions: in every
speech, in every conversation, even in my commercial transactions
class. I have talked so much about her that I finally had to ask myself
what it was I was looking for in this dogged pursuit of family history.
Was I being merely indulgent, looking for roots in the pursuit of
some genetic heraldry, seeking the inheritance of being special,
different, unique in all that primogeniture hath wrought?

I decided that my search was based in the utility of such a quest,
not mere indulgence, but a recapturing of that which had escaped
historical scrutiny, which had been overlooked and underseen. I,
like so many blacks, have been trying to pin myself down in history,
place myself in the stream of time as significant, evolved, present
in the past, continuing into the future. To be without documentation
is too unsustaining, too spontaneously ahistorical, too dangerously
malleable in the hands of those who would rewrite not merely the
past but my future as well. So I have been picking through the ruins
for my roots.

What I know of my mother's side of the family begins with my
great-great-grandmother. Her name was Sophie and she lived in
Tennessee. In 1850, she was about twelve years old. I know that
she was purchased when she was eleven by a white lawyer named

This essay originally appeared in *Signs*, vol. 14, no. 1, Autumn 1988.

Austin Miller and was immediately impregnated by him. She gave birth to my great-grandmother Mary, who was taken away from her to be raised as a house servant.[1] I know nothing more of Sophie (she was, after all, a black single mother—in today's terms—suffering the anonymity of yet another statistical teenage pregnancy). While I don't remember what I was told about Austin Miller before I decided to go to law school, I do remember that just before my first day of class, my mother said, in a voice full of secretive reassurance, "The Millers were lawyers, so you have it in your blood."[2]

When my mother told me that I had nothing to fear in law school, that law was "in my blood," she meant it in a very complex sense. First and foremost, she meant it defiantly; she meant that no one should make me feel inferior because someone else's father was a judge. She wanted me to reclaim that part of my heritage from which I had been disinherited, and she wanted me to use it as a source of strength and self-confidence. At the same time, she was asking me to claim a part of myself that was the dispossessor of another part of myself; she was asking me to deny that disenfranchised little black girl of myself that felt powerless, vulnerable and, moreover, rightly felt so.

In somewhat the same vein, Mother was asking me not to look to her as a role model. She was devaluing that part of herself that was not Harvard and refocusing my vision to that part of herself that was hard-edged, proficient, and Western. She hid the lonely, black, defiled-female part of herself and pushed me forward as the projection of a competent self, a cool rather than despairing self, a masculine rather than a feminine self.

I took this secret of my blood into the Harvard milieu with both the pride and the shame with which my mother had passed it along to me. I found myself in the situation described by Marguerite Duras, in her novel *The Lover:* "We're united in a fundamental shame at having to live. It's here we are at the heart of our common fate, the fact that [we] are our mother's children, the children of a candid creature murdered by society. We're on the side of society which has reduced her to despair. Because of what's been done to our mother, so amiable, so trusting, we hate life, we hate ourselves."[3]

Reclaiming that from which one has been disinherited is a good thing. Self-possession in the full sense of that expression is the companion to self-knowledge. Yet claiming for myself a heritage

---

[1] For a more detailed account of the family history to this point, see Patricia Williams, "Grandmother Sophie," *Harvard Blackletter* 3 (1986): 79.

[2] Patricia Williams, "Alchemical Notes: Reconstructing Ideals from Deconstructed Rights," *Harvard Civil Rights–Civil Liberties Law Review* 22 (1987): 418.

[3] Marguerite Duras, *The Lover* (New York: Harper & Row, 1985), 55.

the weft of whose genesis is my own disinheritance is a profoundly troubling paradox.

Images

A friend of mine practices law in rural Florida. His office is in Belle Glade, an extremely depressed area where the sugar industry reigns supreme, where blacks live pretty much as they did in slavery times, in dormitories called slave ships. They are penniless and illiterate and have both a high birth rate and a high death rate.

My friend told me about a client of his, a fifteen-year-old young woman pregnant with her third child, who came seeking advice because her mother had advised a hysterectomy—not even a tubal ligation—as a means of birth control. The young woman's mother, in turn, had been advised of the propriety of such a course in her own case by a white doctor some years before. Listening to this, I was reminded of a case I worked on when I was working for the Western Center on Law and Poverty about eight years ago. Ten black Hispanic women had been sterilized by the University of Southern California–Los Angeles County General Medical Center, allegedly without proper consent, and in most instances without even their knowledge.[4] Most of them found out what had been done to them upon inquiry, after a much-publicized news story in which an intern charged that the chief of obstetrics at the hospital pursued a policy of recommending Caesarian delivery and simultaneous sterilization for any pregnant woman with three or more children and who was on welfare. In the course of researching the appeal in that case, I remember learning that one-quarter of all Navajo women of childbearing age—literally all those of childbearing age ever admitted to a hospital—have been sterilized.[5]

---

[4] *Madrigal v. Quilligan*, U.S. Court of Appeals, 9th Circuit, Docket no. 78-3187, October 1979.

[5] This was the testimony of one of the witnesses. It is hard to find official confirmation for this or any other sterilization statistic involving Native American women. Official statistics kept by the U.S. Public Health Service, through the Centers for Disease Control in Atlanta, come from data gathered by the National Hospital Discharge Survey, which covers neither federal hospitals nor penitentiaries. Services to Native American women living on reservations are provided almost exclusively by federal hospitals. In addition, the U.S. Public Health Service breaks down its information into only three categories: "White," "Black," and "Other." Nevertheless, in 1988, the Women of All Red Nations Collective of Minneapolis, Minnesota, distributed a fact sheet entitled "Sterilization Studies of Native American Women," which claimed that as many as 50 percent of all Native American women of childbearing age have been sterilized. According to "Surgical Sterilization Surveillance: Tubal Sterilization and Hysterectomy in Women Aged 15–44, 1979–1980," issued

As I reflected on all this, I realized that one of the things passed on from slavery, which continues in the oppression of people of color, is a belief structure rooted in a concept of black (or brown, or red) anti-will, the antithetical embodiment of pure will. We live in a society in which the closest equivalent of nobility is the display of unremittingly controlled will-fulness. To be perceived as unre- mittingly will-less is to be imbued with an almost lethal trait.

Many scholars have explained this phenomenon in terms of total and infantilizing interdependency of dominant and oppressed.[6] Consider, for example, Mark Tushnet's distinction between slave law's totalistic view of personality and the bourgeois "pure will" theory of personality: "Social relations in slave society rest upon the interaction of owner with slave; the owner, having total domin- ion over the slave. In contrast, bourgeois social relations rest upon the paradigmatic instance of market relations, the purchase by a capitalist of a worker's labor power; that transaction implicates only a part of the worker's personality. Slave relations are total, engaging the master and slave in exchanges in which each must take account of the entire range of belief, feeling, and interest embodied by the other; bourgeois social relations are partial, requiring only that par- ticipants in a market evaluate their general productive character- istics without regard to aspects of personality unrelated to production."[7]

Although such an analysis is not objectionable in some general sense, the description of master-slave relations as "total" is, to me,

---

by the Centers for Disease Control in 1983, "In 1980, the tubal sterilization rate for black women . . . was 45 percent greater than that for white women" (7). Further- more, a study released in 1984 by the Division of Reproductive Health of the Center for Health Promotion and Education (one of the Centers for Disease Control) found that, as of 1982, 48.8 percent of Puerto Rican women between the ages of 15 and 44 had been sterilized.

[6] See, generally, Stanley Elkins, *Slavery* (New York: Grosset & Dunlap, 1963); Kenneth Stampp, *The Peculiar Institution* (New York: Vintage, 1956): Winthrop Jordan, *White over Black* (Baltimore: Penguin Books, 1968).

[7] Mark Tushnet, *The American Law of Slavery* (Princeton, N.J.: Princeton Uni- versity Press, 1981), 6. There is danger, in the analysis that follows, of appearing to "pick" on Tushnet. That is not my intention, nor is it to impugn the body of his research, most of which I greatly admire. The choice of this passage for analysis has more to do with the randomness of my reading habits; the fact that he is one of the few legal writers to attempt, in the context of slavery, a juxtaposition of political theory with psychoanalytic theories of personality; and the fact that he is perceived to be of the political left, which simplifies my analysis in terms of its presumption of sympathy, i.e., that the constructions of thought revealed are socially derived and unconscious rather than idiosyncratic and intentional.

quite troubling. Such a choice of words reflects and accepts—at a very subtle level, perhaps—a historical rationalization that whites had to, could do, and did do everything for these simple, above-animal subhumans. It is a choice of vocabulary that fails to acknowledge blacks as having needs beyond those that even the most "humane" or "sentimental" white slavemaster could provide.[8] In trying to describe the provisional aspect of slave law, I would choose words that revealed its structure as rooted in a concept of, again, black anti-will, the polar opposite of pure will. I would characterize the treatment of blacks by whites in whites' law as defining blacks as those who had no will. I would characterize that treatment not as total interdependency, but as a relation in which partializing judgments, employing partializing standards of humanity, impose generalized inadequacy on a race: if pure will or total control equals the perfect white person, then impure will and total lack of control equals the perfect black man or woman. Therefore, to define slave law as comprehending a "total" view of personality implicitly accepts that the provision of food, shelter, and clothing (again assuming the very best of circumstances) is the whole requirement of humanity. It assumes also either that psychic care was provided by slave owners (as though a slave or an owned psyche could ever be reconciled with mental health) or that psyche is not a significant part of a whole human.

Market theory indeed focuses attention away from the full range of human potential in its pursuit of a divinely willed, invisibly handed economic actor. Master-slave relations, however, focused attention away from the full range of black human potential in a somewhat different way: it pursued a vision of blacks as simple-

[8] In another passage, Tushnet observes: "The court thus demonstrated its appreciation of the ties of sentiment that slavery could generate between master and slave and simultaneously denied that those ties were relevant in the law" (67). What is noteworthy about the reference to "sentiment" is that it assumes the fact that emotions could grow up between slave and master is itself worth remarking: slightly surprising, slightly commendable for the court to note (i.e., in its "appreciation")—although "simultaneously" with, and presumably in contradistinction to, the court's inability to take official cognizance of the fact. Yet, if one really looks at the ties that bound master and slave, one has to flesh out the description of master-slave with the ties of father-son, father-daughter, half-sister, half-brother, uncle, aunt, cousin, and a variety of de facto foster relationships. And if one starts to see those ties as more often than not intimate family ties, then the terminology "appreciation of . . . sentiment . . . between master and slave" becomes a horrifying mockery of any true sense of family sentiment, which is utterly, utterly lacking. The court's "appreciation," from this enhanced perspective, sounds blindly cruel, sarcastic at best. And to observe that courts suffused in such "appreciation" could simultaneously deny its legal relevance seems not only a truism; it misses the point entirely.

minded, strong-bodied economic actants.[9] Thus, while blacks had an indisputable generative force in the marketplace, their presence could not be called activity; they had no active role in the market. To say, therefore, that "market relations disregard the peculiarities of individuals, whereas slave relations rest on the mutual recognition of the humanity of master and slave"[10] (no matter how dialectical or abstracted a definition of humanity one adopts) is to posit an inaccurate equation: if "disregard for the peculiarities of individuals" and "mutual recognition of humanity" are polarized by a "whereas," then somehow regard for peculiarities of individuals must equal recognition of humanity. In the context of slavery this equation mistakes whites' overzealous and oppressive obsession with projected specific peculiarities of blacks for actual holistic regard for the individual. It overlooks the fact that most definitions of humanity require something beyond mere biological sustenance, some healthy measure of autonomy beyond that of which slavery could institutionally or otherwise conceive. Furthermore, it overlooks the fact that both slave and bourgeois systems regarded certain attributes as important and disregarded certain others, and that such regard and disregard can occur in the same glance, like the wearing of horseblinders to focus attention simultaneously toward and away from. The experiential blinders of market actor and slave are focused in different directions, yet the partializing ideologies of each makes the act of not seeing an unconscious, alienating component of seeing. Restoring a unified social vision will, I think, require broader and more scattered resolutions than the simple symmetry of ideological bipolarity.

Thus, it is important to undo whatever words obscure the fact that slave law was at least as fragmenting and fragmented as the bourgeois worldview—in a way that has persisted to this day, cutting across all ideological boundaries. As "pure will" signifies the whole bourgeois personality in the bourgeois worldview, so wisdom, control, and aesthetic beauty signify the whole white personality in slave law. The former and the latter, the slavemaster and the burgermeister, are not so very different when expressed in those terms. The reconciling difference is that in slave law the emphasis is really

---

[9] "Actants have a kind of phonemic, rather than a phonetic role: they operate on the level of function, rather than content. That is, an actant may embody itself in a particular character (termed an acteur) or it may reside in the function of more than one character in respect of their common role in the story's underlying 'oppositional' structure. In short, the deep structure of the narrative generates and defines its actants at a level beyond that of the story's surface content" (Terence Hawkes, *Structuralism and Semiotics* [Berkeley: University of California Press, 1977], 89).

[10] Tushnet, 69.

on the inverse rationale: that irrationality, lack of control, and ugliness signify the whole slave personality. "Total" interdependence
is at best a polite way of rationalizing such personality splintering;
it creates a bizarre sort of yin-yang from the dross of an oppressive
schizophrenia of biblical dimension. I would just call it schizo-
phrenic, with all the baggage that that connotes. That is what sounds
right to me. Truly total relationships (as opposed to totalitarianism)
call up images of whole people dependent on whole people; an
interdependence that is both providing and laissez-faire at the same
time. Neither the historical inheritance of slave law nor so-called
bourgeois law meets that definition.

None of this, perhaps, is particularly new. Nevertheless, as precedent to anything I do as a lawyer, the greatest challenge is to allow
the full truth of partializing social constructions to be felt for their
overwhelming reality—reality that otherwise I might rationally try
to avoid facing. In my search for roots, I must assume, not just as
history but as an ongoing psychological force, that, in the eyes of
white culture, irrationality, lack of control, and ugliness signify not
just the whole slave personality, not just the whole black personality,
but me.

Vision

Reflecting on my roots makes me think again and again of the young
woman in Belle Glade, Florida. She told the story of her impending
sterilization, according to my friend, while keeping her eyes on the
ground at all times. My friend, who is white, asked why she wouldn't
look up, speak with him eye to eye. The young woman answered
that she didn't like white people seeing inside her.

My friend's story made me think of my own childhood and ad-
olescence: my parents were always telling me to look up at the
world; to look straight at people, particularly white people; not to
let them stare me down; to hold my ground; to insist on the right
to my presence no matter what. They told me that in this culture
you have to look people in the eye because that's how you tell them
you're their equal. My friend's story also reminded me how very
difficult I had found that looking-back to be. What was hardest was
not just that white people saw me, as my friend's client put it, but
that they looked through me, that they treated me as though I were
transparent.

By itself, seeing into me would be to see my substance, my anger,
my vulnerability, and my wild raging despair—and that alone is
hard enough to show, to share. But to uncover it and to have it
devalued by ignore-ance, to hold it up bravely in the organ of my

eyes and to have it greeted by an impassive stare that passes right through all that which is me, an impassive stare that moves on and attaches itself to my left earlobe or to the dust caught in the rusty vertical geysers of my wiry hair or to the breadth of my freckled brown nose—this is deeply humiliating. It re-wounds, relives the early childhood anguish of uncensored seeing, the fullness of vision that is the permanent turning-away point for most blacks.

The cold game of equality-staring makes me feel like a thin sheet of glass: white people see all the worlds beyond me but not me. They come trotting at me with force and speed; they do not see me. I could force my presence, the real me contained in those eyes, upon them, but I would be smashed in the process. If I deflect, if I move out of the way, they will never know I existed.

Marguerite Duras, again in *The Lover*, places the heroine in relation to her family. "Every day we try to kill one another, to kill. Not only do we not talk to one another, we don't even look at one another. When you're being looked at you can't look. To look is to feel curious, to be interested, to lower yourself."[11]

To look is also to make myself vulnerable; yet not to look is to neutralize the part of myself which is vulnerable. I look in order to see, and so I must look. Without that directness of vision, I am afraid I will will my own blindness, disinherit my own creativity, and sterilize my own perspective of its embattled, passionate insight.

On ardor

The child

One Saturday afternoon not long ago, I sat among a litter of family photographs telling a South African friend about Marjorie, my god-mother and my mother's cousin. She was given away by her light-skinned mother when she was only six. She was given to my grand-mother and my great-aunts to be raised among her darker-skinned cousins, for Marjorie was very dark indeed. Her mother left the family to "pass," to marry a white man—Uncle Frederick, we called him with trepidatious presumption yet without his ever knowing of our existence—an heir to a meat-packing fortune. When Uncle Frederick died thirty years later and the fortune was lost, Marjorie's mother rejoined the race, as the royalty of resentful fascination—Lady Bountiful, my sister called her—to regale us with tales of gracious upper-class living.

---

[11] Duras, 54.

My friend said that my story reminded him of a case in which a swarthy, crisp-haired child was born, in Durban, to white parents. The Afrikaner government quickly intervened, removed the child from its birth home, and placed it to be raised with a "more suitable," browner family.

When my friend and I had shared these stories, we grew embarrassed somehow, and our conversation trickled away into a discussion of laissez-faire economics and governmental interventionism. Our words became a clear line, a railroad upon which all other ideas and events were tied down and sacrificed.

The market

As a teacher of commercial transactions, one of the things that has always impressed me most about the law of contract is a certain deadening power it exercises by reducing the parties to the passive. It constrains the lively involvement of its signatories by positioning enforcement in such a way that parties find themselves in a passive relationship to a document: it is the contract that governs, that "does" everything, that absorbs all responsibility and deflects all other recourse.

Contract law reduces life to fairy tale. The four corners of the agreement become parent. Performance is the equivalent of obedience to the parent. Obedience is dutifully passive. Passivity is valued as good contract-socialized behavior; activity is caged in retrospective hypotheses about states of mind at the magic moment of contracting. Individuals are judged by the contract unfolding rather than by the actors acting autonomously. Nonperformance is disobedience; disobedience is active; activity becomes evil in contrast to the childlike passivity of contract conformity.

One of the most powerful examples of all this is the case of Mary Beth Whitehead, mother of Sara—of so-called Baby M. Ms. Whitehead became a vividly original actor *after* the creation of her contract with William Stern; unfortunately for her, there can be no greater civil sin. It was in this upside-down context, in the picaresque unboundedness of breachor, that her energetic grief became hysteria and her passionate creativity was funneled, whorled, and reconstructed as highly impermissible. Mary Beth Whitehead thus emerged as the evil stepsister who deserved nothing.

Some time ago, Charles Reich visited a class of mine.[12] He discussed with my students a proposal for a new form of bargain by

---

[12] Charles Reich is author of *The Greening of America* (New York: Random House, 1970) and professor of law at the University of San Francisco Law School.

which emotional "items"—such as praise, flattery, acting happy or sad—might be contracted for explicitly. One student, not alone in her sentiment, said, "Oh, but then you'll just feel obligated." Only the week before, however (when we were discussing the contract which posited that Ms. Whitehead "will not form or attempt to form a parent-child relationship with any child or children"), this same student had insisted that Ms. Whitehead must give up her child, because she had *said* she would: "She was obligated!" I was confounded by the degree to which what the student took to be self-evident, inalienable gut reactions could be governed by illusions of passive conventionality and form.

It was that incident, moreover, that gave me insight into how Judge Harvey Sorkow, of New Jersey Superior Court, could conclude that the contract that purported to terminate Ms. Whitehead's parental rights was "not illusory."[13]

(As background, I should say that I think that, within the framework of contract law itself, the agreement between Ms. Whitehead and Mr. Stern was clearly illusory.[14] On the one hand, Judge Sorkow's opinion said that Ms. Whitehead was seeking to avoid her *obligations.* In other words, giving up her child became an actual obligation. On the other hand, according to the logic of the judge, this was a service contract, not really a sale of a child; therefore delivering the child to the Sterns was an "obligation" for which there was no consideration, for which Mr. Stern was not paying her.)

Judge Sorkow's finding the contract "not illusory" is suggestive not just of the doctrine by that name, but of illusion in general, and delusion, and the righteousness with which social constructions are conceived, acted on, and delivered up into the realm of the real as "right," while all else is devoured from memory as "wrong." From this perspective, the rhetorical tricks by which Sara Whitehead became Melissa Stern seem very like the heavy-worded legalities by which my great-great-grandmother was pacified and parted from her child. In both situations, the real mother had no say, no power; her powerlessness was imposed by state law that made her and her child helpless in relation to the father. My great-great-grandmother's

---

[13] See, generally, In the Matter of Baby "M," A Pseudonym for an Actual Person, Superior Court of New Jersey, Chancery Division, Docket no. FM-25314-86E, March 31, 1987. This decision was appealed, and on February 3, 1988, the New Jersey Supreme Court ruled that surrogate contracts were illegal and against public policy. In addition to the contract issue, however, the appellate court decided the custody issue in favor of the Sterns but granted visitation rights to Mary Beth Whitehead.

[14] "An illusory promise is an expression cloaked in promissory terms, but which, upon closer examination, reveals that the promisor has committed himself not at all" (J. Calamari and J. Perillo, *Contracts,* 3d ed. [St. Paul: West Publishing, 1987], 228).

powerlessness came about as the result of a contract to which she was not a party; Mary Beth Whitehead's powerlessness came about as a result of a contract that she signed at a discrete point of time—yet which, over time, enslaved her. The contract-reality in both instances was no less than magic: it was illusion transformed into not-illusion. Furthermore, it masterfully disguised the brutality of enforced arrangements in which these women's autonomy, their flesh and their blood, were locked away in word vaults, without room to reconsider—*ever.*

In the months since Judge Sorkow's opinion, I have reflected on the similarities of fortune between my own social positioning and that of Sara Melissa Stern Whitehead. I have come to realize that an important part of the complex magic that Judge Sorkow wrote into his opinion was a supposition that it is "natural" for people to want children "like" themselves. What this reasoning raised for me was an issue of what, exactly, constituted this "likeness"? (What would have happened, for example, if Ms. Whitehead had turned out to have been the "passed" descendant of my "failed" godmother Marjorie's mother? What if the child she bore had turned out to be recessively and visibly black? Would the sperm of Mr. Stern have been so powerful as to make this child "his" with the exclusivity that Judge Sorkow originally assigned?) What constitutes, moreover, the collective understanding of "un-likeness"?

These questions turn, perhaps, on not-so-subtle images of which mothers should be bearing which children. Is there not something unseemly, in our society, about the spectacle of a white woman mothering a black child? A white woman giving totally to a black child; a black child totally and demandingly dependent for everything, for sustenance itself, from a white woman. The image of a white woman suckling a black child; the image of a black child sucking for its life from the bosom of a white woman. The utter interdependence of such an image; the selflessness, the merging it implies; the giving up of boundary; the encompassing of other within self; the unbounded generosity, the interconnectedness of such an image. Such a picture says that there is no difference; it places the hope of continuous generation, of immortality of the white self in a little black face.

When Judge Sorkow declared that it was only to be expected that parents would want to breed children "like" themselves, he simultaneously created a legal right to the same. With the creation of such a "right," he encased the children conforming to "likeliness" in protective custody, far from whole ranges of taboo. Taboo about touch and smell and intimacy and boundary. Taboo about ardor, possession, license, equivocation, equanimity, indifference, intol-

erance, rancor, dispossession, innocence, exile, and candor. Taboo
about death. Taboos that amount to death. Death and sacredness,
the valuing of body, of self, of other, of remains. The handling
lovingly in life, as in life; the question of the intimacy versus the
dispassion of death.

In effect, these taboos describe boundaries of valuation. Whether
something is inside or outside the marketplace of rights has always
been a way of valuing it. When a valued object is located outside
the market, it is generally understood to be too "priceless" to be
accommodated by ordinary exchange relationships; when, in contrast, the prize is located within the marketplace, all objects outside
become "valueless." Traditionally, the Mona Lisa and human life
have been the sorts of subjects removed from the fungibility of
commodification, as "priceless." Thus when black people were
bought and sold as slaves, they were placed beyond the bounds of
humanity. And thus, in the twistedness of our brave new world,
when blacks have been thrust out of the market and it is white
children who are bought and sold, black babies have become
"worthless" currency to adoption agents—"surplus" in the salvage
heaps of Harlem hospitals.

The imagination

"Familiar though his name may be to us, the storyteller in his living
immediacy is by no means a present force. He has already become
something remote from us and something that is getting even more
distant. . . . Less and less frequently do we encounter people with
the ability to tell a tale properly. . . . It is as if something that seemed
inalienable to us, the securest among our possessions, were taken
from us: the ability to exchange experiences."[15]

My mother's cousin Marjorie was a storyteller. From time to time
I would press her to tell me the details of her youth, and she would
tell me instead about a child who wandered into a world of polar
bears, who was prayed over by polar bears, and in the end eaten.
The child's life was not in vain because the polar bears had been
made holy by its suffering. The child had been a test, a message
from god for polar bears. In the polar bear universe, she would tell
me, the primary object of creation was polar bears, and the rest of
the living world was fashioned to serve polar bears. The clouds
took their shape from polar bears, trees were designed to give shel-

---

[15] Walter Benjamin, "The Storyteller," in *Illuminations,* ed. Hannah Arendt (New
York: Schocken, 1969), 83.

ter and shade to polar bears, and humans were ideally designed to provide polar bears with meat.[16]

The truth, the truth, I would laughingly insist as we sat in her apartment eating canned fruit and heavy roasts, mashed potatoes, pickles and vanilla pudding, cocoa, Sprite, or tea. What about roots and all that, I coaxed. But the voracity of her amnesia would disclaim and disclaim and disclaim; and she would go on telling me about the polar bears until our plates were full of emptiness and I became large in the space which described her emptiness and I gave in to the emptiness of words.

On life and death
Sighing into space

There are moments in my life when I feel as though a part of me is missing. There are days when I feel so invisible that I can't remember what day of the week it is, when I feel so manipulated that I can't remember my own name, when I feel so lost and angry that I can't speak a civil word to the people who love me best. Those are the times when I catch sight of my reflection in store windows and am surprised to see a whole person looking back. Those are the times when my skin becomes gummy as clay and my nose slides around on my face and my eyes drip down to my chin. I have to close my eyes at such times and remember myself, draw an internal picture that is smooth and whole; when all else fails, I reach for a mirror and stare myself down until the features reassemble themselves like lost sheep.

Two years ago, my godmother Marjorie suffered a massive stroke. As she lay dying, I would come to the hospital to give her her meals. My feeding her who had so often fed me became a complex ritual of mirroring and self-assembly. The physical act of holding the spoon to her lips was not only a rite of nurture and of sacrifice, it was the return of a gift. It was a quiet bowing to the passage of time and the doubling back of all things. The quiet woman who listened to my woes about work and school required now that I bend my head down close to her and listen for mouthed word fragments, sentence crumbs. I bent down to give meaning to her silence, her wandering search for words.

She would eat what I brought to the hospital with relish; she would reject what I brought with a turn of her head. I brought fruit

---

[16] For an analysis of similar stories, see Richard Levins and Richard Lewontin, *The Dialectical Biologist* (Cambridge, Mass.: Harvard University Press, 1985), 66.

and yogurt, ice cream and vegetable juice. Slowly, over time, she stopped swallowing. The mashed potatoes would sit in her mouth like cotton, the pudding would slip to her chin in slow sad streams. When she lost not only her speech but the power to ingest, they put a tube into her nose and down to her stomach, and I lost even that medium by which to communicate. No longer was there the odd but reassuring communion over taste. No longer was there some echo of comfort in being able to nurture one who nurtured me.

This increment of decay was like a little newborn death. With the tube, she stared up at me with imploring eyes, and I tried to guess what it was that she would like. I read to her aimlessly and in desperation. We entertained each other with the strange embarrassed flickering of our eyes. I told her stories to fill the emptiness, the loneliness, of the white-walled hospital room.

I told her stories about who I had become, about how I had grown up to know all about exchange systems, and theories of contract, and monetary fictions. I spun tales about blue-sky laws and promissory estoppel, the wispy-feathered complexity of undue influence and dark-hearted theories of unconscionability. I told her about market norms and gift economy and the thin razor's edge of the bartering ethic. Once upon a time, I rambled, some neighbors of mine included me in their circle of barter. They were in the habit of exchanging eggs and driving lessons, hand-knit sweaters and computer programming, plumbing and calligraphy. I accepted the generosity of their inclusion with gratitude. At first, I felt that, as a lawyer, I was worthless, that I had no barterable skills and nothing to contribute. What I came to realize with time, however, was that my value to the group was not calculated by the physical items I brought to it. These people included me because they wanted me to be part of their circle, they valued my participation apart from the material things I could offer. So I gave of myself to them, and they gave me fruit cakes and dandelion wine and smoked salmon, and in their giving, their goods became provisions. Cradled in this community whose currency was a relational ethic, my stock in myself soared. My value depended on the glorious intangibility, the eloquent invisibility of my just being *part* of the collective; and in direct response I grew spacious and happy and gentle.

My gentle godmother. The fragility of life; the cold mortuary shelf.

Dispassionate deaths

The hospital in which my godmother died is now filled to capacity with AIDS patients. One in sixty-one babies born there, as in New

York City generally, is infected with AIDS antibodies.[17] Almost all
are black or Hispanic. In the Bronx, the rate is one in forty-three.[18]
In Central Africa, experts estimate that, of children receiving trans-
fusions for malaria-related anemia, "about 1000 may have been infected with the AIDS virus in each of the last five years."[19] In Congo,
5 percent of the entire population is infected.[20] The *New York Times*
reports that "the profile of Congo's population seems to guarantee
the continued spread of AIDS."[21]

In the Congolese city of Pointe Noir, "the annual budget of the
sole public health hospital is estimated at about $200,000—roughly
the amount of money spent in the United States to care for four
AIDS patients."[22]

The week in which my godmother died is littered with bad
memories. In my journal, I made note of the following:

> *Good Friday:* Phil Donahue has a special program on
> AIDS. The segues are:
>   a. from Martha, who weeps at the prospect of not
> watching her children grow up
>   b. to Jim, who is not conscious enough to speak just
> now, who coughs convulsively, who recognizes no one in his
> family any more
>   c. to Hugh who, at 85 pounds, thinks he has five years
> but whose doctor says he has weeks
>   d. to an advertisement for denture polish ("If you love
> your Polident Green/then gimmeeya SMILE!")
>   e. and then one for a plastic surgery salon on Park
> Avenue ("The only thing that's expensive is our address")
>   f. and then one for what's coming up on the five o'clock
> news (Linda Lovelace, of *Deep Throat* fame, "still recovering
> from a double mastectomy and complications from silicone
> injections" is being admitted to a New York hospital for a
> liver transplant)
>   g. and finally one for the miracle properties of all-
> purpose house cleaner ("Mr. Cleeean/is the man/behind the

[17] B. Lambert, "Study Finds Antibodies for AIDS in 1 in 61 Babies in New York
City," *New York Times* (January 13, 1988), sec. A.

[18] Ibid.

[19] "Study Traces AIDS in African Children," *New York Times* (January 22, 1988),
sec. A.

[20] J. Brooke, "New Surge of AIDS in Congo May Be an Omen for Africa," *New
York Times* (January 22, 1988), sec. A.

[21] Ibid.

[22] Ibid.

shine/is it wet or is it dry?" I note that Mr. Clean, with his gleaming bald head, puffy musculature and fever-bright eyes, looks like he is undergoing radiation therapy). Now back to our show.

h. "We are back now with Martha," (who is crying harder than before, sobbing uncontrollably, each jerking inhalation a deep unearthly groan). Phil says, "Oh honey, I hope we didn't make it worse for you."

Easter Saturday: Over lunch, I watch another funeral. My office windows overlook a graveyard as crowded and still as a rush-hour freeway. As I savor pizza and milk, I notice that one of the mourners is wearing an outfit featured in the window of Bloomingdale's (59th Street store) only since last weekend. This thread of recognition jolts me, and I am drawn to her in sorrow; the details of my own shopping history flash before my eyes as I reflect upon the sober spree that brought her to the rim of this earthly chasm, her slim suede heels sinking into the soft silt of the graveside.

Resurrection Sunday: John D., the bookkeeper where I used to work, died, hit on the head by a stray but forcefully propelled hockey puck. I cried copiously at his memorial service, only to discover, later that afternoon when I saw a black rimmed photograph, that I had been mourning the wrong person. I had cried because the man I *thought* had died is John D. the office messenger, a bitter unfriendly man who treats me with disdain; once I bought an old electric typewriter from him which never worked. Though he promised nothing, I have harbored deep dislike since then; death by hockey puck is only one of the fates I had imagined for him. I washed clean my guilt with buckets of tears at the news of what I thought was his demise.

The man who did die was small, shy, anonymously sweet-featured and innocent. In some odd way I was relieved; no seriously obligatory mourning to be done here. A quiet impassivity settled over me and I forgot my grief.

Holy communion

A few months after my godmother died, my Great Aunt Jag passed away in Cambridge, at ninety-six the youngest and the last of her siblings, all of whom died at ninety-seven. She collapsed on her way home from the polling place, having gotten in her vote for "yet another Kennedy." Her wake was much like the last family gathering at which I had seen her, two Thanksgivings ago. She was a little hard of hearing then and she stayed on the outer edge of the conversation, brightly, loudly, and randomly asserting enjoyment of her meal. At the wake, cousins, nephews, daughters-in-law, first wives, second husbands, great-grand-nieces gathered round her casket and got acquainted all over again. It was pouring rain outside. The funeral home was dry and warm, faintly spicily clean-smelling; the walls were solid, dark, respectable wood; the floors were cool stone tile. On the door of a room marked "No Admittance" was a sign that reminded workers therein of the reverence with which each body was held by its family and prayed employees handle the remains with similar love and care. Aunt Jag wore yellow chiffon; everyone agreed that laying her out with her glasses on was a nice touch.

Afterward, we all went to Legal Seafoods, her favorite restaurant, and ate many of her favorite foods.

On candor

Me

I have never been able to determine my horoscope with any degree of accuracy. Born at Boston's now-defunct Lying-In Hospital, I am a Virgo, despite a quite poetic soul. Knowledge of the *hour* of my birth, however, would determine not just my sun sign but my moons and all the more intimate specificities of my destiny. Once upon a time, I sent for my birth certificate, which was retrieved from the oblivion of Massachusetts microfiche. Said document revealed that an infant named Patricia Joyce, born of parents named Williams, was delivered into the world "colored." Since no one thought to put down the hour of my birth, I suppose that I will never know my true fate.

In the meantime, I read what text there is of me.

My name, Patricia, means patrician. Patricias are noble, lofty, elite, exclusively educated, and well mannered despite themselves. I was on the cusp of being Pamela, but my parents knew that such a me would require lawns, estates, and hunting dogs too.

I am also a Williams. Of William, whoever he was: an anonymous white man who owned my father's people and from whom some escaped. That rupture is marked by the dark-mooned mystery of utter silence.

Williams is the second most common surname in the United States; Patricia is *the* most common prename among women born in 1951, the year of my birth.

Them

In the law, rights are islands of empowerment. To be un-righted is to be disempowered, and the line between rights and no rights is most often the line between dominators and oppressors. Rights contain images of power, and manipulating those images, either visually or linguistically, is central in the making and maintenance of rights. In principle, therefore, the more dizzyingly diverse the images that are propagated, the more empowered we will be as a society.

In reality, it was a lovely polar bear afternoon. The gentle force of the earth. A wide wilderness of islands. A conspiracy of polar bears lost in timeless forgetting. A gentleness of polar bears, a fruitfulness of polar bears, a silent black-eyed interest of polar bears, a bristled expectancy of polar bears. With the wisdom of innocence, a child threw stones at the polar bears. Hungry, they rose from their nests, inquisitive, dark-souled, patient with foreboding, fearful in tremendous awakening. The instinctual ferocity of the hunter reflected upon the hunted. Then, proud teeth and warrior claws took innocence for wilderness and raging insubstantiality for tender rabbit breath.

In the newspapers the next day, it was reported that two polar bears in the Brooklyn Zoo mauled to death an eleven-year-old boy who had entered their cage to swim in the moat. The police were called and the bears were killed.[23]

In the public debate that ensued, many levels of meaning emerged. The rhetoric firmly established that the bears were innocent, naturally territorial, unfairly imprisoned, and guilty. The dead child (born into the urban jungle of a black, welfare mother and a Hispanic alcoholic father who had died literally in the gutter only six weeks before) was held to a similarly stern standard. The police were captured, in a widely disseminated photograph,[24] shooting helplessly, desperately, into the cage, through three levels of bars, at a pieta of bears; since this image, conveying much pathos, came nevertheless not in time to save the child, it was generally felt that the bears had died in vain.[25]

In the egalitarianism of exile, pluralists rose up as of one body, with a call to buy more bears, control juvenile delinquency, eliminate all zoos, and confine future police.[26]

[23] J. Barron, "Polar Bears Kill a Child at Prospect Park Zoo," *New York Times* (May 20, 1987), sec. A.
[24] *New York Post* (May 22, 1987), p. 1.
[25] J. Barron, "Officials Weigh Tighter Security at Zoos in Parks," *New York Times* (May 22, 1987), sec. B.
[26] Ibid.

In the plenary session of the national meeting of the Law and Society Association, the keynote speaker unpacked the whole incident as a veritable laboratory of emergent rights discourse. Just seeing that these complex levels of meaning exist, she exulted, should advance rights discourse significantly.[27]

At the funeral of the child, the presiding priest pronounced the death of Juan Perez not in vain, since he was saved from growing into "a lifetime of crime." Juan's Hispanic-welfare-black-widow-of-an-alcoholic mother decided then and there to sue.

The universe between

How I ended up at Dartmouth College for the summer is too long a story to tell. Anyway, there I was, sharing the town of Hanover, New Hampshire, with about two hundred prepubescent males enrolled in Dartmouth's summer basketball camp, an all-white, very expensive, affirmative action program for the street-deprived.

One fragrant evening, I was walking down East Wheelock Street when I encountered about a hundred of these adolescents, fresh from the courts, wet, lanky, big-footed, with fuzzy yellow crew cuts, loping toward Thayer Hall and food. In platoons of twenty-five or so, they descended upon me, jostling me, smacking me, and pushing me from the sidewalk into the gutter. In a thoughtless instant, I snatched off my brown silk headrag, my flag of African femininity and propriety, my sign of meek and supplicatory place and presentation. I released the armored rage of my short nappy hair (the scalp gleaming bare between the angry wire spikes) and hissed: "Don't I exist for you?! See Me! And deflect, godammit!" (The quaint professionalism of my formal English never allowed the rage in my head to rise so high as to overflow the edges of my text.)

They gave me wide berth. They clearly had no idea, however, that I was talking to them or about them. They skirted me sheepishly, suddenly polite, because they did know, when a crazed black person comes crashing into one's field of vision, that it is impolite to laugh. I stood tall and spoke loudly into their ranks: "I have my rights!" The Dartmouth Summer Basketball Camp raised its collective eyebrows and exhaled, with a certain tested nobility of exhaustion and solidarity.

I pursued my way, manumitted back into silence. I put distance between them and me, gave myself over to polar bear musings. I allowed myself to be watched over by bear spirits. Clean white wind and strong bear smells. The shadowed amnesia; the absence

---

[27] Patricia Williams, "The Meaning of Rights" (address to the annual meeting of the Law and Society Association, Washington, D.C., June 6, 1987).

of being; the presence of polar bears. White wilderness of icy meat-eaters heavy with remembrance; leaden with undoing; shaggy with the effort of hunting for silence; frozen in a web of intention and intuition. A lunacy of polar bears. A history of polar bears. A pride of polar bears. A consistency of polar bears. In those meandering pastel polar bear moments, I found cool fragments of white-fur invisibility. Solid, black-gummed, intent, observant. Hungry and patient, impassive and exquisitely timed. The brilliant bursts of exclusive territoriality. A complexity of messages implied in our being.

School of Law
City University of New York

PART II

CHALLENGING DICHOTOMIES
THE INTERSECTION OF
WORK AND FAMILY

A RESPONSE TO INEQUALITY:
BLACK WOMEN, RACISM, AND SEXISM

DIANE K. LEWIS

Introduction

The women's liberation movement has generated a number of theories about female inequality. Because the models usually focus exclusively upon the effects of sexism, they have been of limited applicability to minority women subjected to the constraints of both racism and sexism.[1] In addition, black women have tended both to see racism as a more powerful cause of their subordinate position than sexism and to view the women's liberation movement with considerable mistrust.[2]

Yet there are recent indications that a growing number of black women have become more responsive to the issue of women's rights.[3]

I am indebted to Oscar Berland and Naomi Katz for comments on an earlier draft of this paper.

1. For example, *Women, Culture and Society,* ed. Michelle Z. Rosaldo and Louise Lamphere (Stanford, Calif.: Stanford University Press, 1974), proposes several models of female subordination, but none considers fully the structural position and theoretical implications of women subject to both racism and sexism.

2. See Linda J. M. LaRue, "Black Liberation and Women's Lib," *Transaction* 8 (November–December 1970): 59–64; Nathan and Julia Hare, "Black Women 1970," ibid., pp. 68, 90; Jean Cooper, "Women's Liberation and the Black Woman," *Journal of Home Economics* 63 (October 1971): 521–23; Toni Cade, ed., *The Black Woman* (New York: New American Library, Signet Books, 1970); Mae C. King, "The Politics of Sexual Stereotypes," *Black Scholar* 4 (March–April 1973): 12; Inez Smith Reid, *"Together" Black Women* (New York: Third Press, 1972).

3. A 1972 poll showed that black women were more sympathetic than white women to efforts to upgrade women's status in society (62 percent to 45 percent, respectively) and that black women were also more supportive than white women of the attempts by women's liberation groups to do so (67 percent and 35 percent, respectively) (see Louis Harris & Associates, *The 1972 Virginia Slims American Women's Opinion Poll: A Survey of the Attitudes of Women on Their Roles in Politics and the Economy,* pp. 2, 4). Interestingly, Lucy Komisar notes that black organizations such as the Urban League and the National Association for the

This essay originally appeared in *Signs,* vol. 3, no. 2, Winter 1977.

During the past few years black women's organizations have emerged whose specific aim is to combat both sexism and racism. In January 1973 fifteen women formed the San Francisco–based Black Women Organized for Action (BWOA). It now has between 300 and 400 members.[4] In December 1973 the first conference of the National Black Feminist Organization (NBFO) met on the east coast in New York. It attracted 400 women. Though its leadership acknowledged difficulties in organizing black women around feminist issues,[5] the group stressed that many goals central to the women's liberation movement—day care, abortions, maternity leaves—were of critical importance to black women. Indeed, some were of greater intrinsic concern to them than to white women because of their more severe economic disadvantage.

This paper attempts to explain the initial rejection and then more favorable reaction to the women's movement on the part of black women. To do so, it develops a model of inequality which may illuminate the situation of women in complex societies who experience discrimination because of race and sex. A trend toward a greater acceptance of feminism may be due to changes in black women's perception of oppression, which in turn reflects changes in the social order. In the 1960s the black liberation movement began to generate important structural shifts in the relationship between blacks and whites in America. Blacks began to participate more fully in public activities previously reserved for whites. In such domains they encountered patterns of sexual discrimination. As the bulk of the higher-status, authoritative positions meted to

---

Advancement of Colored People, which formerly had little interest in feminist issues, have, in recent years, worked jointly with the National Organization of Women to further both minority and women's rights (see Lucy Komisar, "Where Feminism Will Lead," *Civil Rights Digest* 6 [Spring 1974]: 9).

4. Patsy G. Fulcher, Aileen C. Hernandez, and Eleanor R. Spikes, "Sharing the Power and the Glory," *Contact* 4 (Fall, 1974): 52. Eleanor Spikes, a cofounder of the organization, gave the recent estimate of membership (personal communication, April 1976) (see also, *What It Is,* the BWOA Newsletter which can be obtained from P.O. Box 10572, San Francisco, California 94115). Other black women's groups recently organized to eliminate both racism and sexism are League of Black Women (in Chicago), Black Women Concerned (in Baltimore), National Black Women's Political Leadership Caucus (in Detroit), and Sisters Getting Ourselves Together (in Davis, Calif.). (List compiled by Hernandez Associates, 4444 Geary Boulevard, San Francisco, California 94118). The BWOA is dedicated to involving black women in the political process, to helping them get jobs, and to supporting them in business, the arts, and all areas where they face discrimination and exclusion.

5. For example, when Eleanor Holmes Norton, Commissioner of Human Rights for New York City and a NBFO board member stated, "Five years ago you couldn't have gotten five women to come here," a welfare mother said, "Five years ago! . . . We tried to start a consciousness raising group four months ago and nobody was interested" (see "Feminism: 'The Black Nuance,' " *Newsweek* [December 17, 1973], p. 89).

blacks went to black men, a number of black women, particularly in the middle class, became more sensitive to the obstacle of sexism and to the relevance of the women's movement.[6]

Structural Inequality and Black Americans

Michelle Rosaldo has offered a model of female inequality. It proposes that (*a*) women are universally subordinate to men, (*b*) men are dominant due to their participation in public life and their relegation of women to the domestic sphere, and (*c*) the differential participation of men and women in public life gives rise not only to universal male authority over women but to a higher valuation of male over female roles.[7] The point that female inequality is inseparable from differential male/female activity in the public sphere is well taken. Nevertheless, a careful look at the relationship between black men and women and between blacks and whites in this society casts doubt on the full validity of Rosaldo's model.

Historically, black men, like black women, have been excluded from participation in the dominant society's politico-jural sphere and denied access to authority. Moreover, special measures have been needed to reaffirm black male inferiority. Since slavery coexisted with male dominance in the wider society, black men, as men, constituted a potential threat to the established order of white superiority. Laws were formulated that specifically denied black men normal adult prerogatives.[8] Such covertly sanctioned acts as lynchings and the rape and sexual exploitation of black women further intensified black male powerlessness.

Stringent institutionalized barriers to male participation continued for almost 100 years after slavery. These included the refusal of membership in national trade unions, which effectively barred black men from the job market;[9] prejudicial welfare laws, which undermined the

6. Eudora Pettigrew concluded more bluntly: "The black man grapples to achieve social justice and parity with the white male—essentially to attain white male power, privilege and status—while black women are shoved to the back of the bus." Quoted in Geraldine Rickman, "A Natural Alliance: The New Role for Black Women," *Civil Rights Digest* 6 (Spring 1974): 62 (see also Pauli Murray, "The Liberation of Black Women," in *Women: A Feminist Perspective*, ed. Jo Freeman [Palo Alto, Calif.: Mayfield Publishing Co., 1975], p. 354).

7. Rosaldo, "Women, Culture and Society: A Theoretical Overview," in Rosaldo and Lamphere, pp. 17–42.

8. Even Moynihan notes that black exclusionary laws were aimed primarily at defining and keeping the black *man* in his place (see Daniel Moynihan, *The Negro Family: The Case for National Action* [Washington, D.C.: Department of Labor, 1965], p. 62; Lerone Bennett, Jr., *Before the Mayflower* [Baltimore: Pelican Books, 1968], pp. 70–71, 92–93).

9. Andrew Billingsley, *Black Families in White America* (Englewood Cliffs, N.J.: Prentice-Hall, Inc., 1968), pp. 85–90.

man's status as husband and father;[10] and vigorous tactics to block black participation in the political process.[11] The systematic exclusion of black men from the public sphere suggests that black sex-role relationships cannot be adequately explained by the notion of a structural opposition between the domestic and public spheres or the differential participation of men and women in the public sphere.[12]

Rosaldo also suggests that egalitarian sex relationships can only develop in a society at a time when both sexes share equal participation in the public and domestic spheres.[13] There is growing evidence of strong egalitarianism in black sex-role relationships.[14] However, black men and

10. For a discussion of how modern public welfare functions to replace the male in low-income families, a process which affects a still-sizable number of blacks on welfare, see Helen Icken Safa, "The Female-based Household in Public Housing," *Human Organization* 24 (Summer 1965): 135–39 (see also Johnnie Tillmon, "Welfare Is a Woman's Issue," in *Marriage and the Family: A Critical Analysis and Proposals for Change*, ed. Carolyn C. Perrucci and Dena B. Targ [New York: David McKay Co., 1974], p. 109).

11. In the past, this took the form of intimidation and poll tax laws in the South and gerrymandering and cooptation in the North. For an analysis of other establishment bars to effective black political participation, see Stokely Carmichael and Charles V. Hamilton, *Black Power: The Politics of Liberation in America* (New York: Random House, Vintage Books, 1967).

12. Among racially oppressed groups it is important to distinguish between the public life of the dominant and the dominated societies. Using this framework, we recognize a range of male participation from token admittance to the public life of the dominant society to its attempts to destroy the public life within a dominated society. Mexican-American men, for example, have played strong public roles in their own dominated society, and, in fact, as Mexican-Americans have become more assimilated to the dominant society, sex roles have become less hierarchical (see Leo Grebler, Joan W. Moore, and Ralph C. Guzman, *The Mexican American People: The Nation's Second Largest Minority* [New York: Free Press, 1970], pp. 361–72). On the other hand, Afro-American men historically faced attempts at exclusion, enforced by the dominant society, from participation in a public life even among their own people (see Bennett, pp. 70–71, 92–93, and also Robert Staples, "The Myth of the Impotent Black Male," *Black Scholar* 2 [June 1971]: 3).

13. Rosaldo, pp. 40–42.

14. Virginia Heyer Young, "Family and Childhood in a Southern Negro Community," *American Anthropologist* 72 (April 1970): 269–88; Peter Kunkel and Sara Sue Kennard, *Spout Spring: A Black Community* (New York: Holt, Rinehart & Winston, 1971); Diane K. Lewis, "The Black Family: Socialization and Sex Roles," *Phylon* 36 (September 1975): 221–37; Robert B. Hill, *The Strengths of Black Families* (New York: Emerson Hall, 1972), p. 18. It has been pointed out that the notion of women's universal inferiority may be a reflection of our own Western cultural bias (see Nancy Tanner, "Matrifocality in Indonesia and Africa and among Black Americans," in Rosaldo and Lamphere, pp. 129–56, and Ruby Rohrlich Leavitt, *Peaceable Primates and Gentle People: Anthropological Approaches to Women's Studies* [New York: Harper & Row, 1975]). After developing most of the ideas in this paper, I was interested to see further critiques of the thesis of worldwide female inequality by the contributors to *Women Cross-culturally: Change and Challenge*, ed. Ruby Rohrlich Leavitt (The Hague: Mouton & Co., 1975), particularly the articles "Women, Knowledge and Power," by Constance Sutton, Susan Makiesky, Daisy Dwyer, and Laura Klein (pp. 581–600), and "Class, Commodity, and the Status of Women," by Eleanor Leacock (pp. 601–16).

women shared equal exclusion from, rather than equal participation in, the public sphere. What the black experience suggests is that differential participation in the public sphere is a symptom rather than a cause of structural inequality. While inequality is *manifested* in the exclusion of a group from public life, it is actually *generated* in the group's unequal access to power and resources in a hierarchically arranged social order. Relationships of dominance and subordination, therefore, emerge from a basic structural opposition between groups which is reflected in exclusion of the subordinate group from public life. This process may be further accentuated by increasing differentiation between the public and domestic spheres.[15] Members of a subordinate group, moreover, constitute a potential common-interest group whose interests derive from their shared powerlessness.[16] Their interests remain latent, however, until the power relations between themselves and a dominant group begin to shift and the structural opposition between them erupts into conflict.

Black women, due to their membership in two subordinate groups that lack access to authority and resources in society, are in structural opposition with a dominant racial and a dominant sexual group. In each subordinate group they share potential common interests with group comembers, black men on the one hand and white women on the other. Ironically, each of these is a member of the dominant group: black men as men, white women as whites. Thus, the interests which bind black women together with and pull them into opposition against comembers crosscut one another in a manner which often obscures one set of interests over another. Historically, their interests as blacks have taken precedence over their interests as women. A shift in the power relations between the races had to come before changes in the structural relationship between the sexes.

It has been noted that the latent interests shared by members of a subordinate group become manifest when they have been formulated into a conscious ideology.[17] Ideology, I suggest, articulates increasing

15. See Louise Lamphere, "Strategies, Cooperation and Conflict among Women in Domestic Groups," in Rosaldo and Lamphere, p. 100; and Leacock, pp. 610–11. Lamphere notes the relationship between sex egalitarianism and the merging of public and private spheres, and Leacock suggests that it is the imposition of hierarchical social forms that give rise to a division between public and domestic domains.

16. This model derives from ideas in Ralf Dahrendorf, "Toward a Theory of Social Conflict" in *Social Change: Sources, Patterns, Consequences,* ed. Amitai Etzioni and Eva Etzioni (New York: Basic Books, 1964), pp. 98–111, and in Denton E. Morrison, "Some Notes toward Theory on Relative Deprivation, Social Movements, and Social Change," *American Behavioral Scientist* 14 (May 1971): 675–90. "Power" here refers to "having great influence or control over others" (*The American Heritage Dictionary* [New York: Houghton Mifflin Co., 1969], p. 1027); "interests" refers to common values, objectives, and definitions of a situation.

17. See Dahrendorf, p. 107.

discontent, which emerges as a group's members perceive that their legitimate expectations are being frustrated. Frustration arises as they experience a sense of relative deprivation vis-à-vis other groups, a process occurring when (1) members of a subordinate group perceive the possibility of their own improved, more equitable position in the social system by comparing themselves with another group of structurally equivalent status whose members are improving their positions, and (2) members of a dominant group continue to frustrate their legitimate expectations for improved position while granting privileges and resources to members of the other subordinate group. The set of potential interests most clearly perceived as illegitimately blocked will become manifest first through the process of structural conflict. The black women's reactions to the black liberation and feminist movements described below reflect, I feel, their changing interests as they have become manifest through shifts in power relations between the races and between the sexes. Their response suggests that, as a subordinate group's interests change, the lines of conflict and structural opposition between groups tend to shift correspondingly.

The Structural Position of Black Women and White Women in America

Both white and black women in America have been excluded from the politico-jural domain and from positions of authority and prestige which have been reserved mainly for white men. Their joint exclusion as women would place them structurally in the same subordinate group, sharing potential common interests. Yet, due to racism, black women have occupied a structural position subordinate to white women in society.[18] They have had less access to deference, power, and authority. Sanday, noting the difference between deference and power as a basis of women's position, finds that Western women may receive deference in their "often highly valued roles as helpmate, sex object, the 'driving force behind every successful man,' etc." She contrasts this with women

18. Class, a third mitigating factor, is purposely omitted from this section in order to highlight the contrasts between white and black women which stem from racism. That white women represent on the whole a far more privileged group than black women is shown in census data which reveal that 64 percent of employed white women but only 42 percent of black and other minority women hold professional, clerical, or sales jobs, while 19 percent of white women and 37 percent of black and other minority women work in low-paying service-related and domestic occupations (see U.S. Bureau of the Census, *The Social and Economic Status of the Black Population in the United States, 1974,* Current Population Reports, Series P-23, No. 54 [Washington, D.C.: Government Printing Office, 1975], table 49, p. 74). Thus, while poor white women occupy a subordinate position, a greater percentage of black women are poor, and their inequality is compounded by race as well as class and sex.

who, playing important economic roles in other societies, may have power over critical resources but who lack deference and may be resented and feared by their husbands.[19] Black women, on account of male exclusion from the job market, have been forced to share with black men marginal participation in the public work world of the dominant society through menial and ill-paying jobs. Their economic contributions have often been essential to their families. Their important economic role has assured them power over the limited resources available to a racially excluded group. On the basis of power over crucial resources, black women have held a relatively high position within a dominated society.[20] This contrasts with the deference accorded white women in the dominant society. For, unlike white women, black women have lacked deference in the dominant society principally because of the stigma of race. Within the dominated society, their source of power has become one basis of denial of deference. Black writers have noted that black men, unable to get and keep jobs, display resentment toward black women who assume the role of "provider."[21] Concomitantly, the roles played by white women which are highly valued, that is, "the driving force behind every successful man," the valued sex object, are frequently denied black women: the first because of the exclusion of black men from the public world, and the second because of the impossibility of attaining a white standard of beauty.

19. Peggy R. Sanday, "Female Status in the Public Domain," in Rosaldo and Lamphere (n. 1 above), p. 191.

20. See Clyde W. Franklin, Jr., and Laurel R. Walum, "Toward a Paradigm of Substructural Relations: An Application to Sex and Race in the United States," *Phylon* 33 (Fall 1972): 249.

21. For example, William A. Blakey, a black man who is Director of Congressional Liaison for the U.S. Commission on Civil Rights, writes that the attitude of many black men toward black women is one of disrespect and a desire to dominate. He suggests that black men feel they must persecute black women in order to repudiate the myth of the " 'castrating' black matriarch" (see William A. Blakey, "Everybody Makes the Revolution: Some Thoughts on Racism and Sexism," *Civil Rights Digest* 6 [Spring 1974]: 19). Alice Walker also noted the prevailing antogonism of black men when she stated: "Black women are called matriarchs, called castraters of the men, and all kinds of things by black men. . . . [However black women] don't [*sic*] realize that they were all these ugly things that people said they were. They thought they were just providing for their families, that they were just surviving" (see Alice Walker, quoted in "Women on Women," *American Scholar* 972 [Autumn 1972]: 601–2. See also Frances Beale, "Double Jeopardy: To Be Black and Female," in Cade (n. 2 above), p. 92; Toni Cade, "On the Issue of Roles," ibid., p. 106; W. H. Grier and Price M. Cobb, *Black Rage* (New York: Basic Books, 1968). The contrast between female power over resources and male attitudes toward women that vary from resentment to lack of deferential treatment, which is characteristic not only of black Americans but of a number of other societies as well (e.g., Nupe, Iroquois; see Sanday, p. 191), suggests the complex factors involved in assessing sex-role relationships. Thus, structural egalitarianism may or may not be paralleled by mutual respect and deference just as male dominance may coexist with female deference or with women's fear and resentment toward men.

White women have not only been given deference. They have also had some access to power and authority.[22] While they themselves lacked authority in the dominant society, they have had a route to power through their kinship and marital ties with men (e.g., fathers, husbands, and sons) who do exercise authority in the public sphere. Moreover, white women, as members of the dominant group, formerly held both considerable authority and power vis-á-vis the subordinate racial group.

The variance in deference and access to power and authority between black and white women have proven to be critical factors underlying the black woman's perception of common group interests with black men and distrust of white women. During the long period of male exclusion from the public sphere, black women shared the experience of racial oppression with black men. From their perspective as members of a subordinate and powerless racial group, white women wielded greater power and garnered more respect than black men and far more than black women. In fact, attributes of the white woman's status currently criticized by many feminists as examples of sexism were seen (and are still seen) by many black women as representative of the unique privileges of women of the dominant group. For example, women who were forced to take menial jobs (often, in the past, and still to some extent in the present, as domestics in white women's homes) and who were unable to care for their own children or to rely on men for economic support contrasted themselves with white women who were not required to work outside their own homes and who were well provided for by their husbands.

A Response to Inequality

During the protest political movements of the sixties, radical white women became discontented at the subordinate position assigned them by white male activists. They formulated an ideology of female liberation to express their common interests as members of a powerless group in conflict with men, whom they perceived as blocking their legitimate aspirations to authority and resources in society.[23] Significantly, their sense of deprivation grew as they saw black people demanding and acquiring an improved and more equitable position in the wider society. The women's liberation movement emerged, in part, to acquire for women the same

22. Authority can be defined as the legitimate right to make decisions and command obedience. It contrasts with power where influence and control over others are not institutionalized but rest informally with individuals or their roles (see Rosaldo, p. 21, n. 2).

23. Jo Freeman, "The Origins of the Women's Liberation Movement," in *Changing Women in a Changing Society*, ed. Joan Huber (Chicago: University of Chicago Press, 1973), pp. 37–39.

access to authority and resources that the civil rights movement was fighting to obtain for blacks.[24]

The reaction of white women to traditional female subordination did not go unnoticed by black women. They, however, initially began to crystallize their interests as women at the same time that they continued to perceive obstacles to their most legitimate interests primarily in racial terms. In the remarkable anthology edited by Toni Cade, black women warn that the patterning of sex roles in white society offers a dangerous and stultifying model for blacks.[25] They note the detrimental effect of the dominant society on black man-woman relations.[26] They clearly establish that their aim is not so much to demand rights as women as to clarify issues or to "demand rights as Blacks first, women second."[27] In fact, the shared interests of black women seem to have little in common with white women. Cade asks: "How relevant are the truths, the experiences, the findings of White women to Black women? I don't know that our priorities are the same, that our concerns and methods are the same."[28]

Three years after publication of the Cade anthology, however, black women began clearly to formulate their interests as women concomitantly with their interests as members of an oppressed racial group. At the NBFO conference in 1973 a participant stated: "While we share with our men a history of toil and dignity, it is categorically different to be Black and a woman in this society than it has been to be Black and male."[29] The emergence of a feminist movement among black women, signaled by formation of the NBFO, the BWOA, and other organizations concerned with the special problems of being female and black,[30] indicates that some contemporary black women have begun to perceive the way both sex inequality and race inequality affect their lives.

In order to understand the structural factors which account for the black women's growing responsiveness to feminism it is necessary to

24. Catharine Stimpson, " 'Thy Neighbor's Wife, Thy Neighbor's Servants': Women's Liberation and Black Civil Rights," in *Women in Sexist Society*, ed. Vivian Gornick and Barbara K. Moran (New York: New American Library, Signet Books, 1971), pp. 622–57.

25. E.g., Cade, "On the Issue of Roles," pp. 102–3.

26. Beale, pp. 90–92.

27. "Preface," in Cade, *The Black Woman*, p. 10.

28. Ibid., p. 9.

29. Eleanor H. Norton, quoted on p. 86 in Bernette Golden, "Black Women's Liberation," *Essence* 4 (February 1974): 35–36, 75–76, 86.

30. Patricia Bell Scott, "Black Female Liberation and Family Action Programs: Some Considerations" (unpublished paper, n.d., p. 4), suggests that most black women's organizations are now concerned with the issue of black feminism, that is, the plight of black women who are oppressed by both sexism and racism. Among groups she cites, in addition to the NBFO, are the National Welfare Rights Organization, the National Committee on Household Employment, Domestics United of North Carolina, and the Black Women's Community Development Foundation.

analyze the effect of the race struggle on the position of black women. The worldwide black struggle against oppression heightened the discontent of American blacks at their subordinate position. As African countries gained independence from European colonizers, Afro-Americans experienced a growing sense of relative deprivation and perceived the possibility of changing power relationships between whites and blacks in the United States. While for many years the conflict between black and white was waged at the covert level and expressed in an ideology of gradual "race" advancement, black Americans became increasingly impatient at obstacles to their legitimately perceived expectations. Their interests became manifest, their ideology "militant." Civil rights activity in the 1950s spawned the "Black Power" movement, aimed at direct black participation in the political process, and the "Black Is Beautiful" movement, focused on a legitimation of black standards of beauty and physical worth. While black women easily perceived their own interests expressed in these political and cultural ideologies, and while they played a critical role in civil rights activities,[31] these movements, significantly, were seen as primarily male inspired and male led. According to some, the black woman's alleged place was "a step behind" the man's, and her proper role was the bearing and rearing of warriors for the struggle. Many women activists interpreted this attitude as an understandable reaction by black men, who had been duped by proposed white models of black matriarchy and male castration. They counseled patience and conciliation at what they perceived as deliberate divisive tactics by the dominant society.[32] Consequently, Pauli Murray noted, in spite of the black women's broad participation in the civil rights movement ". . . the aspirations of the black community have been articulated almost exclusively by black males. There has been very little public discussion of the problems, objectives or concerns of black women."[33] The black liberation movement resulted in the passage of such federal laws as the Civil Rights Act of 1964 and the Voting Rights Act of 1965. They were to provide institutional support for the termination of black exclusion from the public sphere. The laws, which had a dominoes effect, began to knock down barriers in many American institutions. Edu-

31. For a discussion of some of the significant contributions of black women to the black liberation movement, see Phyl Garland, "Builders of a New South," *Ebony* 21 (August 1966): 27–30, 34–37.

32. See Beale, p. 93; Cade, "On the Issues of Roles," pp. 107–8; Jean Carey Bond and Patricia Perry, "Is the Black Male Castrated," in Cade, *The Black Woman*, pp. 113–18; and Gwen Patton, "Black People and the Victorian Ethos," ibid., pp. 143–48. Francis Beale in a 1970 newspaper interview noted: "Often, as a way of escape . . . black men have turned their hostility toward their women. But this is what we have to understand about him . . . as black women we have to have a conciliatory attitude" (see Charlayne Hunter, "Many Blacks Wary of Women's Liberation Movement in U.S.," *New York Times* [November 17, 1970], p. 47).

33. Murray (n. 6 above), p. 354.

cation, direct political participation, and jobs began to become more accessible to "upwardly mobile" blacks. However, as blacks began to participate in the wider society they moved into a public arena sharply characterized by sex inequality. This situation, together with male domination of the black movement, signaled a significant differentiation in the participation of black men and women in the public sphere. Observing this situation, another black women, corroborating Murray, notes: "It is clear that when translated into actual opportunities for employment and promotional and educational benefits the civil rights movement really meant rights for black men. . . ."[34]

This differentiation is apparent in a comparison of the relative educational levels of black men and women. Education for blacks appears to have shifted in favor of men during the past few years, preceding apace with greater black inclusion in institutions of higher learning. Formerly, sociological studies of black communities showed that black women had higher rates of literacy and more years of schooling than males.[35] They were expected to go into higher education more often than men and had different aspirations,[36] which were linked primarily to the job market for adult blacks in the past. For example, in the South in the 1940s black men aspired to some independence through working their own farms or learning a skilled trade like bricklaying, plastering, or painting, skills transmitted from father to son. Black women, however, were offered higher education so they could become schoolteachers in the segregated school systems of the South and thereby get "out of the white folk's kitchen," the only other job possibility for black females.[37]

In the past, black women were also given greater educational opportunities than men by their families because "educational achievement for black men did not mean the opening up of economic opportunities."[38] Census data show that black women have more median years of schooling and more often graduate from high school than black men. The median years of formal education for black women and men twenty-five years of age and older between 1940 and 1970 are given in table 1.

In 1966, for blacks between twenty-five and thirty-four years of age women more often had a college degree than men; 5.2 percent of the men and 6.1 percent of the women had completed four or more years of

34. Constance M. Carroll, "Three's a Crowd: The Dilemma of the Black Woman in Higher Education," in *Academic Women on the Move,* ed. Alice Rossi and Ann Calderwood (New York: Russell Sage Foundation, 1973), p. 177.

35. Charles Johnson, *Shadow of the Plantation* (Chicago: University of Chicago Press, 1969), pp. 129–30.

36. Hylan Lewis, *Blackways of Kent* (New Haven, Conn.: College and University Press, 1964), pp. 105–6.

37. Ibid.

38. Gerda Lerner, ed., *Black Women in White America: A Documentary History* (New York: Random House, Pantheon Books, 1972), p. 220.

college. However, by 1974 the situation had reversed, and 8.8 percent of the men and 7.6 percent of the women had achieved that level of education.[39] Recent figures also show a sharp rise in the numbers of black men currently enrolled in college. While in 1970 16 percent of black men and 15 percent of black women between eighteen and twenty-four years of age were enrolled in college, by 1974 the figures were 20 percent and 16 percent, respectively.[40] The data indicate a decided shift in favor of black men in higher education over the past few years.[41]

Even in the late 1960s, however, when black women were enrolled in college in somewhat greater proportions than black men, black men were more likely to obtain graduate degrees beyond the M.A. than black women.[42] Jackson's 1968 study of black institutions found that 91 percent of the professional degrees granted in the combined fields of medicine, dentistry, law, veterinary medicine, and theology went to black

Table 1

Median Years of Schooling for Ages 25
and Over

Year	Black Women	Black Men
1940	6.1	5.3
1960	8.5	7.9
1970	10.0	9.3

SOURCES.—Figures for 1940 are from U.S. Department of Commerce, Bureau of the Census, *Sixteenth Census of the United States: 1940. Population: Characteristics of the Nonwhite Population by Race* (Washington, D.C.: Government Printing Office, 1943), table 6, p. 34; for 1960 are for "nonwhite" and are from U.S. Bureau of the Census, *U.S. Census of Population: 1960. Educational Attainment of the Population of the United States: 1960.* Supplementary Reports PC (S1)-37. (Washington, D.C.: Government Printing Office, 1972), table 173, p. 6; for 1970 are from U.S. Bureau of the Census, *Census of Population: 1970. Subject Reports. Educational Attainment.* Final Report PC(2)-5B (Washington, D.C.: Government Printing Office, 1973), table 1, pp. 3, 6.

39. U.S. Bureau of the Census (n. 18 above), table 68, p. 97.
40. Ibid., table 65, p. 94.
41. See Cynthia Fuchs Epstein, "Positive Effects of the Multiple Negative: Explaining the Success of Black Professional Women," in Huber (n. 23 above), pp. 152–53. See also a study by Elias Blake, Linda Jackson Lambert, and Joseph L. Martin, "Degrees Granted and Enrollment Trends in Historically Black Colleges: An Eight Year Study" (Washington, D.C.: Institute for Services to Education, 1974), table 9a, p. 31, which shows that in black four-year colleges, as well, black male enrollment has gradually increased from 45.4 percent in 1966 to 47.8 percent in 1973.
42. Carroll, pp. 174–75.

men and only 9 percent to black women.[43] Two surveys of blacks with doctorates in all fields from all institutions in 1969 and 1970 suggest that black women hold roughly 21 percent of these advanced degrees.[44] Moreover, black men attend more prestigious institutions than black women, and this factor, along with their greater monopoly of advanced professional degrees, affects occupational patterns.[45]

For, according to figures of the U.S. Census Bureau, black women are the poorest paid in the occupational structure. Black men earn more than both black women and white women. The median earnings for year-round, full-time workers in 1963, 1970, and 1974 show an interesting trend over the eleven-year span (see table 2). Note that the wage differential between black women's and black men's salaries went from $1,739 in 1963 to $2,334 in 1974. Although the gap between the dollar earnings of black women and black men widened, there was some improvement in the ratio of female to male income, black women earning 57 percent of the income of black men in 1963 and 74 percent in 1974. In the past, the low pay of black women was related to their frequent employment as domestics. In 1963, as shown in table 3, one out of three black women was a private household worker, but by 1974 only 11 per-

Table 2

Median Earnings Year-round Full-Time Workers
($)

Group	1963	1970	1974
White males	6,245	9,447	12,434
Black males	4,019	6,435	8,705
White females	3,687	5,536	7,021
Black females	2,280	4,536	6,371

SOURCES.—Figures for 1963 are from U.S. Bureau of the Census, *Income of Families and Persons in the United States, 1963*, Current Population Reports, Series P-60, No. 43 (Washington, D.C.: Government Printing Office, 1964), table 18, p. 34 (the table compares whites and nonwhites; the latter are predominantly black); for 1970 are from U.S. Bureau of the Census, *Money Income in 1973 of Families and Persons in the United States*, Current Population Reports, Series P-60, No. 97 (Washington, D.C.: Government Printing Office, 1975), table F, p. 12, for 1974 are from U.S. Bureau of the Census, *Money Income in 1974 of Families and Persons in the United States*, Current Population Reports, Series P-60, No. 101 (Washington, D.C. Government Printing Office, 1975), pp. 106–7.

43. Jacqueline J. Jackson, "Black Women and Higher Education" (unpublished paper, 1973), cited ibid., table 9.1, p. 174. Jackson's figures show that 62 percent of these professional degrees were in the fields of medicine and law and that 85.6 percent of the M.D.'s and 90.4 percent of the LL.B.'s were granted to black men.

44. See Kent G. Mommsen, "Career Patterns of Black American Doctorates" (Ph.D. diss., Florida State University, 1970), table 1, p. 41.

45. Jacqueline J. Jackson, "But Where Are the Men?" *Black Scholar* 3 (December 1971): 30–41.

Table 3

Occupation of Men and Women, 1963, 1970, 1974 (Annual Averages, in Percentages)

	1963 Women White	1963 Women Negro and Other Races*	1963 Men White	1963 Men Negro and Other Races*	1970 Women White	1970 Women Negro and Other Races*	1970 Men White	1970 Men Negro and Other Races*	1974 Women White	1974 Women Negro and Other Races*	1974 Men White	1974 Men Negro and Other Races*
White-collar workers:	61	21	41	15	64	36	43	22	64	42	42	24
Professional and technical	14	8	13	5	15	11	15	8	15	12	15	9
Managers and administrators except farm	5	2	15	4	5	2	15	5	5	2	15	5
Sales workers	8	2	6	2	8	3	6	2	7	3	6	2
Clerical workers	34	10	7	5	36	21	7	7	36	25	6	7
Blue-collar workers:	17	15	46	57	16	19	46	60	15	20	46	57
Craft and kindred workers	1	0.5	20	11	1	1	21	14	2	1	21	16
Operatives, including transport	15	14	20	25	14	17	19	28	13	17	18	26
Non-farm laborers	0.3	0.7	6	21	...	1	6	18	1	1	7	15
Service workers	15	22	6	16	15	26	6	13	17	26	7	15
Private household workers	5	34	...	...	3	18	...	...	3	11	...	...
Farm workers	3	7	8	11	2	2	5	6	2	1	5	4

SOURCES.—Figures for 1963 taken from U.S. Bureau of the Census, *The Social and Economic Status of the Black Population in the United States, 1973*, Current Population Reports, Special Studies Series P-23, No. 48 (Washington, D.C.: Government Printing Office, 1974), table 38, p. 54 and table 39, p. 55; for 1970 and 1974 taken from U.S. Bureau of the Census, *The Social and Economic Status of the Black Population in the United States, 1974*, Current Population Reports, Series P-23, No. 54 (Washington, D.C.: Government Printing Office, 1975), table 48, p. 73, and table 49, p. 74.

*Nearly 90 percent are Negro.

cent of black women were domestics. However, a comparison of jobs held by black women with those held by black men in 1974 shows that while black women have been moving out of domestic work 37 percent or over one-third were still in low-paying service and household jobs not covered by the federal minimum wage, as compared with only 15 percent of black men. Moreover, while black women white-collar workers relative to black men have been highly represented in teaching, nursing, and social work—occupations which are extensions of their domestic roles and traditional careers for women—black men, as they have moved into the public sphere, have been more often found than women in the more prestigious and better-paid professions of medicine, law, science, and college teaching.[46]

Figures showing gradual black inclusion in the field of higher education clearly indicate that black women are either poorly represented or relegated to the lower-status and lower-paid jobs. For example, Carroll found that at the University of Pittsburgh in 1970 black and white women were disproportionately represented in nontenured academic positions and that black men, as well as white men, in relationship to their total numbers, monopolized the higher and tenured ranks (see table 4). Carroll notes that for the University of Pittsburgh, "Clearly, sex is more of a handicap than race . . . and the disproportion between the sexes is far greater for blacks than for whites."[47] Five years later, the occupational profile of the University of California, one of the largest educational complexes in the United States, shows that continued recruitment of blacks and other minorities has resulted in a marked sex inequality in high-level positions. The figures for April 1975 show employment in administration and in tenured and nontenured ladder-faculty positions for black men and women in the nine-campus system (see table 5).[48]

Table 4

Full-Time Professional Staff at University of Pittsburgh, 1970

Rank	White Men	White Women	Minority Men	Minority Women
Full professor	420	25	21	0
Associate professor	355	42	17	1
Nontenured	792	268	83	31

SOURCE.—Figures compiled from Constance M. Carroll, "Three's a Crowd: The Dilemma of the Black Woman in Higher Education," in *Academic Women on the Move*, ed. Alice Rossi and Ann Calderwood (New York: Russell Sage Foundation, 1973), table 9.3, p. 175.
NOTE.—"Minority" refers to predominantly black.

46. See Epstein, pp. 153–54, and Jackson, "But Where Are the Men?" p. 32.

47. Carroll, pp. 174–75 (see also William Moore, Jr., and Lonnie H. Wagstaff, *Black Educators in White Colleges* [San Francisco: Jossey-Bass, Inc., 1974], pp. 154–77).

48. It should be stressed that blacks and other minorities (Asian/Asian-Americans, American Indians and Mexican/Spanish-Americans) are still greatly underrepresented in

Information on black law-faculty members, nationwide, shows a similar skewing in favor of black men. The 1976 directory of minority law professors reveals that there are 226 blacks and thirty-eight nonwhite women out of a total of 282 minority professors. A check of the directory turned thirty-seven women who could be identified by name and judging by surname the majority of these were probably black (see table 6).

The situation in institutions of higher learning is paralleled in government jobs and in the business world generally. In 1974 black women were 19.8 percent of all women and 63.7 percent of all blacks working full time as GS-graded federal employees. While they were generally underrepresented among women in the higher-level jobs, among blacks they were both markedly overrepresented in the lower-ranking jobs and underrepresented in the higher-ranking jobs, as shown in table 7.

Similarly, the 1975 California State Personnel Board's report to the governor and legislature on state employees, which gave monthly salary by sex and race, showed that while the percentages of black men and women were approximately the same (i.e., 3.7 and 3.4 percent, respectively, of the total numbers employed) black men were more highly represented than black women at the higher salary ranges (see table 8). A recent survey of minorities in the mass-media industry indicates that 82 percent were males.[49] In the business-management training field as well, men, regardless of race, have been given a decided preference over women.[50]

---

higher education. The point here is that their gradual inclusion into the system has been proceeding along sex discriminatory lines. This was especially evident in the employment figures for April 1974 (see the table below for figures for April 1974). Comparison with table 5 shows that there has been some improvement for minority women over the ensuing eighteen months. A total of twelve additional black women were hired while seven "other minority" women were added.

	Black Men	Black Women	Other Minority Men	Other Minority Women
Deans and provosts	5	1	1	...
Tenured faculty	41	...	178	7
Nontenured ladder faculty	51	9	84	21

Source.—University of California computer printout, PER 1096, "Summary of Ethnic and Sex Employment, as of April 30, 1974," pp. 1–3.

49. Abigail Jones Nash, Marilyn Jackson-Beeck, Leverne Tracy Regan, and Vernon A. Stone, "Minorities and Women in Broadcast News: Two National Surveys" (paper presented at the annual convention of the Association for Education in Journalism, San Diego, 1974), p. 7.

50. See Bird McCord, "Identifying and Developing Women for Management Positions," *Training and Development Journal* 25 (November 1971): 2.

Table 5

Total Minorities at the University of California, October 1975

Rank	Black Men	Black Women	Other Minority Men	Other Minority Women	Total Men	Total Women
Deans and provosts................	6	1	1	2	155	16
Full professors	24	3	126	...	2,947	124
Associate professors	21	3	82	10	1,398	135
Nontenured ladder faculty	47	15	91	23	1,146	290

SOURCE.—University of California Computer printout, PER 1023, "Summary of Ethnic and Sex Employment, Academic Group/Rank, All Campuses, as of October 31, 1975," pp. 1–3.

Table 6

Minority Law-Faculty Members

Rank	Total Blacks	Minority Women
Professor	37	4
Associate professor	39	6
Assistant professor	51	8
Administrator	24	6
Teacher/administrator	22	5
Part time	49	6
Teaching fellow	4	2
Total	226	37

SOURCE.—*1976 Directory of Minority Law Faculty Members,* Section on Minority Groups, Association of American Law Schools, pp. 9, 25–48.

Table 7

Full-Time Federal Employment of Black Women

General Schedule Grade Grouping	Total Black	Black Women		
		N	All Blacks *(%)*	All Women *(%)*
GS-1–4	66,999	50,143	74.8	12.7
GS-5–8	67,316	45,147	67.1	19.5
GS-9–11	20,772	8,591	41.4	15.8
GS-12–15	11,429	2,206	19.3	12.2
GS-16–18	149	16	10.7	13.3
Total	166,665	106,103	63.7	19.8

SOURCE.—From U.S. Bureau of the Census, *The Social and Economic Status of the Black Population in the United States, 1974* (see table 3 above), table 53, p. 78.

Direct black participation in the political process through election to office has increased over the past five years. While blacks are still woefully underrepresented in government, they moved from 1,230 to 2,630 elected officials between 1969 and 1974. However, movement of blacks into politics, as into higher-paying jobs generally, replicates the wider societal pattern of unequal female inclusion in the politico-jural domain. In 1974, while 2,293 black men were elected officials only 337 black women held that position.[51] This is a significant shift toward disparity, given the tradition of egalitarianism between the sexes and the former importance of women in black public life.[52]

51. U.S. Bureau of the Census, *The Social and Economic Status of the Black Population in the United States, 1973,* Current Population Reports, Special Studies Series P-23, No. 48, (Washington, D.C.: Government Printing Office, 1974), table 74, p. 103. In 1974 blacks held 0.5 of 1 percent of the elective offices (see Herrington J. Bryce and Alan E. Warrick, "Black Women in Elective Offices," *Black Scholar* 6 [October 1974]: 17–20).

52. Lerner (n. 38 above), pp. 319–22, shows that in the past black women, although not holders of elective office, were active in politics.

Table 8

California State Employees: Percentage Distribution
of Monthly Salary for Black Workers, March 1975

Monthly Salary Rate ($)	Black Men	Black Women
Under 500	3.6	12.5
500–699	2.6	7.9
700–899	5.2	5.3
900–1,099	5.7	2.8
1,100–1,299	2.9	1.1
1,300–1,599	2.4	0.9
1,600–2,099	2.4	0.7
Over 2,099	1.8	0.2

SOURCE.—"Minority Women: Triple Discrimination," *Affirmative Action in Progress* 2 (April 1976): 6.

If, as an aftermath of the 1960s, a number of black men were recruited into higher-paying, more authoritative, and prestigious positions, black women generally moved into the lower-status and lower-paying jobs traditionally reserved for women in the dominant society. During this process they made significant strides relative to white women. Although the difference in earnings between black men and women has widened, the income gap between black women and white women has tended to narrow (see table 9). Black women earned 62 percent of the median income of white women in 1963; this increased to 90 percent in 1974.[53] Similarly, recent census data indicate that the overall occupational distribution of black women has improved relative to white women. Since 1963 black women have moved out of domestic work and into clerical positions in greater numbers. Thus, in 1963, 34 percent of black women were domestics, and only 10 percent were clerical workers; in 1974, 11 percent were domestics and 25 percent were clerical workers. Since the percentages for white women clerical workers have remained relatively stable between 1963 and 1974 (34 percent and

Table 9

Wage Differential between Black Women, Black Men
and White Women
($)

	1963	1970	1974
Between black women and black men	1,739	1,899	2,334
Between black women and white women	1,407	1,000	650

53. For a comparison of increases in the ratio of black to white median income from 1967 to 1973 for men and women, see U.S. Bureau of the Census, *Money Income in 1973 of Families and Persons in the United States*, Current Population Reports, Series P-60, No. 97 (Washington, D.C.: Government Printing Office, 1975), table F, p. 12.

36 percent, respectively), black women appear to be moving toward parity with white women in that occupation (see table 3). Although the position of black women has improved in relationship to white women, the data show that for women as a whole sexism continues to constitute a major barrier in the wider society. In fact, the ratio of white female to white male earnings has *decreased* slightly between 1963 and 1974, women earning 59 percent of the male's median income in 1963 and only 56 percent in 1975 (computed from table 3). The existence of sex bias in the wider society explains the observation that the civil rights movement elicited active efforts to provide career opportunities for black men, while little attention was paid to the employment needs of black women.[54]

Class and Sexism

The black liberation movement began to generate important structural changes in the relationship between blacks and whites in American society. For black women, these changes serve to heighten their perception of sexism, since they experience deep-seated sex discrimination as they engage in increased participation in the public sphere. Middle-class black women, in particular, are becoming more sensitive to the obstacle of sexism as racial barriers begin to fall and as the bulk of the higher-status, authoritative positions reserved for blacks have gone to black men. Nevertheless, if the leadership of black organizations recently formed to combat both racism and sexism appears to be middle class, the membership in these black women's groups seems to crosscut class lines. Thus the BWOA notes that its members include welfare recipients, maids, and the unemployed as well as high-income earners. In recognition of this diversity, the organization has adopted a flexible membership policy.[55] Similarly, the NBFO conference attracted domestic workers, welfare mothers, and other poor black women as well as students, housewives, and professionals. As one participant put it, "We were able to do what white feminists have failed to do: transcend class lines and eradicate labels."[56]

A further examination of the structural position of black women suggests why not only upwardly mobile black women but also poor black women will become more responsive to feminist issues. They, along with

54. See Pauli Murray, "Jim Crow and Jane Crow," in Lerner, p. 596.

55. Dues are computed on a sliding scale from $5.00 to $25.00 a year, but members pay when and what they can. Moreover, a woman can become a member *either* by paying dues *or* attending meetings *or* working on a committee (see Fulcher et al. [n. 4 above], pp. 52, 63).

56. Ashaki Habiba Taha, letter *MS* 3 (August 1974): 12 (see also Golden [n. 29 above], p. 36).

middle-class black women, are seriously affected by sex discrimination on the job. For example, Dietrich and Greiser in a study of black blue-collar workers found sexism to be an important factor in black poverty.[57] Furthermore, demographic and occupational trends, which affect all black women, should also elicit among them a sense of common interest which crosscuts class lines. There has been a steadily declining sex ratio from 95.0 in 1940 to 90.8 in 1970.[58] This probably contributes to the fact that black women are more often single than white women, more often work, and are more often heads of household. Thus, in 1974 about one half of minority women worked compared with 44 percent of white women.[59] In 1973, while 77 percent of white women who were fourteen years old and over and ever married were married and living with their husbands, only 54 percent of black women in the same category were married and residing with their spouses.[60] In 1975, while only 11 percent of white families were female headed, 35 percent of black families were supported by women.[61] Black women with preschool-aged children were also more likely to work than white mothers; in 1973, 49 percent of black women as compared with 32 percent of white women with small children were in the labor force.[62]

Black women, then, are more often self-supporting than white women and far more likely to carry single-handedly responsibilities for dependent children. These factors, together with their continued greater concentration in lower-paying service-related jobs than either white women or black men, cause poor black women, particularly, to be vitally affected by matters of inadequate income and child-care facilities, both major issues in the women's movement. For poor women, as a black welfare mother notes, women's liberation is "a matter of survival," a perception increasingly held by such groups devoted to removing obstacles to the legitimate interests of poor black women as the National Welfare Rights Organization.[63]

Since both poor and middle-class black women participate in and have been aware of some of the successes of the black liberation move-

57. Kathryn Dietrich and Lee Greiser, "The Influence of Sex on Wage-Income of Black, Blue-Collar Workers in Selected Non-metropolitan and Metropolitan Areas of Texas" (paper presented at the annual meeting of the Southern Association of Agricultural Scientists, Memphis, Tennessee, February 1974).

58. Jackson, "But Where Are the Men?" table 3, p. 39. The sex ratio among whites has also declined steadily but in 1970 was, at 95.3, far more favorable for whites.

59. U.S. Bureau of the Census, *The Social and Economic Status of the Black Population in the United States, 1973*, p. 93.

60. Ibid., table 64, p. 90.

61. U.S. Bureau of the Census, *The Social and Economic Status of the Black Population in the United States, 1974*, table 72, p. 107.

62. U.S. Bureau of the Census, *The Social and Economic Status of the Black Population in the United States, 1973*, table 68, p. 95.

63. Tillmon (n. 10 above), pp. 108, 109, 111.

ment, their expectations of greater access to resources have been raised. As these expectations have been frustrated, a sense of common interest is beginning to emerge which may increasingly include all classes of black women. A study of race and class factors affecting women's attitudes toward the women's liberation movement in Cleveland found that white working-class women were far less likely than white middle-class women to be interested in women's rights, while black working-class women were somewhat *more* receptive than black middle-class women to efforts to change women's status[64] (see table 10).

The shared experience of racism has also tended to blur class lines among blacks. This, too, probably will contribute to a greater tendency for both poor and middle-class black women to agree regarding women's rights. For example, middle-class black families are in a more precarious position than middle-class white families because of racism. Especially in times of economic recession and high unemployment, they may find themselves in economic straits similar to lower-class blacks.[65]

Whether black women develop a sense of common interests that is manifested more in opposition to sexism or to racism will depend upon the structural relationship between the sexes and between the races. With growing black participation in the wider society some black women, experiencing frustration of their interests primarily as women, now probably share the viewpoint a member of NBFO expressed. "White women are our natural allies; we can't take on the system alone."[66] Middle-class black women will increasingly feel their interests as women illegitimately frustrated if a combination of factors continues: (1) the

Table 10

Percentage of Black and White Women Manifesting a High or
Low Degree of Interest in Women's Rights

Degree of Interest	Black Women		White Women	
	Middle Class	Working Class	Middle Class	Working Class
High	44	48	54	27
Low	56	52	46	73

SOURCE.—From Willa Mae Hemmons, "Toward an Understanding of Attitudes Held by Black Women on the Women's Liberation Movement" (Ph.D. diss., Case Western Reserve University, 1973), tables 7 and 8, p. 101.

64. Willa Mae Hemmons, "Toward an Understanding of Attitudes Held by Black Women on the Women's Liberation Movement" (Ph.D. diss., Case Western Reserve University, 1973). Her sample for this exploratory study was a purposive one, including eighty-three women, forty-five black and thirty-seven white. She notes that she sought women from different classes and residential and occupational areas; however the size of her sample makes her results more suggestive than conclusive (see her discussion of the sample, pp. 80–86).

65. Cf. Billingsley (n. 9 above), pp. 10–15.

66. Eleanor H. Norton, quoted in Golden, p. 86.

income gap between themselves and white women narrows even more, (2) the overall position of women remains low, and (3) the white male hierarchy persists in admitting minority males but excluding minority females from equitable participation in the wider society. Middle-class black women, even more than middle-class white women, occupy a structural position likely to generate a pervasive sense of relative deprivation and an ideology of discontent.

However, on the other hand, black women may see that racism still affects a considerable number of blacks, including black men. Jessie Bernard, analyzing occupations and earnings for black and white men and women for the period 1939–70, concluded: ". . . racism tends to be more serious for black men than black women . . . (and) sexism tends to be more serious for black women than racism."[67] While some middle-class black men have made significant advances, a careful inspection of the trends of the ratio of black to white earnings shows that black men, as a whole, are making much slower headway in closing the income gap between them and white men than are black women relative to white women. Black men earned 64 percent of the median income of white men in 1967; 67 percent of the income of white men in 1973.[68] This would appear to matter to black women. For example, if they marry, there will probably be more pressure on them to work in order to supplement the family income than on married white women. Indeed, now black married women are more likely to work outside the home than their white counterparts.[69]

Perpetuation of a situation in which all black men, irrespective of their socioeconomic status, are subject to racism, might well propel increasing numbers of black women, irrespective of their class backgrounds into overt opposition to both sexism and racism. Their way of doing so, however, might involve organizations concerned with women's rights, but limited to blacks and strongly racially oriented.[70] The concern with racism would preclude too exclusive a concern with sexism.

Department of Anthropology
University of California, Santa Cruz

67. Jessie Bernard, "The Impact of Sexism and Racism on Employment Status and Earnings, with Addendum," Module 25 (New York: MSS Modular Publications, Inc., 1974), p. 5.

68. U.S. Bureau of the Census, *Money Income in 1973 of Families and Persons in the United States*, table F, p. 12. This was similar to the rate of growth of black female income to the black male's, i.e., black women earned 67 percent of the income of black men in 1967 and 70 percent of the income of black men in 1973.

69. U.S. Bureau of of the Census, *The Social and Economic Status of the Black Population in the United States, 1973*, table 67, p. 95.

70. For an alternate thesis on the possible direction of change in the relationship between blacks and whites, males and females, see Franklin and Walum (n. 20 above), pp. 247–52. See also Rickman (n. 6 above), pp. 57–65, for an interesting discussion of the black professional woman's structural position which enables her to act as catalyst for change in the position of both women and blacks.

THE DIALECTICS OF BLACK WOMANHOOD

BONNIE THORNTON DILL

A new scholarship about black women, strengthened by the growing acceptance of black and women's studies as distinct areas of academic inquiry and by the need to refute myths and stereotypes about black women and black family life which helped shape social policies of the mid-1960s, is examining aspects of black family life that have been overlooked or distorted. Several studies have argued that a historical tradition of work forms an essential component in the lives of Afro-American women.[1] Beginning from that premise, this paper seeks to demonstrate that the emphasis on women's work role in Afro-American culture has generated alternative notions of womanhood contradictory to those that have been traditional in modern American society.[2]

This is a revision of a paper presented at the Seventieth Annual Meetings of the American Sociological Association, August 25–29, 1975, San Francisco, California. I would like to thank Elizabeth Higginbotham and Carroll Seron for their helpful comments and criticism.

　　1. See Delores Aldridge, "Black Women in the Economic Marketplace: A Battle Unfinished," *Journal of Social and Behavioral Scientists* 21 (Winter 1975): 48–61; Jacqueline Jackson, "Family Organization and Ideology," in *Comparative Studies of Blacks and Whites in the United States*, ed. Kent Miller and Ralph Dreger (New York: Seminar Press, 1973); and Diane K. Lewis, "A Response to Inequality: Black Women, Racism, and Sexism," *Signs* 3 (Winter 1977): 339–61.
　　2. Natalie J. Sokoloff, "The Economic Position of Women in the Family," in *The Family*, ed. Peter J. Stein, Judith Richman, and Natalie Hannon (Reading, Mass.: Addison-Wesley Publishing Co., 1977).

This essay originally appeared in *Signs*, vol. 4, no. 3, Spring 1979.

These new models project images of female sexual and intellectual equality, economic autonomy, and legal as well as personal parity with men. While they represent a new direction in the social ideology, they reflect an aspect of life that has been dominant for generations among many Afro-American women. Dialectical analysis enables us to clarify and illuminate this contradiction, and could provide theoretical direction to the new scholarship. But understanding the dialectics of black womanhood first requires rethinking several areas of scholarship about black women and their families.

Black Women in Black Family Literature

Four major problems pervade the literature on Afro-American families. The first of these derives from the use of inadequate historical data and/or the misinterpretation of that data. The second entails erroneous or partially conceived assumptions about the relationship of blacks to white society. The third problem is a direct result of the second and arises because of the differences between the values of the researcher and those of the subject. Fourth is the general confusion of class and culture.

Problem One: Issues in Black Family History

The dominant influence on the study of the black family and the role of black women was Frazier's *The Negro Family in the United States.*[3] While his major contribution was to provide a historical and sociological analysis of black family life in a period when psychological and biological theories of racial inferiority abounded, his historical methodology had serious shortcomings.

According to Gutman, Frazier did not explain the conditions he studied but "read that condition back into the past and linked it directly to the nineteenth-century slave experience."[4] He concluded that female-headed families, which he termed the "matriarchate," had developed during the slave period and gained prominence after emancipation among those blacks who were economically unstable or otherwise removed from the direct influence of Euro-American culture. In his view, poverty and limited assimilation into the dominant culture inhibited their adopting the normative family patterns of the society. Since

3. E. Franklin Frazier, *The Negro Family in the United States* (Chicago: University of Chicago Press, 1966).
4. Herbert Gutman, "Persistent Myths about the Afro-American Family," *Journal of Interdisciplinary History*, vol. 6, no. 2 (Autumn 1975).

these conditions were characteristic of most black families, he concluded that female-headed households were prototypical of black family life. Using a linear model of historical change, Frazier argued that the subsequent crises of reconstruction and urbanization served only to intensify this type of family disorganization.

The overriding image of black women that emerged from his work is that of a strong and independent person who placed little value on marriage, engaged without conscience in free sexual activity, and had no notion of male supremacy. As a grandmother, she is depicted as the "oldest head" in a maternal family organization, ideotypically defined as a three-generation household. Thus, while Frazier identified some of the historical conditions which encouraged the development of self-reliance and autonomy in black women, the limitations of his historical interpretation resulted in his evaluating these qualities negatively, suggesting that they were contributory factors in the disorganization of Afro-American family life.

Probably the most debated of recent studies which drew heavily on Frazier's history is "The Moynihan Report."[5] Moynihan accepted, without examination, Frazier's linear model of the historical development of the black family and used it as an explanation for contemporary data. The effect of his work, focusing on marital dissolution, illegitimacy rates, female-headed families, and welfare dependency, was to "prove" that Frazier's interpretation was still relevant. However, Frazier's analysis of black family history is being refuted, not only because of its methodological weakness but also because of its findings.

Gutman's recent study of black families suggests the breadth and detail required for a more accurate understanding of the history of black families, particularly with regard to its structure and normative patterns.[6] He contends that the female-headed household, while a recurrent pattern, was atypical in the period before 1925 and generally exaggerated in studies of black family life. His findings indicate that: (1) there is little evidence of a matriarchal form of household; (2) the typical household everywhere was a simple nuclear household headed by a male; (3) there is no significant difference in the household structure of field hands as opposed to artisans and house servants (this finding addresses itself directly to the issue of assimilation); (4) some of the physical movement associated with emancipation involved the reconstruction of broken slave households; and (5) sustained marriage among slaves, common everywhere, meant that the role models of marriage and family

5. U.S. Department of Labor, Office of Policy Planning and Research, *The Negro Family: The Case for National Action* (Washington, D.C.: Government Printing Office, March 1965).

6. Herbert Gutman, *The Black Family in Slavery and Freedom* (New York: Pantheon Books, 1976).

existed *within* the slave world and were constantly available to younger slaves.[7]

Gutman's work is important in developing a dialectical analysis of black women and their families because he has begun the process of examining the detailed components of family structure at specific historical moments. This permits us to begin an analysis of why and how the family and women's roles therein have changed over time. Of particular interest is the fact that he explains this trend in terms of distinct Afro-American cultural norms which emphasized marriage while refraining from stigmatizing women who gave birth out of wedlock. Since the establishment of paternity has had so profound an influence on the social position of Euro-American women, Gutman's documentation of the existence of norms which differed radically from those of the dominant culture supports the potential of Afro-American culture to generate alternative notions of womanhood and poses this contradiction as an important problem for further study.

Problem Two: Black Families in a White World

Fundamental to the proposal of a dialectical framework to analyze the condition of black women in the family is a conviction that the relationship of blacks to white society is dialectical in nature. This contention, while not new, has yet to be systematically applied to the study of black families. Frazier, influenced by the theories of Robert Park, determined that incomplete assimilation and isolation of blacks from white society explained their divergent family forms. The matriarchate was the result of the failure to assimilate, while patriarchal forms developed among those who had not been isolated from Euro-American norms and values.

A different theoretical position about the relationship of blacks to white society has been proposed by Billingsley.[8] He adopted Parson's social systems model and argued that the black family must be viewed as a separate but interrelated social system within the nexus of the larger society. The functionality of black families depends on the smooth interrelationship of these systems. Applying Billingsley's model, one could analyze black women in their complex of social roles: first in terms of

---

7. These finding were quoted in Clarence Turner, "Some Theoretical and Conceptual Considerations for Black Family Studies," *Blacklines* 2 (Winter 1972): 16. The assumption that slavery was a closed system (item no. 5) without any influences from outside the plantation or from traditional African life has been hotly debated. Two people who have presented findings to the contrary are Melville Herskovitz (*The Myth of the Negro Past* [Boston: Beacon Press, 1941]) and John Blassingame (*The Slave Community* [New York: Oxford University Press, 1972]). In general, revisionist history seeks to examine the existence and influence of African survivals in Afro-American culture.

8. Andrew Billingsley, *Black Families in White America* (Englewood Cliffs, N.J.: Prentice-Hall, 1968).

their roles within the family—mother, daughter, or sister; second, within the community—church member, PTA president, etc.; and third, within the wider society—secretary, housekeeper, teacher, or welfare recipient.

While this model recognizes the existence of a distinct Afro-American culture, its focus on the lives of black women as a set of interacting roles provides only a limited understanding of the dynamic and contradictory nature of their experience. Emphasis on functionality and dysfunctionality of their roles predisposes us to view black women more in relationship to the dominant culture than within Afro-American culture itself.

Valentine has suggested the concept of "biculturation" to describe the relationship of blacks to white society.[9] This concept assumes that blacks have been simultaneously socialized into two different cultural systems: white Euro-American and black Afro-American. However, much of the learning about Euro-American culture remains latent because discrimination prohibits blacks from achieving many mainstream values. While this concept may be particularly useful in explaining role conflict where role expectations derived from Afro-American culture contradict those derived from Euro-American culture, its major weakness is failure to account for the interrelatedness of these two cultural streams or to explain the basis of their unequal interaction.

Ladner's study of adolescent black girls, rather than emphasizing the shared and interacting norms which link Afro- and Euro-American traditions, illuminated the conflicts and dualities which the young women in her sample coped with as maturing adolescents.[10] She argued that the attitudes, behaviors, and interpersonal relationships of these women were adaptations to a variety of factors, including the harsh realities of their environment, Afro-American cultural images of black womanhood, and the sometimes conflicting values and norms of the wider society. This is exemplified in her discussion of attitudes toward premarital sex:

> Often in the absence of material resources, . . . sex becomes the resource that is exchanged. . . . It is here that sexual involvement transcends any conventional analysis because the standards that the individuals apply to their actions are created out of their own situations. Although many girls found it to be a means of expression in a variety of ways, they were still influenced by the conventional codes of morality. Some of them were more influenced by the conventional codes of morality than others and experienced conflict and sometimes trauma over whether or not they should defy these

9. Charles Valentine, "Deficit, Difference and Bicultural Models of Afro-American Behavior," *Harvard Educational Review*, vol. 41, no. 2 (May 1971).

10. Joyce A. Ladner, *Tomorrow's Tomorrow* (Garden City, N.Y.: Doubleday & Co., 1971).

codes. The sharp conflict . . . had a profound effect upon their lives.[11]

At the same time, she describes the reciprocal effects of distinctive aspects of black life upon the wider society.

Ladner's work comes closest to the perspective which we are proposing in this paper. By self-consciously applying the dialectical mode of analysis to the experiences of black women, we may make explicit the complex interaction of political, social, and economic forces in shaping the broad historical trends that characterize black women as a group as well as the particular lives of individual women. In this way, we move beyond the deficit models of Frazier and Moynihan and even beyond the models of Billingsley and Valentine. These models illuminate the complexities of black and white social roles but have limitations in accounting for the impact of racial oppression on the economic, political, or social life of black Americans and in explaining the historical or geographic variations in the black experience. The dialectic permits us to focus on the dynamic and contradictory aspects of black American life and to account for the simultaneity of conflict and interdependence which characterize black-white relations in American society.

Problem Three: Value Discrepancies between Researcher and Subject

The third problem is a direct result of the second and arises because of the differences between the values of the researcher and those of the subject. The values about family life underlying the work of Frazier and Moynihan are those that form the foundation of the bourgeois family: monogamy, nuclearity, and patriarchy. Female independence of male authority and economic control is viewed as destructive of this family form. This analysis denied the existence of a distinct Afro-American culture and ignored the meaning that these behaviors might have for the people being studied. To a large extent, the matriarchy thesis was based on the combination of erroneous historical interpretation with the actualities of black female labor-force participation.

As Aldridge, Jackson, Lewis and others have pointed out, black females have historically had high participation rates in the labor force—higher than their white counterparts, even with children (see tables 1 and 2 and fig. 1). Moynihan combined these high levels of labor-force participation with notions of female dominance in husband-wife families and with the large (relative to white families) percentage of female-headed families in the black community to conclude that matriarchy was characteristic of black family life.

As a result, in much of the social science literature on black families, black women became scapegoats, responsible for the psychological emasculation of black men and for the failure of the black community to gain parity with the white community.

11. Ladner, pp. 212–13.

Table 1

Labor-Force Participation Rates of Women by Race and Year

Selected Years	All Women	Black	White
1900	20.4	41.2	...
1910	25.2	58.2	...
1920	23.3	43.7	...
1930	24.3	...	...
1940	25.4	37.3	...
1950	29.0	46.9	32.6
1960	34.5	48.2	36.5
1970	...	49.5	42.6
1974	...	49.1	45.2

SOURCES.—Joe Feagin, "Black Women in the American Work Force," in *The Family Life of Black People*, ed. Charles Willie (Columbus, Ohio: Charles E. Merrill Publishing Co., 1970), pp. 23–24; Valerie K. Oppenheimer, *The Female Labor Force in the United States*, Population Series Monographs no. 5 (Berkeley: University of California, 1970); U.S. Commerce Department, *Negro Population 1790–1915* (Washington, D.C.: Government Printing Office, 1918).

Table 2

Percentage of Mothers in Labor Force by Age of Children, Color, and Marital Status (March 1967)

Age of Children (years)	Race of Mother		Differential
	Nonwhite	White	
Under 6*	44	27	+17
6–17	58	48	+10
Under 18	50	37	+13

SOURCE.—Adapted from Joe Feagin, "Black Women in the American Work Force" in *The Family Life of Black People*, ed. Charles Willie (Columbus, Ohio: Charles E. Merrill Publishing Co. 1970).
*Percentage participation of black and white mothers for 1973 are 54 and 31, respectively, a differential of +23.

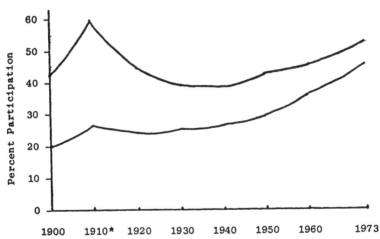

FIG. 1.—Trends in labor-force participation for all women and black women, 1900–1973. *The sharp increase in 1910 has been accounted for by differing instructions to the census takers for that year.

Ryan has labeled this type of reasoning "blaming the victim." It is an ideology which, he says, "... attributes defect and inadequacy to the malignant nature of poverty, injustice, slum life, and racial difficulties. The stigma that marks the victim ... is an acquired stigma, a stigma of social, rather than genetic, origin. But the stigma ... is still located *within* the victim, inside his skin. ... It is a brilliant ideology for justifying a perverse form of social action designed to change, not society, as one might expect, but rather society's victims."[12] In general, the justification of the matriarchy thesis has been based on the combination of erroneous historical interpretation with the actualities of black female participation in the labor force. Ten Houten states: "In modern urban society the subdominance of the black husband to the wife is attributed to employment behaviors."[13]

It is a cruel irony that the black woman's role as a worker has been used to represent dominance over and emasculation of black men. This predisposition ignores both historical and socioeconomic realities. Black women were brought to this country for two economic reasons: to work and to produce workers. Although they were valued for their reproductive function, as were white women settlers, it was only of equal importance with their labor.

There was no concern about the legitimacy of their children because there was nothing for them to inherit. The protective barriers which gradually forced white women out of production and changed their relationship to labor and society did not exist for most black women. Davis, in an analysis of the historical significance of black women's relationship to labor, emphasizes this point.

> It is true that she was a victim of the myth that only the woman, with the diminished capacity for mental and physical labor, should do degrading household work. Yet, the alleged benefits of the ideology of femininity did not accrue to her. She was not sheltered or protected; she would not remain oblivious to the desperate struggle for existence unfolding outside the "home." She was also there in the fields, alongside the man, toiling under the lash. ... This was one of the supreme ironies of slavery: In order to approach its strategic goal—to extract the greatest possible surplus from the labor of slaves—the black woman had to be released from the chains of the myth of femininity. ... The black woman shared the deformed equality of equal oppression with the black man.[14]

12. William Ryan, *Blaming the Victim* (New York: Vintage, 1971), pp. 7–8.
13. Warren Ten Houten, "The Black Family: Myth and Reality," in *The Family in Transition*, ed. Arlene Skolnick and Jerome Skolnick (Boston: Little, Brown & Co., 1971) p. 420.
14. Angela Davis, "Reflections on the Black Woman's Role in the Community of Slaves," *Black Scholar* 3 (December 1971): 7.

Problem Four: Class and Culture

Too often, social science researchers have sought to describe black women and their families as if they were a monolithic whole, without regard for differences in social class. At the other extreme is the contention that social class differences obliterate distinctions of race. In other words, social science has generally supported the idea that Afro-American culture is synonymous with lower class culture and that it disappears as black Americans gain middle class status.

To illuminate the complexities of the interaction of class and culture, Billingsley adopts Milton Gordon's concept of "ethnic subsociety." According to Gordon, "the ethnic group is the locus of a sense of *historical identification,* while the eth-class (the intersection of ethnicity and social class) is the locus of a sense of *participational identification.* With a person of the same social class but of a different ethnic group, one shares behavioral similarities but not a sense of peoplehood. With those of the same ethnic group but of a different social class, one shares the sense of peoplehood but not behavioral similarities. The only group which meets both these criteria are people of the same ethnic group *and* social class."[15]

The concept of "eth-class" is useful in that it communicates a sense of the ways in which ethnic differences interact with social class. However, it has serious limitations because it ignores the elements of domination and oppression which are at the root of black-white relations in the United States and which account for the high concentration of blacks in the lower class.

Blauner argues that black culture is not merely a phenomenon of lower-class life but a product of the experience of discrimination which cuts across all social classes.[16] More important, he links racial oppression to economic exploitation and the structure of classes within a capitalist economy. Thus his analysis goes beyond a merely descriptive portrayal of the interaction of the two variables, class and race, and focuses on the dynamic and contradictory influence that each has on the other. Thus, while he sees race as a form of stratification which has economic, political, and ideological dimensions, he argues that it is a basic rather than epiphenomenal aspect of American industrial capitalism. He concludes: "In American society, races and classes interpenetrate one another. Race affects class formation and class influences racial dynamics in ways that have not yet been adequately investigated."[17]

15. Quoted in Billingsley, p. 10.
16. Robert Blauner, *Racial Oppression in America* (New York: Harper & Row, 1972), chap. 4.
17. Blauner, pp. 28–29.

Dill

Implications for the Study of Black Women and Their Jobs

It is the contention of this paper, therefore, that the study of the black women and their families requires serious revision. First, it must be placed within a historical framework which is carefully researched, documented, and reinterpreted. Gutman, Pleck, Lammermeier, and others have only recently begun to provide this data.[18] Serious historical research promises to provide new information regarding the structure and organization of black families at different historical periods and in different regions of the United States. Information about values, attitudes, and the vicissitudes of daily life will remain, however, to be pieced together from oral history and other descriptive reports.

Second, black women must be studied within a dynamic and contradictory framework to understand the complexities of their relations to all aspects of society. Thus, an examination of the impact of work on the family life of women whose occupational categories result in class differences would be expected to yield important distinctions. At the same time, however, the experience of slavery, whether house servant or field hand, and the continued economic precariousness of most black families which has resulted in high rates of female labor-force participation, would be expected to have a particular impact on the growth and development of women in Afro-American culture.

Third, we must continue to research and provide good descriptive studies of the lives of black women and their families across the social class spectrum. Studies such as Stack's offer considerable insight into the ways in which economic oppression impacts on daily life, family patterns, and women's self-concepts.[19] Her work and Ladner's are examples of studies which provide the data necessary for concept development and theory building in this area.[20] They reveal the ways in which black

18. Particular attention is called to the work of Elizabeth Pleck, "The Two Parent Household: Black Family Structure in Late Nineteenth Century Boston," *Journal of Social History*, vol. 6 (Fall 1972); Paul Lammermeier, "The Urban Black Family of the Nineteenth Century: A Study of Black Family Structure in the Ohio Valley, 1850–1880," *Journal of Marriage and the Family*, vol. 35 (August 1973); and the developing activity in oral history of the Kinte Foundation.

19. Carol Stack, *All Our Kin* (New York: Harper & Row, 1974).

20. See forthcoming Ph.D. dissertations by Bonnie Dill (New York University), which explores the meanings of work and its perceived impact on the family lives of black female household workers; and Elizabeth Higginbotham (Brandeis University), which examines the interrelationship of education, career, and family among college-educated black women. Both studies focus on the women's self-presentations, their goals and strategies for survival, upward mobility, and its relationship to their family lives. An article by Robert D. Abrahams ("Negotiating Respect: Patterns of Presentation among Black Women," *Journal of American Folklore* 88 [January–March 1975]: 58–80) utilizes the data in novels and several sociological studies in an attempt to develop a systematic analysis of the manner in which black women attain respect. It is a preliminary step in the direction of concept development using descriptive data.

women conceptualize work, its meaning in their lives, and its importance in the development of their models of womanhood.

Conclusion: Toward a New Model

We began developing a historical framework for the study of black women by focusing on the contradiction cited at the outset: the historical role as a laborer in a society where ideals of femininity emphasized domesticity. A dominant image of black women as "beasts of burden"[21] stands in direct contrast to American ideals of womanhood: fragile, white, and not too bright. The impact of this contradiction is profound. It has already been alluded to in discussions of the values pervading much of the pejorative literature on black women. It can also be expected to have affected self-images as well as their interpretations and expectations of various role relationships.

In concluding, however, it is important to explore the implications of this historical tradition for contemporary models of black womanhood. Ladner suggests several in her study of adolescent black girls. These revolve around the girls' images of womanhood, goals for themselves, and their relationships to their families and to boys. In developing their ideals of womanhood, Ladner reports that "the strongest conception of womanhood that exists among all pre-adult females is that of how the woman has to take a strong family role."[22] The pervasiveness of this image of an economically independent, resourceful, and hardworking woman was resented by some, adopted by others, and accepted with resignation by still others. Nevertheless, its overriding importance remained even though Ladner observed other models which existed alongside it. One of these other models, which appears to me as a variation, is that of an upwardly mobile middle-class woman. Ladner points out that education was most frequently seen as the means to this end. The choice of this model had a serious impact on the entire life of girls who chose it, particularly as it affected their relationship with boys. These girls most often avoided serious involvement with boys, particularly premarital sex and the risk of pregnancy which represented a definite end to their aspirations. Success in attaining their middle class goals was not only measured in terms of the training or job acquired but also "by the extent to which one can not only care for himself, but help others in the family."[23]

21. This conceptualization is drawn from the writings of Jeanne L. Noble. It was presented in a draft of an article being prepared for the *World Encyclopedia of Black Peoples* which the author generously shared with me.

22. Ladner, p. 127.

23. Ladner, p. 121.

Girls who rejected the dominant model often adopted a model which Ladner calls a "carefree, laissez-faire, egalitarian model of womanhood." Different though this model was, it too encompasses a sense of self-reliance, strength, and autonomy. This image, as described by Ladner, was primarily directed toward relationships with boys. Inherent in it was an attitude of equality between men and women, a rejection of the sexual double standard, and a general belief that a woman can do whatever a man does. This practical attitude toward male-female relations was not without conflict, particularly as it was confronted by the ideals of the wider society. Neither, however, were the other models. They, too, support an image of womanhood which, until recently, has been out of step with the values of white society.

The image of independent, self-reliant, strong, and autonomous women which pervades the models of the young black women in Ladner's study has been reinforced by the work experience and social conditions of black women throughout history. The image, therefore, represents both the oppressive experiences of work and the liberating attitudes of personal autonomy and sexual equality. It may explain the findings of the *1970 Virginia Slims American Women's Opinion Poll* that "an essentially urban coalition of black women and the young and the educated of both races are ready to follow the examples of blacks and the young and challenge the status quo in American society."[24] This finding is particularly interesting in light of the goals of the women's liberation movement and the relationship of black women to this movement. It has been acknowledged that black women have not identified strongly with what many have seen as a movement of middle-class white women.[25] I would suggest that the image of women—as more than housewives and as sexual equals—toward which white women strive is, in large part, synonymous with the dominant image and much of the experience of black women. Ladner says it well in the closing statement of one of the chapters of *Tomorrow's Tomorrow:* "*Black womanhood* has always been the very essence of what American womanhood is attempting to become on some levels."[26] And again in her final chapter:

> . . . much of the current focus on being liberated from the constraints and protectiveness of the society which is proposed by

24. Louis Harris and Associates, *The Virginia Slims American Women's Opinion Poll* (1970), p. 78.

25. For discussions of black women's responses to the women's liberation movement see Robert Staples, *The Black Woman in America* (Chicago: Nelson-Hall Co., 1973); Inez Reid, *"Together" Black Women* (New York: Emerson Hall, 1972); selections in Toni Cade, ed., *The Black Woman: An Anthology* (New York: New American Library, 1970); Linda LaRue, "The Black Woman and Women's Liberation," *Black Scholar*, vol. 1 (May 1970); and Lewis (n. 1 above) for a discussion of the structural factors affecting the variety of responses that have been noted among black women.

26. Ladner, p. 239.

Women's Liberation groups has never been applied to Black women, and in this sense, we have always been "free," and able to develop as individuals even under the most harsh circumstances. This freedom, as well as the tremendous hardships from which Black women suffered, allowed for the development of a female personality that is rarely described in scholarly journals for its obstinate strength and ability to survive. Neither is its peculiar humanistic character and quiet courage viewed as the epitome of what the American model of femininity should be.[27]

Thus the contradiction between the subjection of women from West Africa to the harsh deprivations of slavery, farm, factory, and domestic work and the sense of autonomy and self-reliance which developed, points in the direction of a new avenue for studying black American women. And it is the potential synthesis of these contradictions which embraces the future problems and possibilities of a new definition of femininity for *all* American women.

Department of Sociology
Memphis State University

27. Ladner, p. 280.

FAMILY ROLES, OCCUPATIONAL STATUSES, AND ACHIEVEMENT ORIENTATIONS AMONG BLACK WOMEN IN THE UNITED STATES

WALTER R. ALLEN

As members of two minority groups,[1] black women represent excellent subjects for research into the dynamics of discrimination, motivation, and occupational achievement. Paradoxically, the study of black female occupational achievement is made problematic by their shared minority group memberships. Black women are a minority hidden within two more conspicuous minority groups. As a result, scholars tend to overlook them; their experiences, needs, and realities are assumed to be identical with those of blacks and women in general. Many point out the fallacy of such assumptions and show that the realities of black women depart in marked, fundamental ways from those of both white women and black men.[2] Thus the occupational achievement experiences of black women are best understood as a special class of events. This is not to ignore their commonalities with other similarly placed individuals; rather, these commonalities—along with differences—are taken into account.

Despite the established tradition of black female labor-force participation, black women workers represent a relatively neglected research topic. Many questions remain concerning the attitudes, motivations,

An early version of this paper was presented during the Rockefeller Foundation Conference, "Women, Family, and Work," New York City, September 21–22, 1978. Helpful discussions with and comments from the following people are gratefully acknowledged: Edgar Epps, Bruce Hare, Jacquelyne Jackson, Genna Rae McNeil, Gail Thomas, other conference participants, and the editors. Kris Anderson assisted with the analysis.

1. Here the term "minority group" refers to issues surrounding a group's relative possession of societal power, prestige, and resources.
2. Pauli Murray, "The Liberation of Black Women," in *Women: A Feminist Perspective,* ed. Jo Freeman (Palo Alto, Calif.: Mayfield Publishing Co., 1975); Diane K. Lewis, "A Response to Inequality: Black Women, Racism, and Sexism," *Signs* 3 (Winter 1977): 339–61; William H. Chafe, *Women and Equality* (New York: Galaxy Books, 1977), pp. 52–54.

This essay originally appeared in *Signs*, vol. 4, no. 4, Summer 1979.

roles, and statuses of black women in the labor force. If answered, they could tell us about black women and about our society's occupational attainment machinery in general. This paper contributes to a clarification of these questions through a comparative analysis of occupational status and achievement orientation among black women. Specifically, census and survey data are employed to investigate differences in the occupational statuses of black women relative to white females and males of both races. Achievement orientations among black women are then compared with those of the other sex-race groupings in order to ascertain whether the measured differences in internalized attitude, value, or belief sets seem to substantiate observed occupational status differences. The practical significance of such research is clear: Our findings should contribute to the identification and eventual removal of barriers which deny black women, and other disenfranchised groups, equal opportunity for occupational advancement.

To introduce family roles at this point in the discussion may appear incongruous, even potentially stereotypic. However, prevailing views of black women's familial roles condition the way(s) in which their occupational roles are perceived and evaluated by researchers. For the most part the marriage and family literature has been unflattering in its treatment of black women.[3] "Black matriarchy" theorists have implicitly, and at times explicitly, attributed responsibility for social problems in black communities to black women and their purported social, economic, and psychological dominance over black men. Such negative evaluations of black women's familial roles inevitably distort perceptions of their work roles. For instance, while careful analysis of statistics suggests otherwise, the idea of a black female occupational advantage is still rather widespread.[4] Prior research on black women in the labor force, however, shows them to be seriously disadvantaged relative to white women and men who work.[5] It suggests that: Some black women

3. Works claiming that black society is matriarchal or female dominated include E. Franklin Frazier, *The Negro Family in the United States* (Chicago: University of Chicago Press, 1939); Daniel P. Moynihan, *The Negro Family: The Case for National Action* (Washington, D.C.: Department of Labor, 1965); Lee Rainwater, *Behind Ghetto Walls* (Chicago: Aldine Publishing Co., 1970). That view is convincingly refuted in Robert Hill, *The Strengths of Black Families* (New York: Emerson Hall Publishers, 1971); Robert Staples, "Towards a Sociology of the Black Family," *Journal of Marriage and the Family* 33 (February 1971): 19–38; Jerold Heiss, *The Case of the Black Family: A Sociological Inquiry* (New York: Columbia University Press, 1975).

4. Edwin Harwood and Claire Hodge, "Jobs and the Negro Family: A Reappraisal," *Public Interest* 23 (Spring 1971): 125–31; Jacquelyne Jackson, "But Where Are the Men?" *Black Scholar* 4 (December 1971): 30–41.

5. Valerie Oppenheimer, *The Female Labor Force in the United States: Demographic and Economic Factors Governing Its Growth and Changing Composition* (Berkeley: Institute of International Studies, University of California, 1970); James Sweet, *Women in the Labor Force* (New York: Seminar Press, 1973); Louise Howe, *Pink Collar Workers* (New York: G. P. Putnam's Sons, 1976).

have benefited professionally from their double-negative status;[6] others experience disproportionate difficulty with increasing socioeconomic status in finding similarly located black male mates;[7] black women have steadily relocated from household service jobs to other occupations over time;[8] and black women are systematically channeled into low status, low mobility opportunity, first jobs.[9]

Traditional stereotypes of blacks and women as underachievers have hampered the study of achievement orientation among black women. Where their achievement orientations have been compared with those of other race-sex groups, several interesting findings emerge. Gurin and Epps studied black college students and found that black females displayed lower mobility aspirations and aspired to stereotypic occupations with lower prestige, ability demand, and financial compensation.[10] According to the authors this fact suggests the presence of sex-role constraints which operate to decrease the educational and occupational role choices available to black women. Rosenberg and Rosenberg explain such occupational sex typing by noting that these choices go beyond assignment of occupations by sex; rather, choice of occupation is tied to fundamental definitions of sex identity.[11] This class of socialization and personality development theories about the emergence of sex-stereotypic occupational choices has been appropriately referred to as "pink blanket" theory.[12] Findings from several studies also demonstrate that black women consistently gravitate toward careers and positions within the female sector of the occupational system.[13] As numerous researchers note, this fact must convey a recognition of the occupational realities which blacks and women are forced to confront and conform to in this society.[14]

Related research indicates that achievement orientation is highest

6. C. F. Epstein, "Positive Effects of the Multiple Negative: Explaining the Success of Black Professional Women," *American Journal of Sociology* 78 (January 1973): 912–35.

7. Jackson.

8. Oppenheimer; Sweet.

9. Judith Treas, "Differential Achievement: Race, Sex, and Jobs" (paper presented at the American Sociological Association Meetings, San Francisco, August 30 to September 3, 1976).

10. Patricia Gurin and Edgar Epps, *Black Consciousness, Identity and Achievement* (New York: John Wiley & Sons, 1975).

11. Morris Rosenberg and Florence Rosenberg, "The Occupational Self: A Developmental Study" (paper presented at the Self-Concept Symposium, Boston, September 28 to October 1, 1978).

12. Howe.

13. Sweet; Kelly Hamilton, *Goals and Plans of Black Women* (Hicksville, N.J.: Exposition Press, 1975); Gail Thomas, "Equality of Representation of Race and Sex Groups in Higher Education: Institutional and Program Enrollment Statuses" (paper presented at the American Educational Research Association Meetings, Toronto, March 27–31, 1978).

14. Gurin and Epps; Walter R. Allen, "Preludes to Attainment: Race, Sex, and Student Achievement Orientations," mimeographed (University of North Carolina, 1977).

among black adolescent females where successful adult female role models are present.[15] Black parents establish and stress the attainment of high occupational goals during child socialization.[16] Lewis suggests that black parents are less sex stereotypic than their white counterparts and routinely instill children of both sexes with attitudes and skills believed to be conducive to successful competition.[17] Despite this fact, black females are less likely than black males (and whites) to structure their worlds in achievement terms. Yet when they do so, they are less anxious about failing and more gratified by the anticipation of success.[18] Finally, the dynamics underlying the development of achievement orientation among black females seem to differ from those for the other sex-race groups. The power of family background, personal attitude, and school-setting variables in predicting achievement orientations varies across groups, suggesting that the processes underlying the formation of these also vary across sex-race lines.[19]

The relationship of black female occupational attainments and achievement orientations has yet to be investigated using nationally representative samples. Detailed analyses focused upon black women's occupational statuses per se are also lacking in the literature. Finally, studies comparing black female achievement orientations with those of black men and whites are relatively sparse. This study analyzes the current occupational statuses of black women as these relate to the achievement orientations of a group of black females just entering the adult work world. Results from these analyses will allow us to draw inferences about the interaction of psychological (e.g., personal achievement motives) and structural factors (e.g., institutionalized sex and/or race discrimination) in the determination of eventual occupational attainments among black women.

Occupational status refers to the positions and roles that characterize black female involvement in the labor force. The concept is operationalized by information on their labor-force participation rates, distribution throughout the occupational hierarchy, unemployment rates, and earnings from employment. Such statistics on the national employment situation for black women measure how their labor market placements, experiences, mobility rates, and compensations differ from those of the other three major sex-race categories. Achievement orientation is an unmeasured construct represented by student personality

15. Joyce Ladner, *Tomorrow's Tomorrow* (Garden City, N.Y.: Doubleday & Co., 1971).
16. Hill; John Scanzoni, *The Black Family in Modern Society* (Boston: Allyn & Bacon, 1971).
17. Diane Lewis, "The Black Family: Socialization and Sex Roles," *Phylon* 36 (Fall 1975): 221–37.
18. Joseph Veroff, Lou McClelland, and David Ruhland, "Varieties of Achievement Motivation" in *Women and Achievement*, ed. M. S. Mednick, S. S. Tangri, and L. W. Hoffman (Washington, D.C.: Hemisphere Publishing Co., 1975), pp. 172–205.
19. Gurin and Epps; Allen.

traits shown in past research to be predictive of expected and actual attainments.[20] Here, the achievement orientations of black women are approximated using standard interview measures of characteristics usually correlated with individual achievements: self-esteem, locus of control, academic self-concept, educational expectations, and occupational aspirations.

The data for this research are drawn from two separate, though for our purposes compatible, sources. Data used to assess occupational status come from U.S. government public statistics (e.g., Bureau of the Census, Bureau of Labor Statistics). Discussions of occupational statuses apply, therefore, to the entire universe of female and male, black and white workers in the U.S. labor force. The data used to measure achievement orientation, however, are more restricted. They come from the "National Longitudinal Study of the High School Class of 1972," a study of 21,000 high school seniors enrolled in U.S. public and private secondary schools.[21] Discussions of achievement orientation apply, therefore, to the universe of recent female and male, black and white high school seniors. The selected sources of data are appropriate for this study because they are both recent and nationally representative.[22] Using these data we can draw inferences, within reasonable limits, about the relationship of high school seniors' achievement orientations to their eventual occupational status attainments.

Secondary data analysis is our primary investigative tool. Analysis of government statistics on occupational status involves percentage com-

20. Bernard Rosen, "The Achievement Syndrome: A Psycho-Social Dimension of Social Stratification," *American Sociological Review* 21 (1956): 203–11; Chad Gordon, *Looking Ahead: Self Conceptions, Race and Family as Determinants of Adolescent Orientation to Achievement* (Washington, D.C.: American Sociological Association, 1972); Alan Kerckhoff, *Ambition and Attainment: A Study of Four Samples of American Boys* (Washington, D.C.: American Sociological Association, 1974).

21. The study was conducted by the Educational Testing Service under the auspices of the National Center for Educational Statistics. The sampling plan involved selecting a random sample of eighteen senior class students (plus five alternates) from 1,200 national representative schools. Participants completed an hour-long questionnaire concerning school plans, aspirations, family background, and attitudes; afterward they took an hour-long aptitude test. Other data on students were obtained from school records and interviews with school personnel. Additional information on the NLS study is available through the following sources: William Fetters, *National Longitudinal Study of the High School Class of 1972: A Capsule Description of High School Seniors* (Washington, D.C.: Office of Education, 1974); Rhett Hilton et al., *The Base-Year Survey of the National Longitudinal Study of the High School Class of 1972* (Washington, D.C.: Office of Education, 1973).

22. These data are limited by the fact that measures of attainment and motivation come from different samples. Since data on the achievement orientations of all U.S. workers are not available and the occupational achievement histories of 1972 high school seniors are not yet complete (most are just beginning their careers), merger of the two data sources seemed a reasonable compromise. We know, however, that the current occupational statuses of women and men, blacks and whites as aggregates are predictive of their statuses in the near future, given the relatively static character of the occupational system.

parisons across the four sex-race groups. Percentage comparisons and contingency table analysis are used to examine achievement orientations across the various sex-race groups. Contingency table analysis involves cross classification of two variables (e.g., occupational aspirations by female's race), followed by computation of statistics that estimate the relationship's statistical significance (i.e., probability that an observed relationship is a "chance" occurrence) and level of association (i.e., the strength or magnitude of covariation between two variables).

Roughly half of black women sixteen years or older have found employment outside the home since 1950.[23] Until recently, black female labor-force participation (LFP) rates far exceeded those for white females. The black-white difference in female LFP rates in 1950 was 14 percentage points (46.9 percent vs. 32.6 percent), but this difference shrank by 1974 to 4 percentage points (49.1 percent vs. 45.2 percent). The implicit conclusion that black female LFP rates are now equaled by those of white females requires qualification in that more black than white women are full-time members of the labor force (88 percent vs. 67 percent in 1974). Throughout the twenty-five-year period in question, black male LFP rates exceeded those for black females by anywhere from 32 (1964) to 24 percentage points (1974). The corresponding differences between black women's and white men's LFP rates were 34 and 30 percentage points.

Table 1 reveals additional features which distinguish the occupational statuses of black women from those of others. For the years 1964, 1970, and 1974 the occupational distributions of black women differ from those of men and white women. Computed indices of displacement,[24] our measure of aggregate differences, show that in 1974 roughly 23 percent of white females, 40 percent of black males, and 34 percent of white males would have to be shifted to different occupational categories in order to make their occupational distribution comparable with that of black females. While these occupational disparities are considerably reduced from their 1964 levels—where the corresponding displacement indices were 40 percent, 46 percent, and 51 percent, respectively—they still remain sizable.

Black female shifts out of service work into other employment represent the most prominent change in sex-race group occupational distributions over the 1964–74 period. By 1974 the percentage of black

23. U.S. Bureau of the Census, *The Social and Economic Status of the Black Population in the United States, 1974* (Washington, D.C.: Government Printing Office, 1975), table 54.

24. The index of displacement summarizes percentage differences. The index defines the percentage of a comparison population which needs to be reassigned to make its distribution identical with that of the standard population. The formula for this index is: index of displacement = $\frac{1}{2} \Sigma \left| r_{2a} - r_{1a} \right|$ where Σ = the sum of, r_{2a} = percent of comparison population in category, r_{1a} = percent of standard population in category, and $\left| \; \right|$ = the absolute value of (see H. Shryock and J. Siegel, *The Methods and Materials of Demography* [Washington, D.C.: Government Printing Office, 1971], p. 232, for more detail).

Table 1

Occupation of Employed Men and Women
(%, Annual Averages)

Occupation	1964		1970		1974	
	Black and Other Races	White	Black and Other Races	White	Black and Other Races	White
			Employed Men			
White-collar workers:	16	41	22	43	24	42
Professor and technical..........	6	13	8	15	9	15
Managers and administrators, except farm	3	15	5	15	5	15
Sales workers	2	6	2	6	2	6
Clerical workers	5	7	7	7	7	6
Blue-collar workers:	58	46	60	46	57	46
Craft and kindred workers	12	20	14	21	16	21
Operatives, except transport	18	15	21	14	17	12
Transport equipment operatives	8	5	7	5	9	6
Nonfarm laborers	22	6	18	6	15	7
Service workers	16	6	13	6	15	7
Farm workers	10	7	6	5	4	5
Total employed (thousands)	4,359	41,114	4,803	44,457	5,179	47,340

Table 1 *(Continued)*

Occupation	1964 Black and Other Races	1964 White	1970 Black and Other Races	1970 White	1974 Black and Other Races	1974 White
			Employed Women			
White-collar workers:	22	61	36	64	42	64
Professional and technical	8	14	11	15	12	15
Managers and administrators, except farm	2	5	2	5	2	5
Sales workers	2	8	3	8	3	7
Clerical workers	11	34	21	36	25	36
Blue-collar workers:	15	17	19	16	20	15
Craft and kindred workers	1	1	1	1	1	1
Operatives, except transport	14	15	17	14	17	12
Transport equipment operatives	*	*	*	*	*	*
Nonfarm laborers	1	*	1	*	1	1
Service workers	56	19	43	19	37	19
Farm workers	6	3	2	2	1	2
Total employed (thousands)	3,024	20,808	3,642	26,025	4,136	29,280

Source.—U.S. Bureau of the Census. *The Social and Economic Status of the Black Population in the United States, 1974* (Washington. D.C.: Government Printing Office, 1975), tables 48 and 49

Note.—Indexes of displacement for 1964 and 1974. respectively, are: black women vs. white women, 40 and 23: black women vs. black men, 46 and 40: black women vs. white men, 51 and 34

*Base too small for percentage to be shown.

females in service work had dropped to 37 percent as compared with 19 percent, 15 percent, and 7 percent, respectively, for the other sex-race groups. Concurrent with the diminished presence of black women in service work has been their increased entry into white collar positions. The proportion of black women in white collar positions nearly doubled between 1964 (22 percent) and 1974 (42 percent). However, these increases were largely concentrated within the clerical worker subcategory where the proportion of black women so employed rose from roughly 10 percent in 1964 to 25 percent by 1974. Despite the improved occupational status implied by such a shift, black women remained at a clear disadvantage relative to other groups and were concentrated in the least prestigious and lowest-paying occupations.[25]

During the 1964 through 1975 period when black women were the least favorably employed, relative to other sex-race groups, they were also the most frequently unemployed. As table 2 shows, black female unemployment rates equaled or exceeded those for males and white females in each of the five years cited and presumably throughout the period in question. Further, the data in table 3 for an illustrative year (1974) suggest that unemployment rates are highest for black women regardless of occupational category.

Table 2

Unemployment Rates, by Sex, Age, and Race
(%, Annual Averages)

	1964	1970	1973	1974	1975
Black and other races:					
Men, 20 yr and over	7.7	5.6	5.7	6.8	11.1
Women, 20 yr and over	9.0	6.9	8.2	8.4	11.0
Both sexes, 16–19 yr	27.2	29.1	30.2	32.9	39.8
Total	9.6	8.2	8.9	9.9	13.7
White:					
Men, 20 yr and over	3.4	3.2	2.9	3.5	5.8
Women, 20 yr and over	4.6	4.4	4.3	5.0	7.8
Both sexes, 16–19 yr	14.8	13.5	12.6	14.0	18.0
Total	4.6	4.5	4.3	5.0	7.6

SOURCE.—U.S. Bureau of the Census, *The Social and Economic Status of the Black Population in the United States*, 1974 (Washington, D.C.: Government Printing Office, 1975), table 39.

25. Howe's idea of an "internal labor market," i.e., the job structure within a company which is typically as segregated by sex (and presumably race) as is the labor market as a whole (p. 17), suggests that the observed occupational discrepancies represent only the iceberg's tip. More sensitive and detailed figures would probably reveal even greater occupational advantages of men, whites, and other sex-race groups over women, blacks, and black women, respectively. Such occupational advantages obtain not only across but within occupational categories as well. Black women can be expected to be concentrated not only in the lower positions of the occupational hierarchy but also in the lowest positions within a particular occupational category where they are located.

Table 3

Unemployment Rates by Occupation, Sex, and Race, 1974 (%)

Major Occupational Group	Men		Women		Total	
	Black	White	Black	White	Black	White
White-collar workers:	5.5	2.0	7.7	4.2	7.0	3.1
Professional and technical	4.3	1.7	4.3	2.8	4.3	2.1
Managers and administrators, except farm	3.1	1.5	4.0	3.2	3.3	1.8
Sales workers	12.7	2.8	15.1	5.5	13.9	3.9
Clerical workers	6.7	3.1	8.8	4.6	8.2	4.3
Blue-collar workers:	9.3	5.6	13.5	9.0	10.2	6.2
Craft and kindred workers	6.5	4.1	*	6.1	6.7	4.2
Operatives, except transport	10.2	6.3	13.8	9.6	11.8	7.6
Transport equipment operatives	5.9	4.9	*	4.8	5.8	4.9
Nonfarm laborers	12.7	9.5	*	9.0	12.9	9.5
Service workers	9.8	5.2	8.1	6.0	8.7	5.7
Private household	*	4.4	5.3	3.7	5.4	3.8
Other	9.6	5.2	9.4	6.4	9.5	5.9
Farm workers	5.6	2.0	*	3.1	5.9	2.2
Total, all civilian workers	9.7	4.4	11.2	6.2	10.4	5.1
Experienced labor force	8.5	3.9	9.1	5.3	8.7	4.4

Source.—U.S. Bureau of the Census, *The Social and Economic Status of the Black Population in the United States, 1974* (Washington, D.C.: Government Printing Office, 1975), table 43

*Statistics not available

When attention is shifted to a comparison of earnings, we see yet another dimension of the black female occupational status disadvantage. As table 4 shows, black women earned less than men and white women from 1970 through 1974. While reduced somewhat when only full-time workers were considered, the income disadvantage of black women remained. Earnings for white females over the period were most comparable with those of black females. The earnings for black males exceeded black women's by from one-quarter to a third during the period, with white male earnings being twice as high as black female earnings on average. Figures for an illustrative year (table 5) show that these discrepancies in black female earnings persist irrespective of occupational category.

Since the overwhelming majority of black women who work are either sole or substantial contributors to family support, it is instructive to look at income in terms of family units. Black families have consistently lost ground relative to white families in the median income race since 1967 when their income of $4,875 was $3,400 less; the 1971 figure of $6,440 was $4,200 less; and the 1974 figure of $7,808 was $5,600 less.[26] These general income differentials repeat themselves within the various subcategories of families. Thus the 1967 ($5,808), 1971 ($8,178), and 1974 ($10,530), incomes of families headed by a black male and with wife present are, respectively, $2,800, $3,000, and $3,600 below those of

Table 4

Median Income ($), 1970 to 1974, of Persons Fourteen Years Old and Over, by Sex, Work Experience

	Men		Women	
	Year-round Full-Time Workers	Total	Year-round Full-Time Workers	Total
Black:				
1970	6,435	4,157	4,536	2,063
1971	6,771	4,316	5,092	2,145
1972	7,373	4,733	5,280	2,444
1973	7,953	5,113	5,595	2,548
1974	8,705	5,370	6,371	2,806
White:				
1970	9,447	7,011	5,536	2,266
1971	9,902	7,237	5,767	2,448
1972	10,918	7,814	6,172	2,616
1973	11,800	8,453	6,598	2,823
1974	12,434	8,794	7,021	3,133

SOURCE.—U.S. Bureau of the Census, *The Social and Economic Status of the Black Population in the United States*, 1974 (Washington, D.C.: Government Printing Office, 1975), Table 13.

26. U.S. Bureau of the Census, table 16.

Table 5

Median Earnings ($) in 1973 of Civilians Fourteen Years Old and Over, by Occupation of Longest Job, Work Experience, and Sex

Occupation	Men		Women	
	Black	White	Black	White
All Workers				
Professional, technical, and kindred workers	9,668	13,142	7,543	6,790
Managers and administrators, except farm	9,394	13,831	8,021	5,605
Farmers and farm managers	*	5,590	*	1,408
Clerical and kindred workers	8,007	8,905	4,170	4,409
Sales workers	4,270	8,952	1,405	1,637
Craft and kindred workers	7,346	10,111	4,446	4,357
Operatives, including transport workers	6,539	7,985	3,629	3,618
Private household workers	*	*	1,072	364
Service workers, except private household	4,562	4,609	2,773	1,663
Farm laborers and supervisors	855	1,384	370	463
Laborers, except farm	4,052	3,146	*	1,938
Total, with earnings	5,785	9,046	3,030	3,299
Year-round Full-Time Workers				
Professional, technical, and kindred workers	10,682	14,455	9,015	9,076
Managers and administrators, except farm	11,498	14,662	*	7,602
Farmers and farm managers	*	6,824	*	*
Clerical and kindred workers	9,241	10,811	6,522	6,462
Sales workers	*	12,415	*	4,632
Craft and kindred workers	8,857	11,387	*	6,224
Operatives, including transport workers	7,830	9,782	4,824	5,449
Private household workers	*	*	2,232	1,827
Service workers, except private household	6,397	8,618	4,595	4,577
Farm laborers and supervisors	*	5,104	*	*
Laborers, except farm	6,554	8,423	*	4,722
Total, with earnings	7,880	11,516	5,487	6,434

SOURCE.—U.S. Bureau of the Census, The Social and Economic Status of the Black Population in the United States, 1974 (Washington, D.C.: Government Printing Office, 1975), table 55.
*Base too small for figure to be shown.

similarly defined white families. The median incomes of black families headed by a male and with the wife in the labor force in 1967 ($7,272), 1971 ($10,274), and 1974 ($12,982) are $2,900, $2,800, and $3,800 less, respectively. A similar pattern holds for families with female heads, thus discounting arguments which would attribute these race discrepancies in family income solely to white male and black male income differentials. The 1967 ($3,004), 1971 ($3,645), and 1974 ($4,465) incomes of families headed by a black female are $1,900, $2,200, and $2,900 less than similarly situated white families for these same years.

It is logical to ask whether these observed occupational status discrepancies result from inherent differences between black women and the other sex-race groups. Given the slowness with which occupational and stratification systems change, we suggest that the observed occupational status patterns will probably hold—at least initially—for the black women currently entering the world of work. Let us look, therefore, at the relative achievement orientations of a sample from this group of new work-force entrants for clues which might explain the occupational status discrepancies sure to emerge. Can the occupational status disadvantages, likely to be perpetuated in the next generation of black female workers, be validly attributed to differences in their achievement orientations vis-à-vis male and white female workers? Or are these occupational status disadvantages best attributed to external, structural processes?

Table 6 summarizes results from our comparison of sex-race achievement orientation differences among high school seniors in the class of 1972.[27] Black female educational expectations, though somewhat lower, did not differ substantially from those of males: Comparable numbers expected to receive four or more years of college. Black female educational expectations were, however, much higher than those for white females, where only 44.1 percent expected to receive four or more years of college. The proportion of white females who sought only a high school education was also much higher than among black females. One explanation may be that black females, knowing that in all probability they will have to work, are intent upon going beyond a high school education in order to improve their marketability.

Dissimilarities in the occupational aspirations of the various sex-race groups are probably the most pronounced feature of table 6. The occupational aspirations of black women are significantly different from those of white women, black men, and white men. Specifically, over a

27. The χ^2 statistic is computed to test the significance of relationships or the chance that they are random occurrences. Cramer's V and gamma statistics are computed to measure the association of the relationships or degree of covariation between variables (maximum association = 1.00) (see Hubert M. Blalock, *Social Statistics* [New York: McGraw-Hill Book Co., 1972] or any other introductory statistics book for expanded discussion).

third of the black females aspired to clerical jobs, compared with a quarter of white women and less than a tenth of men. Roughly twice the proportion of white, compared with black, females aspire to service, sales, and full-time homemaker roles. A substantially larger percentage of women than men aspire to professional occupations.

In all probability, more detailed examination of these aspirations would reveal the professional occupations to which black women aspire to be sex typed (e.g., nurse, teacher). These occupational aspirations suggest some redundancy: Black women aspire to occupations where their like members are concentrated, and black women concentrate in certain occupations because these are jobs to which they aspire.

Few, if any, noteworthy differences emerge when black females are compared with males and white females on the remaining dimensions of achievement orientation. Black female levels of reported academic self-concept are comparable with those reported by the other sex-race groups. Predictably, in our society, blacks are much less confident than whites of their abilities to control their own lives. What is surprising in this study is that white females are more confident in this respect than white males. A sex effect, in addition to the observed race effect, may be possible, since black women also have higher senses of personal control than black men. It is possible that individuals whose lives are more predictable (i.e., whites as the dominant racial group and women because of societal stereotypes of and limits on their choices) feel more in control of their lives. Black females, and blacks in general, display higher self-esteem levels than the other sex-race groups and whites respectively, possibly because of socialization patterns which emphasize the development of high self-esteem as a protective mechanism against societal attempts to devalue the self-worth of blacks.[28]

Simply put, this paper asks whether the probable occupational status attainments of black women about to enter the labor force will accurately reflect their orientations toward achievement. The unequivocal conclusion is no. Some will, of course, argue that this conclusion holds for men and white women as well, to which the only reply is, "Yes, but not with the same force!" Black women have been, are, and will likely be in the near future disproportionately represented in menial, low-paying, low-prestige occupations. Where black women's achievement orientations did differ from those of other sex-race groupings, these differences were of insufficient consistency and magnitude to justify their large, persistent disadvantage in occupational status.

Where, then, can we turn in search of factors which account for the continued disparities between black women's achievement orientations and occupational status attainments? Given that status attainment is a

28. Bruce R. Hare, "Relationship of Social Background to the Dimensions of Self-Concept" (Ph.D. diss., University of Chicago, 1975).

Table 6

Sex, Race, and Student Achievement Orientation
(Percent Distributions, Significance Tests, and Measures of Association)

Achievement-Orientation Components	Black Females Percent Distribution	White Females Percent Distribution	White Females Comparison Statistics	Black Females Percent Distribution	Black Females Comparison Statistics	White Males Percent Distribution	White Males Comparison Statistics
Educational expectations:							
Less than high school graduation	3.5	1.9		4.6		2.0	
High school graduation only	10.9	21.6	$\chi^2=83.6^*$	11.6	$\chi^2=4.9$	13.8	$\chi^2=33.3^*$
Voc-tech, business or trade school after high school	25.4	18.8	$V=.121$	22.3	$V=.07$	17.5	$V=.08$
Go to junior college	10.0	13.6	$\gamma=-.127$	10.0	$\gamma=.02$	11.1	$\gamma=.07$
Go to 4-yr college/university	35.4	35.6		39.6		38.8	
Graduate, professional degree after college	14.9	8.5		11.8		16.8	
N	653	5,091		439		4,927	
Occupational aspirations:							
Clerical	37.0	25.8	$\chi^2=71^*$	7.3	$\chi^2=286^*$	1.5	$\chi^2=1699^*$
Craftsman	.3	.5	$V=.109$	10.6	$V=.519$	15.3	$V=.548$
Farmer, farm manager	.2	.4	$\gamma=.165$	.8	$\gamma=-.267$	3.2	$\gamma=.283$
Homemaker or housewife	3.2	6.2		0		0	
Laborer	.8	.2		4.3		5.0	
Manager, administrator	.9	1.4		7.0		4.7	
Military	1.5	.8		7.0		4.1	
Operative	.9	.8		5.0		4.1	
Professional	43.8	47.8		34.2		42.0	
Proprietor or owner	.5	.5		2.3		3.3	
Protective service	.5	.4		1.3		4.1	
Sales	1.8	3.4		2.8		2.8	
Service	3.3	7.1		2.8		1.4	
Technical	5.6	4.6		14.8		8.5	
N	665	5,296		398		5,002	

Table 6 *(Continued)*

Achievement-Orientation Components	Black Females Percent Distribution	White Females Percent Distribution	White Females Comparison Statistics	Black Females Percent Distribution	Black Females Comparison Statistics	White Males Percent Distribution	White Males Comparison Statistics
Academic self-concept:							
Definitely cannot complete college							
Doubt can complete college	38.0	41.6		40.9		43.3	
Unsure of ability to complete college	35.3	34.6	$\chi^2=10.6*$	31.9	$\chi^2=4.5$	31.3	$\chi^2=13.8*$
Probably can complete college	19.6	16.2		21.2		17.9	
Definitely can complete college	4.4	4.7	$V=.04$	3.5	$V=.05$	5.0	$V=-.04$
	2.7	3.0	$\gamma=-.06$	2.4	$\gamma=.03$	2.5	$\gamma=-.07$
N	1,158	6,225		877		6,293	
Locus of control:							
Low	11.7	3.4	$\chi^2=152*$	15.1	$\chi^2=8.1*$	5.2	$\chi^2=55.1*$
Medium	55.2	48.6		57.9		56.3	
High	33.1	48.0	$V=.159$	27.0	$V=.07$	38.5	$V=.10$
N	854	5,180	$\gamma=.329$	608	$\gamma=-.135$	4,951	$\gamma=.163$
Self-esteem:							
Low	1.9	2.7	$\chi^2=130*$	.9	$\chi^2=4.5$	1.8	$\chi^2=86*$
Medium	34.1	54.3		38.0		51.2	
High	64.0	42.9	$V=.150$	61.1	$V=.05$	47.0	$V=.121$
N	853	4,954	$\gamma=-.389$	664	$\gamma=.05$	4,983	$\gamma=-.317$

NOTE.—Table percentages may not add to 100.0 because of rounding error; χ^2 = chi square statistic; V = Cramer's V statistic; γ = gamma statistic.
*Significant at the .05 level or lower.

two-step process involving (1) development of appropriate achievement-related skills and attitudes, and (2) gained access to societal vehicles (e.g., higher education, employment networks) which facilitate the translation of acquired skills and attitudes into high status, both stages of the process need to be studied more thoroughly. Past research has tended to overemphasize step one in this process while neglecting step two. The majority of such research concentrates on the personal characteristics or family backgrounds of black women as the basis for understanding their attainment histories. Meanwhile, established societal practices and norms which systematically deny black women equal opportunity to achieve at levels commensurate with their abilities are ignored. A more viable approach to the study of continued black female occupational inequities involves scrutiny of institutions (their norms, personnel, and procedures) which impact on the achievement process. This information could then be combined with existing knowledge about black female socialization experiences and outcomes, thereby identifying critical personal and societal factors in the occupational achievement histories of black women.

In conclusion, many profoundly important issues in the study of race, sex, ambition, and occupational achievement are not dealt with here. Limitations in space, data, resources, and expertise serve to necessarily restrict the focus of this study. Several intriguing questions remain. How are black women's marital and family roles affected by their occupational status? Do the other sex-race groups perceive black women's occupational ambitions as potentially threatening? Will black women's occupational prospects suffer or prosper in this paradoxical era of economic conservatism and affirmative action pressures? Needless to say, it will be years before these and related questions receive definitive, empirically based answers. However, if this paper serves to clarify the empirical realities underlying the disjunction between black women's achievement orientations and occupational achievements, its major purpose has been fulfilled. It is hoped that the accumulated findings of this genre of studies will ultimately permit creation of a society which allows people the space to affirm and assert their humanity through pursuit of those life goals which they set for themselves, restricted only by limitations in their own vision and capabilities.

Department of Sociology
University of North Carolina at Chapel Hill

THE ECONOMIC FORTUNES OF WOMEN AND CHILDREN:
LESSONS FROM THE PANEL STUDY OF INCOME DYNAMICS

MARY CORCORAN, GREG J. DUNCAN, AND MARTHA S. HILL

Most of our knowledge about the economic fortunes of women and children comes from case studies, special-purpose surveys such as National Longitudinal Surveys, or cross-sectional data. Each source has certain limitations. Case studies often provide richly detailed pictures of a few individuals who may not, however, be representative of larger groups. Analyses of special-purpose longitudinal surveys may yield generalizations about only limited segments of the population. Cross-sectional data provide snapshot pictures of an entire population but tell us little about the dynamic processes that affect their lives.

Because most social science theories of human behavior are dynamic rather than static, they must be tested through repeated observations of the same people. An extra year of data on one set of individuals is considerably more valuable than new data on a different cross section. This is particularly important when the process under analysis takes an extended period of time. For instance, investigations of the causes, extent, and consequences of long-run welfare dependency must be conducted over an extended period and even across generations if competing theories are to be tested adequately. This requirement also holds for studies of changes in family composition (e.g., marriage, childbirth, marital breakups), which should be based on comparisons of a family's situation before and after change.

Equally important, any study of the economic well-being of women

The research reported in this article was supported by the Department of Labor, the Sloan Foundation, the National Science Foundation, the Ford Foundation, the Department of Health and Human Services, and the National Academy of Science. None of these institutions is responsible for any opinions or errors within.

This essay originally appeared in *Signs*, vol. 10, no. 2, Winter 1984.

and children should look at entire families—particularly at any male adults present, for they are often key economic influences. Because families change over time through marriage, childbirth, children's departure from home, and marital disruptions, monitoring economic well-being requires following all family members as these changes occur.

Each year since 1968, the Panel Study of Income Dynamics (PSID) has followed the economic fortunes of a nationally representative sample of American families.[1] Since the PSID tracks all individuals who have left the homes of the original 1968 sample, it is an unbiased, self-replacing, and representative sample of families each year. The procedure of following all original family members also makes the PSID a unique data set for monitoring the causes and effects of family composition change. Further, since the study originally oversampled poor and minority households, it provides a large enough black subsample to permit separate analyses by race.

The main content of the PSID interviews is an annual measurement of a set of trend items that indicate changes in income sources, family composition, employment, earnings, and hours spent working, commuting, doing housework, and caring for children. While these variables have been elaborated and changed somewhat over time, most are comparable from year to year. Also, PSID interviewers collected extensive background information about the head, and some about the spouse, of each original family, a procedure repeated for the head and spouse of each new family surveyed. Information about children's schooling, about housing and transportation, and about income and occupation are available each year. Finally, in 1976, the PSID added a special interview with wives that included questions about their past work history and fertility.

Thus, the Panel Study of Income Dynamics is unique among longitudinal data sets in combining a national sample, years of annual interviews with many similar questions about work and income, and information about all members of the initial sample of families. These factors give the PSID a versatility unparalleled by other studies and also make it an exceptionally good vehicle for exploring the economic situations of women and children, as the findings reported below indicate.

Sex-based Differences in Wages

The Lord spoke to Moses and said, "When a man makes a special vow to the Lord which requires your valuation of living persons, a male between twenty and sixty years old shall be valued at fifty silver

1. The design and content of the PSID are described in an 8-vol. set of documentation available from the Institute for Social Research, University of Michigan, Ann Arbor, Michigan 48106.

shekels. If it is a female, she shall be valued at thirty shekels."
[Lev. 27:1–4]

The biblical practice of setting the value of a woman's work at about three-fifths that of a man's seems to persist in modern times. Census Bureau figures show that on average, for every dollar men earned per hour, women earned $.63 in 1949, $.65 in 1959, and $.63 in 1969.[2] Some attribute this wage gap to discrimination. An alternative explanation—popular with employers, emphasized by economists, and prevalent in recent government policy statements—is that men's higher earnings reflect their higher level of job-related skills. Because women allegedly choose to sacrifice career advancement for home responsibilities, they are thought to lack equal skills.

Demands of child care and other home responsibilities may influence women's acquisition of job skills in several ways. First, most women do not work continuously after leaving school but, instead, fulfill family and child care responsibilities by interspersing periods of employment with periods of nonmarket work. If women expect to have a less regular pattern of labor-force participation, then they will have a shorter wage-earning career than will men. Reducing the period during which a woman will benefit from her investment in job-related skills may produce a clear economic incentive for her to acquire fewer of those skills.[3] Second, women may find that their skills become rusty (and hence less valuable) if they temporarily leave the labor force to have and raise children. Third, many women workers must balance the demands of work and family and may be forced to accept lower-paying jobs in order to be closer to home, to have suitable work schedules, or to allow for high absenteeism when their children are ill.

In sum, the human capital explanation posits that most, if not all, of the earnings gap between the sexes is a consequence of the home responsibilities assumed by women. Saying that the wage differentials are justifiable, however, in no way implies that the choices made by women are unwise. Women's actions are seen merely as responses to the incentives

2. U.S. Department of Labor, *Manpower and Training Report of the President* (Washington, D.C.: Department of Labor, 1973). These ratios have been adjusted for differences in educational attainment. Victor R. Fuchs finds that adjustments for schooling and age produce hourly wage ratios of .61 in 1959 and .64 in 1969 ("Recent Trends and Long-Run Prospects for Female Earnings," *American Economic Review* 64 [1974]: 236–42). Fuchs is also responsible for uncovering the biblical verse that opens this section.

3. This result follows from the view that job skills are acquired at some cost to the worker and can therefore be considered an investment. Costs can be direct (tuition for formal course work) or indirect (the opportunity cost of forgoing a high salary in a job with little future in favor of an initially lower salary in a job that does promise future advancement).

created by their current responsibilities and future plans. Men faced with similar incentives would be expected to make similar choices.[4]

The PSID data are well suited to testing this explanation.[5] In 1976 a special questionnaire asked male and female household heads and spouses explicitly about work history, interruptions in work, absenteeism, and self-imposed restrictions on work hours and job location. Thus, the PSID provides measures of an extensive number of qualifications for a nationally representative sample of men and women across a broad age range.

We investigated the human capital explanation by calculating the difference in average skill levels of men and women as measured by five criteria: education, work experience, work continuity, self-imposed work restrictions, and patterns of absenteeism (see table 1). Then we calculated the economic value of each particular factor, that is, the extent to which it increased earnings. The degree to which a particular attribute contributed to the wage gap was measured by multiplying the economic value of that attribute by the actual difference in the average amounts of that attribute possessed by men and women.[6] If the sex-based wage differential is "justifiable" and our list of factors is complete and well measured, then sex differentials in these factors should "explain" most of the gap.

Many of the differences between women and white men were consistent with cultural stereotypes. A majority of the women surveyed had not worked continuously after school completion; much of their work experience was part-time; a substantial minority of those who did work placed limits on when, how much, or where they worked; and a substantial

4. Women's low incentive to acquire skills may be reinforced by the expectation that discrimination will reduce the likely value of those skills in the workplace. This argument is not an integral part of the skills explanation, although some proponents may support it.

5. The research summarized below is reported in Mary Corcoran, "The Structure of Female Wages," *American Economic Review* 68, no. 2 (May 1978): 165–70, and "Work Experience, Labor Force Withdrawals, and Women's Earnings: Empirical Results Using the 1976 Panel Study of Income Dynamics," in *Women in the Labor Market*, ed. Cynthia Lloyd, Emily Andrews, and Curtis Gilroy (New York: Columbia University Press, 1979); Mary Corcoran and Greg J. Duncan, "Work History, Labor Force Attachment, and Earnings Differences between the Races and Sexes," *Journal of Human Resources* 14, no. 1 (Winter 1979): 3–20; Mary Corcoran, Greg J. Duncan, and Michael Ponza, "Work Experience, Job Segregation and Wages," in *Sex Segregation in the Work Place: Trends, Explanations, Remedies* (Washington, D.C.: National Academy Press, in press), and "A Longitudinal Approach to White Women's Wages," *Journal of Human Resources* 18, no. 4 (Fall 1983): 497–520.

6. For example, suppose that men's average education level exceeded that of women by one year. The influence of that difference on the wage gap would depend on the value of a year's worth of education. If average wages of men and women differed by $2.00 per hour and an additional year of education were "worth" $2.00 per hour, then all of the wage gap could be explained by the education difference. If additional years of education were worth $.25 per hour, then one-eighth of the gap would be accounted for by the education difference.

Table 1

Effect of Differences in Human Capital Measures on Wage Gaps between White Men and Women

	Mean Values of Human Capital Measures			Percent of Wage Gap Accounted for by Human Capital Measures*	
	For White Men	For White Women	For Black Women	Between White Men and White Women	Between White Men and Black Women
Education (years)	12.9	12.7	11.8	2	10
Work experience:					
Years of experience prior to present job	11.3	8.1	9.3	4	2
Years in present job	8.7	5.7	6.5	16	10
Proportion of total working years employed full-time	.91	.79	.83	9	5
Work continuity:					
Years out of the labor force after completing school	.7	3.2	3.1	2	1

Length in years of most recent work interruption	1.0	2.5	.5	1	0
Percent who interrupted work two or more times	2.8	11.8	3.7	1	0
Self-imposed job restrictions:					
Percentage who placed limitations on work hours or location	15	34	22	3	0
Percentage working part-time voluntarily	1	15	9	-2	0
Annual rates of absenteeism (hours):					
Due to own illness	37	43	58	0	0
Due to illness of family members	4	12	25	-1	-2
Total				35	26

NOTE.—Our sample consisted of male heads of households, female heads of households, and wives aged sixteen to sixty-four in 1976 who were employed at least 500 hours in 1975. The table reads (e.g., across the first row): "Schooling of white men averaged 12.9 years, compared with averages of 12.7 and 11.8 years for white and black women, respectively. The schooling differences between white men and white women accounted for 2 percent of the earnings gaps between them. This difference explained 10 percent of the gap between white men and black women."

* This figure is calculated by the following formula: $G_Z = (\bar{Z}_{WM} - \bar{Z}_{WW})\beta_{WM}(\ln \bar{W}_{WM} - \ln \bar{W}_{WW})$, where G_Z = proportion of wage gap between white men and women accounted for by variable Z, $\bar{Z}_{WM}$ = white male mean on Z, $\bar{Z}_{WW}$ = white female mean on Z, $\bar{W}_{WM}$ = white male mean on hourly wage, $\bar{W}_{WW}$ = white female mean on hourly wage, β_{WM} = coefficient obtained from regressing ln (hourly wages) on a set of independent predictors containing Z. For details, see Mary Corcoran and Greg J. Duncan, "Work History, Labor Force Attachment, and Earnings Differences between the Races and Sexes," *Journal of Human Resources* 14, no. 1 (Winter 1979): 3–20.

minority stayed home from work to care for sick children. Also, black women averaged a year less schooling than did white men. Yet these differences in work patterns and experience will explain wage differences only if those factors in themselves have a substantial effect on earnings. If, for example, workers who placed restrictions on work hours or job location were not paid less than other workers, then women's tendency, on average, to self-impose more restrictions would not explain why they earned less than white men.

The last two columns of table 1 show the results of combining information on differences in education, work experience, work continuity, job restrictions, and absenteeism within the race-sex subgroups with the estimated effects of these factors on earnings. We reached these estimates through a statistical analysis that adjusts for differences in all other variables listed in table 1. The figures in the right-hand columns represent the fraction of the wage gaps explained by each of the skill measures. The totals shown indicate the overall explanatory power of all skills combined.

As expected, differences in work experience explained a significant portion of the wage gap between white men and women, largely because women had acquired less tenure and were more likely to have worked part-time. Altogether, differences in work experience accounted for 29 percent of the wage gap between white men and white women and 17 percent between white men and black women.

Surprisingly, the large differences that existed in male and female patterns of job tenure did little to explain the wage gap between white and black women and white men. Although discontinuous employment did reduce women's work experience, they apparently were not handicapped by having "rusty" skills when they returned to the work force. After adjusting for the effects of lost experience, we found that labor-force interruptions never significantly lowered wages for either women or white men. Delays in starting work after school completion did lower white women's wages slightly.

It is also surprising that the large sex differences in male and female decisions to self-impose job restrictions and to stay home to care for family members explained almost none of the wage gap. Women and white men who were frequently absent from work or who had restricted work hours or job locations did not earn consistently less than did equally qualified workers who imposed no limitations and had attended work regularly.[7]

---

7. Since it takes time for employers to reflect their evaluation of individual performance in salary and promotion decisions, it may not be surprising that we found no relation between current pay and records of absenteeism. However, additional analysis has also shown that wages are not related to past absenteeism (see Richard D. Coe, "Absenteeism from Work," in *Five Thousand American Families—Patterns of Economic Progress*, vol. 6, ed. Greg J. Duncan and James M. Morgan [Ann Arbor, Mich.: Institute for Social Research, 1978]).

Even women who voluntarily chose to work part-time earned no less per hour than other women.

Perhaps our most important finding is that, taken together, all these large differences between women and men explain only about one-third of the wage gap between white men and white women and only about one-quarter of the wage gap between white men and black women. Even after accounting for sex differences among a wide range of factors that influence skill measures, we still see that white men enjoy a large advantage in earnings over women. This casts considerable doubt on the argument that women "deserve" to earn less than men because women sacrifice career advancement in order to meet family responsibilities.

Family Composition and Economic Well-Being

A woman's earnings may, however, represent only one component of her overall economic status. Many women live in families in which a male wage earner contributes the largest component of family income; family income dynamics, then, is the key to understanding their economic position.[8] Some might argue that if the economic benefits provided by marriage were added to married women's earnings, their overall economic position might be quite similar to that of men.

The PSID provides longitudinal data on family incomes, which enables those studying economic inequality not only to determine the structure of a family's income and to compare it at multiple points in time but also to analyze the economic mobility of the family as a whole and of its individual members. By following a panel of families over time, the PSID

8. This section summarizes research from Mary Jo Bane, *Here to Stay: American Families in the Twentieth Century* (New York: Basic Books, 1976); Jacob Benus and James N. Morgan, "Time Period, Unit of Analysis, and Income Concept in the Analysis of Income Distribution," in *The Personal Distribution of Income and Wealth,* ed. James D. Smith (New York: Columbia University Press, 1975); Richard D. Coe, Greg J. Duncan, and Martha S. Hill, "Dynamic Aspects of Poverty and Welfare Use in the United States" (paper delivered at the Conference on Problems of Poverty, Clark University, August 1982); Greg J. Duncan, "The Implications of Changing Family Composition for the Dynamic Analysis of Family Well-Being" (paper delivered at the Conference on Analysis of Panel Data on Income, London, June 1982); Martha S. Hill, "Trends in the Economic Situation of U.S. Families and Children" (paper delivered at the Conference on Families and the Economy, National Academy of Science, Washington, D.C., 1982); Jonathan P. Lane and James N. Morgan, "Patterns of Change in Economic Status and Family Structure," in *Five Thousand American Families—Patterns of Economic Progress,* vol. 3, ed. Greg J. Duncan and James N. Morgan (Ann Arbor, Mich.: Institute for Social Research, 1975); George Masnick and Mary Jo Bane, *The Nation's Families: 1969–1990,* Joint Center Outlook Reports (Cambridge, Mass.: Joint Center for Urban Studies of MIT and Harvard University, 1980); James N. Morgan, "Change in Global Measures," in *Five Thousand American Families—Patterns of Economic Progress,* vol. 1, ed. James N. Morgan et al. (Ann Arbor, Mich.: Institute for Social Research, 1974).

also raises a whole new set of questions about our conception and analysis of the "family." In a cross-sectional study, determining family composition is not problematic since at any point, all individuals can be classified uniquely as members of a particular family. However as the PSID demonstrates, a family can at any time splinter through divorce, separation, or the departure of children. Two distinct families can merge through marriage, cohabitation, the return of a child after a temporary absence, or more complicated rearrangements. In fact, one major finding of this study is that families do undergo considerable change over time. By the thirteenth year of the PSID, only 11.9 percent of the existing families had not changed in composition, and 57.1 percent were headed by someone other than the original sample head.

These fluctuations in family structure have important implications. Although measures of the level of family economic status (e.g., family income, family per capita income) may be the outcomes of interest, the family itself is not usually the appropriate unit of analysis. If, however, we choose to look at individuals, then each can be associated with a family at a given point in time and with the economic well-being of that family. This strategy has the added advantage of allowing us to test whether changes in family composition predict changes in economic well-being for women and children.

Greg J. Duncan examined the level, trend, and stability of family income for men, women, and children from 1974 to 1979.[9] Both the level and stability of per capita family income (measured as income relative to needs)[10] were greater for white men than for either women or children. The economic benefits of marriage did not, on average, compensate women for their low relative earnings. Black children had the least per capita income and the least financial stability.

Family composition changes were important in determining changes in economic well-being. Duncan estimated growth rates in family income and in family income relative to needs over the period 1971–78 for male heads of household, female heads of household, and children.[11] He then used dummy variable regression to estimate the effect of family composition changes on family income growth after adjusting for education, age, and race. For men, such changes had a negligible effect on per capita income growth; in contrast, a shift in family composition had a powerful effect on the economic status of women and children. Indeed, the ex-

9. See Duncan (n. 8 above).

10. Needs are defined using the Orsansky Poverty Index, explained in Molly Orshansky, "Counting the Poor," in *Poverty in America*, ed. L. Ferman, J. Hornblack, and A. Haberc (Ann Arbor: University of Michigan Press, 1968).

11. See Duncan (n. 8 above).

planatory power of family change variables was many times higher than the explanatory power of changes in the labor-force participation of men and women. The effects of four major changes in family makeup are explained below in order of importance.

Divorce and remarriage.—Divorce often leads to a sharp drop in family income and per capita income for an ex-wife and, if present, her children. She loses her former husband's wages for the support of her newly formed family, which in almost all instances includes the divorced couple's children as well. Alimony and child support payments from an ex-husband are rare and, even if paid, usually do not represent more than a fraction of the lost income. Although most divorced women enter or remain in the labor force, their low level of earnings and part-time work arrangements result in a dramatically lower income level for the family. Private transfer payments from other relatives or friends are rare. Roughly one-fifth of ex-wives receive public transfer payments in the year following a divorce, but they do not replace much of the lost income.

The ex-wife's new family is smaller following her husband's departure, but the loss of his income is much greater than the drop in needs, producing almost as sharp a decline in per capita family income as in family income alone. The economic status of the ex-husband, in contrast, typically improves substantially for the same reasons. His newly formed family (which usually comprises just himself for a brief period, then another spouse) has fewer needs, since it is greatly reduced in size.

Marriage or remarriage sharply improves the economic status of female-headed households because a male wage earner's contribution to the total family income is typically much greater than the growth in family needs following his arrival. Remarriage is much more common for divorced men than for divorced women and considerably more frequent for white women than for black women.

Departure of children.—Children departing their parental homes experience a sharp drop in family income level but little net change, on average, in their per capita family income level. The newly formed family loses the parents' income but proportionately lowers its needs standards as well. The economic well-being of family members left behind typically increases modestly since, on average, the departing children have added more to the family's needs than to its income.

Birth.—Births often lead to modest reductions in a family's economic well-being. Needs increase with the addition of a new family member, and income often falls if a mother drops out of the labor force to care for the child.

Widowhood.—The death of a spouse is most common for an elderly woman, whose income and needs both decrease so that her economic position changes very little.

Poverty

The "culture of poverty" thesis, dominant both in social science research on poverty and in public policy debate, was developed from anthropological case studies of poor, urban families in a number of countries. It contends that the qualities developed and reinforced in the environment in which the poor live prevent them from taking advantage of economic opportunities. Poverty is seen as a self-perpetuating state; the present generation of poor locked into it bequeath it to their children. Proponents of this argument vary in their estimates of the proportion of poor people to which this pattern applies.

Bradley Schiller has classified this argument as a "flawed character" explanation of poverty. The problem is seen not as a lack of opportunities for the poor but as their failure to seize opportunities because they lack diligence and initiative. According to this argument, poverty is more a function of the way people think than of their physical environment; the implication is that to cure poverty one has to change the attitudes of the poor. As Oscar Lewis put it: "Once [the culture of poverty] comes into existence, it tends to perpetuate itself from generation because of its effects on children. By the time slum children are age six or seven, they have usually absorbed the basic values and attitudes of their subculture and are not psychologically geared to take full advantage of changing conditions or increased opportunities which may occur in their lifetime."[12]

A new flawed-character argument has now become prominent in public debate on poverty. In a recent *New Yorker* series and in a new book, Ken Auletta writes about the "underclass"—a group permanently mired in poverty.[13] He primarily describes relatively young, able-bodied adults and leaves the impression that many of the long-term poor fall into four subgroups: "hostile street criminals," "hustlers," welfare mothers, and the "traumatized." Much of Auletta's work is based on case studies of participants in a supported work program for the hard-core poor.

Lewis and Auletta present compelling and eloquent descriptions of a set of poor people; such case studies easily command public attention—particularly when few data exist about the dynamics of poverty. But the individuals they describe may be very unrepresentative of the larger groups with which the public tends to identify them. A major advantage of the PSID is its more complete picture of the nature, extent, and

12. Bradley R. Schiller, *The Economics of Poverty and Discrimination*, 2d ed. (Englewood Cliffs, N.J.: Prentice-Hall, Inc., 1976); Oscar Lewis, *La Vida* (New York: Random House, 1966), p. 50.
13. Ken Auletta, *The Underclass* (New York: Random House, 1982).

duration of poverty as experienced by real but representative families over time.[14]

We find that poverty is more widespread but much less persistent than is popularly imagined. Poverty spells often begin with a job loss or a marital breakup and end when an individual takes a new job or remarries. Even the small group of persistently poor individuals do not reflect the demographic makeup or economic experiences of either Auletta's "underclass" or Lewis's slum families.

For example, consider the incidence of poverty over the ten-year period 1969–78. In 1978, 6.8 percent of the PSID sample were poor.[15] If poverty were permanent, then those individuals—and thus 6.8 percent of the entire population—should have been poor for every one of those ten years. Similarly, if poverty were entirely transitory, then poverty in one year would be no predictor of later poverty, and 52 percent of the population would have been poor at least once.[16] In fact, one-quarter of the population were poor at some time during the years from 1969 to 1978, suggesting that poverty is a widespread risk. But of that group, the majority were only poor one or two years, and only about one-tenth (2.6 percent of the entire population) were poor at least eight years.[17]

The persistently poor were thus only a small subset of those who ever experienced poverty, and they did not fit easily into the underclass stereotype. One-third were elderly or lived in households headed by an elderly person. More than one-quarter were children, fewer than one-third lived in large urban areas, and more than one-quarter lived in families in which the head had worked a substantial amount in at least five out of the ten years. By following the economic fortunes of both children

14. This section summarizes research by Richard D. Coe, "A Preliminary Empirical Examination of the Dynamics of Welfare Use," in *Five Thousand American Families—Patterns of Economic Progress*, vol. 9, ed. Daniel H. Hill, Martha S. Hill, and James N. Morgan (Ann Arbor, Mich.: Institute for Social Research, 1981), "Dependency and Poverty in the Short and Long Run," in *Five Thousand American Families—Patterns of Economic Progress*, vol. 6, ed. Greg J. Duncan and James N. Morgan (Ann Arbor, Mich.: Institute for Social Research, 1978), and "The Poverty Line: Its Functions and Limitations," *Public Welfare* (Winter 1978), pp. 32–36; Coe, Duncan, and Hill (n. 8 above); Hill (n. 8 above); Martha S. Hill, "Some Dynamics of Poverty," in Hill, Hill, and Morgan, eds.; Frank Levy, "The Intergenerational Transfer of Poverty," Working Paper 1241–02 (Washington, D.C.: Urban Institute, January 1980, mimeographed), and "How Big Is the American Underclass?" rev. version (Urban Institute, Washington, D.C., 1976, mimeographed).

15. This figure is based on the PSID. The Census Bureau reported a higher incidence of poverty for 1978—11.4 percent of the population. For a number of reasons, however, these figures are not comparable.

16. The 52 percent figure is equal to $\sum_{i=1}^{N} (.068)(.932)^{i-1}$.

17. This one-tenth figure is the ratio of experiencing long-term poverty (2.6 percent) to ever experiencing poverty (25 percent).

and parents with PSID data, Frank Levy found that, after forming their own households, at least four-fifths of the children from poor families moved out of poverty; many had incomes substantially above the poverty line. This offers little support for the idea that, among most of the poor, poverty is transmitted from one generation to the next. PSID data on the achievement motivation, sense of personal efficacy, and future orientation of all household heads in the early years of the survey also indicate that these attitudes had small and generally insignificant effects on later changes in individuals' economic status; at least as measured in the PSID, these factors did not account for failure to achieve, as some flawed-character theories might predict.

If the culture-of-poverty and underclass arguments do not apply to many of the long-term poor, then what does explain persistent poverty, and how might one combat it? One way to answer this is to look at the demographic characteristics of the persistently poor.

First, one-third of the persistently poor are elderly, a group in which women are overrepresented. Second, the remaining 65 percent live in households headed by a woman, and 70 percent of these are headed by a black woman. Most of these heads of household have the double economic burden of children at home who increase needs and decrease a single parent's ability to work.

This overrepresentation of female-headed households among the persistently poor underscores our earlier conclusion that changes in family composition greatly affect women's and children's economic well-being. Given Norton and Glick's prediction that 40 percent of all first marriages will end in divorce, we could expect considerable damage to the standard of living of women and children in these homes.[18] In fact, Richard Coe, Greg Duncan, and Martha Hill report that for children, divorce is the strongest single predictor of poverty.[19] Remarriage does considerably improve women's and children's standard of living; but of course not all divorced women do remarry. The period during which they head households without access to a man's income—whether brief or extended—is financially difficult. Frank Levy's analyses suggest that even if poor women who head households were able to work, many of them would be unlikely to find a job paying enough to remove them from poverty. Thus again, we need to understand more about women's low wage rates if we are to help them and their children move out of poverty.

Using PSID data to examine the economic experiences of children over a ten-year period, Martha Hill found that they were slightly more likely to experience poverty than the general population.[20] But her most

18. Arthur J. Norton and Paul C. Glick, "Marital Instability: Past, Present and Future," *Journal of Social Issues* 32 (1976): 5–20.

19. Coe, Duncan, and Hill (n. 8 above).

20. Hill, "Trends in the Economic Situation of U.S. Families and Children" (n. 8 above).

dramatic finding was that black children were considerably more likely to live in poverty than white children. Over a ten-year period, 70 percent of black children were poor at some time, and 30 percent were poor in at least six of the ten years; comparable estimates for white children were 30 percent and 2 percent, respectively. Clearly we are far from eliminating the gap between black and white children's economic experiences during childhood, an aim of the social programs of the 1960s and 1970s.

Welfare Dependency

Central to the recent conservative attack on welfare programs—particularly AFDC and food stamps—is the argument that these programs foster the growth of a "welfare class," people trapped in a system that perpetuates their poverty and dependency. Martin Anderson, former domestic policy advisor to Reagan, summarizes this view: "In effect we have created a new caste of Americans—perhaps as much as one-tenth of this nation—a caste of people free from basic wants but almost totally dependent on the State, with little hope or prospects of breaking free. Perhaps we should call them the Dependent Americans."[21]

Understanding welfare dependency is clearly important for an understanding of women's and children's well-being, since they form the majority of AFDC recipients. Conservatives argue that typical welfare recipients live in families headed by a woman, who persistently depends on welfare and raises children who will do the same. They also suggest that welfare discourages working and remarriage and encourages divorce, separation, and illegitimate births.

The PSID data on long-run patterns of welfare use simply do not support many of these stereotypes, also found in case-study accounts such as Auletta's.[22] Like poverty, welfare use is widespread; between 1969 and 1978 one-fourth of the population lived in families that received welfare income at some point.[23] But welfare dependency was not extensive. If dependency is defined as reliance on welfare income for more than half of total family income in any year, then only one-third of those receiving

21. Martin Anderson, *Welfare* (Stanford, Calif.: Hoover Institution Press, 1978), p. 56.
22. This section reviews research by Coe, "A Preliminary Empirical Examination . . . ," "Dependency and Poverty . . . ," and "The Poverty Line" (all in n. 14 above); Coe, Duncan, and Hill (n. 8 above); Martha Hill and Michael Ponza, "The Intergenerational Transfer of Welfare: Does Dependency Beget Dependency?" (paper delivered at the Southern Economic Association meeting, Washington, D.C., November 1983); Levy, "The Intergenerational Transfer of Poverty," and "How Big Is the American Underclass?" (both in n. 14 above); Martin Rein and Lee Rainwater, "Patterns of Welfare Use," *Social Science Review* (December 1978), pp. 511–34; Isabel V. Sawhill et al., *Income Transfers and Family Structure* (Washington, D.C.: Urban Institute, 1975).
23. This group of welfare recipients overlaps with, but is not identical to, the group of poor individuals identified between 1969 and 1978.

welfare throughout this period were dependent on it. Using this definition, only 2 percent of the population were dependent on welfare for eight or more of the ten years between 1969 and 1978. (About 1 percent were dependent in all ten years.) Thus, most welfare recipients are not on the rolls for a long time, and most are not completely dependent on welfare income. Instead, welfare recipients are more likely to mix work and welfare or to alternate between them.

The PSID data also give little or no support to the contention that patterns of welfare dependency are intergenerational. Most women who had left the homes of parents who received welfare income were not likely to be receiving welfare themselves. Nor did they appear more likely to receive public aid than otherwise similar women whose parents did not receive welfare income. In general, parents' overall economic status proved a more powerful determinant of their children's welfare use than did their history of welfare assistance.

Another important charge leveled against the current welfare system is that it has the unintended side effects of encouraging divorce and separation, discouraging remarriage, or encouraging illegitimate births. The PSID evidence indicates few, if any, effects of this kind.[24]

We conclude that the welfare system successfully reaches a large number of the poor without promoting dependency. But admittedly there is a small group persistently dependent on welfare. As with the persistently poor, these welfare recipients are disproportionately female, black, and with children in the home. Any solutions for this group must deal with the burdens of child care and the low wage positions of blacks and women. Without major societal changes, direct income transfers may be the most efficient solution.

Conclusion

The PSID data have enabled a more complete description and analysis of the long-term economic processes affecting the economic fortunes of women and children and have been useful in dispelling some prominent myths about poverty, welfare, women's wages, and race differences. In summary, this research indicates the following:

1. The argument that women earn less than men because they acquire fewer work skills does not hold up under empirical scrutiny. Although there are large differences between men's and women's work

24. Evidence from the negative income tax experiments suggests that these income maintenance plans may lead to higher rates of marital dissolution than the current system of AFDC, SSI, and other welfare programs. Evidence from the PSID provides little support for the hypothesis that couples living in states with the most generous AFDC benefits are more likely to split up than couples living in less generous states.

skills, our data show that two-thirds of the wage gap between white men and white women and three-quarters of the gap between white men and black women cannot be accounted for by sex differences in skills, work participation, or labor-force attachment.

2. Families change considerably over time, which profoundly affects the economic fortunes of women and children. Often a divorced mother faces the double economic bind of assuming complete responsibility for her children's care while attempting to make up for her ex-husband's lost income with small child support payments and poorly paid wage labor.

3. Arguments about the culture of poverty and the underclass are not consistent with evidence from the PSID about the extent, duration, and nature of poverty. Poverty and welfare use are more pervasive, but much less persistent, than is commonly thought. There is little evidence of extensive welfare dependence or of the transmission of poverty and welfare status from parents to children. There is also little evidence that good attitudes enable people to overcome poverty or that welfare encourages family instability.

4. Women and children have a much lower and more unstable per capita family income over time—and a higher risk of falling into poverty—than do white men. Black children are the group most at risk. Their six-year average per capita income is less than half that of white men. Clearly race differences have not narrowed to the point that black and white children enjoy similar economic security during childhood.

These findings have important implications for public policy debate. Arguments for welfare cuts on the grounds that the poor are "undeserving" and lack initiative are contradicted by our evidence that many recipients of public aid mix work with welfare; the long-term poor most in need of aid, in fact, tend to be elderly people and women with children. Even if we were willing to compel female heads of household to work full-time, our study suggests that they could not make enough to escape poverty. Welfare reform proposals based on assumptions that the availability of AFDC funds encourages welfare dependency within and across generations or that it causes marital instability are simply untenable in light of our research.

Evidence from the PSID also challenges the notion that women's low earnings are due to the voluntary sexual division of labor in the home, a claim often used to justify abandoning equal opportunity and affirmative action programs for women. Such a strategy, we believe, would most likely further exacerbate the economic inequalities based on sex and age reported here. One route to improving women's and children's economic well-being would be to reduce "undeserved" sex differences in earnings. Another might be some kind of social insurance program for divorced women that provided more generous benefits than those currently available from alimony or AFDC.

Finally, our findings confirm that it is not yet time to pull back on compensatory and affirmative action programs for blacks. Policies that discontinue the government's role in alleviating or redressing race-based childhood inequalities could be very costly politically for a society that places great symbolic value on "equal opportunity."

Institute for Social Research
University of Michigan

EXPLODING THE MYTH OF AFRICAN-AMERICAN PROGRESS

JAMES A. GESCHWENDER AND RITA CARROLL-SEGUIN

Recent social science scholarship has given rise to a popular myth that asserts African-Americans have made a great deal of progress toward achieving economic equality in American society and that this progress may be expected to continue into the indefinite future. We assert that this myth is both dangerous and false. It is dangerous because the myth has supported the rationale for public policies that deemphasize government action to overcome racial inequality. It is false because the optimism is based upon an inaccurate and incomplete analysis of the data that has not taken into account the differential impact of women's participation in the labor market. The historical experiences of African-Americans created different patterns of female labor-force participation from those that developed among European-Americans.[1] Consequently, African-American women have

[1] Their participation may best be analyzed using the concept of "ethgender." This concept implies that people should be analyzed in terms of the jointly occupied social space that is created by the intersection of gender and ethnicity. For a more complete discussion of the development of the concept, see H. Edward Ransford and Jon Miller, "Race, Sex and Feminist Outlooks," *American Sociological Review* 48, no. 1 (February 1983): 46–59; Vincent Jeffries and H. Edward Ransford, *Social Stratification: A Multiple Hierarchy Approach* (Boston: Allyn & Bacon, 1980), 265–93. We use the term "European-American" to contrast with "African-American" and to emphasize the theoretical point that race is a social construct that is largely defined in terms of region of origin. We do not mean to imply that all European-Americans are identical in either origin or social characteristics. It is clear that they differ considerably from one another in ethnic origin. This deserves analysis but is beyond the scope of the present manuscript. We wish herein to concentrate our

This essay originally appeared in *Signs*, vol. 15, no. 2, Winter 1990.

always been more likely than European-American women to work outside the home and they have always contributed significantly more to the economic support of their families.[2] Any analysis of past trends in racial inequality and any prediction of future developments must take into account these trends and their impact on the standard of living for both groups.

A large part of the foundation for an optimistic appraisal of African-American advances was provided by Ben Wattenberg and Richard Scammon, who, using an income criterion to define class, argued that a majority of African-Americans were located in the middle class by the early 1970s.[3] They were not alone in their interpretation of developments. Daniel Moynihan stated that there was little racial difference in the incomes of young, husband-wife, nonsouthern, families.[4] Nathan Glazer found a convergence in the incomes of two-parent African-American and European-American families in all regions of the country, and Richard Freeman found little difference in employment and earnings between college-educated African-Americans and European-Americans.[5] A number of scholars found that African-Americans still lagged behind European-Americans in dollar returns for additional years of education but concluded that they had considerably closed the gap after 1960.[6] In fact, George Gilder was so impressed with apparent

---

attention upon gross behavioral differences between African-Americans and European- Americans.

[2] Phyllis A. Wallace, *Black Women in the Labor Force* (Cambridge, Mass.: MIT Press, 1980), 10–11.

[3] Ben J. Wattenberg and Richard M. Scammon, "Black Progress and Liberal Rhetoric," *Commentary* 55, no. 4 (April 1973): 35–44. Some of the authors cited herein defined class in terms of income levels, while most used an occupational criterion—usually a white collar/blue collar split. When citing the work of others, we will indicate those using an income criterion. All others may be assumed to define class in terms of occupation. When we use the term "middle class," or "middle-class life-style," we will be referring to those persons who hold white-collar occupations that generally require education beyond the high school level, who have a reasonable degree of economic security, and who are compensated well enough to obtain decent quality housing, adequate food, clothing, medical care, and education beyond high school for their children. This definition lacks precision but is adequate for our purposes since we are not doing the type of survey research that would require classification of individuals.

[4] Daniel Patrick Moynihan, "The Schism in Black America," *Public Interest* 27 (Spring 1972): 3–24.

[5] Nathan Glazer, *Affirmative Discrimination: Ethnic Inequality and Public Policy* (New York: Basic, 1975); Richard B. Freeman, *Black Elite: The New Market for Highly Educated Black Americans* (New York: McGraw-Hill, 1976), 33.

[6] Reynolds Farley, "Trends in Racial Inequalities: Have the Gains of the 1960s Disappeared in the 1970s?" *American Sociological Review* 42, no. 2 (April 1977):

gains that he concluded, "Gaps in income between truly comparable blacks and whites have nearly closed."[7]

A large part of the scholarly work finding significant advances
for African-Americans focused upon developments during the
1960s. Vernon Jordan and Robert Hill were the first to dampen that
optimism when they demonstrated that the economic gap between
African-Americans and European-Americans not only failed to
close but widened significantly during the 1970s.[8] Michael Reich
argued that most of African-Americans' relative economic gain was
actually the result of structural changes such as migration from
the South to the North or from rural to urban areas and their
movement out of agricultural work and into industry.[9] Edward
Lazear believed, to the contrary, that observed improvement was
real but that it would be only temporary in its impact. He argued
that employers responded to governmental affirmative-action policies by making desirable entry-level jobs available to African-
Americans but that European-Americans would continue to have
much greater opportunities for promotion and advancement.[10] Still
others argued that the summary statistics that indicated advances for
African-Americans obscured the reality of differential experiences
and increasing class polarization within the African-American
community.[11] They noted that the gap between educated middle-

189–208; David L. Featherman and Robert M. Hauser, *Opportunity and Change* (New
York: Academic Press, 1978); Richard B. Freeman, "Decline of Labor Market Discrimination: An Economic Analysis," *American Economic Review* 63, no. 2 (May 1973):
280–86; Stanley H. Masters, *Black-White Income Differentials: Empirical Studies
and Policy Implications* (New York: Academic Press, 1975); James P. Smith and Finis
R. Welch, "Black/White Male Earnings and Employment: 1960–1970," in F. Thomas
Juster, ed. *The Distribution of Economic Well-Being* (Cambridge, Mass.: Ballinger,
1977), 233–96; Leonard Weiss and Jeffrey Williamson, "Black Education, Earnings
and Interregional Migration: Some New Evidence," *American Economic Review* 62,
no. 2 (June 1972): 372–83; Finis R. Welch, "Black-White Differences in Returns to
Schooling," *American Economic Review* 63, no. 5 (December 1973): 893–907.

[7] George Gilder, *Wealth and Poverty* (New York: Basic, 1981), 128.

[8] Vernon Jordan, "Introduction," in *The State of Black America, 1979*, ed. James
D. Williams (Washington, D.C.: National Urban League, 1979), and "Introduction,"
in *The State of Black America, 1980*, ed. James D. Williams (Washington, D.C.:
National Urban League, 1980); Robert B. Hill, *Economic Policies and Black
Progress: Myths and Realities* (Washington, D.C.: National Urban League, 1981).

[9] Michael Reich, *Racial Inequality: A Political-Economic Analysis* (Princeton,
N.J.: Princeton University Press, 1981).

[10] Edward Lazear, "The Narrowing of Black-White Differential Is Illusory,"
American Economic Review 69, no. 4 (September 1979): 553–64.

[11] Ken Auletta, *The Underclass* (New York: Random House, 1982); Gilder, 12;
Daniel Patrick Moynihan, *The Negro Family: The Case for National Action* (Wash-
ington, D.C.: Government Printing Office, 1965); William J. Wilson, *The Declining
Significance of Race*, 2d ed. (Chicago: University of Chicago Press, 1980).

class African-Americans and their European-American counterparts was closing while the African-American underclass grew in size and sank further into poverty.

Perhaps the most extensive attempt to evaluate these conflicting interpretations has been carried out by Reynolds Farley, who provided the major impetus for a rebirth of optimism.[12] He found that in 1959 the median income of African-American families was equivalent to 53 percent of the median income of European-American families. African-American families gained ground throughout the 1960s, and by 1970 African-American median family income was 61 percent of European-American family income. Then African-American families lost ground in the decade that followed; their family income declined to 55 percent of European-American family income in 1982. However, Farley notes that this decline can be explained by considering separately two-parent families and families headed by women. When he compares African-American two-parent families to corresponding European-American families, he finds that African-American families exhibited a more rapid rate of improvement than did European-American families during both the 1960s and the 1970s. African-American families headed by single women showed similar relative economic gains during the 1960s and then held their own during the 1970s; but Farley notes that while the proportion of families headed by women increased for both African-Americans and European-Americans during this time period, it increased far more rapidly among African-Americans.[13] Farley concludes that two-parent African-American families have indeed made major advances in American society, both absolutely and relative to European-Americans, and that the apparent relative decline in family income for African-Americans was simply a consequence of an increase in the number and proportion of female-headed families. He also finds a convergence in the earnings of African-Americans and European-Americans once factors such as gender, education, and years of work experience are considered.[14] Thus, he remains optimistic about the eventual complete elimination of racial inequality in America.

William J. Wilson is not as convinced as Farley that African-Americans are closing the earnings and income gap relative to European-Americans. He has consistently argued that the portion of the African-American community that he calls the underclass is still falling further behind middle-class African-Americans eco-

---

[12] Reynolds Farley, *Blacks and Whites: Narrowing the Gap?* (Cambridge, Mass.: Harvard University Press, 1984), 131–32.

[13] Ibid., 137–42.

[14] Ibid., 57–129.

nomically and is certainly not closing the gap relative to European-Americans.[15] In his earlier work, Wilson argued that the type of analysis Farley presented is misleading because it is based upon the experience of employed persons between ages 25 and 64, and this ignores African-Americans between ages 16 and 24 who have been the most excluded from the labor market.[16] In his most recent work, Wilson concentrates his attention on the plight of the growing number of female-headed families in the African-American community and does not question the widespread assumption, represented here by Farley, that two-parent African-American families are doing well relative to comparable European-American families. He demonstrates that the number of female-headed families is increasing, at least in part in response to economic conditions that make it impossible for large numbers of African-American males to get jobs paying wages large enough to allow them to marry. Consequently, he developed policy recommendations that urge strengthening the economy to create more and better-paying jobs.[17]

Though Wilson's conclusions regarding the plight of the underclass are well founded, he and his colleagues overstate or misinterpret the degree of economic progress of the African-American two-parent family. These authors have failed to recognize the extent to which this apparent progress is a function of a racial difference in patterns of women's participation in the paid labor force. There is abundant evidence that historically the survival of African-American families has depended in large part on the strength of women in holding families together, rearing children, and preserving and passing on traditions.[18] Equally important has been African-American women's income. European-American women's paid labor has been essential to the survival of European-American families, but the labor and earnings of African-American women have made a much greater relative contribution to the economic survival of the African-American family.

[15] William J. Wilson, *The Truly Disadvantaged: The Inner City, the Underclass and Public Policy* (Chicago: University of Chicago Press, 1987), 6–13; 143, for a discussion of his use of the term underclass; and chap. 2 for a summary of his view on the relative position of the African-American underclass *vis-à-vis* both other African-American groups and European-American poor.

[16] Wilson, *The Declining Significance of Race*, 174–75 (the criticism is actually directed toward an earlier work of Farley's, but it applies equally well to Farley's work cited here).

[17] See Wilson, *The Truly Disadvantaged*, 90–92, 104–6, for a summary of his views on the relationship between unemployment and female-headed households, and see his *The Declining Significance of Race*, 121–24, for his specific policy recommendations.

[18] See Jacqueline Jones, *Labor of Love, Labor of Sorrow: Black Women, Work, and the Family from Slavery to the Present* (New York: Basic, 1985).

It is obvious that women's earnings are important to the female-headed family. However, the earnings of women who pooled their income with that of their husbands in order to support the family may be of equal or greater importance. African-American men are not as well compensated as comparable European-Americans.[19] They are less able to translate their educational achievements into the more desirable occupations, and they earn less at each level of education. Consequently, it is not possible for families dependent entirely upon the earnings of an African-American man to achieve the same standard of living or life-style as that of male-supported European-American families. In some cases a working wife is essential in order that the family unit might survive and perhaps prosper.[20] For many African-American women, it is now less of a case of working to meet subsistence needs and more a case of working in order to achieve and maintain quality-of-life goals.

The decision to have both parents active in the labor force may be an attempt to enable the family to live in a safe, attractive, and convenient neighborhood; to be well dressed; to eat foods that are both nourishing and enjoyable; to have good medical and dental care; to have the opportunity and money to enjoy recreational activities; and, perhaps most important of all, to be able to educate children to a point that will enable them to consolidate present levels of economic security and, perhaps, even improve upon them in the future.

African-American wives have traditionally exhibited a much greater propensity than European-American wives to be active in the labor force, but the size of the racial difference has been reduced over time.[21] In 1950 the labor-force participation rate of African-American wives was 62 percent larger than the corresponding rate for European-American wives; by 1988 that gap had been

[19] Hill (n. 8 above); Jordan, 1980 (n. 8 above); Farley, *Blacks and Whites*, 86–88; Paul M. Siegel, "On the Cost of Being a Negro," *Sociological Inquiry* 35, no. 1 (Winter 1965): 41–57; Lester C. Thurow, *Poverty and Discrimination* (Washington, D.C.: Brookings Institution, 1969).

[20] Ronald Angel and Marta Tienda, "Determinants of Extended Household Structure: Cultural Pattern or Economic Need?" *American Journal of Sociology* 87, no. 3 (November 1982): 1360–83.

[21] Howard Hayghe, "Married Couples: Work and Income Patterns," in *Families at Work: The Jobs and the Pay* (Washington, D.C.: Government Printing Office, 1986), 11–14. There were dramatic increases in the labor-force participation rate of European-American women in the twenty-five years prior to 1978 (about fifteen percentage points compared to 5 percent for African-American). The racial difference in female labor-force participation rates decreased to only 3.8 percent in 1978 and 2.0 percent in 1985 and may have completely disappeared by now.

reduced to 18 percent.[22] Racial differences in participation rates also vary by class. The 1970 U.S. Census revealed that African-American wives were more active in the labor market than European-American wives at all levels of the husbands' income. In addition, there is variation in the magnitude of the difference between African-American and European-American wives' labor-force participation rates.[23] The racial gap in labor-force participation rates was smallest at the lowest level of husband's income (7.3 percent), increased with each increase in husband's earnings, and was greatest (24.9 percent) at the highest levels. This positive association between size of racial differences in labor-force partic-ipation rates and size of husband's income holds for wives with children under six years of age and for those whose youngest children were between the ages of six and sixteen.[24]

These findings are consistent with those of Bart Landry and Margaret Platt Jendrek, who used a class-stratified 1976 national sample of two-parent families to explore the simultaneous impact of race and class.[25] They examined employment rather than labor-force participation, but the two variables are related closely enough to draw comparisons. They found that 51.6 percent of working-class African-American wives and 28.8 percent of working-class European-American wives were employed—a 22.8 percent differ-ence. Working-class African-American wives were more likely to be employed full-time than working-class European-American wives (39.8 percent to 18.3 percent—a 21.5 percent difference). Middle-class African-American wives also were more likely to work full-time

[22] In 1950 African-American married women had a labor-force participation rate of 37.0 percent. Comparable European-American women had a rate of 22.8 percent. Thus the African-American rate represented a 62 percent increase over the European-American rate. By 1988 African-American married women had a labor-force participation rate of 66.1 percent and European-American married women had a labor-force participation rate of 55.8 percent. Both rates had increased dramatically over the years. However, the European-American rate increased much more rapidly. The gap remains but has been reduced to 18 percent. The 1988 figures are from *Statistical Abstract of the United States: 1989*, U.S. Bureau of the Census (Wash-ington, D.C.: Government Printing Office, 1989), 386, table 640; data for earlier years are from Phyllis Wallace, *Black Women in the Labor Force* (Cambridge, Mass.: MIT Press, 1980), 10.

[23] William G. Bowen and T. Aldrich Finegan, *The Economics of Labor Force Par-ticipation* (Princeton, N.J.: Princeton University Press, 1969); James A. Sweet, *Women in the Labor Force* (New York: Seminary Press, 1973); Joyce O. Beckett, "Working Wives: A Racial Comparison," *Social Work* 21, no. 6 (November 1978): 463–72.

[24] Bowen and Finegan; Sweet; and Beckett.

[25] Bart Landry and Margaret Platt Jendrek, "The Employment of Wives in Middle-Class Black Families," *Journal of Marriage and the Family* 40, no. 4 (November 1978): 787–97.

than middle-class European-American wives, by a 37.4 percent margin (61.6 percent to 24.2 percent). Thus, not only were African-American wives more active in the labor force and more likely to be employed full-time, regardless of class, but the size of the difference was significantly greater among middle-class than among working-class families. In this portion of the study, the classifications "working class" and "middle class" were distinguished by husband's occupation, not husband's income. When the husband's income was taken into account along with the husband's occupation status, further racial difference emerged. For instance, Landry and Jendrek found that in 1976 African-American middle-class husbands had a mean annual income of $13,866, over $5,000 less than middle-class European-American married men ($19,145 mean annual income).[26] They maintained that a husband's income would have a deterrent effect upon a wife's labor-force activities only if it exceeded an unspecified minimum level, and that many African-American men may not be able to achieve that level of income.[27]

There is a significant racial difference in the impact of children, especially young children, upon female labor-force participation. African-American and European-American women respond differently to conflicting pressures to help pay the bills and to expend a great deal of time in child care. Table 1 presents data for several years on labor-force participation rates by race in two-parent families who have had children. Two things are readily apparent. First, with two exceptions, it appears that African-American married women are more likely to be in the labor force than European-American married women, regardless of children's ages. Second, the presence of children has less of an impact upon African-American married women than upon European-American women. In 1988, for example, 71.7 percent of married African-American women with children under six were in the labor force; the figure for comparable European-American women is 57.4 percent. Table 1 also presents African-American labor-force participation rates as a ratio of European-American labor-force participation rates. This provides a way to express and compare the magnitude of the differences between African-American and European-American rates. The ratio of African-American wives' labor-force participation rates to European-American rates varies over time and across categories but only falls below 1 in two cases; in both 1975 and 1980, African-American married women with children between the ages of fourteen and seventeen were slightly less likely to work than comparable European-American

[26] Ibid., 794.

[27] For similar findings on the differential impact of husbands' earnings by class, see Valerie Kincaid Oppenheimer, *Work and the Family: A Study in Social Demography* (New York: Academic Press, 1982), 215–36.

Table 1 **LABOR-FORCE PARTICIPATION RATES FOR MARRIED WOMEN WITH CHILDREN AND HUSBANDS PRESENT, BY RACE AND AGE OF YOUNGEST CHILD, 1975–88**

Age of Youngest Child	1975			1980		
	African-American	European-American	Ratio	African-American	European-American	Ratio
Under 6 years ...	56.4	35.0	1.61	63.4	43.5	1.46
6–13 years	64.9	50.8	1.28	71.8	61.4	1.17
14–17 years	51.0	53.6	.95	58.4	60.6	.96

Age of Youngest Child	1985			1988		
	African-American	European-American	Ratio	African-American	European-American	Ratio
Under 6 years ...	69.3	53.7	1.29	71.7	57.4	1.25
6–13 years	73.5	67.7	1.08	8.14	71.5	1.14
14–17 years	74.1	60.6	1.22	74.6	72.5	1.02

SOURCE.—*Statistical Abstract of the United States: 1989,* U.S. Bureau of the Census (Washington, D.C.: Government Printing Office, 1989), 386.

women. In every other case African-American wives have higher rates. In every year the increase in labor-force participation associated with the last child's going off to school is much lower for African-American mothers. For example, in 1975 there was little difference in the labor-force activity of African-American wives who had small children and those whose children were over fourteen. The labor-force participation rates for the two groups is 56.4 percent and 51.0 percent. Compare this to the' labor-force activity of European-American women: European-American women with small children had a much lower labor-force participation rate than women with older children (35 percent to 53.6 percent).

Although racial differences in labor-force participation rates have diminished, the earnings of African-American women are still far more important to their life circumstances than is true for European-American women. Table 2 shows this clearly. In 1978 there was a 46.2 percent improvement in median family income associated with the wife's labor-force participation for African-American families, as opposed to a 15.5 percent increase for European-American families. The differential impact of working wives was even more dramatic by 1985, when there was a 101.6 percent improvement associated with African-American wives' labor-force participation.

Table 2 tells an additional story: The increase from 1978 to 1985 was even more dramatic for European-American families where the

Table 2 **IMPACT OF WOMEN'S WAGES ON FAMILY INCOME BY RACE, SELECTED YEARS, IN MEDIAN FAMILY INCOME**

	1978[a]		1985[b]		1987[c]	
	African-American	European-American	African-American	European-American	African-American	European-American
Wife in paid labor force....	16,102	20,357	30,502	36,922	33,333	41,023
Wife not in paid labor force....	11,017	17,620	15,129	25,307	16,822	27,394
Percentage increase..	46.2	15.5	101.6	45.9	98.2	49.8

[a]Elizabeth Waldman, Allyson Sherman Grossman, Howard Hayghe, and Beverly L. Johnson, "Working Mothers in the 1970s: A Look at the Statistics," *Monthly Labor Review* 102, no. 8 (October 1979): 39–49.

[b]*Money Income and Poverty Status of Families and Persons in the United States: 1985* (Advance Data from the March 1986 *Current Population Survey*), U.S. Bureau of the Census, Current Population Reports, Series P-60, no. 154 (Washington, D.C.: Government Printing Office, 1986), 6–8.

[c]*Statistical Abstract of the United States: 1989,* U.S. Bureau of the Census (Washington, D.C.: Government Printing Office, 1989), 446.

improvement in income associated with the wife's labor-force participation tripled to 45.9 percent, thus narrowing the gap between the impact of African-American wives' contribution to family income and comparable European-American contributions.

Table 3 presents data on median family income in 1982 for two-parent families by race, age of children, and presence of the wife in the labor force. African-American women with children under the age of six contributed a larger percentage to household income than African-American women with older children or European-American women with children in any of the age categories. However, it should be noted that regardless of the age of the children, the median income of African-American families with wives in the labor force was less than the median income for European-American families in which the wife is not in the labor force. Working wives and mothers clearly make a difference in the standard of living for all families, but they make a far greater difference for African-American than for European-American families.

The above discussion is based upon median incomes and thus does not address the full range of racial differences across income levels. Table 4 presents data on the number and type of income earners in married-couple families, by race and by total 1982 family income.[28]

[28] All percentages in this table should be taken as approximate since numbers are rounded to the nearest thousand. This table may slightly understate the labor-force participation of wives, as the original publication did not make clear whether the wife was included among the category of multiple income earners when the

Table 3 **LABOR-FORCE PARTICIPATION AND 1982 FAMILY INCOME OF MARRIED WOMEN, HUSBANDS PRESENT, WITH CHILDREN, BY RACE AND AGE OF CHILDREN, 1983**

		Median Family Income		
	Percentage of Wives in Labor Force	Wife Not in Labor Force ($)	Wife in Labor Force ($)	Percentage Increase Associated with Working Wife
With children under 6:				
European-American . . .	48.4	22,022	26,473	20.2
African-American . . .	67.3	13,093	20,895	59.6
No children under 6; one or more 6–13:				
European-American . . .	62.4	27,691	31,850	15.0
African-American . . .	73.1	16,525	25,610	55.0
No children under 14; one or more under 18:				
European-American . . .	65.2	30,916	37,336	20.8
African-American . . .	61.8	15,390	22,967	49.2

SOURCE.—*Families at Work: The Jobs and Pay,* U.S. Department of Labor, Bureau of Labor Statistics, Bulletin 2209 (Washington, D.C.: Government Printing Office, 1984), table B-8.

The percentage of families in the African-American community with the husband as the only earner increased from 25 percent at the under-$5,000 level until reaching its maximum of 35 percent at the $10,000 to $14,999 level. It declined steadily thereafter, reaching its low point of 7 percent at the $50,000 and over level. The percentage of African-American families with both husband and wife as earners increased steadily throughout the family-income hierarchy, from a low of 11 percent at the under-$5,000 level to a high of 91 percent at the $50,000 and over level.

The percentage of European-American families in which the husband was the only earner increased from 23 percent at the

---

husband was not employed. A larger percentage of European-American than African-American families had the husband as the only income earner (30 percent to 22 percent). Conversely, a slightly higher proportion of African-American than European-American families had both husband and wife as income earners (54

Table 4 **PERCENTAGE DISTRIBUTION OF TYPES OF INCOME EARNERS IN TWO-PARENT FAMILIES BY RACE AND INCOME LEVEL, 1982**

	Husband Only Earner	Husband and Wife Both Earners	Wife Only Earner	Other Combination[a]	No Earners	Total Number in Income Bracket (in thousands)
Under $5,000:						
European-American ...	23	12	13	6	46	1,298
African-American ...	25	11	10	2	51	169
$5,000–9,999:						
European-American ...	29	19	7	2	43	3,452
African-American ...	28	14	12	4	42	516
$10,000–14,999:						
European-American ...	32	29	8	3	28	5,067
African-American ...	35	33	13	6	14	540
$15,000–19,999:						
European-American ...	32	41	6	3	17	5,356
African-American ...	26	52	10	5	7	459
$20,000–24,999:						
European-American ...	34	50	4	3	10	5,783
African-American ...	24	62	4	7	3	495
$25,000–34,999:						
European-American ...	30	59	3	3	5	9,810
African-American ...	16	77	3	2	2	716
$35,000–49,999:						
European-American ...	26	67	1	2	3	8,433
African-American ...	9	88	0	2	0	447
Over $50,000:						
European-American ...	30	65	0	1	3	6,074
African-American ...	7	91	0	1	0	161
All income levels:						
European-American ...	30	50	4	3	13	45,273
African-American ...	22	54	7	4	12	3,504

SOURCE.—*Families at Work: The Jobs and Pay,* U.S. Department of Labor, Bureau of Labor Statistics, Bulletin 2209 (Washington, D.C.: Government Printing Office, 1984), table B-6.
[a]Multiple earners in household, excluding husband.

under-$5,000 level to a high of 34 percent at the $20,000 to $24,999 bracket before declining to 26 percent, between $35,000 and $49,999. It increased again to 30 percent for those families earning over $50,000. The percentage of husband-wife income-earner families among European-Americans was 12 percent at the below-$5,000 level and increased steadily from that point, reaching a peak of 67 percent at the $35,000 to $49,999 bracket before declining to 65 percent at the over-$50,000 level.

More African-American than European-American families had husbands as the only income-earners in two of the three income brackets below $15,000. The direction of the difference reversed at that point and increased steadily thereafter until reaching its peak at $50,000 and over. There was a smaller percentage of African-American than European-American families with both husband and wife as earners in the two income brackets below $10,000. However, the pattern of both parents being earners was more common among African-American than European-American families at all levels above $10,000, with the size of the racial difference increasing from 4 percent at the $10,000 to $14,999 level to 27 percent at the $50,000 and over level. Again, it is clear that the income provided by a working wife is important for all families, regardless of race, but here we see that not only is it more important for African-American than for European-American families generally, but also it becomes increasingly crucial as the family income gets larger.

The scholarly literature is replete with statements to the effect that, "like men, most women are employed out of economic necessity."[29] The fact that the smallest racial difference in female labor-force participation rates traditionally has been observed among low-income or working-class families undoubtedly reflects the primary importance of economic need as the reason, regardless of race, that women work. All families at this level find themselves pressured to increase their number of income-earners. Yet the pressure is greatest for African-American families because of the reduced earning capacity of African-American males. The highest rates of labor-force participation among European-American wives traditionally have been found in the working class, with a gradual tendency toward withdrawal from the labor force as the husband's income increased beyond a certain point. Among African-Americans, women's rate of labor-force participation traditionally has increased as the husband's income increased. Thus, until recently, the racial gap in the rates of labor-force participation for

---

percent to 50 percent). However, the size of the overall racial difference is less important than its relation to total family income.

[29] Susan Basow, *Gender Stereotypes* (Monterey, Calif.: Cole, 1986), 286.

wives was greatest at the highest levels of the husband's income. Recent dramatic increases in labor-force participation among middle-class European-American wives appear to be narrowing the gap. The fact that the gap is closing is not, however, necessarily a sign of the economic health of the African-American family.

There is reason to be concerned about the future. African-American families have been able to achieve a standard of living comparable to that of middle-class European-Americans because African-American wives have been far more likely than European-American wives to work, and to work full-time. This difference was greatest at the level where European-American husbands possessed educational and occupational characteristics that would allow them to lay claim to a middle-class standard of living as the household's only income-earner. Thus, the earnings of African-American wives constituted a much greater percentage of total family income than was the case among European-Americans. All of this is changing. The labor-force participation rates of European-American wives—even those with young children—have been increasing rapidly over the last decade or so. The racial difference in labor-force participation rates is rapidly disappearing.

The full implication of these trends hits home when we consider the fact that the African-American woman working full-time in 1987 earned $1,664 less than comparably employed European-American women.[30] In addition, current trends in the American economy show a greater decline in male labor-force participation among African-Americans than among European-Americans, so that the racial earnings gap among males probably will widen in the near future.[31] Given these trends, we can expect a growing racial difference in the standard of living enjoyed by two-parent families—even those headed by males with similar job qualifications.

The precarious hold upon a middle-class standard of living that many African-American families were able to acquire in the 1960s and 1970s is now likely to be lost. As a decline in real wages and reduced state spending combines with racism that continues to discourage educational and economic opportunities for African-Americans, we appear to be in the process of returning to a racially polarized society, with increasing numbers of European-American

[30] Adapted from *Statistical Abstract of the United States: 1989*, U.S. Bureau of the Census (Washington, D.C.: Government Printing Office, 1989), 406, table 666.
[31] Wilson, *The Truly Disadvantaged* (n. 15 above), 81–82.

families experiencing economic strain and increasing numbers of African-American families failing to meet their minimal survival needs.

The policy proposals presented by Wilson in his 1987 study are important but do not go far enough. He urges a series of economic reforms to create more jobs for African-American men, increasing the numbers who can afford to marry and thus reducing the number of female-headed families. This is a laudable objective to the extent that women head families because of shortage of what Wilson calls "marriageable men"—men who are employed and earn an income sufficient to support a family.[32] However, this program does little for two-parent families and nothing for women who head families because that is what they prefer. The evidence is overwhelming that neither European-American nor African-American women have earnings anywhere near as high as comparably qualified European-American men.[33] Women who head families would be most helped by a vigorous push to eliminate gender inequality in wages (e.g., through "comparable worth" legislation). In fact, this would aid all families with female income-earners. All African-American families with male income-earners would benefit from programs designed to eliminate those elements in the economy that cause African-Americans to earn significantly less than comparably qualified European-Americans.[34] In other words, it is clear that we must create a multipronged effort to alter the opportunity structure in American society if we are to reduce racial and gender inequality. There are no shortcuts to equal opportunity in American society.

Department of Sociology (Geschwender)
Institute for Research on Multiculturalism and
International Labor (Carroll-Seguin)
State University of New York at Binghamton

[32] Ibid.
[33] Farley, *Blacks and Whites* (n. 12 above), 72–75.
[34] Ibid., 75–77.

PART III

ALLIANCES ACROSS GENERATIONS
SOCIOHISTORICAL LITERATURE AND CRITIQUES

SLAVERY, SHARECROPPING, AND SEXUAL INEQUALITY

SUSAN A. MANN

One of the main purposes of women's studies, as Joan Kelly succinctly put it, is to "restore women to history and to restore our history to women."[1] This study follows Kelly's suggestions for restoring women to history by examining how changes in major forms of production affected the respective roles of men and women in different classes and racial groups.[2] Specifically, this

This essay is based on work completed as a part of the "Southern Women: The Intersection of Race, Class, and Gender" working paper series cosponsored by the centers for research on women at Memphis State University, Duke University–University of North Carolina–Chapel Hill, and Spelman College. I thank E. Higginbotham, L. Coleman, S. Coverman, M. Heung, C. Greene, L. Weber Cannon, M. Sartisky, G. Welty, H. Benenson, H. Hayes, and two anonymous reviewers for their useful comments and critical insights. I am also grateful to the National Endowment for the Humanities 1985 summer stipend program for funding this research.

[1] Joan Kelly, *Women, History and Theory: The Essays of Joan Kelly* (Chicago: University of Chicago Press, 1984), 1.

[2] Ibid., 9. Kelly uses the term "mode of production," rather than form of production, in her discussion of social change and sexual inequality. Yet, she incorrectly equates changes in the mode of production with less significant economic changes wrought by events like the American Revolution. To be more precise, this paper analytically distinguishes between the mode of production—which represents the dominant form of production in a given historical era—and other specific forms of production which can coexist alongside the dominant mode within a given social formation.

This essay originally appeared in *Signs*, vol. 14, no. 4, Summer 1989.

article examines how the transition from slavery to sharecropping affected the position of freedwomen in the American South.[3]

Since sexism is a distinct form of oppression that can cut across race and class lines, analyzing sexism within oppressed groups has presented feminists with a number of theoretical and political dilemmas. For example, given the central thesis of Marxist theory that private property is the root of women's oppression, socialist feminists have had great difficulty explaining the distinct nature of patriarchal oppression when it has been manifest in both propertied and propertyless classes.[4] Similarly, discussions of Black women's domination by Black men in writings by women of Color have generated a good deal of intraracial controversy and debate. This controversy received national publicity in response to the enormously popular film version of Alice Walker's *The Color Purple*, which candidly portrayed domestic violence and incest within Black households.[5]

Because oppression within a group marked by sex, race, class, or ethnicity is divisive of group solidarity, it must be acknowledged and understood in order to preserve the health of the community. Indeed, the roots of the modern feminist movement stem, in part, from sexism within the civil rights and "new left" movements, just as the women's movement of the nineteenth century arose, in part, from sexism within the abolitionist movement.[6] Recognition of this oppression is thus an integral part of reconstructing women's history. Yet, such recognition can reinforce racist and classist

[3] The term "Black women" is sometimes used in this article interchangeably with "slave" and "sharecropping women." However, not all Black women were slaves since there were also free people of Color living in the southern states during the antebellum era.

[4] For the classical Marxist discussion of the origins of patriarchy, see Frederick Engels, *The Origin of the Family, Private Property, and the State* (New York: International Publishers, 1974). For a modern socialist feminist analysis, see Heidi I. Hartmann, "The Unhappy Marriage of Marxism and Feminism: Towards a More Progressive Union," in *Women and Revolution*, ed. Lydia Sargent (Boston: South End Press, 1981), 1–41.

[5] Trudier Harris, "On *The Color Purple*, Stereotypes, and Silence," *Black American Literature Forum* 18, no. 4 (1984): 155–61; Mel Watkins, "Sexism, Racism and Black Women Writers," *New York Times Book Review* (June 1986), 1 and 35–37. While the film *The Color Purple* had a number of virtues, it also did much to reinforce racist stereotypes, a problem exacerbated by the juxtaposition of slapstick comedy with the serious issues of racist terror and domestic violence. Thus, I am not praising this film but merely recognizing its role in bringing the controversies over oppression by the oppressed to a much larger audience.

[6] Judith Hole and Ellen Levine, "The First Feminists," and Jo Freeman, "The Women's Liberation Movement: Its Origins, Structure, Activities, and Ideas," both in *Women: A Feminist Perspective*, ed. Jo Freeman, rev. ed. (Palo Alto, Calif.: Mayfield, 1984), 533–42, 543–56.

stereotypes or make the just demands of oppressed groups vulnerable to external racist, classist, and sexist manipulation. Moreover, conflict about giving priority to one social critique over another in strategies for political action can itself divide progressive groups and impede social change. Consequently, analyzing oppression within oppressed groups is like "dancing on a minefield."[7]

There are no easy solutions to these political dilemmas. Some feminist theorists, like those in the Combahee River Collective, have sought to resolve these dilemmas by formulating theories about the multiple dimensions of Black women's oppression, arguing against horizontal hostilities that split the solidarity of oppressed groups.[8] Other writers have tried to establish a contextual understanding of multiple oppressions as exemplified by Ann Petry's "Like a Winding Sheet," a moving short story that shows how racism and oppressive working conditions fostered wife abuse.[9] This article looks at historically specific relationships between oppressions experienced by Afro-American women during the transition from slavery to sharecropping, in order to reconsider Joan Kelly's historical work on women. Kelly argues that historical periods traditionally characterized as eras of "progressive" social change, such as the Renaissance or the American Revolution, often have not been progressive for women and instead have entailed greater restrictions on the scope and power of their social roles. Although this thesis calls into question many key assumptions regarding the nature of historical development, it has received a good deal of substantiation from recent scholarship on women.[10]

While the abolition of slavery was clearly a major progressive transformation for both Black men and women, sharecropping was not the most progressive available alternative following the Emancipation. Rather, the sharecropping system was a compromise solution to serious conflicts between landowners and the emanci-

---

[7] This quote is a paraphrase of the title of Annette Kolodny's article, "Dancing through the Minefield: Some Observations on the Theory, Practice, and Politics of a Feminist Literary Criticism," in *The New Feminist Criticism: Essays on Women, Literature, and Theory,* ed. Elaine Showalter (New York: Pantheon, 1985), 144–67. For a discussion of some of these political dilemmas, see Angela Y. Davis, *Women, Race and Class* (New York: Monthly Review Press, 1981).

[8] Combahee River Collective, "A Black Feminist Statement," in *Capitalist Patriarchy and the Case for Socialist Feminism,* ed. Zillah R. Eisenstein (New York: Monthly Review Press, 1979), 362–72.

[9] Ann Petry, "Like a Winding Sheet," in *Women and Fiction: Short Stories By and About Women,* ed. Susan Cahill (New York: New American Library, 1975), 132–42.

[10] Kelly (n. 1 above), 1–15; Nancy Woloch, *Women and the American Experience* (New York: Knopf, 1984), 83.

pated slaves.[11] Indeed, the failure of radical land reform, the demise of any hopes for "forty acres and a mule," and a continuing concentration of land ownership resulted in a strictly controlled system of production and marketing. Sharecroppers had little control over which commodity was produced and sometimes had little control over their labor, depending on the amount of assets, such as land or machinery, furnished by the landowner. In turn, usurious credit arising from the crop-liens system often locked croppers into a system of virtual debt peonage. These factors, when combined with legal and informal controls over Black labor, such as the notorious Black Codes, created production and exchange relations reminiscent of semifeudal or semifree precapitalist forms of labor.[12]

Nevertheless, in relative terms, sharecropping was an important advance over slavery. The legal and institutional rights to human property were abolished so that human beings could no longer legally be bought, sold, tortured, or murdered under the sacred penumbra of private property. The diet, education, leisure time, and general standard of living of the emancipated improved. For example, the per capita reduction in working hours for the Black population after the Emancipation was between 28 and 37 percent.[13] In addition, freedmen and women were able to make their own consumption decisions—an important freedom often taken for granted by a nonslave population.

Kelly has also argued that whenever private and public domains have become more differentiated, sexual inequalities have increased.[14] According to Kelly, the separation of work into "production for subsistence" and "production for exchange" affects the sexual division of labor and women's "equal relations to work or

[11] Gerald David Jaynes, *Branches without Roots: Genesis of the Black Working Class in the American South, 1862–1882* (New York: Oxford University Press, 1986), 141–223.

[12] Jonathan M. Wiener, *Social Origins of the New South: Alabama, 1860–1885* (Baton Rouge: Louisiana State University Press, 1978), 70–73; Susan A. Mann, "Sharecropping in the Cotton South: A Case of Uneven Capitalist Development in Agriculture," *Rural Sociology* 39, no. 3 (1984): 412–29.

[13] R. Ransom and R. Sutch, *One Kind of Freedom: The Economic Consequences of Emancipation* (New York: Cambridge University Press, 1977), 1–39.

[14] Slaves and sharecroppers may not have made these conceptual distinctions between public and private spheres of life. As Lawrence Levine argues, slaves did not subjectively compartmentalize their lives like people do in the modern era. See Lawrence W. Levine, *Black Culture and Black Consciousness: Afro-American Folk Thought from Slavery to Freedom* (Oxford: Oxford University Press, 1977), 157–58. Nevertheless, I have maintained these distinctions because this category scheme is objectively meaningful in terms of power relations arising from the difference between production for use and production for exchange.

property with men of their class."[15] Under both slavery and share-cropping, domestic labor or work inside of the home was labor geared toward production for subsistence, while agricultural labor or work outside of the home was directed primarily toward the production of commodities for exchange.[16]

Sharecropping presents a particularly interesting case for examining Kelly's thesis, since production for exchange under the sharecropping system was often predicated on the labor of the entire family. Relative to other types of production units, family labor enterprises blur the distinction between private and public spheres of social life. However, relative to slavery, Black women's commodity-producing field labor was reduced in sharecropping, even though this labor still made a significant contribution to household income. As in many other family labor enterprises, it also appears that male croppers controlled the labor of family members and, hence, held more power than women held over income and property.[17]

For this comparative analysis of the effect the transition from slavery to sharecropping had on sexual equality, it seems appropriate to use some of the same criteria Kelly suggested for gauging the relative contraction or expansion of the powers of women.[18] Because it is not possible to examine all of the criteria suggested by Kelly in an article-length essay, this study will be limited to an evaluation of how changes in economic roles, domestic power relations, violence against women, reproductive freedom, and access to education affected Afro-American women.[19] Because few

---

[15] Kelly (n. 1 above), 12–13.

[16] Whether domestic labor constitutes production for use or production for exchange has been the subject of long-standing debates in the feminist literature. Indeed, in a previous article I argued that, under certain historical conditions, domestic labor can entail production for exchange, such as when this domestic labor is directed toward reproducing the commodities of labor power or wage labor. See Emily Blumenfeld and Susan Mann, "Domestic Labour and the Reproduction of Labour Power: Towards an Analysis of Women, the Family, and Class," in *Hidden in the Household: Women's Domestic Labour under Capitalism*, ed. Bonnie Fox (Toronto: Women's Press, 1980), 267–307.

[17] Ruth Allen, *The Labor of Women in the Production of Cotton* (Austin: University of Texas Press, 1931), 147; Carolyn E. Sachs, *The Invisible Farmers: Women in Agricultural Production* (Totowa, N.J.: Rowman & Allanheld, 1983), 26.

[18] Kelly, 20. Kelly also suggests an analysis of changes in women's cultural roles, their political roles, and ideologies about women.

[19] Considering the many ways in which Blacks were excluded from economic and political power during these eras, cultural roles might prove extremely important for reassessing sexual inequality in future research. See, e.g., Deborah Gray White's *Ar'n't I a Woman? Female Slaves in the Plantation South* (New York: Norton, 1985) for a discussion of some of the cultural roles of slave women.

historical studies of the post–Civil War South include a sustained account of Black women sharecroppers, my own study is necessarily methodologically exploratory.[20] To overcome some of the methodological difficulties of studying slaves and sharecroppers, whose voices are not a part of the existing historical record, I have interwoven available quantitative data with more qualitative types of data, such as oral histories.[21] Through combining these methodologies, this study attempts to piece together the social fabric of these people's lives and to place their lives within the larger context of economic and social history.

Gender differences in economic roles

An abolitionist sympathizer noted with bitter irony that slaveowners made a "noble admission of female equality" in their attempts to wrench as much labor as possible from *both* female and male slaves.[22] It is estimated that in the Cotton Belt slave women spent approximately thirteen hours a day in fieldwork, engaged in such diverse and traditionally masculine tasks as plowing fields, dropping seeds, hoeing, picking, ginning, sorting, and moting cotton.[23] Yet, as Deborah White points out, those who reported that women and men did the same work seldom reported the ages of the women. White suggests that, although women of childbearing age did plow and do heavy labor, the middle ages or the post-childbearing ages were the most labor-intensive years of a woman's life.[24] In this way slaveowners tried to maximize bondswomen's capacity to labor and to be in labor by matching production demands to family and biological life cycles.

The fact that slaveowners tried to exploit as much profit as possible from both female and male labor did not mean that a

[20] This study relies heavily on a few notable exceptions to the scarcity of research on sharecropping women. These exceptions include the following works: Jacqueline Jones, *Labor of Love, Labor of Sorrow: Black Women, Work, and the Family from Slavery to the Present* (New York: Basic, 1985); Jaynes (n. 11 above); Jack Temple Kirby, *Rural Worlds Lost: The American South, 1920–1960* (Baton Rouge: Louisiana State University Press, 1987).

[21] Although oral histories present problems in terms of the representativeness of such historical evidence, they do provide a more valid means of empathetically understanding the subjects of one's research in keeping with the sociological method of *verstehen*. Moreover, in this particular study, oral histories help to reduce the inherent problems of a social researcher like myself, studying men and women of a different race and class, who also lived in a different historical era.

[22] An abolitionist sympathizer quoted in Jones, 15.

[23] Ibid., 15; Ransom and Sutch (n. 13 above), 233.

[24] White, 114.

division of labor by sex was absent in the slave community. In fieldwork, most women were ranked as three-fourths hands and pregnant or nursing women as one-half hands, regardless of their individual productivity.[25] While women performed many traditionally masculine tasks, those tasks that demanded sheer muscle power were often exclusive to men, such as clearing land or chopping and hauling wood. In addition, very few women served in high-status positions, such as those of skilled artisans and mechanics or supervisors and drivers of male (or even female) slave crews.[26]

Male slaves also regarded many traditionally male tasks as unsuitable for bondswomen, just as they regarded many domestic tasks as unsuitable or degrading for themselves.[27] Leslie Owens describes how one means of humiliating male slaves was to require them to do certain types of domestic labor, such as making them wash clothes. She writes, "So great was their (the male slaves') shame before their fellows that many ran off and suffered the lash on their backs rather than submit to the discipline."[28] Apparently, even slave husbands in cross-plantation marriages, who saw their wives only on weekends, did not do their own laundry. One observer described how on "Saturday night, the roads were . . . filled with men on their way to the 'wife house,' each pedestrian or horseman bearing his bag of soiled clothes."[29]

It has been argued that because the slave's own household was one of the few realms of social life where labor took place outside of the strict supervision and purview of whites, domestic activities, though arduous, offered Black women a degree of personal autonomy and fulfillment. This is exemplified by the remark of one slave about her mother and grandmother, "Dey done it 'cause dey wanted to. Dey wuz workin' for deyselves den."[30] Nevertheless, if

[25] Jones, 15 and 17.

[26] Robert William Fogel and Stanley L. Engerman, *Time on the Cross: The Economics of American Negro Slavery* (Boston: Little, Brown, 1974), 141–42; bell hooks, *Ain't I a Woman: Black Women and Feminism* (Boston: South End Press, 1981), 23; Jones, 18–19.

[27] Eugene Genovese, *Roll, Jordan, Roll: The World the Slaves Made* (New York: Vintage, 1976), 490; hooks, 21–22; Jones, 42.

[28] Leslie H. Owens, *This Species of Property: Slave Life and Culture in the Old South* (New York: Oxford University Press, 1976), 195.

[29] An observer quoted in Christie Farnham, "Sapphire? The Issue of Dominance in the Slave Family, 1830–1865," in *"To Toil the Livelong Day": America's Women at Work, 1780–1980*, ed. Carol Groneman and Mary Beth Norton (Ithaca, N.Y.: Cornell University Press, 1987), 68–83, esp. 79–80. Farnham notes various authors' discussion of men's work within slave households. She concludes that such male domestic labor tended to be an occasional activity.

[30] Jones (n. 20 above), 29. For a discussion of how the slave's own domestic labor provided one of the few spheres of autonomy and meaningful work in the slave

this domestic labor is included in estimates of total labor time expended, slave women worked longer hours per day than slave men.[31]

Moreover, because slaveowners placed a higher priority on agricultural production than on the day-to-day reproduction of their slave labor force, slaves were allowed little time for their own domestic labor.

> On many plantations women did not have enough time to prepare breakfast in the morning and were generally too tired to make much of a meal or to give much attention to their children after a long day's labor. Booker T. Washington's experience was typical: "My mother . . . had little time to give to the training of her children during the day. She snatched a few moments for our care in the early morning before her work began, and at night after the day's work was done. . . ." Fed irregularly or improperly, young black children suffered from a variety of ills.[32]

To increase the efficiency of slave labor time, cooking and child rearing were sometimes carried out communally, particularly on larger plantations.[33] While slaveowners probably cherished their own private life-styles, they preferred these more efficient and less costly communal arrangements for their slaves. In contrast, slaves were quite insistent about their preference for eating in their own separate households. Consequently, even though communal tasks added to the solidarity of the slave community, slave women often felt deprived of their ability to cook for their kinfolk or to discipline their children.[34]

Some feminists may view the existence of collective child care and communal kitchens as fostering improvements in the social position of women, since privatized domestic labor reduces women's ability to participate in the larger community, increases their isolation, and makes them more vulnerable to patriarchal dependency and abuse.[35] However, the communal facilities established by slaveowners were created both to reduce slave subsistence costs

---

community, see Angela Y. Davis, "The Black Woman's Role in the Community of Slaves," *Black Scholar* 3 (December 1971): 3–14.

[31] Genovese, 494–95; White (n. 19 above), 122.

[32] John W. Blassingame, *The Slave Community: Plantation Life in the Antebellum South* (New York: Oxford University Press, 1972), 94.

[33] Ibid., 94; Jones, 29; White, 113.

[34] Jones, 29; Genovese, 544.

[35] There are numerous discussions of this in Fox, ed. (n. 16 above).

and to increase slave labor time—not to benefit slave women. Consequently, the demise of these communal facilities with the rise of sharecropping would suggest a mixture of both gains and losses for freedwomen.

After the Civil War there were numerous abortive attempts to replace slavery with a system of production based on wage and/or share labor organized into gangs or squads. Gerald Jaynes provides an excellent account of the various social and economic factors that resulted in the demise of gang labor and the rise of family sharecropping as a "compromise solution" to ongoing conflicts between white landowners and newly freed Blacks.[36] Along with his discussion of ex-slaves' struggle for more autonomy and their rejection of the centrally controlled wage/gang system, Jaynes also explains how gender-related issues helped to foster the rise of family sharecropping.

One of these gender-related issues involved landowners' acute concerns about the labor shortage that resulted once many women and children left fieldwork after the Civil War. By the 1870s, the number of freedmen, women, and children working in the fields dropped to as low as one-quarter of the antebellum level. Freedwomen often refused to work in the fields because they were paid even lower wages than men and because gang or squad labor put them in close proximity to white landowners and overseers who continued to abuse them.[37]

Blacks preferred the more decentralized system of family sharecropping because it removed them from direct control and supervision by whites. Landowners tolerated sharecropping because it provided a means of dealing with the female and child labor shortage. As one landowner commented, "Where the Negro works for wages, he tries to keep his wife at home. If he rents land, or plants on shares, the wife and children help him in the field."[38] In short, landowners recognized the usefulness of the male sharecropper's patriarchal authority in putting women and children to work in the fields.

Indeed, as Jaynes points out, kinship relations and "an authoritarian paternal figure" proved more powerful for ensuring labor discipline than the impersonal relations between overseers and wage laborers.[39] While no doubt emotional commitments to family well-being may have enhanced labor productivity, the use of force

[36] Jaynes (n. 11 above).
[37] Ibid., 230–32; Ransom and Sutch (n. 13 above), 232–36; Wiener (n. 12 above), 46; Jones, 60.
[38] A landowner quoted in Jaynes, 187.
[39] Ibid., 185–87.

should not be ignored. Unlike landowners and overseers who were now forbidden to use the lash, husbands and fathers could legally use corporal punishment to discipline their wives and children. As an observer noted, "One man, this year, felt obliged to give his own son a tremendous beating, for not performing his share of the labor."[40] Such obligations for disciplining family members were even contractually specified. For example, cropper Thomas Ferguson agreed in his share contract to "control (his) family and make them work and make them behave themselves."[41]

The rise of family sharecropping, then, increased Black women's involvement in field labor in the decades following the Civil War. In this way, sharecropping women were direct victims of this oppressive way of organizing agricultural labor. Sharecropping clearly combined classism, racism, and patriarchy—giving white, well-to-do males control as landowners and giving Black males control as family patriarchs. However, when compared to slavery, the sharecropping system still enabled freedwomen to divide their time between fieldwork and housework in a way that more often reflected their families' needs than the needs of landowners.[42]

If domestic labor is taken into account, sharecropping women probably worked longer hours than men every day. Elizabeth Rauh Bethel's analysis of both domestic and field labor under sharecropping suggests that women's total working hours were longer than those of men, particularly in poorer sharecropping households where women were likely to engage in more field labor than did other sharecropping women.[43] Consequently, while Black women gained some release from field labor and from control and supervision by white males, their gains relative to Black males, in terms of total labor time expended, appear to be directly related to the wealth of sharecropping households.

The decline in female field labor meant that in the Black sharecropping household the sexual division of labor was more marked than in the slave household. Moreover, as compared to slaveowners, sharecropping families placed greater priority on women's role in household labor, which further reinforced a traditional sexual division of labor.[44] Consider, for example, the view of sharecropper Ned Cobb (alias Nate Shaw): "I was a poor colored

[40] An observer quoted in Jaynes, 185.

[41] Thomas Ferguson's contract quoted in Jaynes, 185.

[42] Jones (n. 20 above), 46.

[43] Elizabeth Rauh Bethel, *Promiseland: A Century of Life in a Negro Community* (Philadelphia: Temple University Press, 1981), 45–50.

[44] Kirby (n. 20 above), 157 and 159; Jones, 63; Theodore Rosengarten, *All God's Dangers: The Life of Nate Shaw* (New York: Knopf, 1975), 120–21.

man but I didn't want my wife in the field like a dog. . . . I considered I was the mainline man to look at conditions and try to keep up everything in the way of crops and stock and outside labor."[45]

Despite the fact that freedwomen's fieldwork was generally more seasonal than that of freedmen, Black women in the post–Civil War era worked outside of the home more often than did white women. In 1870 in the Cotton Belt, 98.4 percent of white wives reported to the census that they were "keeping house," while 40 percent of Black wives reported "field laborer" as their occupation.[46] In the poorest sharecropping households, most Black women worked in the fields, with some estimates in later years approximating 90 percent.[47]

However, even though a significant number of Black women worked in the fields, husbands controlled the economic rewards from farm labor. As Ruth Allen observed from her analysis of women in Texan cotton production in the 1920s, "It is practically a universal situation that the money received from the sale of the crop is the man's income."[48] In addition, as in the antebellum era, landowners valued the commodity-producing labor of sharecropping women less than that of men regardless of any individual's productivity. This sexual discrimination is reflected in the fact that landowners allocated land to sharecropping households on the basis of the sex and age of household members, with more land being allocated for men than for women and children.[49] Hence, gender inequalities existed even in labor directed toward production for exchange—inequalities that were buttressed both by the prejudices of landowners and by the power sharecropping husbands gained from controlling the income produced by family labor.

Sharecropping women were more likely than men to switch roles and do traditionally male tasks (particularly in poorer households)—their male counterparts seldom did household tasks.[50] Zora Neale Hurston's fictional account of an exchange between husband and wife captures the complexity of this situation where gender ine-

---

[45] Sharecropper Ned Cobb quoted in Rosengarten, 120.

[46] Jones, 63.

[47] Dolores Janiewski, "Sisters under Their Skins: Southern Working Women, 1880–1950," in *Sex, Race, and the Role of Women in the South*, ed. Joanne V. Hawks and Sheila L. Skemp (Jackson: University Press of Mississippi, 1983), 13–35, esp. 16.

[48] Allen (n. 17 above), 147; see also Sachs (n. 17 above), 26.

[49] Fred A. Shannon, *The Farmer's Last Frontier: Agriculture, 1860–1933* (New York: Farrar & Rinehart, 1945), 88.

[50] Kirby (n. 20 above), 157; Jones (n. 20 above), 63; Rosengarten, 59.

qualities existed alongside the interdependence of husbands' and wives' work:

[Ned, the husband]: "Is dat air supper ready yit?"

[Amy, the wife]: "Naw hit ain't. How you speck me tuh work in de field right long side uh you and den have supper ready jiz az soon ez Ah git tuh de house? Ah helt uh big-eye hoe in my hand jez ez long ez you did, Ned."[51]

While field labor was generally more arduous than household labor, the conditions under which sharecropping women performed household chores were extremely primitive since they owned few pieces of household equipment and lacked running water, adequate insulation, or sanitary facilities. Surplus earnings were more likely to be invested in farm equipment than in domestic labor-saving devices. This could reflect a shared economic interest in investing in types of property that lead to capital accumulation; however, it could also reflect the fact that males controlled farm income.[52]

While the sexual division of labor was more marked in sharecropping than in slavery, oral histories suggest that Black women preferred both the sharecropping system and the ability to devote more time to the reproduction of their own and their families' labor. As one freedwoman remarked when contrasting her work under slavery with her work under sharecropping, "I've a heap better time now'n I had when I was in bondage."[53]

Bethel argues that there were certain advantages for households in which the adult women spent more time in housekeeping tasks. These advantages included the ability to spend more time preparing food, tending gardens, and caring for young children. These reproductive activities not only provided a more varied and balanced diet but also contributed to the material well-being of the family.[54] Yet, while entire families benefited from the time women devoted to domestic activities, it is still not clear whether or not women benefited relative to men. Indeed, there appears to have been a complex contradiction between women's desire to be relieved from the arduous commodity-producing labor of fieldwork and the fact that, by

[51] Zora Neale Hurston, *Jonah's Gourd Vine* (New York: Lippincott, 1971), 16–17.
[52] Joan M. Jensen, *With These Hands: Women Working the Land* (Old Westbury, N.Y.: Feminist Press, 1981), 164–65; Jones, 86–88. For a description of the living conditions of many southern sharecroppers, see Kirby, 174–77.
[53] A freedwoman quoted anonymously in Jones, 60; see also 78.
[54] Bethel (n. 43 above), 47–48; Jaynes (n. 11 above), 231–32.

moving into a traditional household role, Black women enabled Black men to have more control over family income.

Domestic power relations and violence against women

Under both slavery and sharecropping, landowners recognized the Black male as head of his family.[55] Herbert Gutman discusses how religious rules also imposed a submissive role upon married slave women. He describes an incident in which a Black woman had been dropped from a church for refusing "to obey her husband in a small matter." She was readmitted to the church but only after she made "a public apology before the whole congregation."[56] Since slaves were often required to attend the churches of their masters as a means of social control, it is unclear whether these church rules were a product of ruling class hegemony or whether they were in fact part of the slaves' own values and beliefs (as Gutman suggests).[57]

Lawrence Levine provides some insight into American slaves' values and beliefs in his discussion of how slave folk tales often denigrated aggressive women and celebrated the father as the family's chief protector. While he argues that these folk tales must be taken into consideration in any understanding of male-female relations under slavery, he is careful to point out that knowing "one's lot and identity" was a practical necessity for survival and was not confined to women.[58]

This is not to say that slave and sharecropping women were merely passive victims of domestic authority and violence. To the contrary, there is much evidence that individual Black women stood up to their husbands and defended themselves against personal abuse, just as they resisted and fought against the domination and violence wielded by whites.[59] Moreover, relations be-

[55] Blassingame (n. 32 above), 80 and 92; Fogel and Engerman (n. 26 above), 141–42; Genovese (n. 27 above), 489; Jones, 82.

[56] Quoted in Herbert G. Gutman, "Marital and Sexual Norms among Slave Women," in *A Heritage of Her Own: Toward a New Social History of American Women*, ed. Nancy F. Cott and Elizabeth H. Pleck (New York: Simon & Schuster, 1979), 298–310, esp. 304.

[57] Ibid., 304; see also John Hope Franklin, *From Slavery to Freedom: A History of Negro Americans*, 3d ed. (New York: Random House, 1967), 200.

[58] Levine (n. 14 above), 96–97.

[59] Numerous cases where Black women resisted the domination and violence perpetrated by both Black and white males can be found in Gerda Lerner, ed., *Black Women in White America: A Documentary History* (New York: Pantheon, 1972); see also Gutman, 306–7; and White (n. 19 above), 151–52.

tween Black males and females must be viewed within the context of the fact that under both sharecropping and slavery, the oppressions of Black patriarchy paled beside those of racism and classism. Hence, Black males and females depended on each other and their families to work together in solidarity and resistance. Nevertheless, a number of historians (including feminist and Afro-American historians) suggest that it was normative behavior for Black women slaves and sharecroppers to accept male domestic authority.[60]

Modern studies of family decision making generally find that the spouse who makes the major decisions is also the spouse who contributes the most income to the household.[61] If this was also true for the sharecropping era, the facts that women engaged in agricultural commodity production less than men and that they (however voluntarily) did most of the domestic labor would suggest that men held greater decision-making power in sharecropping households, including decision making about family income and property. Since male croppers also were held legally responsible for crop production and for meeting share agreements, this male decision making was buttressed by the state.[62] However, it appears that at least some household property was recognized as belonging to the wife, given the story told by sharecropper Ned Cobb about keeping his wife from signing any share agreements to prevent creditors from "plundering" all of their property.[63] It is possible that ownership of household property was legally recognized if it constituted property the woman brought into the marriage. Nevertheless, personal property, like the household goods Cobb was referring to, must be distinguished from income-producing property, such as land or income from crop production, in terms of relative significance for family power relations.

Though there was a shift from matrilineal descent under slavery to patrilineal descent under sharecropping, this did not prove as significant for Black women as one might expect. Indeed, slave-owners introduced matrilineal descent neither to legitimate African traditions nor to benefit slave women. Rather, they used matrilineality as a formal mechanism for determining property rights over the progeny of cross-plantation unions.[64] Nevertheless, patrilineality and the legalization of marriage for Blacks after the Emancipa-

---

[60] Genovese, 500–501; hooks (n. 26 above), 44 and 47; Jones (n. 20 above), 104; Rosengarten (n. 44 above), 14; Woloch (n. 10 above), 226.
[61] Letty Cottin Pogrebin, *Family Politics: Love and Power on an Intimate Frontier* (New York: McGraw-Hill, 1984), 96.
[62] Jones, 82.
[63] Rosengarten, 32.
[64] Genovese (n. 27 above), 473.

tion allowed Black men to gain control over their wives' property and earnings, to assume custody of children, and to discipline their wives forcefully. Moreover, rights to divorce were limited even in cases of abandonment or domestic violence.[65]

The issue of violence against women raises other serious questions regarding the dominant roles of both white and Black men under American slavery and sharecropping. Clearly, violence was an ever-present threat to slave families.[66] Moreover, slaveowners made no distinctions in meting out physical punishment: neither pregnancy, motherhood, nor physical infirmity precluded this violence. For example, a particularly odious method of whipping pregnant women involved digging a depression in the ground to protect the foetus while ensuring the ability to discipline the mother violently.[67]

Even though the sharecropping system provided greater protection for Blacks than had slavery, violence against Black women by whites was also rampant in the racially motivated terror that accompanied the Reconstruction Era. For example, inadequate legal protection of Black rape victims is reflected in the fact that "from emancipation through more than two-thirds of the twentieth century, no Southern white male was convicted of raping or attempting to rape a Black woman" despite knowledge that this crime was widespread.[68] Given the complacency of the white legal system toward this violence and toward the flagrant lynching of Blacks—female and male—it is not surprising that the Black community placed a much greater emphasis on racism than sexism.

In the face of such violence perpetrated by whites, Black women tended to stay within the confines of their kin, neighbors, and fellow church members. As the daughter of a Black landowner commented, "Women didn't go into town much."[69] Yet some of these women, particularly those in poorer sharecropping households, did private household work to supplement their families' incomes, while others (often widows and single women) migrated to urban areas to do domestic work. Consequently, the risk of sexual

[65] Woloch, 191. As Kirby (n. 20 above), 173, points out, divorce was also a luxury few southern sharecroppers could afford. Moreover, he argues that, because these people viewed marriage as sacred, traditional morality and poverty "conspired" to bind these people together.

[66] Blassingame (n. 32 above), 83; Genovese, 460–61. For a contrasting view on sexual abuse, see Fogel and Engerman (n. 26 above), 130–34.

[67] Davis (n. 30 above), 8; Jones, 20; Lerner, ed. (n. 59 above), 15; hooks (n. 26 above), 23 and 37.

[68] White (n. 19 above), 164. For a more lengthy discussion of violence against Black men and women during the Reconstruction Era, see W. E. B. Du Bois, *Black Reconstruction in America, 1860–1880* (New York: Atheneum, 1975), 670–728.

[69] A Black landowner's daughter quoted in Janiewski (n. 47 above), 15.

abuse by white males was exacerbated by Black women's need to supplement their families' incomes through domestic service. As a Black servant remarked in 1912: "I believe that nearly all white men take, and expect to take, undue liberties with their colored female servants—not only the fathers, but in many cases the sons also. Those servants who rebel against such familiarity must either leave or expect a mightily hard time, if they stay."[70]

It is not possible to determine whether sexual and physical abuse by Black males was normative or whether it increased or decreased following the Emancipation since there are few data on the frequency of abuse during these two eras. However, historical evidence suggests that wife and child abuse by Black husbands was prevalent under both slavery and sharecropping.[71] As one Black woman commented in 1912, "On the one hand, we are assailed by white men, and, on the other hand, we are assailed by black men, who should be our natural protectors."[72] Similarly, Ned Cobb described his parents' relationship: "If I had a twenty-dollar bill this mornin for every time I seed my daddy beat up my mother and beat up my stepmother I wouldn't be settin here this mornin because I'd have up in the hundreds of dollars. Each one of them women—I didn't see no cause for it."[73]

Since social isolation is associated with spouse abuse, it is possible that the greater isolation of sharecropping households, as contrasted to slave quarters and the more centralized plantation system, might have provided less opportunity for community observation or intervention in cases of spouse abuse.[74] Indeed, sharecroppers' voices make clear that domestic misery and violence were frequent components of everyday life in the rural South. Based on thousands of pieces of oral and written testimony documenting the interpersonal lives of southern farm people during the first half of the twentieth century, Kirby concludes: "There are assuredly scenes of satisfaction, security, sometimes bliss. . . . But

[70] A Black servant quoted in Lerner, ed., 156; see also Janiewski, 18; and Jones (n. 20 above), 73, 114, and 127–34. The absence of information on whether these women controlled the income they received from domestic service precludes a complete analysis of the implications of this aspect of sharecropping women's work for Kelly's theses.

[71] Blassingame, 91; Genovese, 483; hooks, 35–36; Jones, 103; Rosengarten (n. 44 above), 10 and 273; White, 151–52.

[72] A Black woman quoted anonymously in Lerner, ed., 157.

[73] Sharecropper Ned Cobb quoted in Rosengarten, 10.

[74] Genovese (n. 27 above), 484. For a discussion of the role of isolation in domestic violence, see David Finkelhor, "Common Features of Family Abuse," in *Marriage and the Family in a Changing Society*, ed. James M. Henslin (New York: Free Press, 1985), 500–507, esp. 504.

the corpus of this large, if haphazard, collection of testimony contains far more instances of unhappiness, *especially among women*. Marriage was a cruel trap, motherhood often a mortal burden; husbands were too often obtuse, unfaithful, drunken, and violent. The collective portrait is less one of bliss than of pathos."[75]

Reproductive freedom under slavery and sharecropping

Reproductive freedom generally refers to the ability to choose when and if one wants to have a child. Today, there is a tendency to focus primarily on family planning issues as the major concerns constituting reproductive freedom.[76] However, information about Afro-American women slaves' and sharecroppers' use of birth control and abortion is scant.[77] Consequently, assessing the reproductive freedom of Black women in these earlier historical eras will have to focus more broadly on identifying when (or if) these women were in a position to make choices about their sexual activities and their sexual partners, as well as evaluating the general health care they received during pregnancy and childbirth.

Because of their interests in the physical reproduction of human capital, slaveowners intervened in even the most intimate of slave family ties. While there is some evidence of slave breeding, this does not appear to have been the norm, although a rudimentary form of eugenics was practiced through the slaveowners' intervention in the marriage ceremonies and broomstick rituals that slaves continued to conduct. The brutality of this class-based control is all too evident in the tragic stories from slave narratives where arranged marriages were forced on unwilling slaves.[78] Since slave marriages had no legal status and property rights over slave children were determined matrilineally (whereby the economic advantage fell to owners of slave women in cross-plantation marriages), in

[75] Kirby (n. 20 above), 169–70; my emphasis. Another researcher found a "bitterness towards men as a class" among the young Black women sharecroppers she interviewed, while older Black women did not express this same "bitterness" as noted in Janiewski, 19.

[76] For a discussion of issues often covered under the rubric of reproductive freedom, see Nadean Bishop, "Abortion: The Controversial Choice," in *Women: A Feminist Perspective*, ed. Jo Freeman (Palo Alto, Calif.: Mayfield, 1979), pp. 64–79.

[77] Gutman (n. 56 above), 307; Kirby, 162–63; White (n. 19 above), 84.

[78] Fogel and Engerman (n. 26 above), 78–86; Herbert G. Gutman, *The Black Family in Slavery and Freedom, 1750–1925* (New York: Pantheon, 1976), 273–77; Blassingame (n. 32 above), 87 and 89–92; Jones, 34–35.

the interests of capital accumulation owners encouraged marriages between slaves on the same plantation.[79]

Another incentive for encouraging slave marriages on the same plantation came from the fact that slaveowners used family affection and solidarity to discipline family members and to reduce the likelihood of escape or rebellion.[80] The fact that more fugitive slaves were male than female may reflect slave women's greater responsibility for child rearing and, hence, a more traditional sexual division of labor.[81]

Most historians agree that relative to other health issues, health care was at its best for pregnant slave women because of slaveowners' direct interests in the physical reproduction of human capital. Prospective mothers' health, along with their work loads and diets, all became more acute investment concerns after Congress outlawed the overseas slave trade in 1807.[82] Despite these concerns, health care for slave women was extremely inadequate. For slaveowners, short-term productive interests generally took priority over long-term reproductive interests. For example, during cotton boom years, there was a significant decline in slave fertility rates and an increase in slave miscarriage rates. Indeed, in general, in the prewar South, the more agriculturally productive regions characteristically had lower than average Black fertility rates.[83]

Compared to slavery, sharecropping arrangements reduced white male control (direct and indirect) over Black women's reproductive activities. Black women were able to choose their mates freely, to spend more time with their children, and to engage in family relations without the constant threat of family separation. These women bore on average five or six children.[84] Such large families did not necessarily reflect ignorance of birth control or irrational family planning. Rather, children were an economic asset—they augmented the household's labor supply and provided security for parents in old age. As one observer noted, "Children thus may be said to cost the cotton farmer less and pay him more."[85]

---

[79] Blassingame, 86; Genovese, 473.

[80] Blassingame, 80–83 and 89–92; Fogel and Engerman; Gutman, *The Black Family*, 318; Genovese, 452–57.

[81] White, 70; see also Gutman, *The Black Family*, 80 and 265.

[82] Blassingame, 93; Fogel and Engerman, 122–23; White, 68.

[83] White, 69, 111–12, and 124; Jones (n. 20 above), 19 and 35.

[84] Jones, 85.

[85] Quoted in Kirby (n. 20 above), 164. As Kirby points out, many of the interviews with southern farm families funded by the New Deal's Federal Writers' Project included questions on birth control. For a discussion of these interviews and various attempts by private and public agencies to distribute birth control information and devices in the 1930s, see 162–69.

Nevertheless, since child rearing was predominantly a female task, young children meant additional demands on women's labor, especially when these children were too young to work.

Some sharecropping landowners arranged for doctors to serve their tenants, but this was not the norm. As under slavery, childbirth was normally attended by midwives who were cheap and nearby, while mothers generally took care of other medical needs. The fact that medical treatment patterns did not change significantly is actually an indication of a relative drop between slavery and sharecropping. That is, the absence of professional medical care for sharecropping families may have been more significant than its absence in the slavery era, since the medical exigencies of Civil War battlefields resulted in major advances in the skills of professional medical practice[86]—advances that did not find their way into sharecropping communities.

Gender inequalities in access to education

According to John Hope Franklin, the Freedmen's Bureau's greatest success came through its efforts on behalf of Black education. By 1867, schools had been set up in even the most remote counties of each of the confederate states.[87] However, schooling for sharecropping children was often merely a brief interlude between infancy and adulthood. Most children never had the opportunity to attend school with any regularity, since they began working in the fields around the age of ten or twelve. Girls were more likely to get a formal education than were boys because of the greater demand for male field labor,[88] but landlords pressured sharecropping families to keep all of their children in the fields.[89]

[86] James C. Mohr, *Abortion in America: The Origins and Evolution of National Policy* (New York: Oxford University Press, 1978), 256–57. It is debatable whether, prior to the Civil War, professional medical practice was any more successful in improving health care than was the lay medical practice of midwives. However, as Mohr points out, the Civil War is often viewed as a transition point for advances in professional medicine, despite the fact that professional medical care for women has been criticized up until the present day. For discussions of the role of wives and midwives in medical care for sharecropping and slave households, see Jones, 56 and 80–81; Federal Writers' Project, *These Are Our Lives* (New York: Norton, 1975), 26; Rosengarten (n. 44 above), 118–19; White (n. 19 above), 111–12.

[87] Franklin (n. 57 above), 308.

[88] Jones, 91; Bethel (n. 43 above), 41; Federal Writers' Project, 19–20; Kirby, 156.

[89] Jones, 64, 76–78, 90, and 96–99; Rosengarten, 19. According to these sources, it appears that fathers had the last word in deciding the allocation of their children's labor between farm and school. Apparently, this decision generated conflict between sharecropping mothers and fathers, with mothers emphasizing school work and fathers emphasizing farm work.

Thus while girls had greater access to formal education than did boys, this education was extremely inadequate, not only in terms of the limited amount of time sharecropping children spent in school but also in terms of the overall quality of the education they received.[90] The introduction of home economics and its ideology of female domesticity into southern public schools in the 1880s and 1890s took place first in Black schools in order to prepare Black women to labor not only in their own households but also as household servants for white families.[91] Though working in white homes was a choice of last resort, there is some evidence that the ideal of female domesticity within Black households had some support among Blacks. Black newspapers urged the "development of a womanly nature" as a means of "elevating and refining" the race, and a number of Black leaders during this era advocated traditional, subservient roles for women.[92]

Despite the inadequate quantity and quality of Black education, the advances in access to education for freedwomen clearly exceeded the slave era when formal instruction in schools was illegal for slaves in most slave states. Franklin captured the class nature of the slave-owners' fear of educating slaves when he pointed out how the laws against teaching individual slaves were often disregarded and viewed as not very serious, "but the instruction of slaves in schools [established specifically] for that purpose was another thing."[93]

Variations in patriarchy

With the rise of sharecropping the position of freedwomen improved, even though the sexual division of labor and women's roles

[90] In eleven southern states, the average expenditure in 1930 for each white child was $44.31 as compared with $12.57 for each Black child. For more information on the quality of education, see Arthur F. Raper and Ira De A. Reid, *Sharecroppers All* (Chapel Hill: University of North Carolina Press, 1941), 110–12.

[91] Druzilla Cary Kent, *A Study of the Results of Planning for Home Economics Education in the Southern States* (New York: Columbia University, Teachers College, Bureau of Publications, 1936), 11.

[92] Woloch (n. 10 above), 226. There are conflicting views in the literature regarding the role that male and female Afro-American leaders played in fostering female subservience and domesticity. Here distinctions should be made between leaders who advocated traditional, patriarchal roles for men and subservient roles for women, those who advocated equal political rights for men and women, and those who included, along with demands for equal political rights, demands for equal social rights and roles. For different views on this subject, see hooks (n. 26 above), 89–102 and 161–84, as contrasted to Elmer P. Martin and Joanne Mitchell Martin, "The Black Woman: Perspectives on Her Role in the Family," in *Ethnicity and Women* (Madison: University of Wisconsin Press, 1986), 184–205, esp. 197–99.

[93] Franklin, 202; see also Blassingame (n. 32 above), 91; Genovese (n. 27 above), 502; Jensen (n. 52 above), 71–75.

in production inside the home became more marked.[94] These women gained more control over their working hours and reproductive freedom than they had in the slave era when white male slaveowners had controlled and/or intervened in these aspects of Black women's lives. It also appears that white males had fewer opportunities to abuse Black women physically and sexually, even though this abuse clearly continued. Relative to Black men, women increased their access to formal education. However, it does not appear that Black sharecropping women experienced an improved quality of life in terms of economic power, domestic authority relations, domestic violence, and their total number of working hours inside and outside the home.

The fact that the postion of Black women appears from this study to be subordinate to that of Black men on certain dimensions under both slavery and sharecropping questions the conclusions of some major feminist historians who have documented women's roles during these eras. For example, Deborah Gray White concludes from her analysis of the lives of female slaves that slave households involved an "equal partnership" between males and females—an equality which was predicated on and buttressed by the absence of property in these households.[95] Yet her description of the lives of female slaves, which included wife battering, black-on-black rape, and husbands who "set 'round talkin' to other mens" while their wives worked even longer hours doing domestic chores, undermines her argument.[96]

---

[94] These findings call into question Kelly's second thesis, since the position of women improved despite the reduction of women's work oustide of the home. Other research provides further anomalous cases. For example, in fascist Germany during the 1930s and 1940s, the increase in women working outside of the home was substantial, in large part as a result of wartime demands. Yet this increase in women's production for exchange, which Kelly predicted would improve women's position, was in fact accompanied by an extensive antifeminist movement which campaigned against women smoking and wearing trousers, closed down birth control centers, and exacted heavy punishments for abortion. See Richard Grunberger, *The 12-Year Reich: A Social History of Nazi Germany, 1933–1945* (New York: Ballantine, 1971), 133, 256–58, 261–62, 278–81, and 288–89. These anomalies would suggest that along with economic roles, the political structures within a given mode of production need to be examined since the extent to which forms of political organization are more democratic or more authoritarian than one another can greatly affect the position of women.

[95] White (n. 19 above), 158–59.

[96] Ibid., 122, 151, and 152. In addition, on pp. 20–22 White notes that her conclusion about equal relations differs from that of many other writers on American slavery whom she claims too often exaggerated male slave masculinity in an effort to negate the derogatory male "Sambo" myth.

White is not alone in offering such contradictory portrayals. Other feminist writers, such as Elmer Martin, Joanne Martin, and Angela Davis, also maintain that slave households were egalitarian units, despite their descriptions of unequal gender roles.[97] For example, Martin and Martin discuss how "slavery equalized the black man and black woman" such that "the black man did not do any work that the black woman did not also do." However, on the very same page they quote Leslie Owens's observation that there "were certain duties considered women's work that men declined to do."[98] Thus it appears that, although slave women experienced a masculinization of their roles, slave men did not experience a corresponding feminization of their roles, despite all the attention academics have paid to the so-called emasculated Black male and the corresponding myth of Black matriarchy in discussing Black family structures. Indeed, rather than either the equality or matriarchy claimed by some writers, it seems that slave households were in fact characterized by patriarchy.[99] As hooks notes, failure to acknowledge this patriarchal reality fosters blindness to the fact that "the damaging effect of racism on black men neither prevents them from being sexist oppressors nor excuses or justifies their sexist oppression of black women."[100]

With few exceptions, patriarchy also has not been adequately acknowledged in writings on sharecropping women. For example, another feminist historian, Jacqueline Jones, is explicitly hesitant to characterize Black sharecropping households as patriarchal. While she admits that there was inequality in "domestic authority," she argues that the use of the term "patriarchy" is inappropriate when Black males had little control over most significant economic resources; when escaping from poverty was often precluded by

[97] See Martin and Martin; and Davis, "The Black Woman's Role" (n. 30 above). Angela Davis's discussion of relations within slave households is particularly interesting because she grounds her analysis in the Hegelian master-slave dialectic, pointing out on pp. 7–8 how the fact that slave women performed both male and female work roles provided these women with "proof of their ability to transform things" as well as a "practical awareness of the oppressor's utter dependence on her"—thus serving to "unharness an immense potential in the black woman." Davis is also careful not to romanticize Black gender relations; she refers to them as a "deformed equality."

[98] Martin and Martin, 193.

[99] Farnham (n. 29 above); hooks. If an analysis of American slavery also takes into account the influence of African culture and heritage, the patriarchal features of traditional African family lives would increase the likelihood that American slave households were patriarchal. For a discussion of the relationship between American slavery and the subjugation of women in traditional African cultures, see Martin and Martin, 188–89 or hooks, 16–20.

[100] hooks, 88.

racism regardless of the amount of an individual's hard work; and when many whites continually tried to deprive Black males of all meaningful types of authority and power.[101]

Both White and Jones tend to base their arguments primarily on the fact that the propertyless nature of slave and sharecropping households, which was persistently maintained by racist restrictions on the accumulation of wealth and power by Blacks, precluded the existence of any meaningful notion of patriarchal domination. In turn, although both of these writers provide evidence of interpersonal inequalities in power, they seem unwilling to equate this with institutional patriarchal domination.

It is possible that due to racist restrictions on the accumulation of wealth or power by Blacks, slaves and Black sharecroppers may have experienced relatively more sexual equality than middle- or upper-class whites. That is, these restrictions precluded Black husbands and wives from being separated by the more extreme gender-based differentials in economic rights and privileges that well-to-do whites experienced. However, this greater relative equality should neither be exaggerated nor romanticized given the fact that it was premised on the poverty and deprivation of both sexes.

Moreover, both slavery and sharecropping existed within the context of a larger capitalist mode of production predicated on private property. Consequently, these propertyless classes were under the hegemony of a legal system and other institutions that were property oriented. Male control over women and children in slave and sharecropping households was backed not merely by individual force but also by mechanisms of social control enforced by ruling classes, churches, and the state. Unfortunately, some feminist thinkers have ignored this more complex relationship between property and patriarchy, presenting instead a rather mechanistic equation that argues that, if an individual lacks property, this precludes the existence of patriarchy. Yet major critics of private property, like Marx, Engels, and Lenin, recognized the existence of patriarchy within propertyless classes, even though these same critics have been accused of being blind to gender issues.[102] Indeed, Marx, Engels, and Lenin all recognized that patriarchy, like private property, was institutionalized and not simply a characteristic of individuals.

Institutionalization entails not only objective constraints on social behavior but also subjective constraints internalized through socialization. Consequently, it is not surprising that male domestic

---

[101] Jones (n. 20 above), 104–5.
[102] Hartmann (n. 4 above).

authority and the relegation of females to traditional sex roles was often fostered by Afro-American folk tales or newspapers and accepted by female slaves and sharecroppers. This is not meant to resurrect either a "blame the victim" approach or the view that the history of Black women is merely a history of passive victimization. Rather, the point of recognizing the subjective dimensions of institutionalization is to highlight the more subtle, yet still coercive, nature of sex-role socialization.

Because property-oriented legal and institutional mechanisms of social control also govern interpersonal life, interpersonal inequalities of power that disadvantage women implement institutional patriarchal domination. Domestic violence and authoritarianism are political forms of institutionalized domination, buttressed by gender inequalities in socialization practices, access to material resources, and existing marriage or family law. While such interpersonal and domestic issues were major concerns of both the nineteenth-century women's movement and the temperance movement,[103] modern feminists have even more emphatically rejected any dichotomy between the public and private spheres of social life when recognizing political oppression. If one takes seriously a major tenet of modern feminist thought that "the personal is political,"[104] then in light of this research on Black women it must also be concluded that the political is personal.

Some writers have argued that because male and female roles are complementary in family labor enterprises, couples are more dependent on each other's labor, and hence, more equal.[105] Though male and female roles may have been complementary under sharecropping, this complementarity was not synonymous with equality.[106] The division of labor under sharecropping was such that female labor was directed more toward production for use, while male labor was directed primarily toward production for exchange.

---

[103] Freeman (n. 6 above), 536–39.

[104] Alison M. Jaggar and Paula S. Rothenberg, *Feminist Frameworks: Alternative Theoretical Accounts of the Relations between Women and Men*, 2d ed. (New York: McGraw-Hill, 1984).

[105] Christina Greene has suggested that the findings of this study would support, rather than critique, Kelly's thesis, if public and domestic spheres were viewed as less differentiated under sharecropping because of the integral and complementary nature of work inside and outside of the home. I thank Ms. Greene for bringing this different interpretation to my attention. However, in my view, this interpretation ignores the importance of the sexual division of labor for determining patriarchal control within family labor enterprises. In this regard, see also Susan A. Mann, review of *Farm Women: Work, Farm and Family in the United States*, by Rachel Ann Rosenfeld, in *American Journal of Sociology* 93, no. 1 (July 1987): 243–45.

[106] Janiewski (n. 47 above), 15.

This differentiation is of particular political and economic significance in a market economy precisely because production for use is by definition unpaid labor, regardless of its intrinsic value. As numerous feminist debates over domestic labor have long recognized, this places women in a subordinate position.[107] Such a sexual divison of labor was a major organizing principle of the American family sharecropping system.

Even when Black women sharecroppers engaged in a significant amount of production for exchange, control over income generated from agricultural production was in the hands of men—even if this income was produced by the labor of the entire family. Male control over this income, coupled with the domestic decision-making power this entailed, meant that Black women could only have been in an inherently unequal relation to Black men. This situation is not unique to sharecropping but, rather, is characteristic of many family labor enterprises—both rural and urban.[108]

Slave and sharecropping households alike were organized patriarchally, and this sexual inequality was buttressed by the larger patriarchal society in which these households existed. This is not to dismiss the cultural and historical specificity of racial or class oppression in the lives of Black women but, rather, to argue that patriarchy should be viewed as historically and culturally diverse. That is, the notion of patriarchy should be reconceptualized to include a number of patriarchies. The degrees of domination characterizing different patriarchies may vary by women's class, race, ethnicity, and sexual orientation, just as various patriarchies may require substantively different political solutions for the liberation of all women. As Audre Lorde points out, recognition of these "many varied tools of patriarchy" will also entail an increased awareness of the many varied differences among women.[109] By recognizing this diversity and the grounds for unity within this diversity, we can take an important step toward restoring women to history and restoring our history to women.

Department of Sociology
University of New Orleans

---

[107] See the introduction or any of the essays in Fox, ed. (n. 16 above).

[108] Harriet Friedmann, "Patriarchal Commodity Production," *Social Analysis* 20 (December 1986): 47–55; Susan George, *How the Other Half Dies: The Real Reasons for World Hunger* (Montclair, N.J.: Allanheld, Osmun, 1981), 20–21.

[109] Audre Lorde, "An Open Letter to Mary Daly," in *Sister Outsider: Essays and Speeches by Audre Lorde*, ed. Audre Lorde (New York: Crossing, 1984), 66–71, esp. 67.

FOR THE GOOD OF FAMILY AND RACE: GENDER, WORK, AND DOMESTIC ROLES IN THE BLACK COMMUNITY, 1880–1930

SHARON HARLEY

The racial restrictions that all blacks face in the paid labor market continually produce similarities in the work experiences of black women and men, yet, there are differences that can largely be attributed to gender.[1] Nowhere are the gender differences more

This article is part of a book-length manuscript on the intersection between gender, class, race, and Afro-American wage-earning women. Financial assistance for the larger study has been provided by a Postdoctoral Fellowship for Minority Group Scholars from the Rockefeller Foundation. The article has benefited from the scholarly advice of Jacquelyn Dowd Hall and James O. Horton, who commented on a version of this paper at the 1987 meeting of the Organization of American Historians (OAH), and from critical readings by Eileen Boris, my copresenter at the OAH, by my colleague William Sabol, and by the anonymous readers for Signs.

[1] Few groups of women have had a longer history of both paid and unpaid work in the United States than black women; yet traditionally, black women have been absent from most published histories of working women, and where they have appeared, they often have been the victims of sweeping generalizations and unfounded stereotypes. The omission has been attributed by some historians to the paucity of sources on black working women and by others to the "uniqueness" of the work experience of black women, which makes it difficult, if not impossible, to offer more than a superficial treatment of black women in histories of (white) women workers. Two recent historical publications that make significant contributions to our understanding of black working women are Jacqueline Jones, *Labor of Love, Labor of Sorrow: Black Women, Work, and the Family from Slavery to the Present* (New York: Basic, 1985); and Dolores Janiewski, *Sisterhood Denied: Race, Gender*

This essay originally appeared in Signs, vol. 15, no. 2, Winter 1990.

evident than in expectations surrounding domestic and work roles. In the late nineteenth and first half of the twentieth centuries, because of widespread and trenchant racial and gender discrimination, black women often found their unpaid domestic work in their own homes and in their community, especially their church, a great source of pride. Accordingly, black women more readily embraced their status as mothers, wives, aunts, and sisters than their more embattled status as wage earners.[2]

The fifty-year period from the closing decades of the nineteenth century to the advent of the Great Depression was a time of

---

and Class in a New South Community (Philadelphia: Temple University Press, 1985). One of the most popular myths about wage-earning Afro-American women is that they represent a monolithic group at the bottom of the occupational structure, whose work and domestic lives have changed very little over time. Recent efforts to correct this picture, especially as it relates to the largest group of black wage-earning women—domestic service workers—have been undertaken by scholars in various disciplines. See, e.g., Bonnie Thornton Dill, "Across the Boundaries of Race and Class: An Exploration of the Relationship between Work and Family among Black Female Domestic Servants" (Ph.D. diss., New York University, 1979); Elizabeth Clark-Lewis, "From 'Servant' to 'Dayworker': A Study of Selected Household Service Workers in Washington, D.C., 1900–1926" (Ph.D. diss., University of Maryland, 1983); David Katzman, Seven Days a Week: Women and Domestic Service in Industrializing America (New York: Oxford University Press, 1978); and Phyllis Palmer, "Household Work and Domestic Labor: Racial and Technological Change," in My Troubles Are Going to Have Trouble with Me: Everyday Trials and Triumphs of Women Workers, ed. Karen Brodkin Sacks and Dorothy Remy (New Brunswick, N.J.: Rutgers University Press, 1984), 80–91. Finally, because of the dominant role that race plays in the lives of all blacks, males and females, and the tendency to assume that black men and women have egalitarian domestic relationships, the role of gender in the domestic and work lives of black women has largely been ignored by Afro-American and women historians. It is not my intention to suggest that race is not an important variable in the lives of black women, but only to suggest that there are other important factors, like gender and class, that simultaneously influence individual lives. Gender is as important a determinant in black women's work lives as it is in the lives of other groups of wage-earning women. For a study of the intersection of gender and work, consult Joseph H. Pleck, "The Work-Family Role System," in Women and Work: Problems and Perspectives, ed. Rachel Kahn-Hut et al. (New York: Oxford University Press, 1982), 101–10; and Ann Game and Rosemary Pringle, Gender at Work (Sydney: Allen & Unwin, 1983). While not focusing on American women, one of the best sources on the relationship between women's work and familial roles remains Louise A. Tilly and Joan W. Scott, Women, Work, and Family (New York: Holt, Rinehart & Winston, 1978). The arguments raised and conclusions reached in this article represent a continuation of those put forward by historian James Oliver Horton in his essay "Freedom's Yoke: Gender Conventions among Antebellum Free Blacks," Feminist Studies 12, no. 1 (Spring 1986): 51–76.

[2] For an informative discussion about the self-perceptions of black women workers and about how the structures of race, gender, and class have influenced these perceptions, see Bonnie Thornton Dill, "Race, Class, and Gender: Prospects

considerable change in the public and private roles of women and in the economic, social, and racial climate in the United States in general and the District of Columbia in particular. At the same time that black and white women assumed larger roles in public life, black women and men experienced a deteriorating racial climate throughout the United States.[3] Despite racial hostilities, the District of Columbia attracted black women workers, especially from Maryland and Virginia, because they usually found better paying and often more prestigious jobs there (even as domestic servants) than in other places.[4] As a result, there was a steady increase in the District in the number of black domestics and washerwomen in

---

for an All-Inclusive Sisterhood," *Feminist Studies* 9, no. 1 (Spring 1983): 131–50; and Micheline Ridley Malson, "Black Women's Sex Roles: The Social Context for a New Ideology," *Journal of Social Issues* 39, no. 3 (1983): 101–13. Also see Jones, "Introduction." Racism in American society allowed and indeed forced black women to play a multiplicity of roles both within and outside the home. Roles outside the home (but closely related to their domestic responsibilities) frequently came under the rubric of their status as "community workers," "church sisters," and "race women." These roles and the cultural and historical underpinnings for them are examined by Evelyn Brooks (Higginbotham) in "The Women's Movement in the Black Baptist Church, 1880–1920" (Ph.D. diss., University of Rochester, 1984); Angela Y. Davis, *Women, Race and Class* (New York: Vintage, 1983); and Cheryl Townsend Gilkes, " 'Holding Back the Ocean with a Broom': Black Women and Community Work," in *The Black Woman*, ed. La Frances Rodgers-Rose (Beverly Hills, Calif.: Sage, 1980), 217–31.

[3] The opening of opportunities in this period for all women, but especially educated black women, is discussed at length by scholars in Bettye Collier Thomas, ed., "Special Issue: The Impact of Black Women in Education," *Journal of Negro Education*, vol. 51, no. 3 (Summer 1982); see especially articles by Cynthia Neverdon-Morton, "Self-Help Programs as Educative Activities of Black Women in the South, 1895–1925: Focus on Four Key Areas," 207–21; and Sharon Harley, "Beyond the Classroom: Organizational Lives of Black Female Educators in the District of Columbia, 1890–1930," 254–65. The deteriorating racial climate for blacks in the United States during this period has been fully documented by American historians. Indicative of the worsening race climate in the nation's capital is the post–World War I race riot in the summer of 1919 and the increased discrimination against and segregation of employees in the federal government on the basis of race. For a historical overview of this period, consult John Hope Franklin, *From Slavery to Freedom: A History of Negro Americans* (New York: Knopf, 1988), chaps. 16 and 17. For information about the race riot and the racial situation in Washington, D.C., see Constance M. Green, *The Secret City: A History of Race Relations in the Nation's Capital* (Princeton, N.J.: Princeton University Press, 1967).

[4] W. E. B. Du Bois noted the attraction that the District of Columbia had for black female domestics in "The Negroes of Farmville, Virginia: A Social Study," *U.S. Department of Labor Bulletin*, no. 14 (January 1898), 20–21. Recent works that examine two groups of women workers in the local economy, the overwhelming majority of whom were white, include Cindy Sondik Aron, *Ladies and Gentlemen of the Civil Service* (New York: Oxford University Press, 1987); and Gloria Moldow, *Women Doctors in Gilded-Age Washington: Race, Gender, and Professionalization* (Urbana: University of Illinois Press, 1987).

private homes, black cleaning-women in office buildings, and unskilled and semiskilled laundry operatives in commercial laundries.

According to published occupational census reports for the District of Columbia, in 1890 54.6 percent of black women worked for pay; by 1910 this figure had risen to 60.1 percent. Ten years later, however, postwar occupation figures reflected a percentage decline to 56.3 percent. In 1930, with the onset of the Depression, the figure had dropped to 52.8 percent. Numerically, there was a steady rise in the number of gainfully employed black women in the District of Columbia during the period from 1880 to 1930.[5]

The District also had a large public school system for blacks and a high concentration of educated black professionals. The District of Columbia public school system for blacks—Miner Normal School, Howard University, the National Training School for Women and Girls, and other black institutions—served as major employers of educated black women and men.[6]

Furthermore, the District's economy centered around the federal and municipal government and consisted primarily of white-collar and professional workers, with a supporting cast of unskilled domestics and laborers. Consequently, the local economy was skewed to the service rather than the production industry, which resulted in a large number of female wage-earners of both races.

[5] See, e.g., U.S. Department of Interior, Census Office, *Compendium of the Eleventh Census, 1890* (Washington, D.C.: Government Printing Office, 1897), pt. 3, p. 446; U.S. Department of Commerce and Labor, Bureau of the Census, *Special Reports—Occupations at the Twelfth Census: 1900* (Washington, D.C.: Government Printing Office, 1904), 248–50; U.S. Department of Commerce, Bureau of the Census, *United States Census of Population: 1910*, vol. 4, *Occupations* (Washington, D.C.: Government Printing Office, 1914), 446–47; and U.S. Department of Commerce, Bureau of the Census, *Fourteenth Census of the United States, 1920: Population*, vol. 4, *Occupations* (Washington, D.C.: Government Printing Office, 1923), 361–62; and U.S. Bureau of the Census, *Negro Population in the United States, 1920–1932* (Washington, D.C.: Government Printing Office, 1935), 300.

[6] Information about local educational institutions for blacks appear in Winfield Scott Montgomery, *Historical Sketch of the Education for the Colored Race in the District of Columbia, 1805–1907* (Washington, D.C.: Smith Bros., 1907); Green, *The Secret City*; and Rayford W. Logan, *Howard University: The First Hundred Years, 1867–1967* (New York: New York University Press, 1969). For a general history of Washington, D.C., consult Constance M. Green, *Washington: Capital City, 1879–1950* (Princeton, N.J.: Princeton University Press, 1967). For an overview of the employment situation of Washington blacks, see Lorenzo Johnston Green and Myra Callis, *Employment of Negroes in District of Columbia* (Washington, D.C.: Association for the Study of Negro Life and History, 1932). For specific information about black workers in the federal bureaucracy, see Laurence J. W. Hayes, *The Negro Federal Government Worker: A Study of His Classification in the District of Columbia, 1883–1938* (Washington, D.C.: Howard University Graduate School, 1941).

Despite this presence in the work force, a smaller percentage of the black female than the black male population labored for wages. In 1900, for instance, 57 percent of the black female population ten years of age and older was gainfully employed compared to 80 percent of the black male population in the same age cohort. In 1910, 60.1 percent of the black female population reportedly worked for wages compared to 81.4 percent of the black male population in Washington, D.C. Twenty years later, 52.8 percent of the black female and 80.6 percent of the black male population was gainfully employed.

A number of gender-related factors explain differences in the proportion of black women and black men represented in the labor force. This participation gap in part reflects the fact that employers (both white and black) often preferred male wage-earners over female wage-earners even though it meant paying slightly higher wages. For example, a study in 1920 of black male and female domestic and personal service workers revealed that male elevator operators averaged between $9.00 and $10.00 per week, compared to $8.00 to $9.00 per week for female elevator operators. Similarly, black male day-workers earned approximately $4.00 per day, while black female day-workers received between $2.50 and $3.00 per day. The inequity in the pay scale was an accepted fact, and employers justified gender-based wage discrimination and hiring practices on the popular assumption that men were the primary breadwinners.[7]

As a result of such attitudes, black women workers also had fewer opportunities than black men to occupy higher-paying (typically more prestigious) positions. Racism in the labor market in general meant that there were fewer white-collar jobs for blacks, male or female; but black males occupied many of the top-level clerical positions reserved for blacks in Washington, D.C., throughout the 1880–1930 period.[8] Prominent black men, such as Frederick Douglass and former Mississippi Reconstruction Senator Blanche K. Bruce, occupied the top clerical and political patronage jobs available to blacks in the federal government. Black women of similar, if not superior, educational training and political connec-

---

[7] The wage figures are taken from Elizabeth Ross Haynes, "Negroes in Domestic Service in the United States," *Journal of Negro History* 8, no. 3 (October 1923): 384–442, esp. 421. Comments about the significance of wage-earning by black women appear throughout the Washington *Bee*. See, for instance, the following issues: November 13, 1897; November 27, 1897; October 20, 1900; February 23, 1901; January 4, 1902; and April 12, 1902.

[8] For a list of the blacks occupying patronage and other top-level jobs in the federal government, see Hayes.

tions, like Mary Church Terrell and Dr. Lucy E. Moten, were never offered any of these top-level positions.[9]

Indeed, between 1920 and 1930, racism in the federal government began to push black women and men out of white-collar job opportunities there. The large number of white female clerks in the federal government by 1920 left little doubt that clerical work was largely white women's work; less than 5 percent of the black female work force occupied clerical positions. Black federal employees who maintained their positions were increasingly victimized by racially inspired policies and practices, such as segregated offices, cafeterias, and restrooms—policies often instituted at the insistence of white female employees.[10] Yet government employment for black women, regardless of the job or its rank, was usually better than personal service in private homes or employment as laundresses. Government employees were paid more, had more prestige, and could spend more time with their families.[11]

For some blacks (and whites) the fact that black *mothers* (especially those who were uneducated and nonprofessional) had jobs was a blatant example of a lack of racial progress and family stability. Giles B. Jackson and D. Webster Davis, authors of *The Industrial History of the Negro Race* (1919) argued: "The race needs wives who stay at home, being supported by their husbands, and then they can spend time in the training of their children."[12]

[9] Ibid., chap. 1 and app. A, 113–15. Also consult Green, *The Secret City*. The deterioration in the racial climate within the federal government and in the city of Washington is documented in these works and other studies specifically dealing with the Wilson administration and blacks. See, e.g., Bert H. Thurber, "The Negro at the Nation's Capital, 1913–1931" (Ph.D. diss., Yale University, 1973).

[10] Hayes, chap. 2.; Green, *The Secret City*, chaps. 7–9.

[11] Outside of teaching, white-collar positions, especially in the federal government, were the most prestigious and highest paying positions available to women. For teachers who married, clerical employment was often the only work available commensurate with their training. During World War I, black women were hired largely for semiskilled and unskilled positions (as elevator operators and as "charwomen"/cleaning women by the federal government). Consult Green and Callis (n. 6 above), 58–64.

[12] Quote taken from Giles B. Jackson and D. Webster Davis, *The Industrial History of the Negro Race of the United States* (Richmond, Va.: Negro Educational Association, 1911), 131. For information about the marital status of black women in the District of Columbia, consult, for instance, U.S. Bureau of the Census, *Negroes in the United States, 1920–1932* (n. 5 above), 151–52, table 11. Based on a comparison of the labor force participation of married Italian and black women, Elizabeth H. Pleck offers several cultural explanations for the larger representation of married black women in the labor force. See her article "A Mother's Wages: Income Earning among Married Italian and Black Women, 1896–1911," in *A Heritage of Her Own: Toward a New Social History of American Women*, ed. Nancy F. Cott and Elizabeth H. Pleck (New York: Simon & Schuster, 1979), 367–92.

This view of the proper role of black mothers, usually (but not always) pronounced by male members of the black community, represented the ideal for many blacks. Yet, the racial barriers that black males faced in the employment market forced a significant number of married black women to join the labor force. According to 1920 census figures, approximately one-half of the married black female population in Washington, D.C., was gainfully employed (compared to less than one-fourth of the local married, white female population). Despite the concern of the reformers, however, most black working women in the District in 1920 were either unmarried (single or widowed) or married with no children or spouse in the home.[13]

For most black husbands, it was nearly impossible to oppose their wives's employment (although some did), when they knew just as well as everyone else in the black community that their family's very survival depended upon the wages, however minimal, that their wives contributed. An examination of federal employment applications and requests for employment for 1890 to 1910, for instance, reveals that women most often mentioned the fulfillment of family obligations as their reason for seeking paid work.[14]

During the immediate post–Civil War years and during World War I, large numbers of unmarried women came to Washington, D.C. In search of better-paying employment, they added to the already large numbers of black women in the District. Indeed, by 1900 slightly over one-half (57.4 percent) of all black women in the District were single or widowed compared to 47.1 percent of the black male population. This uneven sex ratio caused some concern

[13] For a discussion of the diverse, frequently contradictory, attitudes of black males about wage-earning women, consult, e.g., Bonnie Thornton Dill, "The Dialectics of Black Womanhood," *Signs: Journal of Women in Culture and Society* 4, no. 3 (Spring 1979): 543–55; Horton (n. 1 above); Jones (n. 1 above); and E. Pleck, "A Mother's Wages." See also Bonnie Thornton Dill, " 'The Means to Put My Children Through': Child-Rearing Goals and Strategies among Black Female Domestic Servants," in Rodgers-Rose, ed. (n. 2 above), 107–23.

[14] See Dill, " 'The Means to Put My Children Through,' " 108–10. Historian Elizabeth H. Pleck touches on the sacrifice that black mothers willingly make on behalf of their children (see her "A Mother's Wages"). Also see James Borchert, *Alley Life in Washington: Family, Community, Religion, and Folklife in the City, 1850–1970* (Urbana: University of Illinois Press, 1980). The employment applications of job seekers for positions in various federal agencies are located at the National Archives. Because women, especially married women, were required to give compelling reasons for seeking employment, the applications provide invaluable quantitative and qualitative data about female applicants and the myriad reasons they wanted to work. While the race of the applicant is not always given, there are certain federal offices and jobs in which black female job-seekers predominated and race can often be deduced. See, for instance, "Application File—Mrs. Elizabeth B. Meredith," Treasury Department Applications, Charwomen, Laborers, and Messengers, Record Group 56, National Archives, Washington, D.C.

among middle-class black reformers and scholars who predicted that the number of spinsters (and immoral women) would increase as a result of there not being a sufficient number of marriage partners. As Howard University professor Kelly Miller explained in 1908, "Washington and Baltimore have respectively 10,006 and 9,132 hopeless females, for whom there are neither present nor prospective husbands."[15] His predictions about the marital future of what he called "surplus women," however, did little to stem the tide of female in-migrants or to encourage unmarried female city dwellers to leave. Most black women migrants were between thirteen and thirty years of age, and while not opposed to finding a good husband, they came to Washington largely to find jobs in order to support themselves and to help needy kin.[16]

Indeed, there is some evidence that the black community encouraged these women to give their careers priority over making plans to marry. For instance, in 1897 a correspondent for a local black newspaper, the Washington *Bee*, advised young women to pursue some career, not necessarily professional, rather than enter into a "foolish marriage, through the lack of occupation."[17]

For black professional women, especially teachers, the tension between the assumptions that they should marry and that they should work was particularly salient in light of policies that required teachers to quit teaching after they married. In 1923, one

[15] Quote found in Kelly Miller's chapter, "Surplus Negro Women," in his *Race Adjustments: Essays on the Negro in America* (New York: Neale Publishing, 1908), 170; "The preponderance of one sex over the other forebodes nothing but evil to society. The maladjustment of economic and social conditions upsets the scale where nature intended a balance. The argument of Mrs. [Charlotte Perkins] Gilman is as correct as it is courageous. 'Where women preponderate' in large numbers 'there is a proportionate increase in immorality, because women are cheap.' " Miller's discussion of surplus women in large cities refers to an article entitled "The Duty of Surplus Women," by Charlotte Perkins Gilman, *New York Independent*, January 1905, as cited by Miller, 170. In 1900, Washington, D.C., and Baltimore, Maryland, had the highest ratio of females to males (126 females to every 100 males) in the nation.

[16] Based largely on Miller's essay on "Surplus Negro Women," Du Bois offers a brief discussion of the relationship between the marital status, moral character, and the economic conditions of black female migrants to Washington and Baltimore in his *The Negro American Family* (1909; reprint, Cambridge, Mass.: MIT Press, 1970). Although her focus is not specifically on black women, Elizabeth H. Pleck offers a more up-to-date and analytical study of the economics of black migration in *Black Migration and Poverty: Boston, 1865–1900* (New York: Academic Press, 1979). Information about black females who migrated between 1900 and 1927 to Washington, D.C., primarily to work as domestics appears in Clark-Lewis (n. 1 above). Information about the marital status of the black female population can be found in various published census reports. See, e.g., U.S. Bureau of the Census, *Negroes in the United States, 1920–1932* (n. 5 above), p. 152, table 11.

[17] "A Pointer on the Side," *Bee* (January 16, 1897).

female teacher, who wished to remain anonymous for "obvious reasons," wrote a letter to a member of the District of Columbia's board of education expressing her opposition to the campaign to reenact the ban against married female teachers in the school system. Questioning why these women should be penalized for marrying after making tremendous sacrifices in order to advance themselves professionally, the teacher wrote that professional wo- men's "personal obligations—to relatives, for example—do not cease with their marriage and, therefore, [they] have legitimate reasons for continuing to work." Besides, she warned, "in view of the high cost of living, the proposed motion would lead to secret marriages, fewer families, and fewer vacancies."[18]

Even those women who, because they were from upper middle- class black professional families, would not suffer economically from having to choose between work and marriage confronted this tension between ideals for black women. Following her graduation from Oberlin College in 1884, Mary Church, daughter of prominent and well-to-do Memphis black entrepreneurs, took a job as a teacher at Wilberforce University over the objections of her father. Church pursued a career as a teacher because, as she wrote in her autobiography, "All during my college course I had dreamed of the day when I could promote the welfare of my race."[19] Her father wanted her to live the "leisurely" life of a typical "Southern belle," feeling that a teaching position should go to someone who really needed the money.[20] Mary Church continued to teach and in 1887 worked for the District of Columbia's black public school system. Following her marriage to Robert H. Terrell, a prominent Washing- ton educator and jurist, Church Terrell worked as a paid lecturer, as a political organizer for the Republican party, and, for a brief period, as a clerk for the federal government.

[18] "An earnest teacher" to Mrs. Raymond B. Morgan, October 23, 1923, Mary Church Terrell Papers, Box 4, Moorland Spingarn Research Center, Howard Uni- versity, Washington, D.C. Nearly 60 percent of the school boards polled by the National Education Association in the mid-1920s discriminated against married women as new hires. See Nancy Cott, *The Grounding of Modern Feminism* (New Haven, Conn.: Yale University Press, 1987).
[19] For an account of Mary Church Terrell's early work history and her father's initial opposition to her gainful employment, read her autobiography, *A Colored Woman in a White World* (1940; reprint, Washington, D.C.: National Association of Colored Women's Clubs, 1968), 59–63, esp. 60. Based on an analysis of more contemporary data, Bart Landry and Margaret Platt Jendrek discovered that black middle-class wives were more likely to work than both white middle- and black working-class wives (see their article, "The Employment of Wives in Middle-Class Black Families," *Journal of Marriage and Family* 40 [November 1978]: 787–97).
[20] Terrell, 59–60.

Despite her husband's support for her various public activities, she, and not he, was primarily responsible for preparing meals, cleaning the house, and raising the children. Even though she hired a series of live-in domestics and cooks who assisted her with these responsibilities, Terrell was often frustrated, having to chose between fixing dinner, spending time with her two daughters, or working as a civic activist, writer, and paid lecturer. In her autobiography, *A Colored Woman in a White World,* Terrell offered the following explanation for turning down a publisher's request to write a book on lynching: "Even if I had possessed both the ability and the courage, I should have had to surmount many obstacles to find the time, the opportunity for concentration and the peace of mind necessary to write such a book. I had to discharge my duty to my family, to the public schools in my capacity as a member of the Board of Education, and not infrequently I filled lecture engagements."[21]

Mary Church Terrell had a long and successful professional career, despite the tensions between the ideal of the full-time mother and the full-time professional advancing the welfare of black Americans. No doubt this was possible because she could afford to hire people to help her with domestic responsibilities. For the majority of black women, especially those working in low-status jobs (e.g., domestic service and laundry work), the tensions between these ideals were resolved (either by necessity or by choice) by doing their household work themselves.

Describing the difference between how she felt about paid work similar to the work she did for family members and friends on her days off, a woman who had been a domestic remarked:

> Now work can be fun. Remember what I told you about the Thursday get-togethers? That was hard work, but people didn't mind because they wanted to do that and they were working for themselves. . . . One very important difference between white people and black people is that white people think that you *are* your work. . . . Now, a black person . . . knows that what I am doing doesn't have anything to do with what I want to do or what I do when I am doing for myself. Now, black people think that my work is just what I have to do or what I do to get what I want.[22]

---

[21] Ibid., 235.

[22] The quotes are taken from one in a series of personal narratives compiled by anthropologist John Langston Gwaltney in the 1970s. These narratives offer an excellent insight into the thinking of everyday black women and men about their work experiences (see *Drylongso: A Self-Portrait of Black America* [New York: Vintage, 1981], 173–74).

Views similar to those of this former New York black domestic were expressed by current and former black female domestics in the District of Columbia. For instance, a woman identified by the pseudonym Velma Davis was quoted as having said: "When I say 'my job,' I mean a job that you did."[23] These women and others who occupied low status jobs saw the notion that one should focus on a professional or a wage-work identity as irrelevant to the black community.

It was often a source of pride that black mothers with working spouses did not work for wages outside the home. In her autobiography, *Dust Tracks on a Road*, Zora Neale Hurston revealed that her father loved to boast to his male friends that "he had never let his wife hit a lick of work for anybody in her life."[24] The irony, of course, is that Zora's mother took care of a large family (which her father also boasted about) that made it nearly impossible for her to work outside the home. Yet, Zora's father did not consider his wife's unpaid domestic labor to be "real" work.[25]

The debate in the black community in the 1880–1930 period about women's "place" extended into the sex-segregated workplace of the District's public schools. Black male teachers occupied most of the high-paying and prestigious administrative and teaching positions of the District's black public school system, especially at M Street and later at Dunbar High School. The few black women who occupied administrative posts between 1880 and 1930 often endured stinging gender-based attacks.[26] For instance, from the beginning of her appointment in 1902 as principal of M Street High School, Anna Julia Cooper provoked controversy. At the root of the controversy was Cooper's alleged inability as a woman to adequately supervise male students and the male members of her faculty. Though he later reversed his position on Cooper's appoint-

[23] Quote taken from Elizabeth Clark-Lewis, " 'This Work Had a End': African-American Domestic Workers in Washington, D.C., 1910–1940," in *"To Toil the Livelong Day": America's Women at Work, 1780–1980*, ed. Carol Groneman and Mary Beth Norton (Ithaca, N.Y.: Cornell University Press, 1987), 205. The general feeling among blacks and, indeed, among many uneducated, unskilled members of various racial and ethnic groups, was that their work did not represent fundamentally who they were. For an informative discussion of attitudes toward and of black domestics, see Trudier Harris, *From Mammies to Militants: Domestics in Black American Literature* (Philadelphia: Temple University Press, 1982).

[24] Zora Neale Hurston, *Dust Tracks on a Road: An Autobiography* (1942; reprint, Urbana: University of Illinois Press, 1984), 16.

[25] Ibid.

[26] Salaries and rank of District teachers appear in the annual reports of the superintendent of D.C. public schools found in the *Annual Reports of the Commissioners of the District of Columbia* (Washington, D.C.: Government Printing Office) for the period of this study. In 1890, for instance, the average annual salary for grammar and primary school teachers was $588.95 and $984 for high school teachers.

ment, W. Calvin Chase, the outspoken editor of the Washington *Bee*, initially supported her, arguing that "it was a place for a woman."[27] He made similar remarks about practically every "man's" job a woman occupied. Generally these comments included references to some "unique" skill of women, in order to justify their presence. Thus, women in dentistry were praised because female patients could avoid the embarrassment of seeking the services of male dentists. Women embalmers were extolled because they prepared female bodies for burial and provided better comfort to grieving family members.[28]

Some black women advocated sex-segregation because they thought women had superior skills. Alice Strange Davis, a teacher in the District's black public schools, asserted that women, not men, should be assigned to elementary school teaching positions because "they [women] could more easily put themselves in the place of children."[29] From Davis's standpoint, a sex-segregated labor market assured that women would obtain jobs that otherwise might not have been available to them.

Blacks had reasons for supporting separate spheres for women and men that were unique to their history. For a group of people one generation out of slavery, gender-defined work and domestic responsibilities were symbolic of their new status. In addition, because their economic opportunities and employment options continued to be circumscribed by the racism of white American society, sex-segregation helped to protect black women, married or single, from charges of immorality such as those made by nineteenth- and twentieth-century writers and reformers.[30]

Though it often resulted in low-status and low-paying jobs for black women, sex-segregation seems to have been widely accepted in the black community in Washington, D.C., in this period. The tension between the ideal of a full-time mother and respect for and recognition of black working women's abilities and contributions to

[27] Quote appears in "What I Saw and Heard," Washington *Bee* (July 8, 1905). For a discussion of the Cooper controversy, see Louise Daniel Hutchinson, *Anna J. Cooper: A Voice from the South* (Washington, D.C.: Smithsonian Institution Press, 1981); and Sharon Harley, "Anna Julia Cooper: A Voice for Black Women," in *The Afro-American Woman: Struggles and Images*, ed. Sharon Harley and Rosalyn Terborg-Penn (Port Washington, N.Y.: Kennikatt, 1978), 87–96.

[28] See the issues of the *Bee* for May 23, 1896; April 17, 1897; and March 29, 1919.

[29] Alice Strange Davis's comments appear in the Washington *Bee* (September 30, 1899).

[30] By engaging in wage work that involved close contact with male workers, women's morality was regularly called into question. Historian Cindy Sondick Aron examines this issue in *Ladies and Gentlemen of the Civil Service* (n. 4 above). See also her " 'To Barter Their Souls for Gold': Female Clerks in Federal Government Offices, 1862–1890," *Journal of American History* 67 (March 1981): 835–53.

family income existed within a set of attitudes that tended to favor traditional sex roles.

Nevertheless, changes in the District's economy between 1880 and 1930 kept the debate alive. As commercial activity, the number of professional and scientific institutions, and the size of the federal work force grew in the nation's capital, opportunities for married women to work outside the home increased. For instance, as the number of commercial laundries increased, women who had been working in their homes were faced with pressures to work outside the home. As live-in domestic work was replaced by "day work," making it increasingly possible for women to have jobs as domestics and maintain a family life, women faced the pressures of the double day, pressures that could have increased their support for the ideal of the full-time mother.[31]

In addition, the low pay and low status that typified most black women's jobs undermined the overall importance and meaning of paid work and, at the same time, enlarged the importance of their traditional domestic roles. It is clear that a woman's employment was not a detriment to her family's well-being and stability as some race leaders and black middle-class reformers argued. How else were children to be fed, clothed, housed, and educated if mothers did not contribute to the family income? Recognition by family and friends as a good mother, cook, and housekeeper gave many black women a sense of accomplishment and satisfaction not possible in their paid work lives. Testifying to the fruits of her labor, Orra Fisher (a former Washington domestic) remarked: "I worked hard to serve God and to see that my three girls didn't have to serve nobody else like I did except God. . . . My girl's in an office, and the baby—my son—over twenty years in the Army. I get full thinking about it. I had it bad, but look at them."[32]

Indeed, the importance of their labor market activities was that it provided them with the means to fulfill felt personal obligations to family members and needy non-kin. Paid work also provided Afro-American women and men with the ability, however minimal, to assist institutions (primarily the church) and organizations within the black community financially. Key elements of core black culture and religion were (and/are) sharing and giving; paid work allowed black women (and men) to fulfill sharing and giving obligations to those less fortunate.

A clean house, good meals, and well-mannered, responsible children were major sources of pride and status in the black

---

[31] Clark-Lewis, " 'This Work Had a End' " (n. 23 above), 204–7.
[32] Ibid., 212.

community. Women's ideas about their domestic activities, rather than their paid wage-earning activities, were a better indication of their self-perceptions. The elevated social status denied black domestic workers and laundresses by the larger society and even some members of the black community could be found by them in their families and neighborhoods. Not only was women's unpaid labor in their own homes a great source of self-worth and pride, it also provided them with a sense of autonomy and control absent for them in the labor market environment.

Indeed, one self-taught black female domestic aptly summarized the general attitude of many black women about issues of race and gender when she proclaimed: "I can handle black men; what I can't handle is this [racial] prejudice."[33] Her assertion speaks succinctly both to her ability to confront sexism within the black community and the challenges of confronting the racism of twentieth-century America.

Afro-American Studies
University of Maryland, College Park

---

[33] Gwaltney (n. 22 above), 170. Educated, middle-class black professional women generally addressed issues of race and gender equally, viewing discrimination based on either as detrimental to the well-being and advancement of black women. See, e.g., the published works of such Washington black educators as Anna J. Cooper, *A Voice from the South by a Black Woman of the South* (Xenia, Ohio: Aldine Printing House, 1892); Terrell (n. 19 above); and Nannie Helen Burroughs, "Black Women and Reform," *Crisis* 10 (August 1915): 187.

WOMANIST CONSCIOUSNESS:
MAGGIE LENA WALKER AND THE
INDEPENDENT ORDER OF SAINT LUKE

ELSA BARKLEY BROWN

In the first decades of the twentieth century Maggie Lena Walker repeatedly challenged her contemporaries to "make history as Negro women." Yet she and her colleagues in the Independent Order of Saint Luke, like most black and other women of color, have been virtually invisible in women's history and women's studies. Although recent books and articles have begun to redress this,[1] the years of exclusion have had an impact more significant than just the invisibility of black women, for the exclusion of black women has meant that the concepts, perspectives, methods, and pedagogies of

My appreciation is expressed to Mary Kelley, Deborah K. King, Lillian Jones, and the participants in the Community and Social Movements research group of the 1986 Summer Research Institute on Race and Gender, Center for Research on Women, Memphis State University, for their comments on an earlier draft of this article.

[1] The recent proliferation of works in black women's history and black women's studies makes a complete bibliographical reference prohibitive. For a sample of some of the growing literature on black women's consciousness, see Evelyn Brooks, "The Feminist Theology of the Black Baptist Church, 1880–1900," in *Class, Race, and Sex: The Dynamics of Control*, ed. Amy Swerdlow and Hanna Lessinger (Boston: G. K. Hall, 1983), 31–59; Hazel V. Carby, *Reconstructing Womanhood: The Emergence of the Afro-American Woman Novelist* (New York: Oxford University Press, 1987); Elizabeth Clark-Lewis, " 'This Work Had a' End': The Transition from Live-

This essay originally appeared in *Signs*, vol. 14, no. 3, Spring 1989.

women's history and women's studies have been developed without consideration of the experiences of black women. As a result many of the recent explorations in black women's history have attempted to place black women inside feminist perspectives which, by design, have omitted their experiences. Nowhere is this exclusion more apparent than in the process of defining women's issues and women's struggle. Because they have been created outside the experiences of black women, the definitions used in women's history and women's studies assume the separability of women's struggle and race struggle. Such arguments recognize the possibility that black women may have both women's concerns and race concerns, but they insist upon delimiting each. They allow, belatedly, black women to make history as women or as Negroes but not as "Negro women." What they fail to consider is that women's issues may be race issues, and race issues may be women's issues.[2]

Rosalyn Terborg-Penn, in "Discontented Black Feminists: Prelude and Postscript to the Passage of the Nineteenth Amendment," an essay on the 1920s black women's movement, of which Walker was a part, persuasively discusses the continuing discrimination in the U.S. women's movement and the focus of black women on "uplifting the downtrodden of the race or . . . representing people

---

In to Day Work," *Southern Women: The Intersection of Race, Class, and Gender* Working Paper no. 2 (Memphis, Tenn.: Memphis State University, Center for Research on Women, 1985); Patricia Hill Collins, "The Social Construction of Black Feminist Thought," *Signs: Journal of Women in Culture and Society* 14, no. 4 (Summer 1989), forthcoming; Cheryl Townsend Gilkes, " 'Together and in Harness': Women's Traditions in the Sanctified Church," *Signs* 10, no. 4 (Summer 1985): 678–99; Deborah Gray White, *Ar'n't I a Woman? Female Slaves in the Plantation South* (New York: Norton, 1985). Also note: *Sage: A Scholarly Journal on Black Women,* now in its fifth year, has published issues that focus on education, health, work, mother-daughter relationships, and creative artists.

[2] On a contemporary political level, this disassociation of gender concerns from race concerns was dramatically expressed in the 1985 United Nations Decade for Women conference held in Nairobi, Kenya, where the official U.S. delegation, including representatives of major white women's organizations but not one representative of a black women's organization, insisted upon not having the proceedings become bogged down with race and national issues such as apartheid so that it could concentrate on birth control and other "women's" issues. Delegates operating from such a perspective were unable to see African, Asian, and Latin American women who argued for discussion of national political issues as anything other than the tools of men, unfortunate victims unable to discern true women's and feminist struggles. For a discussion of the ways in which these issues were reflected in the Kenya conference, see Ros Young, "Report from Nairobi: The UN Decade for Women Forum," *Race and Class* 27, no. 2 (Autumn 1985): 67–71; and the entire issue of *African Women Rising*, vol. 2, no. 1 (Winter–Spring 1986).

of color throughout the world." Subsequently she argues for the "unique nature of feminism among Afro-American women." The editors of *Decades of Discontent: The Women's Movement, 1920–1940*, the 1983 collection on post–Nineteenth Amendment feminism, however, introduce Terborg-Penn's article by mistakenly concluding that these black women, disillusioned and frustrated by racism in the women's movement, turned from women's issues to race issues. Using a framework that does not conceive of "racial uplift, fighting segregation and mob violence" and "contending with poverty" as women's issues, Lois Scharf and Joan Jensen succumb to the tendency to assume that black women's lives can be neatly subdivided, that while we are both black and female, we occupy those roles sequentially, as if one cannot have the two simultaneously in one's consciousness of being.[3] Such a framework assumes a fragmentation of black women's existence that defies reality.

Scharf and Jensen's conclusion is certainly one that the white feminists of the 1920s and 1930s, who occupy most of the book, would have endorsed. When southern black women, denied the right to register to vote, sought help from the National Woman's Party, these white feminists rejected their petitions, arguing that this was a race concern and not a women's concern. Were they not, after all, being denied the vote not because of their sex but because of their race?[4]

Black women like Walker who devoted their energies to securing universal suffrage, including that of black men, are not widely recognized as female suffragists because they did not separate their struggle for the women's vote from their struggle for the black vote. This tendency to establish false dichotomies, precluding the pos-

[3] See Rosalyn Terborg-Penn, "Discontented Black Feminists: Prelude and Postscript to the Passage of the Nineteenth Amendment," 261–78; Lois Scharf and Joan M. Jensen, "Introduction," 9–10, both in *Decades of Discontent: The Women's Movement, 1920–1940*, ed. Lois Scharf and Joan M. Jensen (Westport, Conn.: Greenwood, 1983).

[4] Terborg-Penn, 267. A contemporary example of this type of dichotomous analysis is seen in much of the discussion of the feminization of poverty. Drawing commonalities between the experiences of black and white women, such discussions generally leave the impression that poverty was not a "feminine" problem before white women in increasing numbers were recognized as impoverished. Presumably, before that black women's poverty was considered a result of race; now it is more often considered a result of gender. Linda Burnham has effectively addressed the incompleteness of such analyses, suggesting that they ignore "class, race, and sex as *simultaneously* operative social factors" in black women's lives ("Has Poverty Been Feminized in Black America?" *Black Scholar* 16, no. 2 [March/April 1985]: 14–24 [emphasis mine]).

sibility that for many racism and sexism are experienced simultaneously, leads to discussions of liberation movements and women's movements as separate entities.

Quite clearly, what many women of color at the United Nations Decade for Women conference held in Nairobi, Kenya, in 1985, along with many other activists and scholars, have argued in recent years is the impossibility of separating the two and the necessity of understanding the convergence of women's issues, race/nationalist issues, and class issues in women's consciousnesses.[5] That understanding is in part hampered by the prevailing terminology: feminism places a priority on women; nationalism or race consciousness, a priority on race. It is the need to overcome the limitations of terminology that has led many black women to adopt the term "womanist." Both Alice Walker and Chikwenye Okonjo Ogunyemi have defined womanism as a consciousness that incorporates racial, cultural, sexual, national, economic, and political considerations.[6] As Ogunyemi explains, "black womanism is a philosophy" that concerns itself both with sexual equality in the black community and "with the world power structure that subjugates" both

[5] See, e.g., Parita Trivedi, "A Study of 'Sheroes,'" *Third World Book Review* 1, no. 2 (1984): 71–72; Angela Davis, *Women, Race, and Class* (New York: Random House, 1981); Nawal el Saadawi, *The Hidden Face of Eve: Women in the Arab World*, trans. Sherif Hetata (Boston: Beacon, 1982); Jenny Bourne, "Towards an Anti-Racist Feminism," *Race and Class* 25, no. 1 (Summer 1983): 1–22; Bonnie Thornton Dill, "Race, Class, and Gender: Prospects for an All-Inclusive Sisterhood," *Feminist Studies* 9, no. 1 (Spring 1983): 131–50; Evelyn Nakano Glenn, *Issei, Nisei, War Bride: Three Generations of Japanese American Women in Domestic Service* (Philadelphia: Temple University Press, 1986); Audre Lorde, *Sister/Outsider: Essays and Speeches* (Trumansburg, N.Y.: Crossing Press, 1984); Barbara Smith, "Some Home Truths on the Contemporary Black Feminist Movement," *Black Scholar* 16, no. 2 (March/April 1985): 4–13; Asoka Bandarage, *Toward International Feminism: The Dialectics of Sex, Race and Class* (London: Zed Press, forthcoming). For a typology of black women's multiple consciousness, see Deborah K. King, "Race, Class, and Gender Salience in Black Women's Feminist Consciousness" (paper presented at American Sociological Association annual meeting, Section on Racial and Ethnic Minorities, New York, August 1986).

[6] Alice Walker's oft-quoted definition is in *In Search of Our Mothers' Gardens: Womanist Prose* (New York: Harcourt, Brace, Jovanovich, 1983), xi–xii: "Womanist. 1. . . . Responsible. In Charge. *Serious*. 2. . . . Appreciates . . . women's strength. . . . Committed to survival and wholeness of entire people, male *and* female. Not a separatist, except periodically, for health. Traditionally universalist. . . . Traditionally capable. . . . 3. . . . Loves struggle. *Loves* the Folk. Loves herself. *Regardless*. 4. Womanist is to feminist as purple is to lavender." Cheryl Townsend Gilkes's annotation of Alice Walker's definition ("Women, Religion, and Tradition: A Womanist Perspective" [paper presented in workshop at Summer Research Institute on Race and Gender, Center for Research on Women, Memphis State University, June 1986]) has been particularly important to my understanding of this term.

blacks and women. "Its ideal is for black unity where every black person has a modicum of power and so can be a 'brother' or a 'sister' or a 'father' or a 'mother' to the other. . . . [I]ts aim is the dynamism of wholeness and self-healing."[7]

Walker's and Ogunyemi's terminology may be new, but their ideas are not. In fact, many black women at various points in history had a clear understanding that race issues and women's issues were inextricably linked, that one could not separate women's struggle from race struggle. It was because of this understanding that they refused to disconnect themselves from either movement. They instead insisted on inclusion in both movements in a manner that recognized the interconnection between race and sex, and they did so even if they had to battle their white sisters and their black brothers to achieve it. Certainly the lives and work of women such as Anna Julia Cooper, Mary Church Terrell, and Fannie Barrier Williams inform us of this. Cooper, an early Africanamerican womanist, addressed the holistic nature of the struggle in her address to the World's Congress of Representative Women:

Let woman's claim be as broad in the concrete as in the abstract. *We take our stand on the solidarity of humanity, the oneness of life,* and the unnaturalness and injustice of all special favoritisms, whether of sex, race, country, or condition. If one link of the chain be broken, the chain is broken. . . . We want, then, as toilers for the universal triumph of justice and human rights, to go to our homes from this Congress, demanding an entrance not through a gateway for ourselves, our race, our sex, or our sect, but a grand highway for humanity. The colored woman feels that woman's cause is one and universal; and that not till . . . race, color, sex, and condition are seen as the accidents, and not the substance of life; . . . not till then is woman's lesson taught and woman's cause won—not the white woman's, nor the black woman's, nor the red woman's, but the cause of every man and of every woman who has writhed silently under a mighty wrong. *Woman's wrongs are thus indissolubly linked with all undefended woe, and the acquirement of her "rights" will mean the final triumph of all right over might,* the supremacy of the moral forces of reason, and justice, and love in the government of the nations of earth.[8]

[7] Chikwenye Okonjo Ogunyemi, "Womanism: The Dynamics of the Contemporary Black Female Novel in English," *Signs* 11, no. 1 (Autumn 1985): 63–80.

[8] May Wright Sewall, ed., *World's Congress of Representative Women* (Chicago, 1893), 715, quoted in Bert James Loewenberg and Ruth Bogin, eds., *Black Women in Nineteenth-Century American Life: Their Words, Their Thoughts, Their Feelings*

One of those who most clearly articulated womanist consciousness was Maggie Lena Walker. Walker (1867–1934) was born and
educated in Richmond, Virginia, graduating from Colored Normal
School in 1883. During her school years she assisted her widowed
mother in her work as a washerwoman and cared for her younger
brother. Following graduation she taught in the city's public schools
and took courses in accounting and sales. Required to stop teaching
when she married Armstead Walker, a contractor, her coursework
had well prepared her to join several other black women in founding
an insurance company, the Woman's Union. Meanwhile, Walker,
who had joined the Independent Order of Saint Luke at the age of
fourteen, rose through the ranks to hold several important positions
in the order and, in 1895, to organize the juvenile branch of the
order. In addition to her Saint Luke activities, Walker was a founder
or leading supporter of the Richmond Council of Colored Women,
the Virginia State Federation of Colored Women, the National Association of Wage Earners, the International Council of Women of
the Darker Races, the National Training School for Girls, and the
Virginia Industrial School for Colored Girls. She also helped direct
the National Association for the Advancement of Colored People,
the Richmond Urban League, and the Negro Organization Society
of Virginia.[9]

(University Park: Pennsylvania State University Press, 1976), 330–31 (emphasis
mine). See also Anna Julia Cooper, *A Voice from the South: By a Black Woman of
the South* (Xenia, Ohio: Aldine, 1892), esp. "Part First."

[9] Although there exists no scholarly biography of Walker, information is available
in several sources. See Wendell P. Dabney, *Maggie L. Walker and The I.O. of Saint
Luke: The Woman and Her Work* (Cincinnati: Dabney, 1927); Sadie Iola Daniel,
Women Builders (Washington, D.C.: Associated Publishers, 1931), 28–52; Sadie
Daniel St. Clair, "Maggie Lena Walker," in *Notable American Women, 1607–1960*
(Cambridge, Mass.: Harvard University Press, Belknap, 1971), 530–31; Elsa Barkley
Brown, "Maggie Lena Walker and the Saint Luke Women" (paper presented at the
Association for the Study of Afro-American Life and History 69th annual conference,
Washington, D.C., October 1984), and " 'Not Alone to Build This Pile of Brick': The
Role of Women in the Richmond, Virginia, Black Community, 1890–1930" (paper
presented at the Midcontinental and North Central American Studies Association
joint conference, University of Iowa, April 1983); Lily Hammond, *In the Vanguard
of a Race* (New York: Council of Women for Home Missions and Missionary Education Movement of the United States and Canada, 1922), 108–18; A. B. Caldwell,
ed., *Virginia Edition*, vol. 5 of *History of the American Negro* (Atlanta: A. B. Caldwell, 1921), 9–11; Rayford Logan, "Maggie Lena Walker," in *Dictionary of American
Negro Biography*, ed. Rayford W. Logan and Michael R. Winston (New York: Norton,
1982), 626–27; Gertrude W. Marlowe, "Maggie Lena Walker: African-American
Women, Business, and Community Development" (paper presented at Berkshire
Conference on the History of Women, Wellesley, Mass., June 21, 1987); Kim Q. Boyd,
" 'An Actress Born, a Diplomat Bred'; Maggie L. Walker, Race Woman" (M.A. thesis,
Howard University, 1987); Sallie Chandler, "Maggie Lena Walker (1867–1934): An

Walker is probably best known today as the first woman bank president in the United States. She founded the Saint Luke Penny Savings Bank in Richmond, Virginia, in 1903. Before her death in 1934 she oversaw the reorganization of this financial institution as the present-day Consolidated Bank and Trust Company, the oldest continuously existing black-owned and black-run bank in the country. The bank, like most of Walker's activities, was the outgrowth of the Independent Order of Saint Luke, which she served as Right Worthy Grand Secretary for thirty-five years.

The Independent Order of Saint Luke was one of the larger and more successful of the many thousands of mutual benefit societies that have developed throughout Africanamerican communities since the eighteenth century. These societies combined insurance functions with economic development and social and political activities. As such they were important loci of community self-help and racial solidarity. Unlike the Knights of Pythias and its female auxiliary, the Courts of Calanthe, societies like the Independent Order of Saint Luke had a nonexclusionary membership policy; any man, woman, or child could join. Thus men and women from all occupational segments, professional/managerial, entrepreneurial, and working-class, came together in the order. The Independent Order of Saint Luke was a mass-based organization that played a key role in the political, economic, and social development of its members and of the community as a whole.[10]

Founded in Maryland in 1867 by Mary Prout, the Independent Order of Saint Luke began as a women's sickness and death mutual benefit association. By the 1880s it had admitted men and had expanded to New York and Virginia. At the 1899 annual meeting William M. T. Forrester, who had served as Grand Secretary since 1869, refused to accept reappointment, stating that the order was in decline, having only 1,080 members in fifty-seven councils, $31.61 in the treasury, and $400.00 in outstanding debts. Maggie Lena

---

Abstract of Her Life and Activities," 1975 Oral History Files, Virginia Union University Library, Richmond, Va., 1975; Maggie Lena Walker Papers, Maggie L. Walker National Historic Site, Richmond, Va. (hereafter cited as MLW Papers). Fortunately, much of Walker's history will soon be available; the Maggie L. Walker Biography Project, funded by the National Park Service under the direction of Gertrude W. Marlowe, anthropology department, Howard University, is completing a full-scale biography of Walker.

[10] Noting the mass base of mutual benefit societies such as the Independent Order of Saint Luke, August Meier has suggested that the activities of these organizations "reflect the thinking of the inarticulate majority better than any other organizations or the statement of editors and other publicists" (*Negro Thought in America, 1880–1915: Racial Ideologies in the Age of Booker T. Washington* [Ann Arbor: University of Michigan Press, 1963], 130).

Walker took over the duties of Grand Worthy Secretary at one-third of the position's previous salary.[11]

According to Walker, her "first work was to draw around me *women*."[12] In fact, after the executive board elections in 1901, six of the nine members were women: Walker, Patsie K. Anderson, Frances Cox, Abigail Dawley, Lillian H. Payne, and Ella O. Waller.[13] Under their leadership the order and its affiliates flourished. The order's ventures included a juvenile department, an educational loan fund for young people, a department store, and a weekly newspaper. Growing to include over 100,000 members in 2,010 councils and circles in twenty-eight states, the order demonstrated a special commitment to expanding the economic opportunities within the black community, especially those for women.

It is important to take into account Walker's acknowledgment of her female colleagues. Most of what we know about the Order of Saint Luke highlights Walker because she was the leader and spokeswoman and therefore the most visible figure. She was able, however, to function in that role and to accomplish all that she did not merely because of her own strengths and skills, considerable though they were, but also because she operated from the strength of the Saint Luke collective as a whole and from the special strengths and talents of the inner core of the Saint Luke women in particular. Deborah Gray White, in her work on women during slavery, underscores the importance of black women's networks in an earlier time period: "Strength had to be cultivated. It came no more naturally to them than to anyone. . . . If they seemed exceptionally strong it was partly because they often functioned in groups and derived strength from numbers. . . . [T]hey inevitably developed some appreciation of one another's skills and talents. This intimacy enabled them to establish the criteria with which to rank and order themselves." It was this same kind of sisterhood that was Walker's base, her support, her strength, and her source of wisdom and direction.[14]

---

[11] *50th Anniversary—Golden Jubilee Historical Report of the R. W. G. Council I. O. St. Luke, 1867–1917* (Richmond, Va.: Everett Waddey, 1917), 5–6, 20 (hereafter cited as *50th Anniversary*).

[12] Maggie L. Walker, "Diary," March 6, 1928, MLW Papers. My thanks to Sylvester Putman, superintendent, Richmond National Battlefield Park, and Celia Jackson Suggs, site historian, Maggie L. Walker National Historic Site, for facilitating my access to these unprocessed papers.

[13] *50th Anniversary*, 26.

[14] White (n. 1 above), 119–41. Although I use the term "sisterhood" here to refer to this female network, sisterhood for black women, including M. L. Walker, meant (and means) not only this special bond among black women but also the ties amongst all kin/community.

The women of Saint Luke expanded the role of women in the community to the political sphere through their leadership in the 1904 streetcar boycott and through the *St. Luke Herald's* pronouncements against segregation, lynching, and lack of equal educational opportunities for black children. Walker spearheaded the local struggle for women's suffrage and the voter registration campaigns after the passage of the Nineteenth Amendment. In the 1920 elections in Richmond, fully 80 percent of the eligible black voters were women. The increased black political strength represented by the female voters gave incentive to the growing movement for independent black political action and led to the formation of the Virginia Lily-Black Republican Party. Walker ran on this ticket for state superintendent of public instruction in 1921.[15] Thus Walker and many other of the Saint Luke women were role models for other black women in their community activities as well as their occupations.

Undergirding all of their work was a belief in the possibilities inherent in the collective struggle of black women in particular and of the black community in general. Walker argued that the only way in which black women would be able "to avoid the traps and snares of life" would be to "band themselves together, organize, . . . put their mites together, put their hands and their brains together and make work and business for themselves."[16]

The idea of collective economic development was not a new idea for these women, many of whom were instrumental in estab-

---

[15] Of 260,000 black Virginians over the age of twenty-one in 1920, less than 20,000 were eligible to vote in that year's elections. Poll taxes and literacy tests disfranchised many; white Democratic election officials turned many others away from the polls; still others had given up their efforts to vote, realizing that even if they successfully cast their ballots, they were playing in "a political game which they stood no chance of winning" (Andrew Buni, *The Negro in Virginia Politics, 1902–1965* [Charlottesville: University of Virginia Press, 1967], 77–88). The high proportion of female voters resulted from whites' successful efforts to disfranchise the majority of black male voters, as well as the enthusiasm of women to exercise this new right; see, e.g., *Richmond News-Leader* (August–October 1920); *Richmond Times-Dispatch* (September–October, 1920). Rosalyn Terborg-Penn (n. 3 above, 275) reports a similarly high percentage of black female voters in 1920s Baltimore. In Richmond, however, black women soon found themselves faced with the same obstacles to political rights as confronted black men. Independent black political parties developed in several southern states where the lily-white Republican faction had successfully purged blacks from leadership positions in that party; see, e.g., George C. Wright, "Black Political Insurgency in Louisville, Kentucky: The Lincoln Independent Party of 1921," *Journal of Negro History* 68 (Winter 1983): 8–23.

[16] M. L. Walker, "Addresses," 1909, MLW Papers, cited in Celia Jackson Suggs, "Maggie Lena Walker," TRUTH: *Newsletter of the Association of Black Women Historians* 7 (Fall 1985): 6.

lishing the Woman's Union, a female insurance company founded in 1898. Its motto was The Hand That Rocks the Cradle Rules the World.[17] But unlike nineteenth-century white women's rendering of that expression to signify the limitation of woman's influence to that which she had by virtue of rearing her sons, the idea as these women conceived it transcended the separation of private and public spheres and spoke to the idea that women, while not abandoning their roles as wives and mothers, could also move into economic and political activities in ways that would support rather than conflict with family and community. Women did not have to choose between the two spheres; in fact, they necessarily had to occupy both. Indeed, these women's use of this phrase speaks to their understanding of the totality of the task that lay ahead of them as black women. It negates, for black women at least, the public/private dichotomy.

Saint Luke women built on tradition. A well-organized set of institutions maintained community in Richmond: mutual benefit societies, interwoven with extended families and churches, built a network of supportive relations.[18] The families, churches, and societies were all based on similar ideas of collective consciousness and collective responsibility. Thus, they served to extend and reaffirm notions of family throughout the black community. Not only in their houses but also in their meeting halls and places of worship, they were brothers and sisters caring for each other. The institutionalization of this notion of family cemented the community. Community/family members recognized that this had to be maintained from generation to generation; this was in part the function of the juvenile branches of the mutual benefit associations. The statement of purpose of the Children's Rosebud Fountains, Grand Fountain United Order of True Reformers, clearly articulated this:

> Teaching them . . . to assist each other in sickness, sorrow and afflictions and in the struggles of life; teaching them that one's happiness greatly depends upon the others. . . . Teach them to live united. . . . The children of different families will know how to . . . talk, plot and plan for one another's peace and happiness in the journey of life.

[17] Four of the women elected to the 1901 Saint Luke executive board were board members of the Woman's Union, which had offices in Saint Luke's Hall; see advertisements in *Richmond Planet* (August 1898–January 3, 1903).

[18] Some of the societies had only women members, including some that were exclusively for the mutual assistance of single mothers. For an excellent discussion of the ties among the societies, families, and churches in Richmond, see Peter J. Rachleff, *Black Labor in the South: Richmond, Virginia, 1865–1890* (Philadelphia: Temple University Press, 1984).

> Teach them to . . . bear each other's burdens . . . to so bind
> and tie their love and affections together that one's sorrow
> may be the other's sorrow, one's distress be the other's dis-
> tress, one's penny the other's penny.[19]

Through the Penny Savings Bank the Saint Luke women were able
to affirm and cement the existing mutual assistance network among
black women and within the black community by providing an
institutionalized structure for these activities. The bank recognized
the meager resources of the black community, particularly black
women. In fact, its establishment as a *penny* savings bank is an
indication of that. Many of its earliest and strongest supporters were
washerwomen, one of whom was Maggie Walker's mother. And the
bank continued throughout Walker's leadership to exercise a special
commitment to "the small depositor."[20]

In her efforts Walker, like the other Saint Luke women, was
guided by a clearly understood and shared perspective concerning
the relationship of black women to black men, to the black community, and to the larger society. This was a perspective that acknowledged individual powerlessness in the face of racism and
sexism and that argued that black women, because of their condition
and status, had a right—indeed, according to Walker, a special duty
and incentive—to organize. She argued, "Who is so helpless as the
Negro woman? Who is so circumscribed and hemmed in, in the
race of life, in the struggle for bread, meat and clothing as the Negro
woman?"[21]

In addition, her perspective contended that organizational activity and the resultant expanded opportunities for black women

[19] W. P. Burrell and D. E. Johnson, Sr., *Twenty-Five Years History of the Grand
Fountain of the United Order of True Reformers, 1881–1905* (Richmond, Va.: Grand
Fountain, United Order of True Reformers, 1909), 76–77.

[20] Saint Luke Penny Savings Bank records: Receipts and Disbursements, 1903–
1909; Minutes, Executive Committee, 1913; Cashier's Correspondence Book, 1913;
Minutes, Board of Trustees, 1913–1915, Consolidated Bank and Trust Company,
Richmond, Va.; *Cleveland Plain Dealer* (June 28, 1914), in Peabody Clipping File,
Collis P. Huntington Library, Hampton Institute, Hampton, Va. (hereafter cited as
Peabody Clipping File), no. 88, vol. 1. See also Works Progress Administration, *The
Negro in Virginia* (New York: Hastings House, 1940), 299.

[21] This analysis owes much to Cheryl Townsend Gilkes's work on black women,
particularly her "Black Women's Work as Deviance: Social Sources of Racial Antagonism within Contemporary Feminism," working paper no. 66 (Wellesley, Mass.:
Wellesley College Center for Research on Women, 1979), and " 'Holding Back the
Ocean with a Broom': Black Women and Community Work," in *The Black Woman*,
ed. LaFrances Rodgers-Rose (Beverly Hills, Calif.: Sage, 1980). Excerpt from speech
given by M. L. Walker at 1901 annual Saint Luke convention, *50th Anniversary* (n.
11 above), 23.

were not detrimental to the home, the community, black men, or the race. Furthermore, she insisted that organization and expansion of women's roles economically and politically were essential ingredients without which the community, the race, and even black men could not achieve their full potential. The way in which Walker described black women's relationship to society, combined with the collective activities in which she engaged, give us some insight into her understanding of the relationship between women's struggle and race struggle.

Walker was determined to expand opportunities for black women. In fulfilling this aim she challenged not only the larger society's notions of the proper place of blacks but also those in her community who held a limited notion of women's proper role. Particularly in light of the increasing necessity to defend the integrity and morality of the race, a "great number of men" and women in Virginia and elsewhere believed that women's clubs, movements "looking to the final exercise of suffrage by women," and organizations of black professional and business women would lead to "the decadence of home life."[22] Women involved in these activities were often regarded as "pullbacks, rather than home builders."[23] Maggie Walker countered these arguments, stressing the need for women's organizations, saying, "Men should not be so pessimistic and down on women's clubs. They don't seek to destroy the home or disgrace the race."[24] In fact, the Richmond Council of Colored Women, of

[22] The prevailing turn-of-the-century stereotype of black women emphasized promiscuity and immorality; these ideas were given prominence in a number of publications, including newspapers, periodicals, philanthropic foundation reports, and popular literature. The attacks by various segments of the white community on the morality of black women and the race at the turn of the century are discussed in Beverly Guy-Sheftall, " 'Daughters of Sorrow': Attitudes toward Black Women, 1880–1920" (Ph.D. diss., Emory University, 1984), 62–86; Darlene Clark Hine, "Lifting the Veil, Shattering the Silence: Black Women's History in Slavery and Freedom," in *The State of Afro-American History: Past, Present, and Future*, ed. Darlene Clark Hine (Baton Rouge: Louisiana State University Press, 1986), 223–49, esp. 234–38; Willi Coleman, "Black Women and Segregated Public Transportation: Ninety Years of Resistance," TRUTH: *Newsletter of the Association of Black Women Historians* 8, no. 2 (1986): 3–10, esp. 7–8; and Paula Giddings, *When and Where I Enter: The Impact of Black Women on Race and Sex in America* (New York: William Morrow, 1984), 82–86. Maggie Walker called attention to these verbal attacks on Negro womanhood in her speech, "Beniah's Valour: An Address for Men Only," Saint Luke Hall, March 1, 1906, MLW Papers (n. 9 above). It was in part the desire to defend black women and uplift the race that initiated the formation of the National Federation of Black Women's Clubs.

[23] Charles F. McLaurin, "State Federation of Colored Women" (n.p., November 10, 1908), Peabody Clipping File, no. 231, vol. 1.

[24] Chandler (n. 9 above), 10–11.

which she was founder and president, and many other women's organizations worked to elevate the entire black community, and this, she believed, was the proper province of women.

In 1908 two Richmond men, Daniel Webster Davis and Giles Jackson, published *The Industrial History of the Negro Race of the United States,* which became a textbook for black children throughout the state. The chapter on women acknowledged the economic and social achievements of black women but concluded that "the Negro Race Needs Housekeepers . . . wives who stay at home, being supported by their husbands, and then they can spend time in the training of their children."[25] Maggie Walker responded practically to those who held such ideas: "The bold fact remains that there are more women in the world than men; . . . if each and every woman in the land was allotted a man to marry her, work for her, support her, and keep her at home, there would still be an army of women left uncared for, unprovided for, and who would be compelled to fight life's battles alone, and without the companionship of man."[26] Even regarding those women who did marry, she contended, "The old doctrine that a man marries a woman to support her is pretty nearly thread-bare to-day." Only a few black men were able to fully support their families on their earnings alone. Thus many married women worked, "not for name, not for glory and honor—but for bread, and for [their] babies."[27]

The reality was that black women who did go to work outside the home found themselves in a helpless position. "How many occupations have Negro Women?" asked Walker. "Let us count them: Negro women are domestic menials, teachers and church builders." And even the first two of these, she feared, were in danger. As Walker perceived it, the expansion of opportunities for white women did not mean a corresponding expansion for black women; instead, this trend might actually lead to an even greater limitation on the economic possibilities for black women. She pointed to the fact that white women's entry into the tobacco factories of the city had "dri-

[25] Daniel Webster Davis and Giles Jackson, *The Industrial History of the Negro Race of the United States* (Richmond: Virginia Press, 1908), 133. Similar attitudes expressed in the *Virginia Baptist* in 1894 had aroused the ire of the leading figures in the national women's club movement. The *Baptist* had been particularly concerned that women, in exceeding their proper place in the church, were losing their "womanliness" and that "the exercise of the right of suffrage would be a deplorable climax to these transgressions"; see discussion of the *Baptist* in *Women's Era* 1, no. 6 (September 1894): 8.

[26] M. L. Walker, "Speech to Federation of Colored Women's Clubs," Hampton, Va., July 14, 1912, MLW Papers (n. 9 above).

[27] M. L. Walker, "Speech to the Negro Young People's Christian and Educational Congress," Convention Hall, Washington, D.C., August 5, 1906, MLW Papers.

ven the Negro woman out," and she, like many of her sisters throughout the country, feared that a similar trend was beginning even in domestic work.[28]

In fact, these economic realities led members of the Order of Saint Luke to discuss the development of manufacturing operations as a means of giving employment and therefore "a chance in the race of life" to "the young Negro woman."[29] In 1902 Walker described herself as "consumed with the desire to hear the whistle on our factory and see our women by the hundreds coming to work."[30] It was this same concern for the economic status of black women that led Walker and other Saint Luke women to affiliate with the National Association of Wage Earners (NAWE), a women's organization that sought to pool the energies and resources of housewives, professionals, and managerial, domestic, and industrial workers to protect and expand the economic position of black women. The NAWE argued that it was vital that all black women be able to support themselves.[31] Drawing on traditional stereotypes in the same breath with which she defied them, Walker contended that it was in the self-interest of black men to unite themselves with these efforts to secure decent employment for black women: "Every dollar a woman makes, some man gets the direct benefit of same. Every woman was by Divine Providence created for some man; not for some man to marry, take home and support, but for the purpose of using her powers, ability, health and strength, to forward the financial . . . success of the partnership into which she may go, if she will. . . . [W]hat stronger combination could ever God make—than the partnership of a business man and a business woman."[32]

[28] Quotations are from M. L. Walker, "Speech to the Federation of Colored Women's Clubs." These ideas, however, were a central theme in Walker's speeches and were repeated throughout the years. See, e.g., "Speech to the Negro Young People's Christian and Educational Congress" and "Beniah's Valour: An Address for Men Only" (n. 22 above). See also the St. Luke Herald's first editorial, "Our Mission" (March 29, 1902), reprinted in 50th Anniversary (n. 11 above), 26.
[29] Excerpt from speech given by M. L. Walker at 1901 annual Saint Luke convention, 50th Anniversary, 23.
[30] See "Our Mission" (n. 28 above).
[31] The NAWE, having as its motto "Support Thyself—Work," aimed at making "the colored woman a factor in the labor world." Much of its work was premised upon the belief that white women were developing an interest in domestic science and other "Negro occupations" to such an extent that the prospects for work for young black women were becoming seriously endangered. They believed also that when white women entered the fields of housework, cooking, and the like, these jobs would be classified as professions. It therefore was necessary for black women to become professionally trained in even domestic work in order to compete. Container 308, Nannie Helen Burroughs Papers, Manuscript Division, Library of Congress.
[32] M. L. Walker, "Speech to Federation of Colored Women's Clubs" (n. 26 above).

By implication, whatever black women as a whole were able to achieve would directly benefit black men. In Walker's analysis family is a reciprocal metaphor for community: family is community and community is family. But this is more than rhetorical style. Her discussions of relationship networks suggest that the entire community was one's family. Thus Walker's references to husbands and wives reflected equally her understandings of male/female relationships in the community as a whole and of those relationships within the household. Just as all family members' resources were needed for the family to be well and strong, so they were needed for a healthy community/family.

In the process of developing means of expanding economic opportunities in the community, however, Walker and the Saint Luke women also confronted white Richmond's notions of the proper place of blacks. While whites found a bank headed by a "Negress" an interesting curiosity,[33] they were less receptive to other business enterprises. In 1905 twenty-two black women from the Independent Order of Saint Luke collectively formed a department store aimed at providing quality goods at more affordable prices than those available in stores outside the black community, as well as a place where black women could earn a living and get a business education. The Saint Luke Emporium employed fifteen women as salesclerks. While this may seem an insignificant number in comparison to the thousands of black women working outside the home, in the context of the occupational structure of Richmond these women constituted a significant percentage of the white-collar and skilled working-class women in the community. In 1900 less than 1 percent of the employed black women in the city were either clerical or skilled workers. That number had quadrupled by 1910, when 222 of the more than 13,000 employed black women listed their occupations as typists, stenographers, bookkeepers, salesclerks, and the like. However, by 1930 there had been a reduction in the numbers of black women employed in clerical and sales positions. This underscores the fact that black secretaries and clerks were entirely dependent on the financial stability of black businesses and in this regard the Independent Order of Saint Luke was especially important. With its fifty-five clerks in the home office, over one-third of the black female clerical workers in Richmond in the 1920s worked for this order. The quality of the work experience was significantly better for these women as compared to those em-

[33] See, e.g., "Negress Banker Says If Men Can, Women Can," *Columbus Journal* (September 16, 1909), Peabody Clipping File (n. 20 above), no. 231, vol. 7; see also Chandler (n. 9 above), 32.

ployed as laborers in the tobacco factories or as servants in private homes. They worked in healthier, less stressful environments and, being employed by blacks, they also escaped the racism prevalent in most black women's workplaces. Additionally, the salaries of these clerical workers were often better than those paid even to black professional women, that is, teachers. While one teacher, Ethel Thompson Overby, was receiving eighteen dollars a month as a teacher and working her way up to the top of the scale at forty dollars, a number of black women were finding good working conditions and a fifty-dollar-per-month paycheck as clerks in the office of the Independent Order of Saint Luke. Nevertheless, black women in Richmond, as elsewhere, overwhelmingly remained employed in domestic service in the years 1890–1930.[34]

Located on East Broad Street, Richmond's main business thoroughfare, the Saint Luke Emporium met stiff opposition from white merchants. When the intention to establish the department store was first announced, attempts were made to buy the property at a price several thousand dollars higher than that which the Order of Saint Luke had originally paid. When that did not succeed, an offer of ten thousand dollars cash was made to the order if it would not start the emporium. Once it opened, efforts were made to hinder the store's operations. A white Retail Dealers' Association was formed for the purpose of crushing this business as well as other "Negro merchants who are objectionable . . . because they compete with and get a few dollars which would otherwise go to the white merchant." Notices were sent to wholesale merchants in the city warning them not to sell to the emporium at the risk of losing all business from any of the white merchants. Letters were also sent to wholesale houses in New York City with the same warning. These letters charged that the emporium was underselling the white merchants of Richmond. Clearly, then, the white businessmen of Rich-

---

[34] In 1900, 83.8 percent of employed black women worked in domestic and personal service; in 1930, 76.5 percent. U.S. Bureau of the Census, *Twelfth Census of the United States Taken in the Year 1900, Population Part 1* (Washington, D.C.: Census Office, 1901), *Thirteenth Census of the United States Taken in the Year 1910*, vol. 4: *Population 1910–Occupation Statistics* (Washington, D.C.: Government Printing Office, 1914), 595, and *Fifteenth Census of the United States: Population*, vol. 4: *Occupations, by States* (Washington, D.C.: Government Printing Office, 1933); Benjamin Brawley, *Negro Builders and Heroes* (Chapel Hill: University of North Carolina Press, 1937), 267–72; U.S. Bureau of the Census, *Fourteenth Census of the United States Taken in the Year 1920*, vol. 4: *Population 1920–Occupations* (Washington, D.C.: Government Printing Office, 1923); Ethel Thompson Overby, *"It's Better to Light a Candle than to Curse the Darkness": The Autobiographical Notes of Ethel Thompson Overby* (1975), copy in Virginia Historical Society, Richmond.

mond found the emporium and these black women a threat; if it was successful, the store could lead to a surge of black merchants competing with white merchants and thus decrease the black patronage at white stores. The white merchants' efforts were ultimately successful: the obstacles they put in the way of the emporium, in addition to the lack of full support from the black community itself, resulted in the department store's going out of business seven years after its founding.[35] Though its existence was short-lived and its demise mirrors many of the problems that black businesses faced from both within and without their community, the effort demonstrated the commitment of the Order of Saint Luke to provide needed services for the community and needed opportunities for black women.

Maggie Walker's appeals for support of the emporium show quite clearly the way in which her notions of race, of womanhood, and of community fused. Approximately one year after the opening of the emporium, Walker called for a mass gathering of men in the community to talk, in part, about support for the business. Her speech, "Beniah's Valour; An Address for Men Only," opened with an assessment of white businessmen's and officials' continuing oppression of the black community. In her fine rhetorical style she queried her audience. "Hasn't it crept into your minds that we are being more and more oppressed each day that we live? Hasn't it yet come to you, that we are being oppressed by the passage of laws which not only have for their object the degradation of Negro manhood and Negro womanhood, but also the destruction of all kinds of Negro enterprises?" Then, drawing upon the biblical allegory of Beniah and the lion, she warned, "There is a lion terrorizing us, preying upon us, and upon every business effort which we put forth. The name of this insatiable lion is PREJUDICE. . . . The white press, the white pulpit, the white business associations, the legislature— all . . . the lion with whom we contend daily . . . in Broad Street, Main Street and in every business street of Richmond. Even now . . . that lion is seeking some new plan of attack."[36]

Thus, she contended, the vital question facing their community was how to kill the lion. And in her analysis, "the only way to kill

[35] The business, which opened the Monday before Easter, 1905, officially closed in January 1912. Information on the emporium is found in *50th Anniversary* (n. 11 above), 55, 76–77; *New York Age*, March 16, 1905, Peabody Clipping File, no. 88, vol. 1, "Maggie Lena Walker Scrapbook," MLW Papers (n. 9 above); Daniels (n. 9 above), 41. The most detailed description of the opposition to the emporium is in M. L. Walker, "Beniah's Valour: An Address for Men Only" (n. 22 above), quote is from this speech.

[36] M. L. Walker, "Beniah's Valour: An Address for Men Only."

the Lion is to stop feeding it." The irony was that the black community drained itself of resources, money, influence, and patronage to feed its predator.[37] As she had many times previously, Walker questioned the fact that while the white community oppressed the black, "the Negro . . . carries to their bank every dollar he can get his hands upon and then goes back the next day, borrows and then pays the white man to lend him his own money."[38] So, too, black people patronized stores and other businesses in which white women were, in increasing numbers, being hired as salesclerks and secretaries while black women were increasingly without employment and the black community as a whole was losing resources, skills, and finances.[39] Walker considered such behavior racially destructive and believed it necessary to break those ties that kept "the Negro . . . so wedded to those who oppress him."[40] The drain on the resources of the black community could be halted by a concentration on the development of a self-sufficient black community. But to achieve this would require the talents of the entire community/ family. It was therefore essential that black women's work in the community be "something more tangible than elegant papers, beautifully framed resolutions and pretty speeches." Rather, "the exercising of every talent that God had given them" was required in the effort to "raise . . . the race to higher planes of living."[41]

The Saint Luke women were part of the Negro Independence Movement that captured a large segment of Richmond society at the turn of the century. Disillusioned by the increasing prejudice and discrimination in this period, which one historian has described as the nadir in U.S. race relations, black residents of Richmond nevertheless held on to their belief in a community that they could collectively sustain.[42] As they witnessed a steady erosion of their civil and political rights, however, they were aware that there was much operating against them. In Richmond, as elsewhere, a system of race and class oppression including segregation, disfranchisement, relegation to the lowest rungs of the occupational strata, and enforcement of racial subordination through intimidation was fully in place by the early twentieth century. In Richmond between 1885 and 1915 all blacks were removed from the city council; the only

[37] Ibid.
[38] Chandler (n. 9 above), 30.
[39] M. L. Walker, "Beniah's Valour: An Address for Men Only."
[40] Chandler, 30.
[41] *New York Age* (June 22, 1909), Peabody Clipping File, no. 231, vol. 1.
[42] Rayford W. Logan, *The Betrayal of the Negro from Rutherford B. Hayes to Woodrow Wilson* (New York: Collier, 1965; originally published in 1954 as *The Negro in American Life and Thought: The Nadir*).

predominantly black political district, Jackson Ward, was gerry-mandered out of existence; the state constitutional convention dis-franchised the majority of black Virginians; first the railroads and streetcars, and later the jails, juries, and neighborhoods were seg-regated; black principals were removed from the public schools and the right of blacks to teach was questioned; the state legislature decided to substitute white for black control of Virginia Normal and College and to strike "and College" from both name and function; and numerous other restrictions were imposed. As attorney J. Thomas Hewin noted, he and his fellow black Richmonders oc-cupied "a peculiar position in the body politics":

> He [the Negro] is not wanted in politics, because his pres-ence in official positions renders him obnoxious to his former masters and their descendants. He is not wanted in the in-dustrial world as a trained handicraftsman, because he would be brought into competition with his white brother. He is not wanted in city positions, because positions of that kind are always saved for the wardheeling politicians. He is not wanted in State and Federal offices, because there is an unwritten law that a Negro shall not hold an office. He is not wanted on the Bench as a judge, because he would have to pass upon the white man's case also. Nor is he wanted on public con-veyances, because here his presence is obnoxious to white people.[43]

Assessing the climate of the surrounding society in 1904, John Mitchell, Jr., editor of the *Richmond Planet*, concluded, "This is the beginning of the age of conservatism."[44] The growing movement within the community for racial self-determination urged blacks to depend upon themselves and their community rather than upon whites: to depend upon their own inner strengths, to build their own institutions, and thereby to mitigate the ways in which their lives were determined by the white forces arrayed against them. Race pride, self-help, racial cooperation, and economic develop-ment were central to their thinking about their community and to the ways in which they went about building their own internal

---

[43] J. Thomas Hewin, "Is the Criminal Negro Justly Dealt with in the Courts of the South?" in *Twentieth Century Negro Literature, or a Cyclopedia of Thought on the Vital Topics Relating to the American Negro*, ed. D. W. Culp (Toronto: J. L. Nichols, 1902), 110–11.

[44] *Richmond Planet* (April 30, 1904).

support system in order to be better able to struggle within the majority system.

The Saint Luke women argued that the development of the community could not be achieved by men alone, or by men on behalf of women. Only a strong and unified community made up of both women and men could wield the power necessary to allow black people to shape their own lives. Therefore, only when women were able to exercise their full strength would the community be at its full strength, they argued. Only when the community was at its full strength would they be able to create their own conditions, conditions that would allow men as well as women to move out of their structural isolation at the bottom of the labor market and to overcome their political impotence in the larger society. The Saint Luke women argued that it was therefore in the self-interest of black men and of the community as a whole to support expanded opportunities for women.

Their arguments redefined not only the roles of women but also the roles and notions of manhood. A strong "race man" traditionally meant one who stood up fearlessly in defense of the race. In her "Address for Men" Walker argued that one could not defend the race unless one defended black women. Appealing to black men's notions of themselves as the protectors of black womanhood, she asked on behalf of all her sisters for their "FRIENDSHIP, . . . LOVE, . . . SYMPATHY, . . . PROTECTION, and . . . ADVICE": "I am asking you, men of Richmond, . . . to record [yourselves] as . . . the strong race men of our city. . . . I am asking each man in this audience to go forth from this building, determined to do valiant deeds for the Negro Women of Richmond."[45] And how might they offer their friendship, love, and protection; how might they do valiant deeds for Negro womanhood? By supporting the efforts of black women to exercise every talent;[46] by "let[ting] woman choose her own vocation, just as man does his";[47] by supporting the efforts then underway to provide increased opportunities—economic, political, and social—for black women.[48] Once again she drew upon tradi-

---

[45] M. L. Walker, "Beniah's Valour: An Address for Men Only" (n. 22 above).

[46] New York Age (June 22, 1909), Peabody Clipping File, no. 231, vol. 1.

[47] M. L. Walker, "Speech to the Federation of Colored Women's Clubs" (n. 26 above).

[48] M. L. Walker, "Beniah's Valour: An Address for Men Only." This appeal for support of increased opportunities for black women permeated all of Walker's speeches. In her last speeches in 1934 she continued her appeal for support of race enterprises (newspaper clipping [n.p., n.d.], "Maggie Laura Walker Scrapbook," MLW Papers [n. 9 above]). Maggie Laura Walker is Walker's granddaughter.

tional notions of the relationship between men and women at the same time that she countered those very notions. Black men could play the role of protector and defender of womanhood by protecting and defending and aiding women's assault on the barriers generally imposed on women.[49] Only in this way could they really defend the race. Strong race consciousness and strong support of equality for black women were inseparable. Maggie Walker and the other Saint Luke women therefore came to argue that an expanded role for black women within the black community itself was an essential step in the community's fight to overcome the limitations imposed upon the community by the larger society. Race men were therefore defined not just by their actions on behalf of black rights but by their actions on behalf of women's rights. The two were inseparable.

This was a collective effort in which Walker believed black men and black women should be equally engaged. Therefore, even in creating a woman's organization, she and her Saint Luke associates found it essential to create space within the structure for men as well. Unlike many of the fraternal orders that were male or female only, the Order of Saint Luke welcomed both genders as members and as employees. Although the office force was all female, men were employed in the printing department, in field work, and in the bank. Principal offices within the order were open to men and women. Ten of the thirty directors of the emporium were male; eight of the nineteen trustees of the order were male. The Saint Luke women thus strove to create an equalitarian organization, with men neither dominant nor auxiliary. Their vision of the order was a reflection of their vision for their community. In the 1913 Saint Luke Thanksgiving Day celebration of the order, Maggie Walker "thank[ed] God that this is a *woman's* organization, broad enough, liberal enough, and unselfish enough to accord equal rights and equal opportunity to men."[50]

Only such a community could become self-sustaining, self-sufficient, and independent, could enable its members to live lives unhampered by the machinations of the larger society, and could raise children who could envision a different world in which to live

---

[49] W. E. B. DuBois, who explored extensively the connection between race struggle and women's struggle in "The Damnation of Women," also challenged men's traditional roles: "The present mincing horror of a free womanhood must pass if we are ever to be rid of the bestiality of a free manhood; *not by guarding the weak in weakness do we gain strength, but by making weakness free and strong*" (emphasis mine; *Darkwater, Voices from within the Veil* [New York: Harcourt, Brace, & Howe, 1920], 165).

[50] M. L. Walker, "Saint Luke Thanksgiving Day Speech," City Auditorium, March 23, 1913, MLW Papers (n. 9 above).

and then could go about creating it. The women in the Order of Saint Luke sought to carve a sphere for themselves where they could practically apply their belief in their community and in the potential that black men and women working together could achieve, and they sought to infuse that belief into all of black Richmond and to transmit it to the next generation.

The Saint Luke women challenged notions in the black community about the proper role of women; they challenged notions in the white community about the proper place of blacks. They expanded their roles in ways that enabled them to maintain traditional values of family/community and at the same time move into new spheres and relationships with each other and with the men in their lives. To the larger white society they demonstrated what black men and women in community could achieve. This testified to the idea that women's struggle and race struggle were not two separate phenomena but one indivisible whole. "First by practice and then by precept"[51] Maggie Lena Walker and the Saint Luke women demonstrated in their own day the power of black women discovering their own strengths and sharing them with the whole community.[52] They provide for us today a model of womanist praxis.

Womanism challenges the distinction between theory and action. Too often we have assumed that theory is to be found only in carefully articulated position statements. Courses on feminist theory are woefully lacking on anything other than white, Western, middle-class perspectives; feminist scholars would argue that this is due to the difficulty in locating any but contemporary black feminist thought. Though I have discussed Maggie Lena Walker's public statements, the clearest articulation of her theoretical perspective lies in the organization she helped to create and in her own activities. Her theory and her action are not distinct and separable parts of some whole; they are often synonymous, and it is only through her actions that we clearly hear her theory. The same is true for the lives of many other black women who had limited time and resources and maintained a holistic view of life and struggle.

More important, Maggie Lena Walker's womanism challenges the dichotomous thinking that underlies much feminist theory and writing. Most feminist theory poses opposites in exclusionary and hostile ways: one is black and female, and these are contradictory/problematical statuses. This either/or approach classifies phenom-

[51] M. L. Walker, "Address—Virginia Day Third Street Bethel AME Church," January 29, 1933, MLW Papers.
[52] Ogunyemi (n. 7 above; 72–73) takes this idea from Stephen Henderson's analysis of the role of the blues and blues women in the Africanamerican community.

ena in such a way that "everything falls into one category or another, but cannot belong to more than one category at the same time."[53] It is precisely this kind of thinking that makes it difficult to see race, sex, and class as forming one consciousness and the resistance of race, sex, and class oppression as forming one struggle. Womanism flows from a both/and worldview, a consciousness that allows for the resolution of seeming contradictions "not through an either/ or negation but through the interaction" and wholeness. Thus, while black and female may, at one level, be radically different orientations, they are at the same time united, with each "confirming the existence of the other." Rather than standing as "contradictory opposites," they become "complementary, unsynthesized, unified wholes."[54] This is what Ogunyemi refers to as "the dynamism of wholeness." This holistic consciousness undergirds the thinking and action of Maggie Lena Walker and the other Saint Luke women. There are no necessary contradictions between the public and domestic spheres; the community and the family; male and female; race and sex struggle—there is intersection and interdependence.

Dichotomous thinking does not just inhibit our abilities to see the lives of black women and other women of color in their wholeness, but, I would argue, it also limits our ability to see the wholeness of the lives and consciousnesses of even white middle-class women. The thinking and actions of white women, too, are shaped by their race and their class, and their consciousnesses are also formed by the totality of these factors. The failure, however, to explore the total consciousness of white women has made class, and especially race, nonexistent categories in much of white feminist theory. And this has allowed the development of frameworks which render black women's lives invisible. Explorations into the consciousnesses of black women and other women of color should, therefore, be a model for all women, including those who are not often confronted with the necessity of understanding themselves in these total terms. As we begin to confront the holistic nature of

[53] The essays in Vernon J. Dixon and Badi G. Foster, eds., *Beyond Black or White: An Alternate America* (Boston: Little, Brown, 1971) explore the either/or and the both/and worldview in relation to Africanamerican systems of analysis; the quote can be found in Dixon, "Two Approaches to Black-White Relations," 23–66, esp. 25–26.

[54] Johnella E. Butler explores the theoretical, methodological, and pedagogical implications of these systems of analysis in *Black Studies: Pedagogy and Revolution: A Study of Afro-American Studies and the Liberal Arts Tradition through the Discipline of Afro-American Literature* (Washington D.C.: University Press of America, 1981), esp. 96–102.

all women's lives, we will begin to create a truly womanist studies. In our efforts Maggie Lena Walker and black women like her will be our guide.

Departments of History and Sociology
State University of New York at Binghamton

BLACK MATRILINEAGE:
THE CASE OF ALICE WALKER
AND ZORA NEALE HURSTON

DIANNE F. SADOFF

In their book on women writers and the nineteenth-century literary imagination, Sandra M. Gilbert and Susan Gubar revise Harold Bloom's psycholiterary model of poetic precedence to make it applicable to the female writer. In Bloom's Freudian model of poetic influence, the poet, like Oedipus, battles his precursor father at the intertextual crossroads and metaphorically kills him: he misreads and so swerves from, completes, or defines his discontinuity with his literary forebear. Bloom defines an author's inevitable dependence on tradition as necessarily anxious because writers deny obligation to precursors; they desire originality yet know it a fiction. The woman poet, however, finds no place in this paradigm of authorial interaction. On the one hand, she has few precursors who resemble herself, and on the other, she must come to terms with her difference from male writers who (metaphorically) beget the text upon the female muse. Gilbert and Gubar therefore posit that for the woman writer the "anxiety of influence" becomes a "primary 'anxiety of authorship.'" Her alienation from the male canonical tradition appears in her text as marks, fissures, and traces of "inferiorization": rebellion masquerades as submission, poetic closure is ambivalent, structure and figurative language undercut stated thematic material.[1] The feminist

---

1. Harold Bloom, *The Anxiety of Influence: A Theory of Poetry* (New York: Oxford University Press, 1973), pp. 5–15; Sandra M. Gilbert and Susan Gubar, *The Madwoman in the Attic: The Woman Writer and the Nineteenth-Century Literary Imagination* (New Haven, Conn.: Yale University Press, 1979), pp. 45–49. In *From Behind the Veil: A Study of Afro-American Narrative* (Urbana: University of Illinois Press, 1979), Robert B. Stepto creates a paradigm for black literature that resembles, but is culturally distinct from, Bloom's. Modern Afro-American narrative, he believes, "revoices" specific tropes from two slave narrative types,

This essay originally appeared in *Signs*, vol. 11, no. 1, Autumn 1985.

study of literary tradition seeks sympathetically to comprehend the strains of gender expectation and difference in texts, to reenvision female possibility, and to right (or rewrite) the wrongs of literary history.

This theoretical perspective on feminism, texts, and literary tradition focuses on the ambivalence and self-deprecation of the white woman writer in nineteenth-century England. Yet modern and contemporary women writers also have precursors. Both Bloom's masculinist and Gilbert and Gubar's Victorian-feminist paradigms of anxiety and influence need further revision once we alter the literary-historical prism through which we view texts. In Virginia Woolf's modern female version of literary influence, moreover, women writers "think back through [their] mothers."[2] This maternal literary precedence means the contemporary woman writer seeks her precursors with enthusiasm and misreads their anxiety so as fully to enable her own enterprise. When we consider contemporary women writers of color, we must again revise Bloom's and Gilbert and Gubar's models of influence. Race and class oppression intensify the black woman writer's need to discover an untroubled matrilineal heritage. In celebrating her literary foremothers, however, the contemporary black woman writer covers over more profoundly than does the white writer her ambivalence about matrilineage, her own misreading of precursors, and her link to an oral as well as a written tradition. Study of Alice Walker's relationship as a writer to Zora Neale Hurston clarifies the relationship of gender and race in a revised theory of literary influence.

I

In numerous and diverse ways Walker proclaims Hurston her precursor and appears to find that precedence a source not of anxiety but of nurturance. For example, she dedicates the whole of *In Love and Trouble: Stories of Black Women* as well as the story in it, "The Revenge of Hannah Kemhuff," to the memory of Hurston. The story's narrator, a young woman who trains as a rootworker under the legendary Tante Rosie, recites a voodoo curse "straight from Zora Neale Hurston's book, *Mules and Men*" against the racist and classist Mrs. Holley; when she finishes her apprenticeship, the narrator, like Tante Rosie, will know this curse "by heart."[3] Central to this passing on of knowledge from one woman to

---

the "generic narrative" and the "authenticating narrative" (p. xi). Stepto's excellent book, however, deals very little with black women writers.

2. Virginia Woolf, *A Room of One's Own* (New York: Harcourt Brace & Co., 1929), p. 79.

3. Alice Walker, *In Love and Trouble: Stories of Black Women* (New York: Harcourt, Brace, Jovanovich, 1973), dedication page, pp. 60, 72; hereafter cited as *LT* in parentheses in the text. See also Gloria T. Hull, "Rewriting Afro-American Literature: The Case for Black Women Writers," *Radical Teacher* 6, no. 1 (1977): 10–14.

another is the quest for identification. For the rootworker, as for other black women, the double oppression of gender and race makes it doubly necessary to celebrate such continuity in the black experience. Reading about black heroines initiates a similar identification. Walker writes that if she were condemned to live on a desert island with only ten books, she would "unhesitatingly" choose as one *Their Eyes Were Watching God*: "I would want to enjoy myself while identifying with the black heroine, Janie Crawford, as she acted out many roles in a variety of settings. . . . *There is no book more important to me than this one.*"[4] The multifaceted liveliness of the black heroine gives rise to Walker's sense of her own resemblance to Janie Crawford, and a similar sense of shared life and knowledge makes Walker identify with Hurston as well. The woman from Eatonton, Georgia, recognizes the woman from Eatonville, Florida, as a "model" for herself.[5]

A tradition depends not only on identification with precursors but also on transmission by the belated or second-generation writer to later readers and writers. Walker writes that she would take *Mules and Men* to her desert island so as to "pass on to younger generations the life of American blacks as legend and myth" ("Zora," p. 86). In *Mules and Men*, Hurston herself has done just this: "Who you reckon want to read all them old-time tales about Brer Rabbit and Brer Bear," George Thomas asks the anthropologist. "Plenty of people," Zora replies; "we want to set them down before it's too late. . . . Before everybody forgets all of 'em.'"[6] Alice Walker later takes *Mules and Men* to New York and Boston, to members of her family who "rapidly forget . . . their southern cultural inheritance." *Mules and Men*, Walker reports, "gave them back all the stories they had forgotten or of which they had grown ashamed (told us years ago by our parents and grandparents). . . . *This is not exaggerated.* . . . No matter how they tried to remain cool toward all Zora revealed, in the end they could not hold back the smiles, the laughter, the *joy* over who she was showing them to be: descendants of an inventive, joyous, courageous and outrageous people: loving drama, appreciating wit, and, most of all, relishing the pleasure of each other's loquacious and *bodacious* company." Walker thus undertakes a "fight for Zora and her work" because it "must not be lost to us"; this campaign Walker views as her "duty" ("Zora," pp. 85, 87). Transmission necessarily retrieves texts from the past and

4. Alice Walker, "Zora Neale Hurston—a Cautionary Tale and a Partisan View," in *In Search of Our Mothers' Gardens: Womanist Prose* (San Diego, Calif.: Harcourt, Brace, Jovanovich, 1983), pp. 83–92, esp. p. 86; hereafter cited in parentheses in the text as "Zora"; the collection is referred to hereafter as *Mothers' Gardens*.

5. Alice Walker, "Saving the Life That Is Your Own: The Importance of Models in the Artist's Life," in Walker, *Mothers' Gardens*, pp. 3–14, esp. p. 12.

6. Zora Neale Hurston, *Mules and Men*, ed. Robert E. Hemenway (Bloomington: Indiana University Press, 1978), p. 10; hereafter cited as *Mules* in parentheses in the text.

restores them to continuous use by later readers and storytellers, creating an intergenerational and contemporary cultural community.

Alice Walker's understanding of poetic history or literary influence, then, appears not at all melancholy or anxiety laden. Her essays about Hurston seem to share none of Woolf's modernist ambivalence about precursors: the "depressing" yet "triumphant" George Eliot, a woman "with no wish for intimacy"; the vehement yet angry and "self-centered" Charlotte Brontë; the discriminating yet "taciturn" and evasive—even dull—Jane Austen.[7] Walker designates her precursor an author of black legend and black female liberation, a woman who facilitates what Adrienne Rich calls "re-vision" and who enables female possibility;[8] her dedication—that is, her inscription and devotion—to Hurston acknowledges that, without predecessors, a writer cannot write, since texts enable other texts.

Walker's enthusiastic battle to restore both Hurston and her texts to the Afro-American literary canon, however, masks an underlying anxiety about the black woman writer's singularity in white America that emerges, although disguised, in Walker's fiction. Needing a precursor to validate her own enterprise as a writer, Walker virtually invents Hurston before she defines herself as indebted to Hurston's example. In her forward to Robert Hemenway's biography of Hurston, Walker says of *Mules and Men*, "I became aware of my need of Zora Neale Hurston's work some time before I knew her work existed. In late 1970 I was writing a story that required accurate material on voodoo practices among rural southern blacks of the thirties; . . . it was then that I discovered *Mules and Men*, Zora's book on folklore, collecting, herself, and her small, all-black community of Eatonville, Florida. . . . Here was this perfect book!" ("Zora," pp. 83–84). This deep need for a predecessor and her knowledge of black culture—in this instance voodoo—makes Walker idealize Hurston as model: *Mules and Men* is "perfect." As though to emphasize Hurston as ideal, Walker underscores that she does "*not exaggerate*" the folktales' effect on their audience, that "*no book is more important*" to her than *Eyes*. Hurston becomes not only predecessor but originator; her work, archetypal. Walker's essays on and editorship of Hurston designate the Renaissance writer precursor and obscure the Second Renaissance writer's fear of her cultural marginality, her own deep need for a foremother.

7. Virginia Woolf, *The Common Reader: First Series* (New York: Harcourt, Brace, & World, 1925), pp. 166–76, 159–65, 137–49.

8. Rich calls such "re-vision" central to a female literary tradition: the woman reader-poet "look[s] back," "see[s] with fresh eyes," and "enter[s] an old text from a new critical direction" ("When We Dead Awaken: Writing as Re-Vision," in *On Lies, Secrets and Silence: Selected Prose* [New York: W. W. Norton & Co., 1979], pp. 31–49, esp. p. 35).

II

A woman who writes knows herself her precursors' metaphorical daughter. In Walker's journey to find Hurston's grave, however, she imagines herself to be Hurston's illegitimate niece. "The lie," as she calls it, is a figurative truth, for her precursor *is* her relation: "As far as I'm concerned, she *is* my aunt—and that of all black people."[9] Yet Hurston is not only Walker's figurative aunt but her metaphorical mother as well. In her essay "In Search of Our Mothers' Gardens" Walker movingly pays tribute to the mute female poets of the enslaved South who are her precursors, her "mothers." Black women who were sexually exploited and politically oppressed by the system of slavery—"the *mule*[s] of the world"—dreamed dreams and saw visions. They could not have dreamed of being artists, but they might have been rootworkers, "saints," or singers. These "great-grandmothers," forbidden by law to read or write, kept alive the creative spirit among their people and passed on to their daughters that "living creativity," the *"notion of song."* Phillis Wheatley, Hurston, and Bessie Smith are among Walker's own "great-grandmothers," women who by their "songs" made it possible for her to "sing." Like Woolf, Walker believes a (black) female tradition includes silence as well as voice.

Walker concludes her essay, however, not with her figurative but with her literal mother. Although her mother spent her days in laborious tasks, she was an artist: she tended her garden daily, with the commitment necessary to art; she experienced the artist's radiance. Her materials were not paints but flower seeds, for like the unsung artists of any working or lower class, she "left her mark in the only materials she could afford, and in the only medium her position in society allowed her to use." Walker's mother also told stories, and Walker preserves these tales: her mother's stories about "strong horse tea" and voodoo curses become part of her own, just as her mother's "garden," her art, passes to her daughter and becomes her garden, her art.[10] The literal and figurative genealogy of artists and storytellers enables and empowers the art of the contemporary black woman.

In this genealogical metaphor, the family resembles the poetic generations: ancestors on a family tree become by analogy literary precursors. In Bloom's original paradigm of such precedence, the Freudian

9. Alice Walker, "Looking for Zora," in Walker, *Mothers' Gardens* (n. 4 above), pp. 93–116, esp. p. 102.

10. Alice Walker, "In Search of Our Mothers' Gardens: The Creativity of Black Women in the South," in Walker, *Mothers' Gardens*, pp. 231–43. See also Mary Helen Washington, "I Sign My Mother's Name: Alice Walker, Dorothy West, Paule Marshall," in *Mothering the Mind: Twelve Studies and Their Silent Partners*, ed. Ruth Perry and Martine Watson Brownley (New York: Holmes & Meier, 1984), pp. 142–63, esp. 144–50.

"family romance" represents oedipal rivalry between the early or prior poet-father and the belated poet-son. Guy Rosolato describes the way in which the oedipal triangle at the heart of the family romance opens into the patriarchal and genealogical situation. If the rivalry between son and father over the mother's love is to conclude without parricide, the son must replace his loyalty to mother with devotion to patrilineage. In Rosolato's paradigmatic patrilineal narrative, God, Abraham, and Isaac battle over love and loyalty, and only by killing his own son, Isaac, can Abraham prove his obedience to his Father, God. When God inserts the ram into the oedipal equation, the mediating sacrifice allows the three generations of males to accept one another's sonhood or fatherhood and so create a patrilineage in which males inherit substance and identity one from another.[11]

These masculine models of family structure and genealogy may be transformed into female-centered paradigms. In Nancy Chodorow's rethinking of oedipal models, the daughter as subject experiences her resemblance to her mother and never rejects the family as firmly as does the son; both girl and boy have their first and primary loving relationship with a woman. The tie between mother and daughter, then, unlike the tie between father and son, is in its beginnings based on love rather than rivalry. Although the later relationship between mother and daughter is often ambivalent, the early tie never is fully denied. The girl's sexual development may be troubled because she shifts the object of her affections from mother to father, but identification is less troubled for her than for the boy; she sees her mother in herself, and views her daughter as repeating—perhaps repairing—that matrilineal resemblance.[12] This female genealogy makes woman the paradigmatic subject and defines her primary intersubjectivity as female.

As a model for literary priority, a female genealogy based on family structure alters Bloom's "anxiety of influence" to "matrilineal anxiety." The nineteenth-century white woman writer, for example, will find in the texts of her "motherly precursors" signs of inferiorization, self-hatred, and suppressed rebellion; she must seek her "lost literary matrilineage" and accept ambivalent matrilineal poetics so as herself to give birth to texts based on her precursors' strengths.[13] The Second Renaissance black

11. Guy Rosolato, "Trois générations d'hommes dans le mythe religieux et la généalogie," in *Éssais sur le symbolique* (Paris: Gallimard, 1969), pp. 59–96.

12. Nancy Chodorow, *The Reproduction of Mothering: Psychoanalysis and the Sociology of Gender* (Berkeley: University of California Press, 1978), pp. 62–67, 92–104, 111–40. See also Dorothy Dinnerstein, *The Mermaid and the Minotaur: Sexual Arrangements and Human Malaise* (New York: Harper & Row, 1976); Juliet Mitchell, *Psychoanalysis and Feminism: Freud, Reich, Laing, and Women* (New York: Vintage Books, 1975); and Judith Herman, *Father-Daughter Incest* (Cambridge, Mass.: Harvard University Press, 1981).

13. Gilbert and Gubar (n. 1 above), pp. 52–53. For an excellent sociohistorical discussion of the British female tradition, see Elaine Showalter, *A Literature of Their Own: British Women Novelists from Bronte to Lessing* (Princeton, N.J.: Princeton University Press, 1977).

woman writer will not wholly fit this pattern, however, partly because of her history, partly her race.

For this paradigm unspokenly assumes the white nuclear family to be universal and without a history. Although radical American white women in the nineteenth century considered themselves metaphorically enslaved, their black sisters endured literal bonds. Moreover, slavery intervened in and altered the black family structure. The slave mother may have enjoyed more affective power in her family than did the white mother (whether northern or southern), yet the myth of "the black matriarch" current among twentieth-century liberals misreads maternal as though it were social authority. With terrible irony, this mystification originates in white resentment of the slave woman's seeming power through her sexual relationship with the master, when that relationship signifies instead her status as chattel. Forced to submit for survival, the black slave woman could yet resist her oppression because the dominant culture failed to define her as stereotypically "feminine." Although the master used rape in an attempt to crush the black woman's resistance and to humble the black man, her ironic freedom from the restraints of submissive white southern ladyhood allowed her to fight both alongside of and apart from the black man. Thus the black (slave) mother represents the contemporary black woman's double history of enslavement and survival.[14]

Notions that the contemporary black family is fatherless, unstable, and ruled by domineering women, like the myth of black "matriarchy," misinterpret matrifocality. Carol B. Stack examines extended clusters of urban black kin and finds that, although men are usually present, women "constitute the core of [the] network." Young women in the clusters, daughters and nieces, move often among households headed by their mothers, aunts, and women friends. Relationships between mothers and children, between women who are friends or kin, strengthen the network and provide its continuity; although the specific "household composition" may and does change, "members are selected or self-selected largely from a single network that has continuity over time." Rooted in slave culture and its adaptive strategies to the involuntary separation of mothers and fathers (exogamous marriage, extended inter- and intragenerational kin

14. Angela Davis, "Reflections on the Black Woman's Role in the Community of Slaves," *Massachusetts Review* 13, nos. 1, 2 (Winter/Spring 1972): 81–100. See also Gerda Lerner, *Black Women in White America: A Documentary History* (New York: Random House, 1972), pp. 150–83; Joyce Ladner, *Tomorrow's Tomorrow: The Black Woman* (Garden City, N.Y.: Doubleday & Co., 1971); Eugene Genovese, *Roll, Jordan, Roll* (New York: Pantheon Books, 1974); and Erlene Stetson, "Studying Slavery: Some Literary and Pedagogical Considerations on the Black Female Slave," in *All the Women Are White, All the Blacks Are Men, But Some of Us Are Brave: Black Women's Studies,* ed. Gloria T. Hull, Patricia Bell Scott, and Barbara Smith (Old Westbury, N.Y.: Feminist Press, 1982), pp. 61–84.

networks, naming of children for consanguineal kin, social acceptance of atypical female-headed families), black matrifocality serves as a response to poverty, urbanization, and oppression.[15]

Her history and her race make the Second Renaissance writer appear less anxious about literary maternity or priority than is the modernist or contemporary white woman writer. She must create a tradition that restores to her people their "forgotten" culture, and so she seeks her motherly precursors without apparent ambivalence or anxiety, with a necessity to survive, even with idealization. Such precedence calls up matrifocal identification of daughter with foremother; it confirms and continues woman's rebellion, courage, and support. Walker's "In Search of Our Mothers' Gardens" transforms Woolf's model of the white female tradition by inserting in brackets the black equivalents for Woolf's exemplary writers and issues: instead of "Emily Brontë," "Zora Hurston"; instead of "wise women," "rootworkers."[16] Yet the black and white female traditions are not, as Walker's substitutions imply, symmetrical or identical. The historical burden of black matrifocality and motherhood—slavery, sexual exploitation, forced loss of children, and economic marginality—also creates the special "duty," as Walker defines it, of black literary matriliny. Walker's own insistent affirmation of her foremother's perfection as example and uniqueness as precursor originates in the pressures of belatedness when superadded to the double bind of race and gender. Black and white women suffer similar oppression as women, but the black woman's double oppression intensifies her suffering and the beauty of her survival. Because she is black and female, Walker celebrates her matriliny with an idealism that counters her anger at her black slave mothers' "disinhertance," a disinheritance about which she knows her own mother can articulate anger only obliquely, about which for similar reasons the educationally deprived middle-aged black women she teaches in an Office for Economic Opportunity program know little. The evasions are strategies to escape the psychic deformity conscious anger entails. For

15. Carol B. Stack, "Sex Roles and Survival Strategies in an Urban Black Community," in *Woman, Culture, and Society,* ed. Michelle Z. Rosaldo and Louise Lamphere (Stanford, Calif.: Stanford University Press, 1974), pp. 113–28, and *All Our Kin* (New York: Harper & Row, 1974); Herbert Gutman, *The Black Family in Slavery and Freedom, 1750–1925* (New York: Pantheon Books, 1976), pp. 115–43, 432–74; Nancy Tanner, "Matrifocality in Indonesia and Africa and among Black Americans," in Rosaldo and Lamphere, eds., pp. 129–56; Alice Walker, "But Yet and Still the Cotton Gin Kept on Working . . . ," in Walker, *Mothers' Gardens* (n. 4 above), pp. 22–32, esp. p. 28. See also Daryl C. Dance, "Black Eve or Madonna? A Study of the Antithetical Views of the Mother in Black American Literature," in *Sturdy Black Bridges: Visions of Black Women in Literature,* ed. Roseann P. Bell, Bettye J. Parker, and Beverly Guy-Sheftall (Garden City, N.Y.: Anchor Press/Doubleday, 1979), pp. 123–32.

16. Walker, "In Search of Our Mothers' Gardens" (n. 10 above), p. 235.

Walker also, in the face of suffering and a history of oppression, idealized but necessary celebration masks anxiety about cultural disinheritance.[17]

In "*One* Child of One's Own," the white female tradition calls up Walker's covert anger and her concomitant anxiety about the fragility of a black literary matrilineage. Articulating feminist theory and ideas about motherhood, Walker asks why white scholarship and art about women exclude the black woman. Judy Chicago, for example, in her feminist art piece "The Dinner Party" does not use for Harriet Tubman's plate the vaginal design found on most others. Walker states: "To think of black women as women is impossible if you cannot imagine them with vaginas. . . . And through that vagina, Children." White feminism obscures black women's sexuality and consequent motherhood. White women feel guilty and resentful about their relationship with black women, Walker theorizes, because they know their children get more from a racist society than do black mothers' children—yet all mothers want the best for their children. Despite shared motherhood, race separates women; racism, not gender or motherhood, oppresses the black woman. Walker believes that her motherhood—surely literal but also metaphorical—will help overcome her oppression: "We are together, my child and I. Mother and child, yes, but *sisters* really, against whatever denies us all that we are."[18] Her conflation of the female generations, while describing the necessary political and cultural alliance of black women across generations, also confuses motherhood with sisterhood and idealizes the mother-daughter bond.

III

The tradition Walker sees passed on by foremothers is oral and southern. In "Looking for Zora," then, Walker seeks in her precursor a writer of the black South and an exemplary black female "voice." The essay's structure and material imitates and so recalls *Mules and Men.* Hurston journeys back to Eatonville in her Chevrolet to seek the "city of five lakes, three croquet courts, three hundred brown skins, three hun-

17. See Alice Walker, "Beyond the Peacock: The Reconstruction of Flannery O'Connor," and "The Cotton Gin," in Walker, *Mothers' Gardens* (n. 4 above), pp. 42–59, 22–32. About idealization, Walker says, "I [feel] a deep reluctance to criticize other black women [writers]. I am much more comfortable praising them" (p. 322).

18. Alice Walker, "*One* Child of One's Own: A Meaningful Digression within the Work(s)," in Walker, *Mothers' Gardens* (n. 4 above), pp. 361–83, esp. pp. 373–74, 382. See also Alice Walker, "Burial," in *Revolutionary Petunias and Other Poems* (New York: Harcourt, Brace, Jovanovich, 1973), pp. 12–15, for an idealized black matrilineage; Nan Bauer Maglin, "'Don't never forget the bridge that you crossed over on': The Literature of Matrilineage," in *The Lost Tradition: Mothers and Daughters in Literature,* ed. Cathy N. Davidson and E. M. Broner (New York: Frederick Ungar Publishing Co., 1980), pp. 257–67.

dred good swimmers, plenty guavas, two schools, and no jail-house";
Walker quotes this passage from *Mules and Men* as she writes about flying
into an Eatonville still free, healthy, and black.[19] In *Mules and Men*, Hurston rediscovers a people of "vivid imagination" (p. 5). She hears the tales
of her childhood about the devil outsmarting God, blacks outsmarting
Ole Massa, and animals allegorizing the black condition. These stories
exist within an oral tradition that encourages both retelling and
embroidering of the basic tale. Such repetition and variation knit the
members of a community in their shared knowledge of their history,
background, and culture, while rewarding individual inspiration and
celebrating the verbal agility and metaphorical storytelling skill of black
people.[20] Storytelling happens socially: while men sit on the porch, while
men and women flirt at a toe-party, while children play, while folks fish or
play cards at a jook joint. Community members participate in telling
"lies"—figurative and often hyperbolic truths about black life; the end of
each story provides a verbal association that creates the next. Shug, for
example, tells "The Quickest Trick" about three men who court one girl;
Robert Williams follows with "How to Write a Letter" about a man and his
daughter; Henry Byrd follows with another about a letter, "A Fast Horse"
(*Mules*, pp. 42–44). Hurston herself participates in this community self-
creation. She urges her neighbors to tell as many stories as they can; one
neighbor replies, "We kin tell you some lies most any old time. We never
run outer lies and lovin'" (p. 15).

The folklorist who returns south, however, is no longer herself
southern. Hurston chooses to collect folklore in Florida to be among black
neighbors who know her: "I hurried back to Eatonville because I knew
that the town was full of material and that I could get it without hurt,
harm or danger," without "seeming acquiescence" or evasion (*Mules*,
p. 4). Yet her northern education provides her a double perspective on
southern black life: "It was only when I was off in college, away from my
native surroundings, that I could see myself like somebody else and stand
off and look at my garment. Then I had to have the spy-glass of Anthropology to look through at that" (p. 3). Such double perspective aligns
Hurston's narrative stance and voice. A white intellectual discipline and
context provide another vantage point from which to examine her old
cultural "garment," which, as Robert Hemenway demonstrates, is Eaton-

19. Walker, *Mothers' Gardens* (n. 4 above), p. 94.
20. On oral and folk traditions in black women's fiction, see Robert E. Hemenway, "Are
You a Flying Lark or a Setting Dove?" in *Afro-American Literature: The Reconstruction of
Instruction*, ed. Dexter Fischer and Robert B. Stepto (New York: Modern Language Association of America, 1979), pp. 122–52; Valerie Lee Gray, "The Use of Folktalk in Novels by
Black Women Writers," *College Language Association Journal* 23, no. 3 (March 1980): 266–72;
and Trudier Harris, "Folklore in the Fiction of Alice Walker: A Perpetuation of Historical
and Literary Traditions," *Black American Literature Forum* 11, no. 1 (Spring 1977): 3–8.

ville idealized and removed from the Depression's economic hardship. To contain the difference between South and North, educated woman and townspeople, Hurston creates, as Hemenway says, a semifictional self-effacing narrator who presents her tales, a poseur. Although this "Zora" participates in porch sittings, parties, and high jinks at jook joints, her paradoxical distance from her ex-neighbors shows in her educated but "innocent" narrative voice;[21] Hurston's record of return south covertly exposes her distance from her home.

Walker, following her foremother back to the latter's home in the South, fails to find Hurston's unknown grave but marks a grave nonetheless in Hurston's memory. She encounters misinformation about and lack of interest in Hurston; she practices "evasion" to get her stories. The Eatonville that lived in her imagination, her self-irony implies, was, like Hurston's, an ideal. For she, like her foremother, has gone north, has become semi-assimilated to a white male literary world; she seeks her rural, southern heritage with an idealism that tempers and compensates for her own lost past. Walker takes her trips back south to look for wholeness because, she believes, experience has fragmented and split apart herself and her people; she needs to confirm their faith and grace under the continuous pressures of racism, but she finds as well cultural disinheritance, symptomized by black cooperation in the neglect of Afro-American literature and of black women's writing. Black literary matriliny, like the structures of the black family, empowers daughters who write in the face of race and gender oppression, but it also sustains and conceals anxiety about the difficulties of writing as a woman of color. The difficulties appear, even if dispersed, in the fictional texts.

Like Hurston's semifictional narrator, Walker's fictional women find returning south bittersweet. Dee, of "Everyday Use," wants to make antique the Civil War quilts, butter churn, and rump-marked bench that are her southern heritage; although Walker sympathizes with her Muslim heroine's "new day" for blacks, she sides with the narrator, Dee's mother, and with Dee's crippled sister Maggie, who will put her ancestors' things to daily use (*LT*, pp. 47–59). The narrator of "To Hell with Dying" returns south to "resurrect" her old childhood friend Mr. Sweet, and, although her childhood "resurrections" worked, this one fails; yet Mr. Sweet lives on in the narrator's memory, in her story, and such figurative resurrection attempts to balance the violence and sexual exploitation other heroines in the stories of *In Love and Trouble* somehow survive (*LT*, pp. 129–38). Sarah Davis, of "A Sudden Trip Home in the Spring," leaves Wellesley to attend her father's funeral; she rediscovers her commitment to family and the South and decides to "come home." Quickly, however,

21. Robert E. Hemenway, *Zora Neale Hurston: A Literary Biography* (Urbana: University of Illinois Press, 1977), pp. 221, 164–66.

she realizes that she must return north to study art so that she later may come home to sculpt a bust of her grandfather.[22] In *Meridian*, Meridian ends up in Mississippi, gradually divesting herself of belongings so as to transcend herself. Lynne, Meridian's white friend and rival for Truman Held, wants to return south to rediscover the meaningful past of civil rights struggles; skeptical about both politics and the South, Truman declines to join her. In short, Walker's fiction reveals her own ambivalence about returning south as she rewrites Hurston's anxiety about separation from a rural past.

IV

The stories in *Mules and Men* articulate sexual politics with race and serve to normalize and regularize conflict between the sexes while permitting the community the appropriate stage on which to enact it. Man and woman, according to Mathilda, were once equal in strength. But the man wanted dominance, so he asked God to make him stronger; the woman got a set of keys from God, and the devil taught her how to use them to lock up the kitchen, the bedroom, and the cradle. For if the woman controls access to food, sex, and reproduction, she has more power than the man despite his strength. When the man "submit[s] hisself to de woman," Mathilda says, she opens the doors; "and dat's why de man makes and de woman takes" (*Mules*, pp. 33-38). This tale of sexual difference portrays the necessity to mythologize such conflict so as to control it. The tale, indeed, follows an exchange between Gene and Gold in which each belittles the sexual prowess and gender privilege of the other:

> [*Gene.*] "De trouble is you women ain't good for nothin' exceptin' readin' Sears and Roebuck's bible and hollerin' 'bout, 'gimme dis and gimme dat' as soon as we draw our pay." . . .
> [*Gold.*] "You mens don't draw no pay. You don't do nothin' but stand around and draw lightnin'." . . .
> "You ain't seen me cryin'." . . .
> "Aw, shut up, Gene, you ain't no big hen's biddy if you do lay gobbler eggs. You tryin' to talk like big wood when you ain't nothin' but brush." [P. 19]

Such hyperbolic and richly metaphorical language inscribes power relationships between the sexes even while joking about them. Moreover, a

22. Walker, *Mothers' Gardens* (n. 4 above), pp. 48, 32; Alice Walker, "A Sudden Trip Home in the Spring," in *You Can't Keep a Good Woman Down* (New York: Harcourt, Brace, Jovanovich, 1981), pp. 124–37.

quick wit often defines a woman's power vis-à-vis men. "When Bertha starts her jawin'," Jim says, "her tongue is hung in de middle and works both ways"; "her tongue is all de weapon a woman got," George Thomas chides. Big Sweet nonetheless knows a woman's speech is authoritative; "Ah got de law in my mouth," she claims (*Mules*, pp. 101, 33, 134).

Hurston's finest novel, *Their Eyes Were Watching God*, examines gender privilege and sexual politics from a feminist perspective. Janie Crawford's Nanny, fearing routine sexual exploitation of her adolescent granddaughter, marries her against her will to a domineering husband, Logan; Janie leaves him to go off with Jody Starks, who promises she won't have to "follow a plow" when she's married to him. But when the radiant attraction to "horizon" and the feeling of possibility wear off between them, the raw power of sexual domination once more appears in Janie's life. Jody founds an all-black town, and, like Hurston's father, writes the laws for it; the account of the bringing of light, the inscribing of laws, parodies biblical creation stories and suggests Jody's exaggerated sense of "godliness." As mayor, Jody demands class status—a "high chair"—for his wife, whom he assumes acquires her social standing through his. "Ah aim . . . tuh be uh big voice," he says; "you oughta be glad, 'cause dat makes uh big woman outa you."[23] Janie disagrees, and the novel relates the ensuing battle for power between husband and wife.

In *Their Eyes Were Watching God* and *Mules and Men*, male community members gather to tell tales on Jody Starks's or Joe Clark's porch, the public arena for sexual ogling, courting, and joking. But Jody denies his wife the privilege of telling stories on his porch, just as he earlier denied her the right to speak in public: "Mah wife don't know nothin' 'bout no speech-makin'. . . . She's uh woman and her place is in de home" (*Eyes*, p. 69). Jody wants Janie's "submission" and will fight to earn it (*Eyes*, p. 111). Jody makes Janie work in his store, forces her to tie her abundant hair up in a headrag—sign of her oppression and self-denial—and slaps her when the bread won't rise. Only slightly less forcefully, the porch tales reveal the men's insistence on female submission and inferiority, while they enhance masculine pride and encourage male solidarity. One day the men heckle Mrs. Robbins for begging groceries when her husband provides for her:

> "If dat wuz *mah* wife," said Walter Thomas, "Ah'd kill her cemetery dead."
>
> "More special after Ah done bought her everything mah wages kin stand, lak Tony do," Coker said. "In de fust place Ah never would spend on *no* woman whut Tony spend on *her*." . . .
>
> "[He] say he can't bear tuh leave her and he hate to kill her," [Jody responds], "so 'tain't nothin' tuh do but put up wid her."

23. Zora Neale Hurston, *Their Eyes Were Watching God*, foreward by Sherley Anne Williams (Urbana: University of Illinois Press, 1978), p. 74; hereafter cited as *Eyes* in parentheses in the text.

"Dat's 'cause Tony love her too good," said Coker. "Ah could break her if she wuz mine. Ah'd break her or kill her. Makin' uh fool outa me in front of everybody." [*Eyes*, pp. 115–16]

As Janie realizes when she hears this exchange, female obedience and chatteldom are a figurative death.

Their Eyes Were Watching God, however, tells about a woman who acquires the power to speak, who finds her voice and so learns to tell stories and create metaphors.[24] Angered by the men's response to Mrs. Robbins, Janie for the first time "thrust[s] herself into the conversation": "It's so easy to make yo'self out God Almighty when you ain't got nothin' tuh strain against but women and chickens," she says, metaphorically describing the sexual pecking order. She's "gettin' too moufy," Jody fumes (*Eyes*, p. 117). Janie follows her verbal assault on male power with one on Jody's sexuality. When he humbles her in front of her store customers by calling her "old," she responds with a tongue lashing: "You big-bellies round here and put out a lot of brag, but 'tain't nothin' to it but yo' big voice. Humph! Talkin' 'bout *me* lookin' old! When you pull down yo' britches, you look lak de change uh life." Jody instinctively understands the challenge to male pride: Janie had "robbed him of his illusion of irresistible maleness that all men cherish" (*Eyes*, p. 123). He goes to bed and never gets up. Janie accuses him of demanding she "bow down" and be "obediant" to him: he was "too busy listening tuh [his] own big voice" (*Eyes*, p. 133). Narrative structure implies that Janie's learning to speak out, her willingness to use her tongue as weapon against masculine domination, kills Jody. Her words about his lack of sexual charisma send him into decline and disease; her verbal assault on his "big voice"—sign of his sexual prowess and political status—does him in. Janie's ability to play the signifying game, to allude indirectly to Jody's sexual inadequacy, instigates as well as insults; her imaginative skill with hyperbolic and metaphoric speech earns her power hitherto reserved for the men in the community, the right to tell tales. For the narrative opens with Janie's return to Hurston's fictional Eatonville and is framed by her telling the story of the novel to her friend Pheoby. Janie tells the community's "lies"—its fictional truths—and her own story as well.

V

Central to Bloom's theory of literary priority and influence is misreading. He believes weak talents "idealize," while strong ones "appropri-

24. See a strong interpretation of Janie's "posture as a storyteller," her knowledge of "tribal tropes," her sisterhood with Pheoby, and the ambivalence of her "voice" in Stepto (n. 1 above), pp. 164–67. See also Hemenway, *Zora Neale Hurston*, pp. 238–39, and "Flying Lark," p. 146.

ate" space for themselves by misreading their precursors. Gilbert and
Gubar view their nineteenth-century literary figures as producing incomplete texts well suited to misreading—texts that simultaneously conform
to and subvert "patriarchal literary standards."[25] These women writers,
with few earlier models, are themselves unsure precursors to a modern
female tradition; they often misrepresent themselves and so invite misinterpretation. As Gilbert and Gubar's revision demonstrates, Bloom's
aggressive, even territorial, masculine model of misreading does not suit a
woman's literary tradition. Female precursors, fearful of overt originality, facilitate misreading by their daughters; as precursor, the black
woman writer, doubly culturally jeopardized by gender and race, will
necessarily represent herself even more ambiguously in her texts than do
white women writers. As literary daughter, meantime, the black woman
writer will overtly idealize foremothers while disguising anxiety and covertly appropriating concealed rebellious thematic material. Her own
texts may nevertheless revise and so expose this process of misreading,
this idealized matriliny that covers over the troubling history of black
women's motherhood.

  Hurston, a first-generation writer in the black female tradition, does
misrepresent herself, as a foremother must. Her texts bear the scars of
disguise or concealment because she is black and female—doubly alienated from a white and patriarchal mainstream literature. Indeed, Arthur
P. Davis judges Hurston's art "dishonest," her racial politics "incredible";
he accuses her of ignoring the effects of racism on the black community
and of playing "darky" to white readers and patrons.[26] Implicit in this
reading is Davis's political rather than literary bias, his inability to regard
concealed female rebellion as itself "political." Davis believes Hurston's
fictional dialect mimics white conceptions of black speech, while on the
contrary her folkloristic dialogue justly renders the rich metaphors,
hyperboles, personifications, and allegorical urge of rural southern black
language of the 1930s.[27] Moreover, Hurston's much-criticized and problematic eccentricity, her posturings and evasions, got a woman of color
published by the white literary establishment of her time, got her funds
from universities and patrons, and so authorized and initiated her literary
career.

  In her autobiography, Hurston represents herself ambiguously by
complying with, while covertly subverting, white male literary expectations. About *Dust Tracks on a Road*, Walker writes, "For me, the most
unfortunate thing Zora ever wrote is her autobiography. After the first

  25. Bloom (n. 1 above), p. 5; Gilbert and Gubar (n. 1 above), pp. 72–73.
  26. Arthur P. Davis, *From the Dark Tower: Afro-American Writers, 1900–1960* (Washington, D.C.: Howard University Press, 1974), pp. 116–19.
  27. See an excellent essay by John Wideman, "Defining the Black Voice in Fiction,"
Black American Literature Forum 11, no. 3 (Fall 1977): 79–82.

several chapters, it rings false. . . . But this unctuousness, so out of character for Zora, is also a result of dependency, a sign of her powerlessness" ("Zora," p. xvii). Hurston's book both justifies and falsifies the self. The slighting of black influence and playing up of white friendships such as those with Fannie Hurst and Mrs. Mason, even the refusal to "kiss and tell" about her love affairs, may originate not only in uneasy self-justification but in the double necessity the black woman is under to write inoffensively about her life. When "looking for Zora," Walker reports, "you have to read the chapters Zora *left out* of her autobiography"; for Hurston truncated and revised her political and racial analysis in *Dust Tracks* in response to comments her editor at Lippincott made on the manuscript. She deleted, as Robert Hemenway demonstrates, discussions of colonial oppression in the Third World, American racism, and the failures of democracy.[28] In the 1940s Hurston's political acuity and her racial bitterness must both have been considered by whites as inappropriate for verbalization by a black woman.

A woman born in an all-black Florida town who lost her mother at nine and left home at fourteen yet grew up to become a well-known writer must understandably have had difficulty reconciling her achievement with her race, class, and family background. In *Dust Tracks*, Hurston portrays herself as a survivor. Having left her family, she says she disregards all emotional ties to them. As a result, she appears to falsify her feelings about her mother's death: her exaggerated metaphors about the prowling "Old Master-Maker" cover over her unexpected loss; her insistence that she failed her mother by not heeding her last promise to Lucy appears to mask a child's normal anger at a dying parent for figuratively "failing" *her*. Hurston also evades knowledge of her oedipal jealousy of her stepmother, her anger so extreme that the sequence about this "skunk" who needed her "behind . . . kicked" gets narrated early and out of sequence.[29] No wonder this "survivor" idealized her long-suffering mother and vilified her womanizing father in the loosely autobiographical first novel, *Jonah's Gourd Vine*; no wonder she sought surrogate family in "godmother" Mason and "Papa" Franz Boas, her patroness and anthropology teacher, respectively. But the jealous and solitary girl must not surface in the successful woman writer's autobiography—the acceptable story of black girlhood and womanhood—and so she gets repressed.

Hurston also portrays her literary success as almost accidental in *Dust Tracks*. She happened to write a story her teacher sent out to *Story Magazine* which happened to get published, and publishers solicited an unwritten novel (she chose Lippincott, she says, because the letter did not

28. Walker repeats the words of a student at the Beinecke Library (Walker, *Mothers' Gardens* [n. 4 above], p. 109); Hemenway, *Zora Neale Hurston*, pp. 286–88.

29. Zora Neale Hurston, *Dust Tracks on a Road* (New York: Arno Press and New York Times, 1969), pp. 94–113; hereafter cited as *Dust Tracks* in parentheses in the text.

frighten her); a friend typed her first manuscript for nothing, and—surprise—Lippincott took it (*Dust Tracks*, pp. 214–22). This account surely masks the drive necessary for a poor black woman to become educated, or, for that matter, to write at all. Hurston plays the passive role she deems proper for the woman of color dependent on others for her economic and literary security. Through her eccentric self-presentation in the 1920s and evasiveness in the 1940s, she was able to act out this sensed marginality to white male culture that her writing itself had to suppress. That repression, however, scars the written text. Robert Hemenway interprets sympathetically the "problem of voice" he perceives in *Dust Tracks*—a problem evident in my opinion even as early as *Mules and Men*—where the northern-educated girl struggles to represent herself and her own speech in her "native village." This problematic voice inscribes Hurston's "contradictory understanding of her own success and her uneasy interpretation of it."[30] Walker designates this double bind, in Virginia Woolf's terms, "contrary instincts" and ascribes it to lack of precursors on the one hand and the necessity to satisfy a white audience and publisher on the other.[31]

Although in *Dust Tracks* Hurston masks her feelings about herself and her family, as well as her opinions about politics, race, and sex, her omitted material about gender appears in fictionalized form in *Their Eyes Were Watching God*. She wrote the novel in seven weeks after her second separation from Arthur Price and so "embalm[ed] all the tenderness of [her] passion for him" (*Dust Tracks*, p. 268). Indeed, many incidents between Janie and Jody, and Janie and Tea Cake are clearly transposed from her troubled relationship with Price. Janie's desire, for example, to tell stories and to achieve verbal power in the face of Jody's denial are figures for Hurston's drive to write novels and essays in the face of Price's insecure demand that she give up her career for their relationship. Like many women before and after her, Hurston used work to manipulate her relationship; when things got tough, she left home to do folklore research, to take her Guggenheim fellowship.[32] But her insistence on writing won out, as does Janie's demand that she be free to tell stories. The committed writer's ambivalence about relationships betrays itself in her choice of language to describe her novel's genesis; it "embalms" her passion—kills and preserves it.

30. Hemenway, *Zora Neale Hurston*, p. 283.
31. Walker, *Mothers' Gardens* (n. 4 above), p. 235. About black women's autobiography, see Ann L. Rayson, "*Dust Tracks on a Road:* Zora Neale Hurston and the Form of Black Autobiography," *Black American Literature Forum* 7, no. 1 (Spring 1973): 39–45; Regina Blackburn, "In Search of the Black Female Self: African-American Women's Autobiographies and Ethnicity," in *Women's Autobiographies: Essays in Criticism*, ed. Estelle C. Jelinek (Bloomington: Indiana University Press, 1980), pp. 133–48; and Stephen Butterfield, *Black Autobiography in America* (Amherst: University of Massachusetts Press, 1974), chap. 10.
32. Hemenway, *Zora Neale Hurston* (n. 21 above), pp. 273–76.

Hurston's ambivalent feelings about Price also appear concealed in the character of Tea Cake. In *Their Eyes Were Watching God*, a woman liberates her sexuality by taking as her third husband a man dedicated not to domination but to equality.[33] The surface of the narrative supports this commonplace reading. Unlike Logan and Jody, Tea Cake asks Janie to participate in men's activities—shooting, playing checkers, and storytelling. He appreciates her achievements and individuality; he awakens her sexuality; he works side by side with her in the Everglades. Yet Hurston makes the reader distrust Tea Cake almost as soon as he and Janie settle down. When Janie discovers he has taken her two hundred dollars, she fears she's been jilted. When he returns, she forgives him. Tea Cake gambles to restore the money; "Ah no need assistance tuh help me feed mah woman," he declares. This incident and Janie's uncertainties unsettle the reader's initial attraction to Tea Cake, even if Janie is temporarily reassured (*Eyes*, pp. 174–92).

Hurston also arouses our suspicions about Tea Cake's dedication to sexual equality. As jealousy becomes an issue in his and Janie's marriage, Tea Cake begins physically to abuse his wife and so to resemble Jody Starks, the manipulator of male power and privilege: "Before the week was over he had whipped Janie. Not because her behavior justified his jealousy, but it relieved that awful fear inside him. No brutal beating at all. He just slapped her around a bit to show he was boss" (*Eyes*, p. 218). Afterward, he pets Janie, and she helplessly hangs on him. Hurston profoundly distrusts heterosexual relationships because she thinks them based on male dominance and willing female submission; yet such inequality appears necessary to the institution of marriage. In her autobiography, for example, Hurston blames her mother for not submitting fully to her father and so robbing him of "that conquesting feeling" (*Dust Tracks*, p. 100). In *Eyes*, Tea Cake rationalizes his jealous beating of Janie as serving to show that she is *his* woman and cannot possibly be attracted to a lighter-skinned man.[34] The reader hardly believes the stated motivation and finds the novel's resolution of the incident unconvincing. The plot has broken down, has lost the link between sequence and consequence, between action and motive.

An event without narrative precedent follows: the flood. The characters interpret this catastrophe as an act of God; the novel places it in a pattern of biblical parody and black folktale. Yet neither the flood nor the

33. See Erlene Stetson, *"Their Eyes Were Watching God*: A Woman's Story," *Regionalism and the Female Imagination* 4, no. 1 (Spring 1978): 30–36; Wendy J. McCredie, "Authority and Authorization in *Their Eyes Were Watching God*," *Black American Literature Forum* 16, no. 1 (Spring 1982): 25–28; and Lloyd W. Brown, "Zora Neale Hurston and the Nature of Female Perception," *Obsidian* 4, no. 3 (Winter 1978): 39–45.

34. For an interpretation of this incident as relating to Afro-American history in *Eyes*, see Mary Helen Washington, "The Black Woman's Search for Identity," *Black World* 21 (August 1972): 68–75.

rabid dog kills Tea Cake: Janie does. Janie kills the rabid man in self-defense; she guiltily accuses the mad dog of killing Tea Cake through her (as Hurston blames herself for failing her mother in *Dust Tracks*); language removes Janie as subject from the narrative description of the shooting (*Eyes*, p. 273). The novel declares Janie's innocence—a white jury acquits her of murder!—yet we remember she figuratively killed her second husband. Although plot and language manipulate events so that the heroine kills off her man metaphorically or unintentionally, Janie is clearly a dangerous woman. At the end of the novel, Janie banishes her male oppressors; although theme appears to affirm Tea Cake's eternal presence to Janie after his death, narrative structure ensures his absence. Pheoby had warned Janie about marrying Tea Cake—"You'se yo' own woman"—and by the end of the novel she is. Hurston has motivated her narrative, perhaps unconsciously, to act out her rage against male domination and to free Janie, a figure for herself, from all men.

The novel covers over this subversive material and so encourages us to misread it. Both literary critics and daughters have thus misread Hurston, their precursor, as a celebrator of liberated heterosexual love. Neither Hurston's subterranean thematic concern to punish dominating males in *Eyes* nor to idealize mothers while vilifying mother substitutes in *Dust Tracks* and *Jonah's Gourd Vine* appears in Walker's rhetoric about her literary foremother because the double bind of race and gender skews literary influence toward creative affirmation. Moreover, Hurston herself here misreads and covertly appropriates material from her contemporary, Nella Larsen, for whom the South, the return "home," and female sexuality were problematic. If Larsen's heroine embraces such goals, Hurston's Janie covertly refutes their force when she returns to her own house, alone, and surrenders her dependence on heterosexual love. While Alice Walker names Larsen—as well as Jean Toomer, whose *Cane* treats similar material—a precursor, her deep dedication to Hurston originates in that foremother's subversive material, which Walker herself covertly appropriates under the guise of idealized matriliny.

For while celebrating literary matrilineage in her essays, Walker subverts that celebration on the margins of her own fictional texts. In *Meridian*, for example, Walker restates yet revises the subterranean theme in Hurston's *Eyes* that women most truly become themselves without men. At seventeen, Meridian has married, divorced, and given up custody of her son; she views sex as a "sanctuary" from male aggression and, having never been aroused, at first refuses her future lover, Truman Held. "And for her part in what happened," the narrator states, "Meridian paid dearly."[35] Consequently Truman dates white exchange stu-

35. Alice Walker, *Meridian* (New York: Pocket Books, 1977), p. 106; hereafter cited as *Meridian* in parentheses in the text. See also Barbara Christian, *Black Women Novelists: The*

dents and eventually marries Lynne Rabinowitz; consequently, when she and Truman have sex once, Meridian has no orgasm, gets pregnant, aborts the fetus, and ties her tubes. Like Janie, Meridian surrenders her sexuality, not, however, for female voice and power but for politics. The novel begins at its story's chronological end when Truman encounters a parodic and corrupted emblem of capitalist endeavor: the circus wagoner who displays his wife's corpse for cash. He allows black children to view only on Thursdays, and to integrate the spectators, Meridian must ironically confront an army tank and stand before its guns. Despite Truman's shock, he and the reader see that the Civil Rights movement served not to eradicate southern racism but to perpetuate parodies of itself, to keep poor black people in their place, and to teach black revolutionaries that racism will end only when the capitalist system alters. The ensuing retrospective narrative reveals the past, the unexpected consequences and complexities of political action: nervous breakdown, acquaintance rape, scapegoating of white (Jewish) women, divorce, and death. The terrible fictional price Walker exacts from her characters and in particular her heroine—Meridian "pays"—originates in Walker's own guilty ambivalence about political action; for despite her supposed apotheosis at the novel's end, Meridian has little visible effect on racist America. Politics becomes "performance," a personal yet powerless volunteer suffering.

The narrator implies and narrative structure confirms that Meridian persists in political performances—takes chances with her life—because she sacrifices her motherhood. As daughter, Meridian feels guilt for having shattered her own mother's frail independence and creativity, her "emerging self" (*Meridian*, p. 51). Now anti-intellectual, prejudiced, and blindly religious, Meridian's mother nonetheless once fought her father's sexism, her own poverty, and the racist system to become a schoolteacher. The cost: *her* mother's life and willing self-sacrifice. As a daughter who becomes a mother and so participates in matrilineage, Meridian's mother represents the history of black motherhood: a legacy of suffering, endurance, and self-sacrifice. Meridian despises this "narrowing of perspective" yet also idealizes its self-righteous uprightness. Caught by such personal and historical guilt, Meridian views her own motherhood as "slavery," her wish to relinquish her child both his "salvation" and proof of her "monstrous" inadequacy (*Meridian*, pp. 69, 90); she desires to "murder" her son but represses such unnatural thoughts and so turns them against herself; she abortively attempts metaphorical and compensatory motherhood in "adopting" an untameable, pregnant, and self-destructive "wild child." A unique woman without "precedent" or precursor, Meridian considers

Development of a Tradition, 1892–1976 (Westport, Conn.: Greenwood Press, 1980), pp. 212–21; Deborah McDowell, "The Self in Bloom: Alice Walker's *Meridian*," *College Literature Association Journal* 24, no. 3 (March 1981): 262–75.

herself unworthy of the black matriliny she idealizes and fails to see that her foremothers, unlike herself, were "compelled by necessity" to endure their suffering (*Meridian*, p. 91). She therefore refutes her own motherhood, despite knowing that her grandmothers—and by implication Meridian herself—defined freedom as keeping their children. Narrative structure exposes Meridian's consequent guilt: she gets ill, takes to bed, whispers "Mama, I *love* you" to her teacher, and rises to undertake her performances only when this mother surrogate responds, "I forgive you" (*Meridian*, pp. 124–25). Walker's fiction covertly exposes her own nonfictional misreading and idealization of matriliny.

In *The Color Purple*, Walker extends the conflation of motherhood and sisterhood she undertook in "*One* Child." In doing so, she appropriates the subterranean gender politics of Hurston's *Eyes*. As Celie reports in her letters to God, paternal incest has figuratively killed her mother and literally gotten her "big." Her father sells her children and barters her to a man who needs household help. Owned, beaten, and degraded by her husband's "climbing on top" of her, Celie survives only by learning her sister-in-law's lesson: fight back against the gender system based on male dominance and female submission that breeds violence against women and wives. Celie sees Sofia beat Harpo and Shug Avery talk back to Mr. _____ and so learns to resist with fist and—as did Janie—with words. In addition she discovers Sofia's "amazon" sisters "stuck together." When Celie decides to leave her husband, she combines these sisterly lessons: she tells Harpo his attempt to make Sofia "mind" indirectly caused the white mayor to throw the uppity, talking-back woman in jail; she threatens Mr. _____ that she, her children, and her sister Nettie "gon whup [his] ass"; she encourages Squeak, Harpo's lover, to laugh at male pride, go north to sing in public, and take back her proper name, Mary Agnes; and she goes off to Memphis with her female lover, Shug Avery.[36]

This idealized sisterhood of women-loving women, however, masks a subterranean narrative violence against men and mothers that restates Hurston's. In *Purple*, Walker rereads and revises Hurston's concealed anxiety about motherhood and distrust of heterosexuality by idealizing sisterhood and economic progress. As Sofia, for example, fights back against Harpo, he begins to overeat and look "big" while Sofia constructs swings and shingles. At the end of the narrative, Mr. _____ sews pants with Celie, and Harpo stays home with the kids while Sofia works in the sisters' dry goods store. Women gain strength by feminizing their men and creating a community of women and men who affirm female values of loving equality. In the same way, Nettie and Celie independently imagine a God neither man nor woman who loves "everything"; this God metaphorically calls Nettie home from Africa so the reunited sisters may

36. Alice Walker, *The Color Purple* (New York: Washington Square Press, 1982).

inherit their rightful estate and become merchants. Walker's romanticized female economics revises the politics expressed in *Meridian* and
misreads Hurston's analysis in which class aspiration and male dominance—Jody's "high chair," Nanny's organ in the parlor—cooperate to
oppress the black woman. Moreover, in *Purple* mothers suffer death early
or see their functions displaced onto sisters. Nettie raises Celie's children
in Africa, where in a political subplot African daughters, like their American counterparts, must combat male violence against women (clitoridec-
tomy, lack of educational and work opportunity) and so depend on
idealized but ineffectual female support networks among mothers and
daughters.

Other contemporary black women writers likewise question anxiety-
free matrilineage. Toni Morrison's novel *Sula* values the black woman
free enough to take her sexual pleasure without the middle-class security
of "nesting," yet the novel rages against mothers as women who sacrifice
contentment, limbs, and lives for their children. Sula watches her mother,
Hannah Peace, burn to death because Hannah loves but does not like her
daughter; Hannah as a child wanted her mother, Eva Peace, to play with
her although the novel defines such play as a middle-class luxury: for a
poor black woman, mother love means ensuring a child's survival. In *Sula*,
black matrilineage breeds resentment and death, not affirmation; these
free and mothering women pay with their lives, even though the author
calls attention to her own motherhood in the book's dedication to her
sons. Another example is *Corregidora* by Gayle Jones, in which black
motherhood is portrayed as a scourge. Ursa's mothering ancestors were
raped by their masters. The terrible knowledge of her history and that of
all black women culminates in the novel's refusal to allow Corregidora
motherhood; she has a hysterectomy. In *Eva's Man*, Jones explores the
concomitant dangers of the black woman's sexuality: she is the queen bee
who poisons men with love.

The black woman's history of suffering, however, necessitates her
survival. Seeking survival and so matrilineal affirmation, the black woman
writer paradoxically marks her texts with a heroine's suffering and the
effects of oppression. Hurston explores the power while covertly disguising the danger of finding her black female voice; as literary precursor, she
inscribes this danger on the margins of her fiction, her folktales, her
autobiography. Yet the double bind of race and gender that scars her text
also enables misreading. White feminist critics may misread narrative
signs of concealment because of their double commitment to interpretation and feminist theory; black feminist critics, because of their commitment to reading, feminism, and affirmation of black community. Yet
misreading, I would argue, makes reading and criticism possible. For a
text inevitably bears scars and contains gaps, as blindness tempers all
critical insight. My own readings here bear the trace of my race, no doubt,

as well as my gender. Yet read we must, for this multiple and unavoidable misreading empowers poetic influence, facilitates understanding between women of color and white women, and creates literary tradition. As her literary daughters—and critics—misread Hurston, they also reread her and encourage other readers to do likewise. As we seek our matrilineage, we too will idealize, covertly appropriate, and conceal as we expose and revise our anxiety, our misreading, our history. Our mothers' gardens, like Hurston's, grow weeds as well as flowers, and rightly so.

Department of English
Colby College

PART IV

INVENTING SELVES AND CONSTITUTING COMMUNITY

"TOGETHER AND IN HARNESS":
WOMEN'S TRADITIONS IN THE SANCTIFIED CHURCH

CHERYL TOWNSEND GILKES

All human communities contain enterprising and historically aware members who struggle to maintain the cherished values, statuses, roles, activities, and organizations of earlier generations that serve to structure the group's presentation of self and, therefore, constitute tradition. Within the black community in the United States, women have been some of the most enterprising agents of tradition. Since sociologists have seriously neglected study of tradition, women, and black people, black women's traditions in community institutions represent the most under-developed topic of social inquiry.

Black women and men have perceived racial oppression to be the most pervasive source of their individual and group suffering, but it has not been the sole catalyst for their collective action. In addition to mounting organized responses to problems of political subordination, economic exploitation, and social exclusion, black people have constructed a historical community that has provided a context for traditions, distinctive ethnic identity, and group consciousness. When pressure to abandon tradition has come from outside the black community, maintaining tradi-

Earlier versions of this article were presented to the Women's Studies in Religion Program of the Harvard Divinity School and to the *Signs* Communities of Women Conference, held February 18–20, 1983, at the Center for Research on Women, Stanford University. I wish to acknowledge the support of Boston University's Faculty Research Program, the Women's Studies in Religion Program of the Harvard Divinity School, the Inter-University Research Group on the Intersection of Gender and Race, and the Bunting Institute of Radcliffe College for their contributions at various stages of the research and writing. I also wish to thank Paule Verdet, Thomas Koenig, and two anonymous *Signs* reviewers for criticisms and editorial suggestions.

This essay originally appeared in *Signs*, vol. 10, no. 4, Summer 1985.

tion has become a matter of political resistance, even though this struggle may take place in parts of the community that typically avoid confrontation with the dominant culture. For example, religion and religious activity have been the most important spheres for the creation and maintenance of tradition. Black women have invested considerable amounts of time, energy, and economic resources in the growth and development of religious organizations.

Recognition of the variety of strong traditions that black women have established in the religious and secular affairs of their community has been obscured by sociologists' exclusive focus on family roles and on black women's deviation from patriarchal expectations in a sexist and racist society. The tendency to view black churches only as agencies of sociopolitical change led by black male pastors also obscures the central and critical roles of black women. Throughout all varieties of black religious activity, women represent from 75 to 90 percent of the participants; yet there is little documentation or analysis of their role in the development of this oldest and most autonomous aspect of black community life.[1] This article examines the place and importance of black women and their traditions within one segment of the black religious experience, the Sanctified Church.

The Sanctified Church, a significant but misunderstood segment of a very pluralistic black church, comprises those independent denominations and congregations formed by black people in the post-Reconstruction South and their direct organizational descendents. In contrast to those Baptist and Methodist denominations organized before the Civil War, the Sanctified Church represents the black religious institutions that arose in response to and largely in conflict with postbellum changes in worship traditions within the black community. Although these congregations and denominations were part of the Holiness and Pentecostal movements of the late nineteenth and early twentieth centuries, the label "Sanctified Church" emerged within the black community to distinguish congregations of "the Saints" from those of other black Christians. This label not only acknowledges the sense of ethnic kinship and consciousness underlying the black religious experience but also designates the part of the black religious experience to which a Saint belongs without having to go through the sometimes dizzying maze of organizational histories involving at least twenty-five denominations.

The importance of the Sanctified Church lies in its relationship to

---

1. Teressa Hoover, "Black Women and the Churches: Triple Jeopardy," in *Black Theology: A Documentary History*, ed. Gayraud Wilmore and James Cone (Maryknoll, N.Y.: Orbis Books, 1979), pp. 377–88; James Tinney, "The Religious Experience of Black Men," in *The Black Male*, ed. Lawrence E. Gary (Beverly Hills, Calif.: Sage Publications, 1981), pp. 269–76. See also Pearl Williams-Jones, "A Minority Report: Black Pentecostal Women," *Spirit: A Journal of Issues Incident to Black Pentecostalism* 1, no. 2 (1977): 31–44.

black history, its normative impact on the larger black religious experience, and its respect for and positive redefinition of black women's historical experience. When black people were first making choices about their
cultural strategies as free women and men, the Sanctified Church rejected
a cultural and organizational model that uncritically imitated Euro-
American patriarchy. In the face of cultural assaults that used the economic and sexual exploitation of black women as a rationale for their
denigration, the Sanctified Church elevated black women to the status of
visible heroines—spiritual and professional role models for their
churches. At a time when Baptist and Methodist denominations relegated
Christian education to the structural margins of their organizations, the
Sanctified Church professionalized this activity, and women were able to
use their roles as educators and the "educated" as a source of power and
career opportunity. At a time when employment opportunities for black
women were the worst possible, the Sanctified Church presented "professional" role models for black working women to emulate. Higher education and work were identified as legitimate means of upward mobility for
black women, and they were encouraged to achieve economic power
through white-collar employment. As a consequence, the women's growing economic power helped to maintain their collective autonomy and
reinforced their heroic role in the church. Finally, taking their cue from
the feminist infrastructure of the black women's racial uplift movement,
churchwomen created an institutional basis for women's self-con-
sciousness. The result was an alternative model of power and leadership
within the most authoritarian and least democratic of formal organizations—the episcopally governed church. These religious organizations
transformed the negative and contradictory experiences of black women
into an aspect of community life that maintained tradition and fostered
social and individual change.

Within the Sanctified Church, black women have created for themselves a variety of roles, careers, and organizations with great influence
but with variable access to structural authority. Their activities and their
consciousness represent a part of the black religious experience that
underscores both the dynamic and unsettled nature of gender relations in
the wider black community and the historical centrality of gender as a
public issue within it. Although the women in the Sanctified Church have
worked within structures that range from egalitarian to purely patriarchal, they have neither ceased nor relaxed their efforts to improve their
status and opportunities within these organizations. In a variety of ways,
their efforts are related to those of women in other black religious and
secular organizations.

Women's experience in the Sanctified Church has been part of the
larger historical role of black women, a role that emphasizes indepen-

dence, self-reliance, strength, and autonomy and that contradicts the dominant culture's expectations and demands of women.[2] Like many of the black community's activities of the late nineteenth and early twentieth centuries, the rise of the Sanctified Church contained a gender-conscious response to the problems of racial oppression. Concern about the status and role of women was reflected in one among a number of cultural debates within the post-Reconstruction black community. In a response to black women's suffering and role demands in the context of violent racial oppression, the Sanctified Church took account of at least four specific aspects of their history when developing churchwomen's roles: the devaluation of black women by dominant culture, the education of black women and their recruitment as educators of "the Race" during the late nineteenth and early twentieth centuries, the "relative" economic independence of black women through sustained participation in the labor force, and the autonomous political organization of black women between 1892 and 1940.[3]

The rise of the Sanctified Church also occurred when "liberation of the race was the immediate goal of blacks, [and] the men attached great importance to the females' roles in the effort."[4] In 1896, black women formed the National Association of Colored Women after several years of autonomous organizing. Their efforts earned them W. E. B. DuBois's admiration and praise as the "intellectual leadership of the Race."[5] The ethic sustaining their efforts supported women's leadership as a necessary part of the overall effort to benefit the community and the world. Club-woman Josephine St. Pierre Ruffin stated this clearly in 1892: "Our women's movement is a woman's movement in that it is led and directed by women for the good of women and men, for the benefit of all humanity. . . . We want, we ask the active interest of our men; . . . we are not alienating or withdrawing, we are only coming to the front, willing to

2. Bonnie Thornton Dill, "The Dialectics of Black Womanhood," *Signs: Journal of Women in Culture and Society* 4, no. 3 (Spring 1979): 543–55.

3. On the dominant culture's devaluation of black women, see Bell Hooks, *Ain't I a Woman: Black Women and Feminism* (Boston: South End Press, 1981). On the role of black women in education, see Linda Perkins, "Black Women and Racial 'Uplift' Prior to Emancipation," in *The Black Woman Cross-culturally*, ed. Filomena Chioma Steady (Cambridge, Mass.: Schenkman Publishing Co., 1981), pp. 317–34; Angela Y. Davis, *Women, Race and Class* (New York: Random House, 1981); and Gerda Lerner, ed., *Black Women in White America: A Documentary History* (New York: Random House, 1971). On the "relative" economic independence of black women, see Dill; and Davis. On the political organization of black women, see Perkins; Davis; and Cheryl Townsend Gilkes, "Living and Working in a World of Trouble: The Emergent Career of the Black Woman Community Worker" (Ph.D. diss., Northeastern University, 1978).

4. Perkins, p. 321.

5. W. E. B. DuBois, "Votes for Women," in *The Crisis Writings*, ed. Daniel Walden (1912; reprint, Greenwich, Conn.: Fawcett Publications, 1972), pp. 339–40, esp. p. 340.

join any others in the same work."[6] "The Saints" carried this ethic and a positive perception of the role of the "Race woman" into their new denominational structures as they separated or were ejected from the more established Baptist and Methodist churches. Specific women's tradition reflected the high value placed on women's political and educational leadership.

Leaders of the early Sanctified Church were also responsive to the fact that the majority of job opportunities for black women were in domestic service and agricultural work. As black people migrated and the church became more urban, this consciousness generated a concern for the problems of black women as household domestics. As household workers, black women were subject to sexual exploitation by white men who assumed that all black women were morally loose and appreciated male advances. Many black parents saw the education of their daughters as a strategy to avoid such risks. As a result, white observers often criticized black parents' failure to discriminate against their daughters. These educated women were expected to play a role in elevating their sisters, and black women's gatherings were the settings of just such "uplifting" socialization. Church and community activities were organized around household domestics' "time off" as alternatives to the entertainments available in the world of "sinners." Churches encouraged both the educated and the uneducated to be "ladies." While not entirely feminist, these strategies fostered a high degree of woman consciousness within the black religious community.

The black women who responded to Holiness and Pentecostal preachers and evangelists represented the broad spectrum of Afro-American women. These women were as militantly pro-black, pro-woman, and pro-uplift as their Baptist and Methodist sisters were, and their political consciousness was fueled by spiritual zeal. They were somewhat more successful than Baptist and Methodist women in gaining access to the pulpit or lectern; in those churches where they failed, the "double pulpit" emerged as a compromise between the women's spiritual militance and biblical patriarchy. In some cases, Baptist and Methodist women defected to the Sanctified Church in order to exercise their gifts.

The militancy of organized women in the Sanctified Church led to the almost total divergence of women's leadership roles from that of the "pastor's wife." Such separation of marital role from leadership status came more slowly in black Baptist and Methodist churches than in the Sanctified Church, where women's opportunities for leadership became more and more diverse, offering a wide choice of religious careers. In

6. Elizabeth Lindsey Davis, *Lifting as They Climb: A History of the National Association of Colored Women* (Washington, D.C.: Howard University, Moorland Spingarn Research Center, 1933), p. 19.

those denominations in which women were unable to become elders, pastors, and bishops, they assumed the roles of church mothers, evangelists, missionaries, prayer band leaders, deaconesses, and, most important, "teachers"; these alternatives were also available in those denominations in which women were eligible for all leadership roles. Where churchwomen were officially "the second sex," they achieved quite powerful positions of influence and structural authority.

The various women's traditions existing within these churches are as much a response to the sociohistorical realities of black womanhood as to perceived biblical mandates and doctrines. One could almost argue that these traditions are more woman-centered than religious. Although all Protestants read the same King James Bible, the black interpretation of scripture had radically different organizational consequences than did the white male reading of the same texts. Whatever the degree of patriarchal control, black churches have been influenced in some way by the militancy of the women of the Sanctified Church.

"Women God Raised Up": The Elevation of Black Women

At the time when white Americans were calling black people a nation of "thieves, liars, and prostitutes,"[7] Sanctified Church members were calling each other "Saints." They perceived themselves to be set apart for sacred purposes; these men and women were confident that God "had raised them up" for a special calling. Regardless of the intensity of racial oppression, it was the responsibility of the "Saints" to do everything in their power to prevent whites from casting them down. Black women represented the overwhelming majority of "Saints" in need of elevation and protection from the physical and cultural assaults of white racism.

The church's resistance strategies have included the adoption of distinctive dress codes and the refusal to use first names in any public settings that could be interracial. Even cornerstones and signs listing church officers give only first initials and surnames. It is important to recognize that this tactic to achieve personhood applies to women as well as men: if male elders are listed with initials, church mothers are similarly listed. In church publications, elders, church mothers, and all others are also identified in this way. All this was (and still is) intended to prevent white racists from calling black Saints by their first names, a white practice used as a strategy to depersonalize and to devalue black people. Although largely overlooked as a tactic in cultural resistance, the Saints' use of initials rather than first names remains a very forceful answer to the daily irritations and abrasions of southern race relations. Accommodation to

7. Ibid.

racism is, in the context of the preaching of the Sanctified Church, an accommodation to sin.

Although white people withheld ordinary titles of respect for blacks, such as Mr., Mrs., and Miss, they relaxed such overt racism when using the religious titles of fellow southern Protestants. In the Baptist and Methodist churches, such courtesies were often extended only to the black preacher. The Sanctified Church, however, saw as ministry those roles reserved exclusively for women and therefore included women when contemplating the problem of interracial protocol. This failure to exclude women from protocol is clear testimony to the woman consciousness of the Sanctified Church, a consciousness evident in the glowing terms used to describe both women's and men's activities in denominational newspapers and reports. If images of the Sanctified Church were derived solely from such reading, one could almost believe that the roles of mothers, evangelists, and missionaries were structurally equivalent to those of the male elders, bishops, and pastors. Unlike men in other churches, men in the Sanctified Church have not ignored or trivialized women's roles. Thus these women with their expanded roles, important careers, and influence have been perceived as "the women God raised up."

The Church of God in Christ (COGIC), largest denomination of the Sanctified Church, ostensibly does not permit the ordination of women, and churchwomen have never let the matter rest. While there is a widespread agreement to disagree within the church, Bishop O. T. Jones represented the quintessence of the truce when he wrote, "The proper place of women in the church is an age old debate and from all appearances it seems that it perhaps will be an eternal one—for most mortals at least."[8] Despite its sexism, the church became the structural paradigm for other denominations. Despite or because of women's exclusion from pulpits, the most powerful Women's Department of any black denomination arose within the COGIC.

The Women's Department is a characteristic feature of the Sanctified Church denominations. James Shopshire argues that a defining characteristic of the power structures of these churches is their control by "a board of bishops" and the prevalence of an independently organized "women's work . . . where female leaders assume much authority, but with deference and loyalty to the bishops." Although these churches adopt the terminology associated with episcopally governed churches, they reflect the Baptist roots of their leadership in a tendency toward a Presbyterian style of more or less sharing power between the laity and the clergy. As a result, "a person may be upwardly mobile . . . to regional and

8. Charles H. Pleas, *Fifty Years of Achievement (History): Church of God in Christ* (Memphis, Tenn.: Church of God in Christ Publishing House, n.d.), p. 35.

national positions of relative independence from local congregations."[9] This is especially true for Women's Departments, which offer career mobility for a wide range of women.

Women leaders include those called to the ministry and denied access to pastoral positions, women who prefer the role of evangelist to that of pastor, women who actually have charge of churches in the absence of a pastor, and women who are Spirit-filled religious activists and congregational leaders. The political skill of the early Women's Department of the COGIC was such that nearly all women's roles, including that of "laywoman," were eventually included in that denomination's official definition of the ministry. The term "layman" was not so included. Thus the avenues of social mobility for women in the church branched out and were officially recognized. The diversity of roles allowed women to exercise influence beyond their congregations, which laymen were not organized to do. Women's Departments today retain unparalleled power in matters of policy and practice for all laywomen and continue to provide ladders of career mobility. They communicate both to the women of the church and to the male leadership and, regardless of restrictions, determine the role models available to churchwomen. This means that the choice of heroines of the Women's Department, and thus of the church as a whole, reflects churchwomen's values and view of reality.

In order to contribute to the construction of those role models in the early days of the Sanctified Church, women needed to attend the regional and national conventions and convocations. For the black women of the late nineteenth and early twentieth centuries, such travel was full of risks, and Jim Crow laws made these undertakings all the more difficult. Since women played a large part in developing individual congregations, the church recognized as issues of common concern the problems of their travel and need for respect in public places. In order to counter the stereotypes used as rationales for the abuse of black women, Sanctified Church women were encouraged to "dress as becometh holiness." One early bishop was convinced that the sight of women of the COGIC dressed according to the dictates of the Women's Department would restrain the most ardent racists.

There was a decided contrast between the ecstatic style of worship of these churches and the formal style of dress. Women wore black or white uniformlike dresses, and evangelists and church mothers devised a uniform or "habit" called "the Saint" to wear in services and on trains. At regional or national meetings, the highest ranking woman—the district missionary, the district supervisor, or the national supervisor—determined the dress of all other women present and decided whether they

9. James Shopshire, "A Socio-historical Characterization of the Black Pentecostal Movement in America" (Ph.D. diss., Northwestern University, 1975), pp. 144–45.

wore white on a particular day. While this may seem a rather trivial matter, the problem of discipline was not, and clergymen were required to adhere to equally stringent dress codes.

Thus the women of the early COGIC and other Sanctified Church denominations achieved such a position of respect and autonomy that they defined the content of their own roles. Furthermore, church members could not advance ideologies of patriarchy that contradicted standards of holiness since "holiness" was the most important achieved status in these churches—and a status not humanly conferred. Biblical debate concerning women was confined to structural norms, not the nature, quality, or character of women per se. Denominations that ordained women to be elders and pastors argued about women becoming bishops; in others in which all roles were open, there was no controversy. However, the egalitarian denominations would not recognize a woman's call at as early an age as they would a man's.[10] Within the COGIC, the church was forced to argue that women were completely capable but that the COGIC did not recognize the feminist biblical argument.[11]

Since women evangelists or revivalists founded or "dug out" many churches, they could not be excluded from church histories; they were too important to the tradition of holiness and to church growth. When male church leaders identified in their spiritual biographies those preachers who effected their conversions, the revivalists were often women. Thus the personal and congregational accounts passed down in written records and oral tradition placed a high value on the contribution of women and men to the most important goal of the church—salvation and holiness.[12]

The extension of women's spiritual contributions into autonomous leadership networks and careers fostered the development of heroines and myth, the most important pillars of tradition. In a social setting that placed a primary value on spirituality, "the women God raised up" as "Mothers in Zion" could not be excluded simply for the sake of male domination. The many tensions created by the intrusion of patriarchal norms were eased by the fact that both men and women placed a high value on holiness, and women played a heroic role in upholding that value. Women's allusion to Deborah who "arose a mother in Israel" in their self-descriptions provided a legitimate counterideology to the pa-

10. Church of the Living God, Christian Workers for Fellowship, *Glorious Heritage: The Golden Book—Documentary and History* (n.p.: Church of the Living God, Christian Workers for Fellowship, 1976).

11. Church of God in Christ (COGIC), *Official Manual with the Doctrines and Discipline of the Church of God in Christ* (Memphis, Tenn.: COGIC Publishing House, 1973).

12. Lucille Cornelius, *The Pioneer History of the Church of God in Christ* (Memphis, Tenn.: COGIC Publishing House, 1975); Church of the Living God; Pleas.

triarchal desires of churchmen.[13] Finally, elevation to clearly articulated roles of spiritual leadership guaranteed that female heroines were part of the culture of the church shared by both men and women.

"Women May Teach": Education as a Source of Power

Education has represented a supreme cultural value in the black church and community. The Sanctified Church arose during the height of the struggle for black education, which led to the expanded role of women as educators. The parents of church founders were slaves who had made their children's education a life's goal that was often not realized. Church officials' personal accounts of conversion echo laments over their own lack of education. Because the Sanctified Church became stereotyped as the sects and cults of illiterate black masses and disaffected urban migrants, both black and white observers failed to apprehend the high value these denominations placed on literacy and higher education. Thus it is important not to view their teaching ministries as a devalued area of female segregation. Male denominational leaders recruited educated women precisely because of their importance to the future.

The Sanctified Church's emphasis on biblical authority made learning "the Word" an important means for living a sanctified life. Educational goals therefore comprised general literacy, biblical literacy, advanced academic and professional achievement, and biblical expository skills, and these goals apparently ranked second in priority after salvation and holiness. The Saints were encouraged to acquire "the learning" without losing "the burning." Those able to teach biblical and general literacy skills and to provide appropriate spiritual role models were chosen as teachers.

The growth in women's roles as teachers resulted from a combination of male decisions and female enterprise. The male church organizers shared the larger cultural value of education, and their decisions to recruit female educators converged with the women's desires for important roles in their churches and with trends toward black women's education in the wider community. Recruitment occurred during that period in black history when the education of women was a conscious response to aspects of their oppression and when they were also being encouraged to act as educators of "the Race." Thus the deployment of women teachers in black education was carried out with almost total disregard for the dominant culture's norms; these women were not limited to teaching children or relegated to roles subordinate to men's. Black women capitalized on their leadership in church education. The early Women's Departments

13. Judg. 5:7.

revolved around the Prayer and Bible Study Bands, which expanded the literacy skills of women collectively; these groups paralleled the clubs and seminar groups that were part of the early National Association of Colored Women. This collective self-education was reflected in the expansion of women's leadership roles in denominations and in the growth of the Women's Departments.

Although engaged in conflict with the larger black community over the importance of ecstatic worship, the Sanctified Church admired the same heroines in racial uplift and black education. The examples of prominent churchwomen such as Mary McLeod Bethune, Nannie Helen Burroughs, Ida B. Wells, and Mary Church Terrell prompted the founder of the COGIC, Bishop C. H. Mason, to recruit Mother Lizzie Woods Roberson, a Baptist teacher and academy matron, to be the first "overseer" of the women's work. Encouraged to travel in order to enlist and appoint women leaders, she also conducted revivals as an organizer. Another woman, Arenia C. Mallory, was hired as a teacher at Saints' Academy in Lexington, Mississippi. Church histories describe her as a protégée of Mary McLeod Bethune. After the death of the first principal of Saints' Academy, Mallory became head of the school, which then grew from a primary academy to an accredited junior college. For a while, she was the only black woman college president. As conflicts over theology, doctrine, biblical interpretation, and church polity fostered differentiation within the Sanctified Church, women's importance as educators and the high value placed on educated women were not diminished. When denominations argued about the ordination of women, those that chose to ordain preserved the teaching roles of evangelist and missionary.[14]

In addition to their role in developing attitudes about and organizations for formal education, Sanctified Church women were permitted to teach the Gospel. Teaching the Gospel involved setting forth biblical doctrine, church polity, and duties; conducting revivals; presenting teachings in the morning service in lieu of and in the style of a sermon; and "having charge of a church in the absence of the pastor."[15] The tasks of the teaching role differed very little from the task of the preaching role reserved for men. In some denominations, evangelists not only could have charge of churches but also, as in the case of Pentecostal Assemblies of the World, could serve communion and perform marriages. In some instances, the difference between women's and men's credentials was merely internal; for all practical and legal purposes, women evangelists were clergy. Often members of particular congregations have been hard-pressed to distinguish between men's preaching and women's teaching. One young woman I interviewed observed, "I went to the service and the

14. COGIC; Church of the Living God.
15. COGIC.

elder preached. Then he invited the women to speak. They preached, and they were much better than the man."

In the COGIC, women developed their own standards for examining and promoting evangelists. While it is conceivable that a COGIC church-man may be ordained as an elder with very little preaching and adminis-trative experience, the Women's Department sets radically different re-quirements for women aspiring to become national evangelists. In order to receive such a license, a woman must preach revival successfully in seven states.[16] COGIC churchwomen are strongly motivated to develop their gifts and to develop a national reputation as revivalists in order to receive approval from the Women's Department.

The most widely shared value in the total black religious experience is the high premium placed on good preaching, which is as important in the black church as good music—another area in which women are not restricted. In the COGIC, the women's system guarantees that their "teaching" skills are superior. The dynamic and effective teaching of these women stands in stark contrast to the official stance of the COGIC that women are not called to preach. The availability of women evangel-ists who are in theory skilled "teachers" but in reality excellent preachers allows the elder with minimal skills in the pulpit to provide good preaching for his congregation. Since black Baptist and Methodist de-nominations tend to call all evangelists "Reverend" and to call male pastors conducting revival away from their own churches "Evangelist," the uninitiated may believe that these women are preachers. In the formative days of the Sanctified Church, the role of evangelist was an alternative for those women in Baptist and Methodist denominations who were unable to exercise their gifts either from the pulpit or from the floor. Such women went "over" into the Sanctified Church. Contemporary changes among Baptists and Methodists have reversed this earlier trend.

Women's concentration in educational roles in the early Sanctified Church was not simply a form of female segregation; instead it was the basis for alternative structures of authority, career pathways, and spheres of influence. More important, those leaders and historical accounts that provide the church with normative legitimacy and modify the stereotype of its members as poor and illiterate credit the influence of women's educational work. Given the overall, sometimes exaggerated, respect and deference that the black community confers on educators, these women have legitimized the image of the "professional" woman throughout the church. As a result, women in the Sanctified Church have established a more differentiated model of social mobility and occupational aspiration than have the men.

16. Women's Department, COGIC, *Women's Handbook* (Memphis, Tenn.: COGIC Publishing House, 1980).

"$10,000 in a Paper Bag":
The Economic Limits of Subordination

In the black community, educated women work outside the home. Contrary to trends in the dominant culture, the higher the social class of black women, the greater their rate of labor force participation.[17] Organizers of the black Holiness and Pentecostal churches were children of freedwomen who worked for wages and thus were more sympathetic to the problems and stereotypes black women faced. These church leaders learned that it was working churchwomen who decided what proportion of their earnings would go to the church. However, black churchwomen did not wait for their pastors to discover their economic importance; they demonstrated their economic power collectively. After 1906, black congregations, conventions, and denominational convocations became acquainted with Women's Day, when women take charge of the program and turn over to the congregation, the convention, or the denomination the money they have raised. In one church I visited, this contribution was one-third of the church's budget for the year. While black congregations also hold Men's Days, men have rarely matched the contributions of the women. The fund-raising ability of women remains a traditional source of male-female rivalry in black churches.

The overwhelming female majorities in the early Sanctified Church meant that women's economic enterprise and labor force participation were essential for church growth and survival. Thus women's financial power was a major contradiction to the ethic of male domination and control. This contradiction was intensified by the dynamics of economic decision making in black families and black women's relatively greater economic independence.

Strong Women's Departments retained control over the disbursement and allocation of their funds. Women paid the expenses of their leaders and staff members, collected offerings for the evangelists and church mothers "teaching" in the churches and representing districts and congregations at national meetings, and provided benevolence for unemployed men, women, and their families. Sanctified Church women raised money for their pastors' and bishops' wives to travel to conventions and simply to have some funds of their own. These women believed in economic cooperation with men, not in economic dependence on them.

Black women have a history of handling financial matters efficiently. Early Women's Departments often assessed each member an equal amount of money to meet goals, one of several monetary practices that paralleled those of the clubs of the National Association of Colored

---

17. Priscilla Douglas, "Black Working Women: Factors Affecting Labor Market Experience," Working Paper (Wellesley College, Center for Research on Women, 1980).

Women. As their activities grew, Sanctified Church women adopted the practice of contributing money throughout the year and then presenting this collection at the end of Women's Day or of a convention. Such practices had their roots in benevolent and mutual aid associations, with the sacred and secular practices becoming mutually influential. In a sense, churchwomen extended their domestic economic practices to their households of racial uplift and their households of faith.

By 1951, the COGIC Women's Department had grown to such an extent that the women began meeting in a separate convention under the leadership of Lillian Brooks Coffey. Using the structure of state and district supervisors, Mother Coffey collected money prior to and during the convention and then presented it to the church at the end of the convention. She inaugurated this practice at a convention where she surprised the church by presenting Bishop Crouch with "thousands of dollars" in a paper bag.[18] The women's importance to the survival of congregations led some to the false belief that black women were better off economically than black men. Since women tithed faithfully and prominently, it was easy to perceive them as the most powerful economic segment of the black community. Such perceptions made the image of the matriarch so believable to black men.

Whatever their beliefs and ideologies concerning female subordination, men in the Sanctified Church ultimately have been confronted with the economic necessity of maintaining good relationships with their female members. At some point during the church year, it has been in the interest of the most sexist and domineering pastor to advocate financial support for the local, district, and national women's work. Like almost all black pastors, these men also have acknowledged the collective economic power of churchwomen on Women's Day—and they often have vacated their pulpits to do so. Finally, the collective economic power of women has been reinforced at the district, jurisdictional, and national levels when the superintendents and bishops receive the quarterly or annual "reports" from the Women's Department.

"The Women Stuck Together": Collective Autonomy

Women's economic power has limited attempts by bishops and pastors to impose themselves directly on the activities of women. Churchwomen have thus been free to discuss issues and problems that churchmen may not have wanted to hear. While the dynamics and degree of male domination of local congregations varies, black women, because of

---

18. Cornelius (n. 12 above), p. 24. Oral tradition and interviews set the amount at a minimum of $10,000.

their autonomous organizations, occasionally remind their brethren, "If it wasn't for the women, you wouldn't have a church."

Although many denominations were formed between 1895 and 1950, those that survived and flourished were those with strong Women's Departments. Structures of female influence enabled denominations with charismatic male founders to grow after those founders died; other denominational movements with high visibility but no structures of female influence almost disappeared. The Women's Department of the COGIC was formed at approximately the same time that the denomination was reconstituted as Pentecostal in 1907 and after women's auxiliaries, missions, societies, and clubs had grown and developed in black Baptist and Methodist churches. The founder of the COGIC, divorced from a woman who was still living, could not remarry. His position as an unmarried head of a church was almost unique in black church history, a marked departure from the traditional pattern of a preacher married to a professional woman leader (usually a teacher). This historical "accident" generated the model of a nearly autonomous women's organization. Mason not only recruited Mother Roberson to head the women's work but also on her advice appointed women's overseers along the same jurisdictional and district lines as the male overseers who later became bishops. The title "overseer," a literal translation of the Greek word usually translated as "bishop," was used in the early days of the church for both men and women leaders in the church. Such usage implied that the founders of the COGIC and other denominations initially envisioned a church organized in parallel structures of both male and female overseers. This vision was closer to the dual sex political systems characteristic of some West African societies than to the patriarchal episcopal polities of European origin.

The founding of the Sanctified Church coincided with the most extensive and energetic period of organizing by black women. In the 1890s, the Fire Baptized Holiness Church of God of the Americas was founded as an egalitarian denomination. The COGIC began as a Holiness church in 1895 toward the end of, but distinct from, the Church of God movement that established an interracial and egalitarian denomination. In the same year, black women began holding national conventions focused on the problems of "the Race" and of black women. Women were eligible for ordination in the A. M. E. Zion Church, the church of Harriet Tubman. During this period, they organized major women's auxiliaries among black Baptists and Methodists, and they formed the National Association of Colored Women, which assembled women across the boundaries of religion, class, and intensity of skin color. By 1907 and the beginning of the Pentecostal Movement, the black woman had a prominent image as Race woman, clubwoman, churchwoman, and educator in the black community. Black clubwomen and schoolteachers in the Sanctified Church were prepared to assume roles of leadership and possessed the skills to do so.

The period between 1895 and World War II was the era of "racial uplift." In addition to race relations, female employment, and the multiple problems of group advancement, black women made the "status of the ministry" a central concern of their national programs, first in the Colored Women's League and the Federation of Afro-American Women and, after the merger of these organizations, in the National Association of Colored Women.[19] Women in the Sanctified Church were committed to the cause of racial uplift. They retained their commitment to ecstatic worship, which black Baptists and Methodists were rejecting. They also retained an emphasis on women's interests, education, professionalism, and the cultivation of a black female image that contradicted the dominant culture's stereotypes.

Some of the organizational features of the Sanctified Church Women's Departments have since disappeared in the black women's clubs where they may have originated. One such example is the Women's Purity Class, where women still learn their "proper place" in their churches and homes. A Baptist clergywoman I interviewed who visited such a class remarked, "Those classes are interesting. One woman told me, 'The Bible says that I should be in subjection to my husband, but that's the *only* man!'" In these classes—as well as the meetings of the evangelists, missionaries, and church mothers; the Prayer and Bible Bands; the Sewing Circles; and the organizations of the Deacons' Wives, the Bishops' Wives, and the Pastors' Wives—women are able to develop a perspective on their position in their churches that includes important critiques of church politics and structure. In such settings, women learn the language of biblical feminism and maintain their collective autonomy, arguing that it is not "proper" for pastors "to teach . . . things that women should know."[20]

In structuring their activities, women in the Sanctified Church retained the features of organizations founded during the most intensive era of Afro-American feminism; the network of small groups they organized around churchwomen's specialized roles formed a feminist infrastructure within a patriarchal organization. Many women belonged to several of these groups, which provided multiple perspectives on women's roles in the form of direct statement and biblical allusions. When churchwomen showed their strength, it arose from these many networks and was described in biblical terms.

The role of the Women's Department in the COGIC during the crisis precipitated by the founder's death illustrates the importance of the

19. Elizabeth Lindsey Davis (n. 6 above).
20. Women's Department, COGIC (n. 16 above), p. 21.

women's infrastructure to the survival of the denomination. During that crisis, while the men were fighting constitutional battles in the court-rooms, the Women's Department continued to function under the leadership of Mother Anna Bailey. While sources are cryptic, the Women's Department seemed to exercise veto power over the direction of policy, structure, and choice of leaders. The women also participated in the election of the bishops, who in turn elected the presiding bishop. Finally, the church's newspaper took special note of Mother Bailey's approval of the final choice of the board.[21]

Writing later in an official church history, Lucille Cornelius emphasized the contribution of the Women's Department to the survival and integrity of the COGIC. She emphasized that "the women stuck together and held the church in harness until the brethren could find their identity in the form of leadership that we must have in this time."[22] The phrase "in harness," a biblical term meaning "prepared or organized for war," referred to the children of Israel leaving Egypt. The statement reflects some of the disdain that the well organized feel for the relatively disorganized; the women knew that they could do better. Cornelius's tone also suggests the frustration of many black women who, regardless of conflicts and inequities, were reluctant to abandon institutions they played a major role in building.

Churchwomen have advanced a public strategy of cooperation with men. While their oral tradition is militant, their written tradition is indulgent, eschewing overt conflict. Recently, church mothers were admonished to "remember . . . [that the pastors] are the Lord's people."[23] It seems that the biblical ethic of love and of church unity has reduced the temptation toward open rebellion. Yet these women are aware that other denominations have been founded by women more militant in opposing subordination. Examples of female leaders within the denomination heighten women's sense that entire congregations and perhaps the entire church could continue in the absence of male leadership. However, racial oppression serves to remind black women of the importance of unity. The tension generated by a hostile dominant culture encourages women to adopt a cooperative model of gender relations and to support male leadership that, as Cornelius wrote, is necessary "in this time."

Men in the early Sanctified Church were aware of the tension between women's leadership skills and the structural realities within their institutions. Although bishops and elders married evangelists and missionaries, historically a woman's marital status did not determine her access to leadership; only one of the four national supervisors of women was married to a man nationally prominent in the church. In a very few but significant cases where pastors died and were therefore "absent" from

21. Cornelius (n. 12 above), p. 27.
22. Ibid.
23. Women's Department, COGIC (n. 16 above), p. 21.

their churches, bishops did not appoint any other male leaders to replace them but left the widows, licensed evangelists, in charge. The COGIC discovered that such congregations were more efficiently managed.[24] Finally, while churchwomen today admonish their sisters to cooperate with pastors, many pastors head congregations that were "dug out" and managed by women until those women sent for a pastor.

In other denominations that do not restrict women, female evangelists have become elders or pastors through the prompting and encouragement of women's organizations. In the Church of the Living God, Christian Workers for Fellowship, for example, women recognized that the sacred traditions of the wider black community did not encourage women in ministry in the way they encouraged men.[25] Both churchwomen and clubwomen depended on their autonomous organizations to achieve positions of leadership.

The women's methods of leadership have evolved in direct contrast to the authoritarian style demanded by the nature of episcopal polity: hierarchical, individualistic, and dominating.[26] In comparison, women's leadership tends to be consensus oriented, collective, and more inclusive, involving larger numbers of people in decision making. Visible women leaders have been able to represent large organizations of women in both sacred and secular settings. Black churchwomen have thus transformed their autonomy into the form of power best described as influence and created a pluralist political structure in an episcopally governed church where pluralism was never intended.

The collectivism and autonomy of organized women has been the most significant historical factor in the survival of denominations within the Sanctified Church. In churches with structures derived from male positions, women's organizations with parallel structures maintain the visibility of female leaders. Finally, this collectivist orientation has also kept alive a cooperative model of gender relations and pluralist political practice in an elitist organization.

Beyond "This Time": Tradition, Cooperation, and Prospects for Change

Women's standing in the Sanctified Church presently ranges from subordination in the COGIC to equality with men in the Fire Baptized Holiness Church of God of the Americas and the Mount Calvary Holy

24. James Tinney, "Black Pentecostals: The Difference Is More Than Color," *Logos Journal* 10, no. 3 (1980): 16–19.

25. Church of the Living God (n. 10 above).

26. Jualynne Dodson, "Black Women as an Unknown Source of Organizational Change" (Providence, R.I., Society for the Scientific Study of Religion, 1982, mimeographed).

Church of America. While access to authority is a problem for these churchwomen, they do not experience structural marginality, a major difficulty for women in white churches. According to Rosemary Ruether, churchwomen were marginalized because they "seldom controlled the processes of the cultural interpretation of their actions," which led to their exclusion from the myths and heroic accounts central to church tradition. Women's exclusion from leadership followed, except "in those areas where roles based on gifts of the Spirit were recognized."[27] Both men and women in the Sanctified Church attain leadership through their expression of gifts of the Spirit, which perhaps explains in part why marginality and exclusion do not characterize the type of subordination women experience in black Pentecostal and Holiness denominations. Where the processes of cultural interpretation have been external to the church, the entire Sanctified Church has suffered. Where the interpretive process was internal to the church, black women influenced and, in some cases, controlled that process.

The politics of sexism in the Sanctified Church are the politics of incomplete male domination, and the politics of feminism are the politics of cooperative protest, collective enterprise, and assertive autonomy. Therefore, strong and visible women's traditions are part of the total church culture that is passed on in the socialization of new members. Recruits and young people learn beliefs, values, and ways of thinking that depart from the dominant culture's notion of women's place in churches and other formal organizations. Church members also learn to admire the distinctive aspects of black women's experience and their historical role without accepting the negative images and stereotypes imposed by the dominant culture.

By writing symbolic accounts of women's participation in the extraordinary events that made the growth and development of these denominations possible, churchwomen continue to reinforce these heroic images. In American society, women have been permitted more expression of gifts of the Spirit, the most important aspect of these denominations' identities. Clearly, women must be included in the symbolic accounts or myths strengthening the norms of holiness that define the unique position of the Sanctified Church on the continuum of black religious experience.

The presence of prominent female heroines in holiness has prevented churchwomen from becoming alienated by their structural subordination in the Sanctified Church. The collective and self-conscious politics of female influence modify the politics and pain of male domina-

---

27. Rosemary Radford Ruether and Eleanor McLaughlin, eds., *Women of Spirit: Female Leadership in the Jewish and Christian Traditions* (New York: Simon & Schuster, 1979), pp. 16–17.

tion. Over time, black women in the Sanctified Church have drawn on the strength of their skills and historical experiences to create structural conditions tending toward equality. Yet even in denominations where women have full access to authority, some of which were formed in protest against discrimination, black women and men have not pursued a course of antagonism or separatism. Instead, a model of dual-career religious leadership has emerged. Where women church members have a higher status than their husbands ("Mr. and Rev.," or "Deacon and Elder," or "Mr. and Elder"), men express pride in their wives' achievements. Through a combination of heroic accounts, symbolic leaders, and an alternative organizational setting, black women have maintained a tradition of protest and cooperation—a dialectical tradition—within the Sanctified Church.

The Sanctified Church and its women's traditions are an important resource for the entire range of the black religious experience. Churchmen cannot ignore the written tradition of women's achievement, and they ignore the oral tradition of cooperative protest with great difficulty. In denominations that do not ordain women, female members point to their tremendous records of service and continue the conflict over their role in the church. If and when these denominations change their stance—and there are a variety of reasons to be pessimistic about this prospect—ordained women will have a greater impact than they now do as unordained evangelists. As has been the case in the area of music, the Sanctified Church continues to have normative impact on the larger black experience greater than would be expected from its actual number of members, and that number is growing.

A major problem exists concerning the values of churchmen, which range from a commitment to patriarchy, domination, and hierarchy to a belief in male-female cooperation and mutual influence. The history of the Sanctified Church demonstrates that both sets of values exist in the world of black men. In the Sanctified Church and beyond, many black men want to achieve the pure patriarchy they have never truly experienced. The functional necessity of women to the very survival of congregations, convocations, and denominations opposes such a tendency. James Tinney suggests that some black men absent themselves from churches precisely because of authoritarian male domination.[28] However, such male resistance to religious patriarchy is undermined by the dominant culture's persistent denigration of black women as matriarchs who are too assertive, powerful, and aggressive. Such labeling feeds a sexist backlash within the black community that encourages a rejection of the

28. Tinney, "The Religious Experience of Black Men" (n. 1 above).

model of womanhood black women represent and deepens intragroup hostilities.[29]

Thus it has become fashionable since the civil rights movement to dismiss the achievements of black women in church, community, and society at large as a mere consequence of economic necessity. Unfortunately, many black men perceived the message of the 1960s to be, If you will be sexist, we white men won't be racist. Such ideological assaults led to attempts to enforce European or dominant culture patriarchy where it had been effectively resisted.

The disestablishment of sexism in the dominant culture remains a threat to many black males who perceive the traditional model of gender relations as a component of the goal of assimilation. In order to persist in this thinking, such men must reject as unseemly and inappropriate any institutional record that suggests a tradition of heroism by black women. They must refuse to transform their observations of women's church and community roles and of the historical records of the churches into an internalized norm of egalitarian gender relationships. The saving grace for black women in the Sanctified Church is that, even in a context of structural subordination, they do control the record books and therefore the written record of their role. As long as women are involved in this process of cultural interpretation, there exists a strong egalitarian potential within the Sanctified Church. Additionally, black women do have their allies among pastors who have never adopted or who have abolished the separate lectern or "double pulpit" and among sympathetic bishops who will ordain them to take a charge outside the church (e.g., military chaplaincies) or to begin new churches.

Racial oppression and its gender-specific racist ideologies still invade the black experience. Black women who do not conform to patriarchal traditions have been particularly victimized. Unless black women's image in the dominant culture changes radically, their struggles against racial oppression must proceed both inside and outside the black community; they will continue to be tied to internal struggles to maintain what power they now have in the face of embarrassed black male opposition, as well as to the external struggles with white racism. As long as racism limits opportunities for black men, black women will continue to express some ambivalence about competing with black men inside the black community and will also strive to avoid direct confrontation and overt conflict. As long as racism and patriarchy operate as combined forces in the oppression of black women and men, black women will not abandon those institutions that are responsive to the shared aspects of the problems. The

29. Dill (n. 2 above); Pauli Murray, "The Liberation of Black Women," in *Voices of the New Feminism*, ed. Mary L. Thompson (Boston: Beacon Press, 1970), and "Jim Crow and Jane Crow," in Lerner, ed. (n. 3 above), pp. 592–99; Hooks (n. 3 above).

history of formal and informal organization within the black community suggests that the cooperative and egalitarian model of male-female leadership would be the preferred outcome. Black women's traditions in the Sanctified Church yield great hope for the transformation of structures that alienate and trivialize women's experiences. In the meantime, black women will maintain their solidarity and organizational strength—"stuck together [holding] the church in harness"—until deliverance comes.

Department of Sociology
Boston University

FAMILY, RACE, AND POVERTY IN THE EIGHTIES

MAXINE BACA ZINN

The 1960s Civil Rights movement overturned segregation laws, opened voting booths, created new job opportunities, and brought hope to Black Americans. As long as it could be said that conditions were improving, Black family structure and life-style remained private matters. The promises of the 1960s faded, however, as the income gap between whites and Blacks widened. Since the middle 1970s, the Black underclass has expanded rather than contracted, and along with this expansion emerged a public debate about the Black family. Two distinct models of the underclass now prevail— one that is cultural and one that is structural. Both of them focus on issues of family structure and poverty.

The cultural deficiency model

The 1980s ushered in a revival of old ideas about poverty, race, and family. Many theories and opinions about the urban underclass rest on the culture-of-poverty debate of the 1960s. In brief, proponents of the culture-of-poverty thesis contend that the poor have a different way of life than the rest of society and that these cultural differences explain continued poverty. Within the current national

This essay originally appeared in *Signs*, vol. 14, no. 4, Summer 1989.

discussion are three distinct approaches that form the latest wave of deficiency theories.

The first approach—culture as villain—places the cause of the swelling underclass in a value system characterized by low aspirations, excessive masculinity, and the acceptance of female-headed families as a way of life.

The second approach—family as villain—assigns the cause of the growing underclass to the structure of the family. While unemployment is often addressed, this argument always returns to the causal connections between poverty and the disintegration of traditional family structure.

The third approach—welfare as villain—treats welfare and antipoverty programs as the cause of illegitimate births, female-headed families, and low motivation to work. In short, welfare transfer payments to the poor create disincentives to work and incentives to have children out of wedlock—a self-defeating trap of poverty.

Culture as villain

Public discussions of urban poverty have made the "disintegrating" Black family the force most responsible for the growth of the underclass. This category, by definition poor, is overwhelmingly Black and disproportionately composed of female-headed households. The members are perceived as different from striving, upwardly mobile whites. The rising number of people in the underclass has provided the catalyst for reporters' and scholars' attention to this disadvantaged category. The typical interpretation given by these social commentators is that the underclass is permanent, being locked in by its own unique but maladaptive culture. This thinking, though flawed, provides the popular rationale for treating the poor as the problem.

The logic of the culture-of-poverty argument is that poor people have distinctive values, aspirations, and psychological characteristics that inhibit their achievement and produce behavioral deficiencies likely to keep them poor not only within generations but also across generations, through socialization of the young.[1] In this argument, poverty is more a function of thought processes than of physical environment.[2] As a result of this logic, current discussions

---

[1] Mary Corcoran, Greg J. Duncan, Gerald Gurin, and Patricia Gurin, "Myth and Reality: The Causes and Persistence of Poverty," *Journal of Policy Analysis and Management* 4, no. 4 (1985): 516–36.

[2] Mary Corcoran, Greg J. Duncan, and Martha S. Hill, "The Economic Fortunes of Women and Children: Lessons from the Panel Study of Income Dynamics," *Signs: Journal of Women in Culture and Society* 10, no. 2 (Winter 1984): 232–48.

of ghetto poverty, family structure, welfare, unemployment, and out-of-wedlock births connect these conditions in ways similar to the 1965 Moynihan Report.[3] Because Moynihan maintained that the pathological problem within Black ghettos was the deterioration of the Negro family, his report became the generative example of blaming the victim.[4] Furthermore, Moynihan dismissed racism as a salient force in the perpetuation of poverty by arguing that the tangle of pathology was "capable of perpetuating itself without assistance from the white world."[5]

The reaction of scholars to Moynihan's cultural-deficiency model was swift and extensive although not as well publicized as the model itself. Research in the sixties and seventies by Andrew Billingsley, Robert Hill, Herbert Gutman, Joyce Ladner, Elliot Leibow, and Carol Stack, to name a few, documented the many strengths of Black families, strengths that allowed them to survive slavery, the enclosures of the South, and the depression of the North.[6] Such work revealed that many patterns of family life were not created by a deficient culture but were instead "a rational adaptational response to conditions of deprivation."[7]

A rapidly growing literature in the eighties documents the disproportionate representation of Black female-headed families in poverty. Yet, recent studies on Black female-headed families are largely unconcerned with questions about adaptation. Rather, they study the strong association between female-headed families and poverty, the effects of family disorganization on children, the demographic and socioeconomic factors that are correlated with single-parent status, and the connection between the economic

[3] Daniel P. Moynihan, "The Negro Family: The Case for National Action," in *The Moynihan Report and the Politics of Controversy*, ed. L. Rainwater and W. L. Yancy (Cambridge, Mass.: MIT Press, 1967), 39–132.

[4] Margaret Cerullo and Marla Erlien, "Beyond the 'Normal Family': A Cultural Critique of Women's Poverty," in *For Crying Out Loud*, ed. Rochelle Lefkowitz and Ann Withorn (New York: Pilgrim Press, 1986), 246–60.

[5] Moynihan, 47.

[6] Leith Mullings, "Anthropological Perspectives on the Afro-American Family," *American Journal of Social Psychiatry* 6, no. 1 (Winter 1986): 11–16; see the following revisionist works on the Black family: Andrew Billingsley, *Black Families in White America* (Englewood Cliffs, N.J.: Prentice-Hall, 1968); Robert Hill, *The Strengths of Black Families* (New York: Emerson-Hall, 1972); Herbert Gutman, *The Black Family in Slavery and Freedom* (New York: Pantheon, 1976); Joyce Ladner, *Tomorrow's Tomorrow: The Black Woman* (New York: Doubleday, 1971); Elliot Leibow, *Talley's Corner: A Study of Negro Street Corner Men* (Boston: Little, Brown, 1967); Carol Stack, *All Our Kin* (New York: Harper & Row, 1974).

[7] William J. Wilson and Robert Aponte, "Urban Poverty," *Annual Review of Sociology* 11 (1985): 231–58, esp. 241.

status of men and the rise in Black female-headed families.[8] While most of these studies do not advance a social-pathology explanation, they do signal a regressive shift in analytic focus. Many well-meaning academics who intend to call attention to the dangerously high level of poverty in Black female-headed households have begun to emphasize the family structure and the Black ghetto way of life as contributors to the perpetuation of the underclass.

The popular press, on the other hand, openly and enthusiastically embraced the Moynihan thesis both in its original version and in Moynihan's restatement of the thesis in his book *Family and Nation*.[9] Here Moynihan repeats his assertion that poverty and family structure are associated, but now he contends that the association holds for Blacks and whites alike. This modification does not critique his earlier assumptions; indeed, it validates them. A profoundly disturbing example of this is revealed in the widely publicized television documentary, CBS Reports' "The Vanishing Family."[10] According to this refurbished version of the old Moynihan Report, a breakdown in family values has allowed Black men to renounce their traditional breadwinner role, leaving Black women to bear the economic responsibility for children.[11] The argument that the Black community is devastating itself fits neatly with the resurgent conservatism that is manifested among Black and white intellectuals and policymakers.

Another contemporary example of the use of the culture of poverty is Nicholas Lemann's two-part 1986 *Atlantic Monthly* article about the Black underclass in Chicago.[12] According to Lemann, family structure is the most visible manifestation of Black America's bifurcation into a middle class that has escaped the ghetto and an underclass that is irrevocably trapped in the ghetto. He explains the rapid growth of the underclass in the seventies by pointing to two mass migrations of Black Americans. The first was from the rural South to the urban North and numbered in the millions during the forties, fifties, and sixties; the second, a migration out of the ghettos by members of the Black working and middle

[8] For a review of recent studies, see ibid.

[9] Daniel Patrick Moynihan, *Family and Nation* (San Diego: Harcourt, Brace, Jovanovich, 1986).

[10] "The Vanishing Family: Crisis in Black America," narrated by Bill Moyers, Columbia Broadcasting System (CBS) Special Report, January 1986.

[11] "Hard Times for Black America," *Dollars and Sense*, no. 115 (April 1986), 5–7.

[12] Nicholas Lemann, "The Origins of the Underclass: Part 1," *Atlantic Monthly* (June 1986), 31–55; Nicholas Lemann, "The Origins of the Underclass: Part 2," *Atlantic Monthly* (July 1986), 54–68.

classes, who had been freed from housing discrimination by the civil rights movement. As a result of the exodus, the indices of disorganization in the urban ghettos of the North (crime, illegitimate births) have risen, and the underclass has flourished.[13] Loose attitudes toward marriage, high illegitimacy rates, and family disintegration are said to be a heritage of the rural South. In Lemann's words, they represent the power of culture to produce poverty:

> The argument is anthropological, not economic; it emphasizes the power over people's behavior that culture, as opposed to economic incentives, can have. Ascribing a society's condition in part to the culture that prevails there seems benign when the society under discussion is England or California. But as a way of thinking about black ghettos it has become unpopular. Twenty years ago ghettos were often said to have a self-generating, destructive culture of poverty (the term has an impeccable source, the anthropologist Oscar Lewis). But then the left equated cultural discussions of the ghetto with accusing poor blacks of being in a bad situation that was of their own making. . . . The left succeeded in limiting the terms of the debate to purely economic ones, and today the right also discusses the ghetto in terms of economic "incentives to fail," provided by the welfare system. . . . In the ghettos, though, it appears that the distinctive culture is now the greatest barrier to progress by the black underclass, rather than either unemployment or welfare.[14]

Lemann's essay, his "misreading of left economic analysis, and cultural anthropology itself"[15] might be dismissed if it were atypical in the debate about the culture of poverty and the underclass. Unfortunately, it shares with other studies the problems of working "with neither the benefit of a well-articulated theory about the impact of personality and motivation on behavior nor adequate data from a representative sample of the low-income population."[16]

The idea that poverty is caused by psychological factors and that poverty is passed on from one generation to the next has been called into question by the University of Michigan's Panel Study of Income Dynamics (PSID), a large-scale data collection project

[13] Lemann, "Part 1," 35.
[14] Ibid.
[15] Jim Sleeper, "Overcoming 'Underclass': More Jobs Are Still the Key," *In These Times* (June 11–24, 1986), 16.
[16] Corcoran et al. (n. 1 above), 517.

conceived, in part, to test many of the assumptions about the psychological and demographic aspects of poverty. This study has gathered annual information from a representative sample of the U.S. population. Two striking discoveries contradict the stereotypes stemming from the culture-of-poverty argument. The first is the high turnover of individual families in poverty and the second is the finding that motivation cannot be linked to poverty. Each year the number of people below the poverty line remains about the same, but the poor in one year are not necessarily the poor in the following year. "Blacks from welfare dependent families were no more likely to become welfare dependent than similar Blacks from families who had never received welfare. Further, measures of parental sense of efficacy, future orientation, and achievement motivation had no effects on welfare dependency for either group."[17] This research has found no evidence that highly motivated people are more successful at escaping from poverty than those with lower scores on tests.[18] Thus, cultural deficiency is an inappropriate model for explaining the underclass.

The family as villain

A central notion within culture-of-poverty arguments is that family disintegration is the source and sustaining feature of poverty. Today, nearly six out of ten Black children are born out of wedlock, compared to roughly three out of ten in 1970. In the 25–34-year age bracket, today the probability of separation and divorce for Black women is twice that of white women. The result is a high probability that an individual Black woman and her children will live alone. The so-called "deviant" mother-only family, common among Blacks, is a product of "the feminization of poverty," a shorthand reference to women living alone and being disproportionately represented among the poor. The attention given to increased marital breakups, to births to unmarried women, and to the household patterns that accompany these changes would suggest that the bulk of contemporary poverty is a family-structure phenomenon. Common knowledge—whether true or not—has it that family-structure changes cause most poverty, or changes in family struc-

---

[17] Martha S. Hill and Michael Ponza, "Poverty and Welfare Dependence across Generations," *Economic Outlook U.S.A.* (Summer 1983), 61–64, esp. 64.

[18] Anne Rueter, "Myths of Poverty," *Research News* (July–September 1984), 18–19.

ture have led to current poverty rates that are much higher than they would have been if family composition had remained stable.[19]

Despite the growing concentration of poverty among Black female-headed households in the past two decades, there is reason to question the conventional thinking. Research by Mary Jo Bane finds that changes in family structure have less causal influence on poverty than is commonly thought.[20] Assumptions about the correlation and association between poverty and family breakdown avoid harder questions about the character and direction of causal relations between the two phenomena.[21] Bane's longitudinal research on household composition and poverty suggests that much poverty, especially among Blacks, is the result of already-poor, two-parent households that break up, producing poor female-headed households. This differs from the event transition to poverty that is more common for whites: "Three-quarters of whites who were poor in the first year after moving into a female-headed or single person household became poor simultaneously with the transition; in contrast, of the blacks who were poor after the transition, about two-thirds had also been poor before. Reshuffled poverty as opposed to event-caused poverty for blacks challenges the assumption that changes in family structure have created ghetto poverty. This underscores the importance of considering the ways in which race produces different paths to poverty."[22]

A two-parent family is no guarantee against poverty for racial minorities. Analyzing data from the PSID, Martha Hill concluded that the long-term income of Black children in two-parent families throughout the decade was even lower than the long-term income of non-Black children who spent most of the decade in mother-only families: "Thus, increasing the proportion of Black children growing up in two-parent families would not by itself eliminate very much of the racial gap in the economic well-being of children; changes in the economic circumstances of the parents are needed most to bring the economic status of Black children up to the higher status of non-Black children."[23]

[19] Mary Jo Bane, "Household Composition and Poverty," in *Fighting Poverty*, ed. Sheldon H. Danziger and Daniel H. Weinberg (Cambridge, Mass.: Harvard University Press, 1986), 209–31.

[20] Ibid.

[21] Betsy Dworkin, "40% of the Poor Are Children," *New York Times Book Review* (March 2, 1986), 9.

[22] Bane, 277.

[23] Martha Hill, "Trends in the Economic Situation of U.S. Families and Children, 1970–1980," in *American Families and the Economy*, ed. Richard R. Nelson and Felicity Skidmore (Washington, D.C.: National Academy Press, 1983), 9–53, esp. 38.

Further studies are required if we are to understand the ways in which poverty, family structure, and race are related.

Welfare as villain

An important variant of the family-structure and deficient-culture explanations, one especially popular among political conservatives, is the argument that welfare causes poverty. This explanation proposes that welfare undermines incentives to work and causes families to break up by allowing Black women to have babies and encouraging Black men to escape family responsibilities. This position has been widely publicized by Charles Murray's influential book, *Losing Ground*.[24] According to Murray, liberal welfare policies squelch work incentives and thus are the major cause of the breakup of the Black family. In effect, increased AFDC benefits make it desirable to forgo marriage and live on the dole.

Research has refuted this explanation for the changes in the structure of families in the underclass. Numerous studies have shown that variations in welfare across time and in different states have not produced systematic variation in family structure.[25] Research conducted at the University of Wisconsin's Institute for Research on Poverty found that poverty increased after the late sixties due to a weakening economy through the seventies. No support was found for Murray's assertion that spending growth did more harm than good for Blacks because it increased the percentage of families headed by women. Trends in welfare spending increased between 1960 and 1972, and declined between 1970 and 1984; yet there were no reversals in family-composition trends during this period. The percentage of these households headed by women increased steadily from 10.7 percent to 20.8 percent between 1968 and 1983.[26]

Further evidence against the "welfare-dependency" motivation for the dramatic rise in the proportion of Black families headed by females is provided by William Darity and Samuel Meyers. Using statistical causality tests, they found no short-term effects of variations in welfare payments on female headship in Black families.[27]

[24] Charles Murray, *Losing Ground* (New York: Basic, 1984).
[25] David T. Ellwood, *Poor Support* (New York: Basic, 1988).
[26] Sheldon Danziger and Peter Gottschalk, "The Poverty of *Losing Ground*," *Challenge* 28 (May/June 1985): 32–38.
[27] William A. Darity and Samuel L. Meyers, "Does Welfare Dependency Cause Female Headship? The Case of the Black Family," *Journal of Marriage and the Family* 46, no. 4 (November 1984): 765–79.

Other research draws similar conclusions about the impact of welfare policies on family structure. Using a variety of tests, David Ellwood and Lawrence Summers dispute the adverse effects of AFDC.[28] They highlight two facts that raise questions about the role of welfare policies in producing female-headed households. First, the real value of welfare payments has declined since the early 1970s, while family dissolution has continued to rise. Family-structure changes do not mirror benefit-level changes. Second, variations in benefit levels across states do not lead to corresponding variations in divorce rates or numbers of children in single-parent families. Their comparison of groups collecting AFDC with groups that were not, found that the effects of welfare benefits on family structures were small.[29] In sum, the systematic research on welfare and family structure indicates that AFDC has far less effect on changes in family structure than has been assumed.

Opportunity structures in decline

A very different view of the underclass has emerged alongside the popularized cultural-deficiency model. This view is rooted in a substantial body of theory and research. Focusing on the opportunity structure of society, these concrete studies reveal that culture is not responsible for the underclass.

Within the structural framework there are three distinct strands. The first deals with transformations of the economy and the labor force that affect Americans in general and Blacks and Hispanics in particular. The second is the transformation of marriage and family life among minorities. The third is the changing class composition of inner cities and their increasing isolation of residents from mainstream social institutions.

All three are informed by new research that examines the macrostructural forces that shape family trends and demographic patterns that expand the analysis to include Hispanics.

Employment

Massive economic changes since the end of World War II are causing the social marginalization of Black people throughout the United States. The shift from an economy based on the manufacture

[28] David T. Ellwood and Lawrence H. Summers, "Poverty in America: Is Welfare the Answer or the Problem?" in *Fighting Poverty* (n. 19 above), 78–105.

[29] Ibid., 96.

of goods to one based on information and services has redistributed work in global, national, and local economies. While these major economic shifts affect all workers, they have more serious consequences for Blacks than whites, a condition that scholars call "structural racism."[30] Major economic trends and patterns, even those that appear race neutral, have significant racial implications. Blacks and other minorities are profoundly affected by (1) the decline of industrial manufacturing sectors and the growth of service sectors of the economy; and (2) shifts in the geographical location of jobs from central cities to the suburbs and from the traditional manufacturing cities (the rustbelt) to the sunbelt and to other countries.

In their classic work *The Deindustrialization of America,* Barry Bluestone and Bennett Harrison revealed that "minorities tend to be concentrated in industries that have borne the brunt of recent closing. This is particularly true in the automobile, steel, and rubber industries."[31] In a follow-up study, Bluestone, Harrison, and Lucy Gorham have shown that people of Color, particularly Black men, are more likely than whites to lose their jobs due to the restructuring of the U.S. economy and that young Black men are especially hard hit.[32] Further evidence of the consequences of economic transformation for minority males is provided by Richard Hill and Cynthia Negrey.[33] They studied deindustrialization in the Great Lakes region and found that the race-gender group that was hardest hit by the industrial slump was Black male production workers. Fully 50 percent of this group in five Great Lakes cities studied lost their jobs in durable-goods manufacturing between 1979 and 1984. They found that Black male production workers also suffered the greatest rate of job loss in the region and in the nation as a whole.

The decline of manufacturing jobs has altered the cities' roles as opportunity ladders for the disadvantaged. Since the start of World War II, well-paying blue-collar jobs in manufacturing have been a main avenue of job security and mobility for Blacks and Hispanics.

[30] "The Costs of Being Black," *Research News* 38, nos. 11–12 (November–December 1987): 8–10.

[31] Barry Bluestone and Bennett Harrison, *The Deindustrialization of America* (New York: Basic, 1982), 54.

[32] Barry Bluestone, Bennett Harrison, and Lucy Gorham, "Storm Clouds on the Horizon: Labor Market Crisis and Industrial Policy," 68, as cited in "Hard Times for Black America" (n. 11 above).

[33] Richard Child Hill and Cynthia Negrey, "Deindustrialization and Racial Minorities in the Great Lakes Region, U.S.A.," in *The Reshaping of America: Social Consequences of the Changing Economy,* ed. D. Stanley Eitzen and Maxine Baca Zinn (Englewood Cliffs, N.J.: Prentice-Hall, 1989), 168–77.

Movement into higher-level blue-collar jobs was one of the most important components of Black occupational advancement in the 1970s. The current restructuring of industries creates the threat of downward mobility for middle-class minorities.[34]

Rather than offering opportunities to minorities, the cities have become centers of poverty. Large concentrations of Blacks and Hispanics are trapped in cities in which the urban employment base is shifting. Today inner cities are shifting away from being centers of production and distribution of physical goods toward being centers of administration, information, exchange, trade, finance, and government service. Conversely, these changes in local employment structures have been accompanied by a shift in the demographic composition of large central cities away from European white to predominantly Black and Hispanic, with rising unemployment. The transfer of jobs away from central cities to the suburbs has created a residential job opportunity mismatch that literally leaves minorities behind in the inner city. Without adequate training or credentials, they are relegated to low-paying, nonadvancing exploitative service work or they are unemployed. Thus, Blacks have become, for the most part, superfluous people in cities that once provided them with opportunities.

The composition and size of cities' overall employment bases have also changed. During the past two decades most older, larger cities have experienced substantial job growth in occupations associated with knowledge-intensive service industries. However, job growth in these high-skill, predominantly white-collar industries has not compensated for employment declines in manufacturing, wholesale trade, and other predominantly blue-collar industries that once constituted the economic backbone of Black urban employment.[35]

While cities once sustained large numbers of less skilled persons, today's service industries typically have high educational requisites for entry. Knowledge and information jobs in the central cities are virtually closed to minorities given the required technological education and skill level. Commuting between central cities and outlying areas is increasingly common; white-collar workers commute daily from their suburban residences to the central business districts while streams of inner-city residents are commuting to their blue-collar jobs in outlying nodes.[36]

[34] Elliot Currie and Jerome H. Skolnick, *America's Problems: Social Issues and Public Policy* (Boston: Little, Brown, 1984), 82.

[35] John D. Kasarda, "Caught in a Web of Change," *Society* 21 (November/December 1983): 41–47.

[36] Ibid., 45–47.

An additional structural impediment inner-city minorities face is their increased distance from current sources of blue-collar and other entry-level jobs. Because the industries that provide these jobs have moved to the suburbs and nonmetropolitan peripheries, racial discrimination and inadequate incomes of inner-city minorities now have the additional impact of preventing many from moving out of the inner city in order to maintain their access to traditional sources of employment. The dispersed nature of job growth makes public transportation from inner-city neighborhoods impractical, requiring virtually all city residents who work in peripheral areas to commute by personally owned automobiles: The severity of this mismatch is documented by John Kasarda: "More than one half of the minority households in Philadelphia and Boston are without a means of personal transportation. New York City's proportions are even higher with only three of ten black or Hispanic households having a vehicle available."[37]

This economic restructuring is characterized by an overall pattern of uneven development. Manufacturing industries have declined in the North and Midwest while new growth industries, such as computers and communications equipment, are locating in the southern and southwestern part of the nation. This regional shift has produced some gains for Blacks in the South, where Black poverty rates have declined. Given the large minority populations in the sunbelt, it is conceivable that industrial restructuring could offset the economic threats to racial equality. However, the sunbelt expansion has been based largely on low-wage, labor-intensive enterprises that use large numbers of underpaid minority workers, and a decline in the northern industrial sector continues to leave large numbers of Blacks and Hispanics without work.

Marriage

The connection between declining Black employment opportunities (especially male joblessness) and the explosive growth of Black families headed by single women is the basis of William J. Wilson's analysis of the underclass. Several recent studies conducted by Wilson and his colleagues at the University of Chicago have established this link.[38] Wilson and Kathryn Neckerman have docu-

[37] John D. Kasarda, "Urban Change and Minority Opportunities," in *The New Urban Reality*, ed. Paul E. Peterson (Washington, D.C.: Brookings Institution, 1985), 33–68, esp. 55.

[38] William J. Wilson with Kathryn Neckerman, "Poverty and Family Structure: The Widening Gap between Evidence and Public Policy Issues," in *The Truly Disadvantaged*, by William J. Wilson (Chicago: University of Chicago Press, 1987), 63–92.

mented the relationship between increased male joblessness and female-headed households. By devising an indicator called "the index of marriageable males," they reveal a long-term decline in the proportion of Black men, and particularly young Black men, who are in a position to support a family. Their indicators include mortality and incarceration rates, as well as labor-force participation rates, and they reveal that the proportion of Black men in unstable economic situations is much higher than indicated in current unemployment figures.[39]

Wilson's analysis treats marriage as an opportunity structure that no longer exists for large numbers of Black people. Consider, for example, why the majority of pregnant Black teenagers do not marry. In 1960, 42 percent of Black teenagers who had babies were unmarried; by 1970 the rate jumped to 63 percent and by 1983 it was 89 percent.[40] According to Wilson, the increase is tied directly to the changing labor-market status of young Black males. He cites the well-established relationship between joblessness and marital instability in support of his argument that "pregnant teenagers are more likely to marry if their boyfriends are working."[41] Out-of-wedlock births are sometimes encouraged by families and absorbed into the kinship system because marrying the suspected father would mean adding someone who was unemployed to the family's financial burden.[42] Adaptation to structural conditions leaves Black women disproportionately separated, divorced, and solely responsible for their children. The mother-only family structure is thus the consequence, not the cause, of poverty.

Community

These changes in employment and marriage patterns have been accompanied by changes in the social fabric of cities. "The Kerner Report Twenty Years Later," a conference of the 1988 Commission on the Cities, highlighted the growing isolation of Blacks and Hispanics.[43] Not only is inner-city poverty worse and more persistent than it was twenty years ago, but ghettos and barrios have become isolated and deteriorating societies with their own econo-

---

[39] Ibid.

[40] Jerelyn Eddings, "Children Having Children," *Baltimore Sun* (March 2, 1986), 71.

[41] As quoted in ibid., 71.

[42] Noel A. Cazenave, "Alternate Intimacy, Marriage, and Family Lifestyles among Low-Income Black Americans," *Alternative Lifestyles* 3, no. 4 (November 1980): 425–44.

[43] "The Kerner Report Updated" (Racine, Wis.: Report of the 1988 Commission on the Cities, March 1, 1988).

mies and with increasingly isolated social institutions, including schools, families, businesses, churches, and hospitals. According to Wilson, this profound social transformation is reflected not only in the high rates of joblessness, crime, and poverty but also in a changing socioeconomic class structure. As Black middle-class professionals left the central city, so too did working-class Blacks. Wilson uses the term "concentration effects" to capture the experiences of low-income families who now make up the majority of those who live in inner cities. The most disadvantaged families are disproportionately concentrated in the sections of the inner city that are plagued by joblessness, lawlessness, and a general milieu of desperation. Without working-class or middle-class role models these families have little in common with mainstream society.[44]

The departure of the Black working and middle classes means more than a loss of role models, however. As David Ellwood has observed, the flight of Black professionals has meant the loss of connections and networks. If successfully employed persons do not live nearby, then the informal methods of finding a job, by which one worker tells someone else of an opening and recommends her or him to the employer, are lost.[45] Concentration and isolation describe the processes that systematically entrench a lack of opportunities in inner cities. Individuals and families are thus left to acquire life's necessities though they are far removed from the channels of social opportunity.

The changing demography of race and poverty

Hispanic poverty, virtually ignored for nearly a quarter of a century, has recently captured the attention of the media and scholars alike. Recent demographic and economic patterns have made "the flow of Hispanics to urban America among the most significant changes occurring in the 1980s."[46]

As the Hispanic presence in the United States has increased in the last decade, Hispanic poverty rates have risen alarmingly. Between 1979 and 1985, the percentage of Latinos who were poor grew from 21.8 percent to 29.0 percent. Nationwide, the poverty rate for all Hispanics was 27.3 percent in 1986. By comparison, the white poverty rate in 1986 was 11 percent; the Black poverty rate was 31.1

[44] Wilson, *The Truly Disadvantaged* (n. 38 above), 62.

[45] Ellwood (n. 25 above), 204.

[46] Paul E. Peterson, "Introduction: Technology, Race, and Urban Policy," in *The New Urban Reality*, ed. Paul E. Peterson (Washington, D.C.: Brookings Institution, 1985), 1–35, esp. 22.

percent.[47] Not only have Hispanic poverty rates risen alarmingly, but like Black poverty, Hispanic poverty has become increasingly concentrated in inner cities. Hispanics fall well behind the general population on all measures of social and economic well-being: jobs, income, educational attainment, housing, and health care. Poverty among Hispanics has become so persistent that, if current patterns continue, Hispanics will emerge in the 1990s as the nation's poorest racial-ethnic group.[48] Hispanic poverty has thus become a trend to watch in national discussions of urban poverty and the underclass.

While Hispanics are emerging as the poorest minority group, poverty rates and other socioeconomic indicators vary widely among Hispanic groups. Among Puerto Ricans, 39.9 percent of the population lived below the poverty level in 1986. For Mexicans, 28.4 percent were living in poverty in 1986. For Cubans and Central and South Americans, the poverty rate was much lower: 18.7 percent.[49] Such diversity has led scholars to question the usefulness of this racial-ethnic category that includes all people of Latin American descent.[50] Nevertheless, the labels Hispanic or Latino are useful in general terms in describing the changing racial composition of poverty populations. In spite of the great diversity among Hispanic nationalities, they face common obstacles to becoming incorporated into the economic mainstream of society.

Researchers are debating whether trends of rising Hispanic poverty are irreversible and if those trends point to a permanent underclass among Hispanics. Do macrostructural shifts in the economy and the labor force have the same effects on Blacks and Latinos? According to Joan W. Moore, national economic changes do affect Latinos, but they affect subgroups of Latinos in different ways:

The movement of jobs and investments out of Rustbelt cities has left many Puerto Ricans living in a bleak ghetto economy. This same movement has had a different effect on Mexican Americans living in the Southwest. As in the North, many factories with job ladders have disappeared. Most of the newer Sunbelt industries offer either high paying jobs for which few Hispanics are trained or low paying ones that provide few opportunities for advancement. Those industries

---

[47] Jennifer Juarez Robles, "Hispanics Emerging as Nation's Poorest Minority Group," *Chicago Reporter* 17, no. 6 (June 1988): 1–3.

[48] Ibid., 2–3.

[49] Ibid., 3.

[50] Alejandro Portes and Cynthia Truelove, "Making Sense of Diversity: Recent Research on Hispanic Minorities in the United States," *Annual Review of Sociology* 13 (1987): 359–85.

that depend on immigrant labor (such as clothing manufacturing in Los Angeles) often seriously exploit their workers,
so the benefits to Hispanics in the Southwest of this influx of
industries and investments are mixed. Another subgroup, Cubans in Miami, work and live in an enclave economy that
appears to be unaffected by this shift in the national
economy.[51]

Because shifts in the subregional economies seem more important
to Hispanics than changes in the national economy, Moore is
cautious about applying William Wilson's analysis of how the
underclass is created.

Opportunity structures have not declined in a uniform manner
for Latinos. Yet Hispanic poverty, welfare dependence, and unemployment rates are greatest in regions that have been transformed
by macrostructural economic changes. In some cities, Puerto Rican
poverty and unemployment rates are steadily converging with, and
in some cases exceeding, the rates of Blacks. In 1986, 40 percent of
Puerto Ricans in the United States lived below the poverty level
and 70 percent of Puerto Rican children lived in poverty.[52]

Family structure is also affected by economic dislocation.
Among Latinos, the incidence of female-headed households is
highest for Puerto Ricans—43.3 percent—compared to 19.2 percent
for Mexicans, 17.7 for Cubans, and 25.5 percent for Central and
South Americans.[53] The association between national economic
shifts and high rates of social dislocation among Hispanics provides
further evidence for the structural argument that economic conditions rather than culture create distinctive forms of racial poverty.

Family, poverty, and gender

The structural model described above advances our understanding
of poverty and minority families beyond the limitations of the
cultural model. It directs attention away from psychological and
cultural issues and toward social structures that allocate economic
and social rewards. It has generated a substantial body of research
and findings that challenge culture-of-poverty arguments.

[51] Joan W. Moore, "An Assessment of Hispanic Poverty: Does a Hispanic
Underclass Exist?" *Tomás Rivera Center Report* 2, no. 1 (Fall 1988): 8–9.

[52] Robles, 3.

[53] U.S. Bureau of the Census, *Current Population Reports,* Series P-20, nos. 416,
422 (Washington, D.C.: Government Printing Office, March 1987).

On matters of gender, however, the structural model would benefit from discussion, criticism, and rethinking. This is not to deny the structural model's value in linking poverty to external economic conditions but, rather, to question the model's assumptions about gender and family structure and to point to the need for gender as a specific analytic category.

Although several key aspects of the structural model distinguish it from the cultural model, both models are remarkably close in their thinking about gender. Patricia Hill Collins, in her viewpoint in this issue, exposes the gender ideologies that underlie cultural explanations of racial inferiority. Those same ideologies about women and men, about their place in the family and their relationship to the public institutions of the larger society, reappear, albeit in modified ways, in the structural model.

Collins shows how assumptions about racial deficiency rest on cultural notions about unfit men and women. In contrast, the structural approach focuses on the social circumstances produced by economic change. It therefore avoids drawing caricatures of men who spurn work and unmarried women who persist in having children. Yet both models find differences between mainstream gender roles and those of the underclass. Indeed, some of the most striking and important findings of the structural approach focus on this difference. Clearly, the reasons for the difference lie in the differing economic and social opportunities of the two groups, yet the structural model assumes that the traditional family is a key solution for eliminating racial poverty. Although the reasons given for the erosion of the traditional family are very different, both models rest on normative definitions of women's and men's roles. Two examples reveal how the structural perspective is locked into traditional concepts of the family and women's and men's places within it.

Wilson identifies male joblessness and the resulting shortage of marriageable males as the conditions responsible for the proliferation of female-headed households. His vision of a solution is a restoration of marital opportunities and the restoration of family structures in which men provide for their families by working in the labor force and women have children who can then be assured of the economic opportunities afforded by two-parent families. He offers no alternative concept of the family, no discussion of lesbian families or other arrangements that differ from the standard male-female married pair. Instead of exploring how women's opportunities and earning capacities outside of marriage are affected by macrostructural economic transformations, instead of calling "for pay equity, universal day care and other initiatives to buttress

women's capacities for living independently in the world . . .
Wilson goes in exactly the opposite direction."[54]

Ellwood's comprehensive analysis of American family poverty
and welfare, *Poor Support: Poverty in the American Family*,
contains a discussion that says a great deal about how women, men,
and family roles are viewed by authoritative scholars working
within the structural tradition. Looking at the work of adults in
two-parent families, Ellwood finds that all families must fulfill two
roles—a nurturing/child-rearing role and a provider role—and that
in two-parent families these responsibilities are divided along
traditional gender lines. Therefore, Ellwood raises the question
"Do we want single mothers to behave like husbands or like wives?
Those who argue that single mothers ought to support their families
through their own efforts are implicitly asking that they behave like
husbands."[55] While Ellwood's discussion is meant to illustrate that
single mothers experience difficulty in having to fulfill the dual
roles of provider and nurturer, it confuses the matter by reverting to
a gendered division of labor in which women nurture and men
provide. By presenting family responsibilities as those of "husbands" and "wives," even well-meaning illustrations reproduce the
ideology they seek to challenge.

Structural approaches have failed to articulate gender as an
analytic category even though the conditions uncovered in contemporary research on the urban underclass are closely intertwined
with gender. In fact, the problems of male joblessness and female-
headed households form themselves around gender. Although
these conditions are the result of economic transformations, they
change gender relations as they change the marital, family, and
labor arrangements of women and men. Furthermore, the economic
disenfranchisement of large numbers of Black men, what Clyde
Franklin calls "the institutional decimation of Black men,"[56] is a
gender phenomenon of enormous magnitude. It affects the meanings and definitions of masculinity for Black men, and it reinforces
the public patriarchy that controls Black women through their
increased dependence on welfare. Such gender issues are vital.
They reveal that where people of Color "end up" in the social order
has as much to do with the economic restructuring of gender as with
the economic restructuring of class and race.

[54] Adolph Reed, Jr., "The Liberal Technocrat," *Nation* (February 6, 1988), 167–70.
[55] Ellwood (n. 25 above), 133.
[56] Clyde W. Franklin II, "Surviving the Institutional Decimation of Black Males:
Causes, Consequences, and Intervention," in *The Making of Masculinities*, ed.
Harry Brod (Winchester, Mass.: Allen & Unwin, 1987), 155–69, esp. 155.

The new structural analyses of the underclass reveal that the conditions in which Black and Hispanic women and men live are extremely vulnerable to economic change. In this way, such analyses move beyond "feminization of poverty" explanations that ignore class and race differences among women and ignore poverty among minority men.[57] Yet many structural analyses fail to consider the interplay of gender-based assumptions with structural racism. Just as the "feminization of poverty" approach has tended to neglect the way in which race produces different routes to poverty, structural discussions of the underclass pay far too little attention to how gender produces different routes to poverty for Black and Hispanic women and men. Many social forces are at work in the current erosion of family life among Black and Hispanic people. Careful attention to the interlocking systems of class, race, and gender is imperative if we are to understand and solve the problems resulting from economic transformation.

Women's Studies
University of Delaware

[57] See Maxine Baca Zinn, "Minority Families in Crisis: The Public Discussion," Working Paper no. 6 (Memphis, Tenn.: Memphis State University, Center for Research on Women, 1987), for an extended critique of the culture-of-poverty model.

MULTIPLE JEOPARDY, MULTIPLE CONSCIOUSNESS: THE CONTEXT OF A BLACK FEMINIST IDEOLOGY

DEBORAH K. KING

Black women have long recognized the special circumstances of our lives in the United States: the commonalities that we share with all women, as well as the bonds that connect us to the men of our race. We have also realized that the interactive oppressions that circumscribe our lives provide a distinctive context for black womanhood. For us, the notion of double jeopardy is not a new one. Near the end of the nineteenth century, Anna Julia Cooper, who was born a slave and later became an educator and earned a Ph.D., often spoke and wrote of the double enslavement of black women and of our being "confronted by both a woman question and a race problem."[1] In 1904, Mary Church Terrell, the first president of the National Association of Colored Women, wrote, "Not only are colored women . . . handicapped on account of their sex, but they are almost everywhere baffled and mocked because of their race. Not only because they are women, but because they are colored women."[2]

I am greatly indebted to Elsa B. Brown, Elaine Upton, Patricia Palmieri, Patricia Hill Collins, Dianne Pinderhughes, Rose Brewer, and *Signs'* referees for their thoughtful and critical comments on this paper.

[1] Gerda Lerner, ed., *Black Women in White America: A Documentary History* (New York: Vintage, 1973), 573.
[2] Mary Church Terrell, "The Progress of Colored Women," *Voice of the Negro* 1, no. 7 (July 1904): 292.

This essay originally appeared in *Signs*, vol. 14, no. 1, Autumn 1988.

The dual and systematic discriminations of racism and sexism remain pervasive, and, for many, class inequality compounds those oppressions. Yet, for as long as black women have known our numerous discriminations, we have also resisted those oppressions. Our day-to-day survival as well as our organized political actions have demonstrated the tenacity of our struggle against subordination. In the mid-nineteenth century, Sojourner Truth, an antislavery activist and women's rights advocate, repeatedly pronounced the strength and perseverance of black women.[3] More than one hundred years later, another black woman elaborated on Truth's theme. In addressing the National Association for the Advancement of Colored People (NAACP) Legal Defense Fund in 1971, Fannie Lou Hamer, the daughter of sharecroppers and a civil rights activist in Mississippi, commented on the special plight and role of black women over 350 years: "You know I work for the liberation of all people because when I liberate myself, I'm liberating other people . . . her [the white woman's] freedom is shackled in chains to mine, and she realizes for the first time that she is not free until I am free."[4] The necessity of addressing all oppressions is one of the hallmarks of black feminist thought.

The theoretical invisibility of black women

Among the first and perhaps most widely used approaches for understanding women's status in the United States has been the race-sex analogy. In essence, the model draws parallels between the systems and experiences of domination for blacks and those for women, and, as a result, it assumes that political mobilizations against racism and sexism are comparable. In 1860, Elizabeth Cady Stanton observed, "Prejudice against color, of which we hear so much, is no stronger than that against sex."[5] Scholars in various disciplines have drawn similar analogies between racism and sexism. Sociologist Helen Hacker and historian William Chafe have both noted

[3] See Lerner, ed., esp. 566–72; and Bert James Loewenberg and Ruth Bogin, eds., *Black Women in Nineteenth-Century American Life* (University Park: Pennsylvania State University Press, 1976), 234–42.

[4] See Lerner, ed., 609, 610, 611.

[5] Elizabeth Cady Stanton as quoted by William Chafe, *Women and Equality: Changing Patterns in American Culture* (New York: Oxford University Press, 1977), 44. Some eighty years after Stanton's observation, Swedish social psychologist Gunnar Myrdal, in an appendix to his *An American Dilemma: The Negro Problem and Modern Democracy* (New York: Harper & Row, 1962), also saw the woman problem as parallel to the Negro problem.

that unlike many ethnic groups, women and blacks possess inerad-
icable physical attributes that function "systematically and clearly
to define from birth the possibilities to which members of a group
might aspire."[6] In the first formal typology of the race-sex analogy,
Helen Hacker identifies four additional dimensions on which the
castelike status of blacks and women are similar: (1) ascribed attributes of emotionality, immaturity, and slyness; (2) rationalizations
of status as conveyed in the notions of appropriate "place" and the
contented subordinate; (3) accommodating and guileful behaviors;
and (4) economic, legal, educational, and social discriminations.[7]
Feminist theorists, including Simone de Beauvoir, Kate Millett,
Mary Daly, and Shulamith Firestone have all drawn extensively on
this analogy in their critiques of the patriarchy.[8]

This analogy has served as a powerful means of conveying an image of women's subordinate status, and of mobilizing women and
men for political action. The social movements for racial equality in
the United States, whether the abolitionist movement in the nineteenth century or the civil rights movement in the mid-twentieth
century, were predecessors, catalysts, and prototypes for women's
collective action. A significant segment of feminist activists came to
recognize and understand their own oppression, as well as to develop important organizing skills through their participation in efforts for racial justice.[9] In sum, the race-sex correspondence has been
used successfully because the race model was a well-established and
effective pedagogical tool for both the theoretical conceptualization
of and the political resistance to sexual inequality.

---

[6] Chafe, 77.

[7] Helen Hacker, "Women as a Minority Group," *Social Forces* 30 (1951): 60–69.

[8] For examples of feminist writings using the race-sex analogy or the master-slave
model, see Simone de Beauvoir, *The Second Sex*, trans. and ed. H. M. Parshley (New
York: Random House, 1974); Kate Millett, *Sexual Politics* (New York: Avon, 1969);
Shulamith Firestone, *The Dialectics of Sex* (New York: Morrow, 1970); and Mary
Daly, *Beyond God the Father: Toward a Philosophy of Women's Liberation* (Boston:
Beacon, 1973).

[9] See Sara Evans, *Personal Politics: The Roots of Women's Liberation in the Civil
Rights Movement and the New Left* (New York: Vintage, 1980); Catharine Stimpson,
"Thy Neighbor's Wife, Thy Neighbor's Servants: Women's Liberation and Black
Civil Rights," in *Woman in Sexist Society: Studies in Power and Powerlessness*, ed.
Vivian Gornick and Barbara Moran (New York: Basic, 1971), 452–79; and Angela
Davis, *Women, Race and Class* (New York: Random House, 1981). Recently, there
has been some debate concerning precisely what lessons, if any, women learned
from their participation in the abolitionist and civil rights movements. For an ar-
gument against the importance of race-oriented movements for feminist politics, see
E. C. DuBois, *Feminism and Suffrage* (Ithaca, N.Y.: Cornell University Press, 1978).

We learn very little about black women from this analogy.[10] The experience of black women is apparently assumed, though never explicitly stated, to be synonymous with that of either black males or white females; and since the experiences of both are equivalent, a discussion of black women in particular is superfluous. It is mistakenly granted that either there is no difference in being black and female from being generically black (i.e., male) or generically female (i.e., white). The analogy obfuscates or denies what Chafe refers to as "the profound substantive differences" between blacks and women. The scope, both institutionally and culturally, and the intensity of the physical and psychological impact of racism is qualitatively different from that of sexism. The group experience of slavery and lynching for blacks, genocide for Native Americans, and military conquest for Mexican-Americans and Puerto Ricans is not substantively comparable to the physical abuse, social discrimination, and cultural denigration suffered by women. This is not to argue that those forms of racial oppressions are greater or more unjust but that the substantive differences need to be identified and to inform conceptualizations. Althea Smith and Abigail Stewart point out that "the assumption of parallelism led to research that masked the differences in these processes [i.e., racism, sexism, and their effects on self-image] for different groups."[11] A similar point has been forcefully made by bell hooks: "No other group in America has so had their identity socialized out of existence as have black women. We are rarely recognized as a group separate and distinct from black men, or a present part of the larger group 'women' in this culture. . . . When black people are talked about the focus tends to be on black men; and when women are talked about the focus tends to be on white women."[12] It is precisely those differences between blacks and women, between black men and black women,

---

[10] Other limitations have been noted by Linda LaRue, who contends that the analogy is an abstraction that falsely asserts a common oppression of blacks and women for rhetorical and propagandistic purposes ("The Black Movement and Women's Liberation," in *Female Psychology: The Emerging Self*, ed. Sue Cox [Chicago: Science Research Assoc., 1976]). In *Ain't I a Woman* (Boston: South End Press, 1981), bell hooks questions whether certain women, particularly those self-identified feminists who are white and middle class, are truly oppressed as opposed to being discriminated against. Stimpson bluntly declares that the race-sex analogy is exploitative and racist. See also Margaret A. Simons, "Racism and Feminism: A Schism in the Sisterhood," *Feminist Studies* 5 (1979): 384–401, for a critical review of this conceptual approach in feminist theorizing.
[11] Chafe, 76; Althea Smith and Abigail J. Stewart, "Approaches to Studying Racism and Sexism in Black Women's Lives," *Journal of Social Issues* 39 (1983): 1–15.
[12] hooks, *Ain't I a Woman*, 7.

between black women and white women that are crucial to understanding the nature of black womanhood.

The promise and limitations of double jeopardy

In 1972, Frances Beale, a founding member of the Women's Liberation Committee of the Student Nonviolent Coordinating Committee (SNCC) and, later, a member of the Third World Women's Alliance, introduced the term "double jeopardy" to describe the dual discriminations of racism and sexism that subjugate black women. Concerning black women, she wrote, "As blacks they suffer all the burdens of prejudice and mistreatment that fall on anyone with dark skin. As women they bear the additional burden of having to cope with white and black men."[13] Beale also astutely observed that the reality of dual discriminations often entailed economic disadvantage; unfortunately she did not incorporate that understanding into the conceptualization. Perhaps she viewed class status as a particular consequence of racism, rather than as an autonomous source of persecution; but such a preponderant majority of black women have endured the very lowest of wages and very poorest conditions of rural and urban poverty that some scholars have argued that economic class oppression must necessarily constitute a third jeopardy.[14] Still others have suggested that heterosexism or homophobia represents another significant oppression and should be included as a third or perhaps fourth jeopardy.[15] The triple jeopardy of racism, sexism, and classism is now widely accepted and used as the conceptualization of black women's status. However, while advancing our understanding beyond the erasure of black

[13] Frances Beale, "Double Jeopardy: To Be Black and Female," in *The Black Woman: An Anthology*, ed. Toni Cade (New York: New American Library, 1979), 90–100.

[14] See, e.g., Beverly Lindsay, "Minority Women in America: Black American, Native American, Chicana, and Asian American Women," in *The Study of Woman: Enlarging Perspectives of Social Reality*, ed. Eloise C. Synder (New York: Harper & Row, 1979), 318–63. She presents a paradigm wherein whiteness, maleness, and money are advantageous; a poor, black woman is triply disadvantaged. Lindsay argues that triple jeopardy, the interaction of sexism, racism, and economic oppression, is "the most realistic perspective for analyzing the position of black American women; and this perspective will serve as common linkage among the discussions of other minority women" (328).

[15] See Barbara Smith, ed., *Home Girls: A Black Feminist Anthology* (New York: Kitchen Table Press, 1983), esp. sec. 3; and Audre Lorde, "Scratching the Surface: Some Notes on Barriers to Women and Loving," *Black Scholar* 13 (Summer 1982): 20–24, and *Sister Outsider: Essays and Speeches* (Trumansberg, N.Y.: Crossing Press, 1984).

women within the confines of the race-sex analogy, it does not yet fully convey the dynamics of multiple forms of discrimination.

Unfortunately, most applications of the concepts of double and triple jeopardy have been overly simplistic in assuming that the relationships among the various discriminations are merely additive. These relationships are interpreted as equivalent to the mathematical equation, racism plus sexism plus classism equals triple jeopardy. In this instance, each discrimination has a single, direct, and independent effect on status, wherein the relative contribution of each is readily apparent. This simple incremental process does not represent the nature of black women's oppression but, rather, I would contend, leads to nonproductive assertions that one factor can and should supplant the other. For example, class oppression is the largest component of black women's subordinate status, therefore the exclusive focus should be on economics. Such assertions ignore the fact that racism, sexism, and classism constitute three, interdependent control systems. An interactive model, which I have termed multiple jeopardy, better captures those processes.[16]

The modifier "multiple" refers not only to several, simultaneous oppressions but to the multiplicative relationships among them as well. In other words, the equivalent formulation is racism multiplied by sexism multiplied by classism. The sexual exploitation of black women in slavery is a historical example. While black women workers suffered the same demanding physical labor and brutal punishments as black men, as females, we were also subject to forms of subjugation only applicable to women. Angela Davis, in *Women, Race and Class,* notes, "If the most violent punishments of men consisted in floggings and mutilations, women were flogged and mutilated, as well as raped."[17] At the same time, our reproductive and child-rearing activities served to enhance the quantity and quality of the "capital" of a slave economy. Our institutionalized exploitation as the concubines, mistresses, and sexual slaves of white males distinguished our experience from that of white females' sexual oppression because it could only have existed in relation to racist and classist forms of domination.

[16] For other attempts at nonadditive models, see Smith and Stewart; Elizabeth M. Almquist, "Untangling the Effects of Race and Sex: The Disadvantaged Status of Black Women," *Social Science Quarterly* 56 (1975): 129–42; Margaret L. Andersen, *Thinking about Women: Sociological and Feminist Perspectives* (New York: Macmillan, 1983). The term "ethnogender" is introduced in Vincent Jeffries and H. Edward Ransford, *Social Stratification: A Multiple Hierarchy Approach* (Boston: Allyn & Bacon, 1980); and Edward Ransford and Jon Miller, "Race, Sex, and Feminist Outlook," *American Sociological Review* 48 (1983): 46–59.
[17] Davis, *Women, Race and Class,* 7.

The importance of any one factor in explaining black women's circumstances thus varies depending on the particular aspect of our lives under consideration and the reference groups to whom we are compared. In some cases, race may be the more significant predictor of black women's status; in others, gender or class may be more influential. Table 1 presents the varied and conditional influence of race and gender and, presumably, of racism and sexism on socioeconomic and educational status. White males earn the highest median incomes, followed in decreasing order by black males, white females, and black females. The educational rankings are different. White males are again on top; but whites, males and females, have more years of schooling than black males and females. While gender is more critical in understanding black women's income ranking, race is more important in explaining their level of educational attainment. But in both examples, black females have the lowest status.

Table 2 shows a more complex relationship between race, gender, and class (here represented by educational attainment), and the influence of these variables on income. Overall, education is an important determinant of income, and despite race or gender, those with more education earn more money than those with less. Men earn more than women at the same level of education, and whites earn more than blacks at the same level of education. But among women, the relationship of education to income is confounded by race. Given our subordinate statuses as female and black, we might expect black women to receive the lowest incomes regardless of their educational attainment. However, the returns of postsecondary education, a college degree or higher, are greater for black females than for white females, while among those with less than a college degree, black females earn less than white females. A similar pattern is not found among males. In this three-way anal-

TABLE 1 **RACE AND GENDER INTERACTIVE EFFECTS ON SOCIOECONOMIC STATUS**

	Economic Status ($)	Educational Status (yrs.)
White males	16,467	12.7
Black males	9,448	12.2
White females	6,949	12.6
Black females	6,164	12.2

NOTE.—Income figures are 1984 median incomes for those fifteen years or older. Educational attainment is for 1984, median years of school completed.

SOURCE.—U.S. Department of Commerce, Bureau of the Census, *Statistical Abstract of the United States, 1987* (Washington, D.C.: Government Printing Office, 1987).

TABLE 2 **MULTIPLICATIVE EFFECTS OF RACE, GENDER, AND CLASS ON INCOME**

	Income ($)			
	White Males	Black Males	White Females	Black Females
Less than a high school diploma	9,525	6,823	3,961	3,618
4 years of high school	13,733	9,260	6,103	5,954
1–3 years of college	14,258	10,532	6,451	6,929
Bachelor's degree	19,783	14,131	9,134	10,692
5 or more years of post-baccalaureate education	23,143	18,970	12,980	14,537

NOTE.—Income is 1979 median income. Educational attainment is used as a measure of economic class.

SOURCE.—*Detailed Population Characteristics*, U.S. Summary, Sec. A, 1980 (Washington, D.C.: Government Printing Office, 1980).

ysis, black women are not consistently in the lowest status, evidence that the importance of the multiple discriminations of race, gender, and class is varied and complex.

In the interactive model, the relative significance of race, sex, or class in determining the conditions of black women's lives is neither fixed nor absolute but, rather, is dependent on the sociohistorical context and the social phenomenon under consideration. These interactions also produce what to some appears a seemingly confounding set of social roles and political attitudes among black women. Sociologist Bonnie Thornton Dill has discussed the importance of scholars' recognizing, incorporating, and interpreting the complex variety of social roles that black women have performed in reaction to multiple jeopardies. She argues that the constellation of "attitudes, behaviors, and interpersonal relationships . . . were adaptations to a variety of factors, including the harsh realities of their environment, Afro-American cultural images of black womanhood, and the sometimes conflicting values and norms of the wider society."[18]

A black woman's survival depends on her ability to use all the economic, social, and cultural resources available to her from both the larger society and within her community. For example, black women historically have had to assume economically productive roles as well as retain domestic ones, and until recently our labor

[18] Bonnie Thornton Dill, "The Dialectics of Black Womanhood," *Signs: Journal of Women in Culture and Society* 4 (1979): 543–55, esp. 547. Smith and Stewart, 1, make a similar point.

force participation rate well exceeded that of white women.[19] Labor, whether unpaid and coerced (as under slavery) or paid and necessary employment, has been a distinctive characteristic of black women's social roles. It has earned us a small but significant degree of self-reliance and independence that has promoted egalitarian relations with black men and active influence within the black family and community.[20] But it also has had costs. For instance, black women have most often had to work in low status and low paying jobs since race and sex discrimination have historically limited our employment options. The legacy of the political economy of slavery under capitalism is the fact that employers, and not black women, still profit the most from black women's labor. And when black women become the primary or sole earners for households, researchers and public analysts interpret this self-sufficiency as pathology, as deviance, as a threat to black family life.[21] Yet, it is black women's well-documented facility to encompass seemingly contra-

[19] In slavery, there was 100 percent labor force participation by black women. In 1910, 34 percent were in the official labor force. In 1960, the figure was 40 percent, and by 1980, it was over 50 percent. Comparable figures for white women are 18 percent in 1890, 22 percent in 1910, 37 percent in 1960, and 51 percent in 1980. For a more detailed discussion, see Phyllis A. Wallace, *Black Women in the Labor Force* (Cambridge, Mass.: MIT Press, 1980).

[20] Angela Davis, "Reflections of the Black Woman's Role in the Community of Slaves," *Black Scholar* 3 (December 1971): 2–16, offers an enlightening discussion of the irony of independence out of subordination. See also Deborah Gray White, *Ar'n't I a Woman? Female Slaves in the Plantation South* (New York: Norton, 1985), for a more detailed analysis of the contradictions of the black female role in slavery. For a discussion of the role of black women in the family, see Robert Staples, *The Black Woman in America* (Chicago: Nelson Hall, 1973); Robert Hill, *The Strengths of Black Families* (New York: Emerson Hall, 1972); Herbert Guttman, *The Black Family in Slavery and Freedom, 1750 to 1925* (New York: Random House, 1976); Carol Stack, *All Our Kin: Strategies for Survival in a Black Community* (New York: Harper & Row, 1974); and Charles Willie, *A New Look at Black Families* (New York: General Hall, 1976). For a discussion of black women's community roles, see Bettina Aptheker, *Woman's Legacy: Essays on Race, Sex, and Class in American History* (Amherst: University of Massachusetts Press, 1982); Paula Giddings, *When and Where I Enter: The Impact of Black Women on Race and Sex in America* (New York: William Morrow, 1983); Lerner, ed. (n. 1 above); Sharon Harley and Rosalyn Terborg-Penn, eds., *The Afro-American Woman: Struggles and Images* (Port Washington, N.Y.: Kennikat Press, 1978); Linda Perkins, "The Impact of the 'Cult of True Womanhood' on the Education of Black Women," *Journal of Social Issues* 39 (1983): 17–28; and the special issue, "The Impact of Black Women in Education," *Journal of Negro Education* 51, no. 3 (Summer 1982).

[21] See Robert Staples, "The Myth of the Black Matriarchy," in his *The Black Family: Essays and Studies* (Belmont, Calif.: Wadsworth, 1971), and *The Black Woman in America*. Also see hooks, *Ain't I a Woman* (n. 10 above); and Cheryl T. Gilkes, "Black Women's Work as Deviance: Social Sources of Racial Antagonism within Contemporary Feminism," Working Paper no. 66 (Wellesley, Mass.: Wellesley

dictory role expectations of worker, homemaker, and mother that has contributed to the confusion in understanding black woman-hood.[22] These competing demands (each requiring its own set of resistances to multiple forms of oppression) are a primary influence on the black woman's definition of her womanhood, and her relationships to the people around her. To reduce this complex of negotiations to an addition problem (racism + sexism = black women's experience) is to define the issues, and indeed black womanhood itself, within the structural terms developed by Europeans and especially white males to privilege their race and their sex unilaterally. Sojourner's declaration, "ain't I a woman?" directly refutes this sort of conceptualization of womanhood as one dimensional rather than dialectical.

Multiple jeopardy within the politics of liberation

In order to understand the concept of multiple jeopardy, it is necessary to look beyond the social structure and process of the dominant society that insidiously pervade even the movements for race, gender, and class liberation. Thus, the confrontations among blacks about sexism and classism, among women about racism and classism, and among the various economic classes about racism and sexism compose a second feature of the context of black feminist ideology. A formidable impediment in these battles is the "monist" approach of most liberation ideologies. In *Liberating Theory,* monism is described as a political claim "that one particular domination precipitates all really important oppressions. Whether Marxist, anarchist, nationalist, or feminist, these 'ideal types' argue that important social relations can all be reduced to the economy, state, culture, or gender."[23] For example, during the suffrage debates, it was routinely asserted that only one group might gain voting privileges—either blacks or women, that is black men or white women. For black women, the granting of suffrage to either group would still mean our disenfranchisement because of either our sex or our

---

College, Center for Research on Women, 1979). However, more recently Robert Staples has argued that black women who are too independent will be unable to find black mates and that black men are justified in their preference for a more traditionally feminine partner ("The Myth of Black Macho: A Response to Angry Black Feminists," *Black Scholar* 10 [March–April 1979]: 24–32).

[22] See White; and Jacqueline Jones, *Labor of Love, Labor of Sorrow: Black Women, Work and the Family, From Slavery to the Present* (New York: Basic, 1985).

[23] Michael Albert et al., *Liberating Theory* (Boston: South End Press, 1986), 6.

race. Faced with this dilemma, many black women and most black men believed that the extension of suffrage to black males was imperative in order to protect race interests in the historical period of postbellum America. But because political empowerment for black women would require that both blacks and women gained the right to vote, some of these same black women also lobbied strenuously for women's suffrage.[24]

The contemporary efforts of black women to achieve greater equal opportunity and status present similar dilemmas, whether in the areas of reproductive rights, electoral politics, or poverty. Our history of resistance to multiple jeopardies is replete with the fierce tensions, untenable ultimatums, and bitter compromises between nationalism, feminism, and class politics. In a curious twist of fate, we find ourselves marginal to both the movements for women's liberation and black liberation irrespective of our victimization under the dual discriminations of racism and sexism. A similar exclusion or secondary status typifies our role within class movements. Ironically, black women are often in conflict with the very same subordinate groups with which we share some interests. The groups in which we find logical allies on certain issues are the groups in which we may find opponents on others. To the extent that we have found ourselves confronting the exclusivity of monistic politics, we have had to manage ideologies and activities that did not address the dialectics of our lives. We are asked to decide with whom to ally, which interests to advance. Should black women's primary ideological and activist commitment be to race, sex, or class-based social movements? Can we afford to be monist? Can we afford not to be?

In the following consideration of the dialectics within each of three liberation movements, I hope to describe the tensions and priorities that influence the construction of a black feminist ideology. To the extent that any politic is monistic, the actual victims of racism, sexism, or classism may be absent from, invisible within, or seen as antagonistic to that politic. Thus, prejudicial attitudes and discriminatory actions may be overt, subtle, or covert; and they may have various manifestations through ideological statements, policies and strategies, and interpersonal relations. That is, black and/or poor women may be marginal to monistic feminism, women's concerns may be excluded from nationalistic activism, and indif-

---

[24] For further discussion of suffrage and racism, see Davis, *Women, Race and Class* (n. 9 above); Giddings; Harley and Terborg-Penn; and Barbara H. Andolsen, *"Daughters of Jefferson, Daughters of Bootblacks": Racism and American Feminism* (Macon, Ga.: Mercer University Press, 1986).

ference to race and gender may pervade class politics. This invisibility may be due to actual exclusion or benign neglect, while marginality is represented in tokenism, minimization, and devalued participation. Antagonism involves two subordinate groups whose actions and beliefs are placed in opposition as mutually detrimental. From this conceptual framework, the following discussion highlights the major aspects of multiple jeopardy within liberation politics.

Intraracial politics

Racial solidarity and race liberation have been and remain a fundamental concern for black Americans. Historically and currently, slavery, segregation, and institutional as well as individual discrimination have been formative experiences in most blacks' socialization and political outlook. The inerasable physical characteristics of race have long determined the status and opportunities of black women in the United States. Since race serves as a significant filter of what blacks perceive and how blacks are perceived, many black women have claimed that their racial identity is more salient than either their gender or class identity.[25] Diane Lewis, an anthropologist, has remarked that when racism is seen as the principal cause of their subordinate status, "their interests as blacks have taken precedence over their interests as women."[26] This political importance of race is evident for other reasons as well. Certainly, the chronological order of the social movements for racial, gender, and class justice in part explains the priority given to racial interests. In both the nineteenth and twentieth centuries, the abolition and civil rights movements predate women's suffrage and the women's movement. Similarly, collective efforts that addressed economic deprivation and exploitation, such as trade unionism beginning in the late 1800s, communist organizing in the 1920s and 1930s, and the anti-imperialist activism of the 1960s were preceded by or simultaneous with race-oriented movements. Considering the order of events, it is reasonable to expect that most black women would have made commitments to and investments in the race movements

[25] See Gloria Joseph and Jill Lewis, *Common Differences: Conflicts in Black and White Feminist Perspectives* (New York: Avon, 1981); Diane K. Lewis, "A Response to Inequality: Black Women, Racism, and Sexism," *Signs* 3 (1977): 339–61; and bell hooks, *Feminist Theory: From Margin to Center* (Boston: South End Press, 1984), for extended discussions of the dynamics of structural subordination to and social conflict with varying dominant racial and sexual groups.
[26] Lewis, 343.

such that they would not or could not easily abandon those for later movements.

Furthermore, through the necessity of confronting and surviving racial oppression, black women have assumed responsibilities atypical of those assigned to white women under Western patriarchy. Black women often held central and powerful leadership roles within the black community and within its liberation politics. We founded schools, operated social welfare services, sustained churches, organized collective work groups and unions, and even established banks and commercial enterprises. That is, we were the backbone of racial uplift, and we also played critical roles in the struggle for racial justice.[27] Harriet Tubman led slaves to freedom on the underground railroad; Ida Wells Barnett led the crusade against lynching; Fannie Lou Hamer and Ella Baker were guiding political spirits of the southern black efforts that gave birth to SNCC and the Mississippi Freedom Democratic Party; the "simple" act of Rosa Parks catapulted Martin Luther King to national prominence. Black women, therefore, did not experience sexism within the race movement in quite the ways that brought many white women to feminist consciousness within either civil rights or New Left politics.[28]

All together this history constitutes a powerful impetus toward a monistic race approach as the means of liberation for black women. Michelle Wallace concludes that black women simply lack a feminist consciousness as a matter of choice, out of ignorance, misguided beliefs, or an inability to recognize sexual domination both within and without the black community.[29] Since the 1800s, however, the writings of such prominent black women as Sojourner Truth, Maria Stewart, Anna Julia Cooper, Josephine St. Pierre Ruffin, Frances Watkins Harper, Pauli Murray, Frances Beale, Audre Lorde, and Angela Davis have described a broader view of black consciousness.[30] Even among those black women who expressed

[27] Giddings; Harley and Terborg-Penn; and Davis, "Reflections on the Black Woman's Role in the Community of Slaves."
[28] See Evans (n. 9 above); and Clayborne Carson, *In Struggle: SNCC and the Black Awakening of the 1960s* (Cambridge, Mass.: Harvard University Press, 1981).
[29] Michelle Wallace, *Black Macho and the Myth of the Superwoman* (New York: Dial, 1979). See also Linda C. Powell, "Black Macho and Black Feminism," in Smith, ed. (n. 15 above), 283–92, for a critique of Wallace's thesis.
[30] For statements by Truth, Stewart, Cooper, Ruffin, and Harper, see Loewenberg and Bogin, eds. (n. 3 above); and Lerner, ed. (n. 1 above); for Lorde, see Lorde (n. 15 above); for Davis, see Davis, *Women, Race and Class;* for Beale, see Frances Beale, "Double Jeopardy" (n. 13 above), and "Slave of a Slave No More: Black Women in the Struggle," *Black Scholar* 12, no. 6 (November/December 1981): 16–24; and for Murray, see Pauli Murray, "The Liberation of Black Women," in *Women: A Feminist Perspective,* ed. Jo Freeman (Palo Alto, Calif.: Mayfield, 1975), 351–63.

grave reservations about participating in the women's movement, most recognized sexism as a factor of their subordination in the larger society and acknowledged sexual politics among blacks. They could identify the sexual inequities that resulted in the images of black women as emasculating matriarchs; in the rates of sexual abuse and physical violence; and in black men assuming the visible leadership positions in many black social institutions, such as the church, the intelligentsia, and political organizations.[31] During the civil rights and black nationalist movements of the 1960s and 1970s, men quite effectively used the matriarchy issue to manipulate and coerce black women into maintaining exclusive commitments to racial interests and redefining and narrowing black women's roles and images in ways to fit a more traditional Western view of women. Black feminists Pauli Murray and Pauline Terrelonge Stone both agree that the debates over this issue became an ideological ploy to heighten guilt in black women over their supposed collusion with whites in the oppression of black men.[32] Consequently, these intraracial tensions worked against the public articulations of a feminist consciousness by most black women. Nevertheless, a point of concern and contention within the black community was how sexual inequalities might best be addressed, not whether they existed. A few black women responded by choosing monistic feminism, others sought a distinct black feminist activism. While many organized feminist efforts within race-oriented movements, some also adopted a strict nationalist view. Over time, there were also transformations of perspectives. For example, the black women of SNCC created within it a women's liberation group which later became an independent feminists-of-color organization, the Third World Women's Alliance, which is today the only surviving entity of SNCC.

The politics of race liberation have rarely been exclusively race-based. Because so many blacks historically have been economically

---

[31] Regarding the church, see Pauline Terrelonge Stone, "Feminist Consciousness and Black Women," in Freeman, ed., 575–88; Joseph and Lewis; Jacqueline Grant, "Black Women and the Church," in *But Some of Us Are Brave: Black Women's Studies*, ed. Gloria T. Hull et al. (Old Westbury, N.Y.: Feminist Press, 1982), 141–52; and Cheryl Townsend Gilkes, " 'Together and in Harness'; Women's Traditions in the Sanctified Church," *Signs* 10, no. 4 (Summer 1985): 678–99. Concerning politics, see LaRue (n. 10 above); Mae C. King, "The Politics of Sexual Stereotypes," *Black Scholar* 4 (March/April 1973): 12–22; and Manning Marable, *How Capitalism Underdeveloped Black America* (Boston: South End Press, 1983), esp. chap. 3. For a discussion of sexual victimization, see Barbara Smith, "Notes for Yet Another Paper on Black Feminism, or Will the Real Enemy Please Stand Up," *Conditions* 5 (1979): 123–27, as well as Joseph and Lewis. For a critique of the notion of the matriarch, see Stone; and Staples, "The Myth of the Black Matriarchy" (n. 21 above).

[32] See Murray; and Stone.

oppressed, race liberation has out of necessity become more pluralistic through its incorporation of economic interests. Whether civil
rights or a nationalist activism, the approach to class injustice generally promotes greater economic opportunities and rewards within
the existing capitalist order. At the turn of the century, for instance,
the collective action known as racial uplift involved the efforts of
educated, middle-class blacks to elevate the moral, physical, social,
and economic conditions of lower income blacks. The National
Association of Wage Earners was established in the 1920s by women
like Nannie Burroughs, Maggie Wallace, and Mary McCleod Bethune to assist black female domestic and factory workers.[33]
    The civil rights movement initially seemed to avoid the value-
laden implications of this pattern of middle-class beneficence toward those with fewer economic resources. Both Aldon Morris, a
sociologist, and Clayborne Carson, a historian, have written of the
genuine grass roots orientation of the black southern strategy in the
1950s and early 1960s.[34] The majority of the participants were rural,
poorly educated, and economically disadvantaged, but more important, these same individuals set the priorities and the strategies
of the movement. The legacy was an affirmation of the strength of
seemingly powerless people, and particularly of the black women
who were among the principal organizers and supporters.[35]
    Despite these auspicious beginnings, Cornell West, a black theo-
logian, described the 1960s as a time when the interests of poor
blacks were often betrayed.[36] Middle-class blacks were better able
to take advantage of the relatively greater opportunities made possible through the race-oriented, legal liberalism of equal opportunity and affirmative action policies and electoral politics. Only such
groups as the Nation of Islam and the League of Revolutionary Black
Workers, like Marcus Garvey's United Negro Improvement Association earlier in this century, continued to represent the interests
of working class and impoverished blacks. The contemporary controversy over class polarization in the black community is a consequence of the movement not effectively addressing the economic

[33] Evelyn Brooks Bennett, "Nannie Burroughs and the Education of Black Woman,"
in Harley and Terborg-Penn (n. 20 above), 97–108.
    [34] Aldon Morris, *The Origins of the Civil Rights Movement: Black Communities
Organizing for Change* (New York: Free Press, 1984); and Carson.
    [35] See the recent publication by Jo Ann Gibson Robinson, *The Montgomery Bus
Boycott and the Women Who Started It* (Knoxville: University of Tennessee Press,
1987).
    [36] Cornell West, "The Paradox of the Afro-American Rebellion," in *The Sixties
without Apology,* ed. Sohnya Sayres, Anders Stephanson, Stanley Aronowitz, Fredric
Jameson (Minneapolis: University of Minnesota Press, 1984).

status of all blacks. Given the particularly precarious economic status of black women, this neglect and marginalization of class is especially problematic for them. The National Welfare Rights Organization, founded in 1967, was one of the few successful, though short-lived, efforts to address the class divisions. Only recently have race-focal groups, including the Urban League and the National Association for the Advancement of Colored People addressed the plight of impoverished black women.

Racial solidarity has been a fundamental element of black women's resistance to domination. However, the intraracial politics of gender and class have made a strictly nationalistic approach overly restrictive and incalculably detrimental to our prospects for full liberation. Given a social condition that is also compounded by other oppressions, black women have necessarily been concerned with affecting, at the very least, an amelioration of economic and gender discriminations. Consequently, some black women have sought an association with feminism as one alternative to the limitations of monistic race politics.

Politics among women

At one level, black women, other women of color, and white women, share many common contemporary concerns about their legal status and rights, encounters with discrimination, and sexual victimization. It is on these shared concerns that feminists have sought to forge a sense of sisterhood and to foster solidarity. This effort is manifest in a variety of ways, but the slogan, "sisterhood is powerful," best exemplifies the importance and the hoped for efficacy of such solidarity in the achievement of women's equality and liberation. For example, all-female restrictions for consciousness-raising sessions, intellectual and artistic programs and publications, organizations, businesses, and communities reflect this singular orientation; and lesbian feminist separatism represents the absolute ideological expression of the monistic tendencies in feminism.

Presumably, black women are included in this sisterhood, but, nonetheless, invisibility and marginality characterize much of our relationship to the women's movement. The assertion of commonality, indeed of the universality and primacy of female oppression, denies the other structured inequalities of race, class, religion, and nationality, as well as denying the diverse cultural heritages that affect the lives of many women. While contending that feminist consciousness and theory emerged from the personal, everyday reality of being female, the reality of millions of women was ignored. The phrase, "the personal is the political" not only reflects a phenomenological approach to women's liberation—that is, of women defining and constructing their own reality—but it has also come to describe the politics of imposing and privileging a few women's personal !ives over all women's lives by assuming that these few could be prototypical. For black women, the personal is bound up in the problems peculiar to multiple jeopardies of race and class, not the singular one of sexual inequality. This has not necessarily meant that black women rejected feminism, but merely that they were not singlemindedly committed to the organizations and some of the agenda that have come to be called the women's movement, that is, the movement of white, often protestant, middle-class women.

Feminism has excluded and devalued black women, our experiences, and our interpretations of our own realities at the conceptual and ideological level. Black feminists and black women scholars have identified and critically examined other serious flaws in feminist theorizing. The assumption that the family is by definition patriarchal, the privileging of an individualistic worldview, and the advocacy of female separatism are often antithetical positions to many of the values and goals of black women and thus are hindrances to our association with feminism.[37] These theoretical blinders obscured the ability of certain feminists first to recognize the multifaceted nature of women's oppressions and then to envision theories that encompass those realities. As a consequence, monistic feminism's ability to foresee remedies that would neither abandon women to the other discriminations, including race and class, nor exacerbate those burdens is extremely limited. Without theories and concepts that represent the experiences of black women, the women's movement has and will be ineffectual in making ideological appeals that might mobilize such women. Often, in fact, this conceptual invisibility has led to the actual strategic neglect and physical exclusion or nonparticipation of black women. Most black women who have participated in any organizations or activities of the women's movement are keenly aware of the racial politics that anger, frustrate, and alienate us.

The case of the struggle for suffrage in the nineteenth century again is an instructive example of the complexity of multiple jeopardy and its politics. Initially, there was an alliance of blacks and

---

[37] Lorde, *Sister Outsider*, esp. 66–71; hooks, *Feminist Theory* (n. 25 above); Linda Burnham, "Has Poverty Been Feminized in Black America?" *Black Scholar* 16, no. 2 (March/April 1985): 14–24; Maria C. Lugones and Elizabeth V. Spelman, "Have We Got A Theory for You! Feminist Theory, Cultural Imperialism and the Demand for 'The Woman's Voice,' " *Women's Studies International Forum* 6, no. 6 (1983): 573–81.

women for universal suffrage. However, as the campaign ensued, opponents of universal suffrage, and of any extension of voting privileges, were successful in transforming the debate into one of whom should receive the vote—women or black males. Many prominent white suffragists, including Elizabeth Cady Stanton, Susan B. Anthony, and Carrie Chapman Catt abandoned the alliance and demanded a "women only" enfranchisement. The question of black women's suffrage should have been especially problematical for them. In fact, it was never seriously considered. More damning, however, were their politics of expediency. They cooperated with avowed racists in order to gain the southern vote and liberally used racial slurs and epithets arguing that white women's superior character and intellect made them more deserving of the right to vote than blacks, Native Americans, and Eastern European and Asian immigrants.

As Angela Davis observes in her examination of race and class in the early women's rights campaign, even the Seneca Falls Declaration "all but ignored the predicament of white working-class women, as it ignored the condition of black women in the South and North alike."[38] Barbara Andolsen, in one of the most comprehensive studies of racism in the woman suffrage movement observed: "[it] had a bold vision and noble principles . . . but this is a story of a vision betrayed. For the white women who led this movement came to trade upon their privilege as the daughters (sisters, wives, and mothers) of powerful white men in order to gain for themselves some share of the political power those men possessed. They did not adequately identify ways in which that political power would not be accessible to poor women, immigrant women, and black women."[39] Yet despite the blatant racism and class bias of the women's suffrage movement, black women, discouraged and betrayed, continued to work for their right to vote, both as blacks and as women, through their own suffrage organizations.

This history of racism in the early women's movement has been sustained by contemporary white feminists. Within organizations, most twentieth-century black women encounter myriad experiences that deny their reality. In some instances, it is the absence of materials, information, speeches, readings, or persons representing black women. When present at all, women of color are underrepresented and have marginal and subordinate roles. Recently, Paula Giddings has reported that the National Organization of Women (NOW) remains insensitive to such problematic issues

[38] Davis, *Women, Race and Class* (n. 9 above), 53–54.
[39] Andolsen (n. 24 above), 78.

as rape, abortion, sterilization, poverty, and unions. Women of color are rarely elected as officers or appointed to major positions, and NOW has actually encouraged minority women's chapters rather than the incorporation of their concerns into the "regular" chapters.[40] Lawyer and educator Mary Frances Berry, in her analysis of the politics of amending the constitution, has argued that one reason for the defeat of the Equal Rights Amendment was the failure of its proponents to campaign, educate, and mobilize the black community, and especially black women.[41]

Many white feminist activists have often assumed that their anti-sexism stance abolished that all racial prejudice or discriminatory behaviors. At best, this presumption is naive and reflects a serious ignorance of the pervasiveness of racism in this society. Many blacks, women and men alike, see such postures as arrogant, racist, and dangerous to their own interests. Diane Lewis concluded that the status of black women and our interests within the women's movement and its organizations essentially replicates our structurally subordinate position to white women in the larger society.[42] Different opportunity structures and life options make interracial alliances and feminist solidarity problematic. Conceptually invisible, interpersonally misunderstood and insulted, and strategically marginal, black women have found that much in the movement has denied important aspects of our history and experience. Yet, despite the critical obstacles and limitations, the imperatives of multiple jeopardy necessitate recognizing and resisting sexism.

Beyond the race politics in feminism, many black women share concerns of impoverished and working-class women about class politics. What has become mainstream feminism rests on traditional, liberal economic aspirations of equal employment opportunities for women. In practice, however, the emphasis is often on the professional careers of those women who are already economically privileged and college educated. It could be argued, for instance, that equal access to all types of vocational training and jobs may not be desirable as a necessary or primary goal. While it is true that men on average earn more than women, all men do not have equally attractive jobs in terms of working conditions, compensation and benefits, prestige, and mobility. Those male jobs may represent, at best, only a minimal improvement over the jobs of many working women. White feminist economic concerns have concentrated on

[40] Giddings (n. 20 above), 348.
[41] Mary Frances Berry, *Why ERA Failed: Politics, Women's Rights, and the Amending Process of the Constitution* (Bloomington: Indiana University Press, 1986).
[42] Lewis (n. 25 above).

primary sector employment, but these are not the positions that are most critical and accessible to lower- or no-income women. Referring to the equal opportunity approach, Karen Kollias points out that "the majority of nonwhite, lower- and working-class women don't have the power to utilize these benefits because their primary, objective economic conditions haven't changed."[43]

Class stratification becomes an insignificant issue if economic disadvantage is seen as only relevant for feminism to the extent that women are unequal vis-à-vis men. The difference between male and female incomes is dramatically less among blacks than among whites (see table 1), suggesting that sex alone is not the sole determinant of economic status. From a monist feminist perspective, class exploitation is not understood as an independent system of oppression. Consequently, broad class dynamics are not addressed in liberal and some radical feminisms. Marxist and socialist feminists have sought to correct this biased view of class.[44] While the Marxists attempted to incorporate a concern for gender within traditional Marxist analysis, socialist feminists tried to develop a nonmonist perspective of feminism that saw sexism and classism as co-equal oppressions. Ellen Willis concludes that within various feminisms there was limited politics beyond an assertion that class hierarchy was oppressive. A radical feminist, she observes that the consciousness-raising, personal politics approach did not effectively challenge the structural, political economy of class oppression. She concludes that as a consequence, "women were implicated in the class system and had real class interests, that women could oppress men on the basis of class, and that class differences among women could not be resolved within a feminist context alone."[45]

First, the memberships of these class-oriented groups remained mostly middle class. Economically disadvantaged women have not directly contributed to a feminist theoretical understanding of class dynamics or the development of programs and strategies. Black feminist and literary critic, bell hooks notes that "had poor women

[43] Karen Kollias, "Class Realities: Create a New Power Base," in *Building Feminist Theory: Essays from Quest*, ed. *Quest* staff (New York: Longman, 1981), 125–38, esp. 134.

[44] See Josephine Donovan, *Feminist Theory: The Intellectual Traditions of American Feminism* (New York: Ungar, 1985); and Lydia Sargent, ed., *Woman and Revolution: A Discussion of the Unhappy Marriage of Marxism and Feminism* (Boston: South End Press, 1981); and Zillah R. Eisenstein, ed., *Capitalist Patriarchy and the Case for Socialist Feminism* (New York: Monthly Review Press, 1979), for fuller discussions.

[45] Ellen Willis, "Radical Feminism and Feminist Radicalism," in Sayres et al., eds. (n. 36 above), 91–118, esp. 110–11.

set the agenda for feminist movement, they might have decided that class struggle would be a central feminist issue."[46] She further contends that class oppression has not become central among women liberationists because their "values, behaviors, and lifestyles continue to be shaped by privilege."[47] In a similar fashion, feminist and race politics have not informed or established ties between poor and working-class black and white women. Phyllis M. Palmer reasons that from the perspective of a poor black woman, white women individually may suffer wage discrimination because of their sex, but their relations to white males, the top income earners, as daughters and wives grants them a relatively better quality of material well-being. "Most white women do not *in reality* live on what they earn; they have access to the resources of white male income earners."[48] Rejecting what she views as the hollow efforts of "slumming" or nonhierarchical organizing, she observes that no serious strategies have been developed for convincing bourgeois women that class liberation is critical for women's liberation or for organizing with poor and working-class women.

This lack of attention to economic issues has significant implications for the participation of black women. Many of the differences of priorities between black and white women are related to class. Issues of welfare, hunger, poor housing, limited health care, and transportation are seldom seen as feminist interests and are rarely the subject of feminist social policies. As Brenda Eichelberger maintains, "the black woman's energy output is more often directed toward such basic survival issues, while the white woman's is more often aimed at fulfillment."[49] The economic concerns of women from lower-income backgrounds are relatively ignored and distorted in the contemporary women's movement. The feminist interpretation of the "feminization" of poverty is a case in point. While noting that some women, again middle class, have indeed experienced a recent drastic decline in life circumstances as a consequence of divorce, the feminization analysis has misrepresented many of the causes of female poverty. For example, most impoverished women have been poor throughout their lives as a consequence of their class position or of racial oppression. Linda Burnham writes that race and class are more significant causative factors in

---

[46] hooks, *Feminist Theory* (n. 25 above), 60–61.

[47] Ibid., 61.

[48] Phyllis Marynick Palmer, "White Women/Black Women: The Dualism of Female Identity and Experiences in the United States," *Feminist Studies* 91 (Spring 1983): 162.

[49] Brenda Eichelberger, "Voices on Black Feminism," *Quest: A Feminist Quarterly* 4 (1977): 16–28, esp. 16.

black women's impoverishment than is gender. In the thesis of the feminization of poverty, she contends, "The vulnerability of white women to impoverishment is overstated; the impoverishment of Black men is ignored or underestimated; and the fundamental basis in working-class exploitation for the continual regeneration of poverty is abandoned for a focus on gender."[50]

In summary, feminism's neglect, misunderstanding, or deemphasis of the politics of race and class have direct implications for the actions of black women in relationship to the movement. Often, our response has been to avoid participation in white female, middle-class dominated organizations and to withhold our support from policies that are not in our race and class interests. Nevertheless, just as the importance of race led many black women to commitments to racially based politics, and gender interests compelled our feminist efforts, economic injustices have brought many to consider class politics as a major avenue of liberation.

Class politics

Economic exploitation is the third societal jeopardy constraining the lives of black women. Historically, the three major movements to address the deprivations of class in the United States have been trade unionism and the anticapitalist politics of the 1930s and 1960s which are colloquially referred to as the Old and the New Left. Having their origins in responses to the degradations that accompanied urbanization and industrialization, labor unionists and leftists organized to address the problems of wage labor and economic stratification in a capitalistic society, including the excessive working hours in poor, unsafe conditions, low pay and limited job security, fluctuations in the labor demand, the decline in work satisfaction, the loss of worker autonomy, and poverty. Each movement, although monistic, possessed different objectives. Unionism was reformist in orientation, seeking to ameliorate the worst of the above conditions. In contrast, the socialist and communist ideologies of the Left were revolutionary in that they aspired to eradicate capitalism and ostensibly to establish a classless society.

Into the first quarter of this century, organized labor's approach to economic disadvantage held little promise for blacks or women, and thus no promise for black women. Samuel Gompers, the leading force of trade unionism and president of the American Federation of Labor (AFL, founded in 1886), believed that the best means of improving wages for Anglo males was to restrict the labor supply.

---

[50] Burnham (n. 37 above), 15.

His strategy was to advocate the return of women to the home and the banning of blacks and Asians from the unions. Although the AFL never formally adopted these restrictions at the national level, many local chapters did so through both formal rules and informal practices.[51] Trade unionists cultivated a cultural image of the worker as a married male who required a family wage to support a wife and children. Labor actively supported protective labor legislation, which effectively excluded women from the jobs that would provide them with sufficient incomes to support themselves and their families. These efforts against women were coupled with the exclusion of blacks, other racial minorities, and initially southern and eastern European immigrant males from the most economically rewarding labor in the unionized crafts and the closed shops. Blacks, in particular, were specifically denied union membership or else relegated to the unskilled, low paying jobs. Consequently, the denial of a family wage to black males exacerbated the circumstances of already economically distressed black families and individuals. In occupations where blacks were well represented, unionization often meant their forceable expulsion. Many of the race riots in the early 1900s were related to the tensions between black laborers and white laborers in competition for employment. So, an effective two-prong strategy for improving white men's income required the demand for a family wage and the restriction of labor competition from women and racial minorities.

In response to union discrimination, white women and black women and men organized. The Working Women's Association, formed in 1868, was one of the earlier attempts at synthesizing feminist and white female workers concerns; the Women's Trade Union League, established in 1903, allied white working- and middle-class women, while the International Ladies' Garment Workers' Union publicized the conditions of white working women,

[51] For discussion of women, employment, and the labor movement, see Diane Balser, *Sisterhood and Solidarity: Feminism and Labor in Modern Times* (Boston: South End Press, 1987); Carol Groneman and Mary Beth Norton, eds., *"To Toil the Livelong Day": America's Women at Work, 1780–1980* (Ithaca, N.Y.: Cornell University Press, 1987); Philip S. Foner, *Women and the American Labor Movement: From World War I to the Present* (New York: Free Press, 1980); Bettina Berch, *The Endless Day: The Political Economy of Women and Work* (New York: Harcourt Brace Jovanovich, 1982); and Mary Frank Fox and Sharlene Hesse-Biber, *Women at Work* (Palo Alto, Calif.: Mayfield, 1984). For blacks, see Marable (n. 31 above); Richard Polenberg, *One Nation Divisible: Class, Race, and Ethnicity in the United States since 1938* (New York: Penguin, 1980); Philip S. Foner, *Organized Labor and the Black Worker, 1619–1973* (New York: International Publishers, 1976); and Dorothy K. Newman et al., *Protest, Politics, and Prosperity; Black Americans and White Institutions, 1940–75* (New York: Pantheon, 1978).

demanded equal pay, demanded female representation in the national labor unions, formed female unions, and organized strikes.[52] Ironically, most of the women's trade union organizations as well as many socialist feminists supported protective legislation but with the mistaken belief that involving the state would ensure safer work environments and reasonable labor requirements for both women and men. However, an unintended consequence of this strategy was that many women's economic situations declined because protective legislation could be used to reinforce occupational segregation and thus limit women's wage earning opportunities.

As the wives and daughters of men who did not earn a family wage, black women's participation in the labor market was crucial to the survival of themselves and their families. Yet, black women benefited little from the unionization efforts among white women. First, they were disproportionately situated in those occupations least likely to be unionized, such as domestic and nonhousehold service and agricultural labor. In large industrial workplaces, they were segregated from white female workers, where the organizing took place, and were often pawns in the labor-management contests.[53] Second, white trade unionists failed actively to recruit black females and they often were denied membership because of their race. The protective legislation further hampered their opportunities by closing off numerous employment opportunities simply on the basis of sex. Black women wanted better paying jobs, but they often had to settle for the jobs that were considered too hazardous, dirty, or immoral for white women, and for which they were not fairly compensated. During the Depression, race-gender discrimination was so pervasive that employment in federal work-relief projects often was closed to them. Thus, significant numbers of black women were unemployed and/or underemployed and, therefore, untouched by union activism.

Despite their exclusion from the major unions, black women and men organized caucuses within predominantly white unions and formed their own unions, such as the Urban League's Negro Workers Councils, African Blood Brotherhood, Negro American Labor Council, National Negro Labor Council, and Dodge Revolutionary Union Movement (DRUM). A. Phillip Randolph, founder of the Brotherhood of Sleeping Car Porters, called for a march on Washington in the 1940s to demand the end of wage and job dis-

[52] See Balser for a detailed consideration of the contemporary union activities of women, especially their efforts to organize clerical and other pink collar workers.

[53] See Jones (n. 22 above); Giddings (n. 20 above); and Davis, *Women, Race and Class* (n. 9 above), for an examination of black women's work roles and labor activism.

crimination, the desegregation of schools and public accommodations, protection of immigrant workers, cessation of lynching, and the unionization of black women. During the Depression, trade unions and unemployed councils held demonstrations demanding immediate cash relief and unemployment compensation, as well as advocating race solidarity. For blacks in the first half of this century, class and race interests were often inseparable. Black women benefited indirectly from black men's labor activism, and they often supported those efforts by participating on picket lines, providing food and clothing for strikers and their families, and, most important, making financial contributions to the households from their own paid labor. Black women also engaged in labor organizing directly, both through existing predominantly white unions and through their own activism. Black domestics, tobacco workers, garment workers, and others organized strikes and fought for union representation.[54]

Not all unions and economic organizations excluded white women and black women and men. The Knights of Labor, established in 1886, the Industrial Workers of the World, created in 1905, and the Congress of Industrial Organizations, formed in 1938, are noted for encouraging the unionization of millions of black men and black and white women workers. But overall, the record of organized labor on issues of import to black women and men and white women has not been outstanding. Until 1971, the major unions opposed the Equal Rights Amendment; and today, many challenge affirmative action and comparable worth policies. The continued need for black and women's labor organizations suggest that the historic barriers remain to their full participation and rewards in unions. But, it is also important to recognize that the trade unionist approach has many limitations, and first among these is its focus on the individual worker. As a result, the broad issues of poverty and economic inequality are perceived as beyond the purview of most labor activism. While seeking to ameliorate the worst of industrial society, unionists seldom challenge the economic order of capitalism.

This challenge was left to the Socialist and Communist activists, but this radical critique of the political economy has never been a part of the political mainstream of the United States as it has in other nations. Nevertheless, a small but significant group of activists and intellectuals have advanced radicalism throughout this century.[55] The

[54] See Dolores Janiewski, "Seeking 'a New Day and a New Way': Black Women and Unions in the Southern Tobacco Industry"; and Elizabeth Clark-Lewis, " 'This Work Had a End': African-American Domestic Workers in Washington, D.C., 1910–1940," both in Groneman and Norton, eds.

[55] See Peter Clecak, *Radical Paradoxes: Dilemmas of the American Left: 1945–1970* (New York: Harper & Row, 1973), for an illuminating analysis of the Old and New Left.

political Left, in general, supported black women and men and white working women during the Progressive Era. In fact, leading intellectuals, including Emma Goldman, Margaret Sanger, Charlotte Perkins Gilman, Elizabeth Gurley Flynn, Langston Hughes, Paul Robeson, W. E. B. DuBois, and C. L. R. James saw socialism as the route for liberation. Two black women, Lucy Parsons and Claudia Jones, were among the early labor activists and Socialists of the Old Left. And even Angela Davis, who describes the important role of individual women within the Socialist and Communist parties during the first half of the twentieth century, does not offer us much insight into the general status of black women, besides noting the Socialist party's indifference to blacks, both males and females.[56]

But even within these efforts, there still were gaps in recognizing the needs of black women. In 1900, the Socialist party was founded and immediately began campaigning for women's suffrage and labor rights through its Woman's National Committee. Because it focused on the industrial proletariat, it paid no particular attention to blacks since they were mostly agricultural laborers. Consequently, the party also paid minimal attention to the black women who were not industrially employed. In contrast, members of the Communist party were actively involved in organizing industrial workers, sharecoppers, and the unemployed during the Depression and in championing racial as well as economic justice for blacks.[57] However, the Communist party remained relatively silent on various feminist concerns. Its vigorous defense of the Scottsboro boys and other victims of racial bigotry linked with its call for black self-determination initially attracted numerous blacks to the party in the 1930s and 1940s. Nevertheless, it became increasingly clear that the international Communist party was concerned with the liberation of blacks only as long as those efforts advanced its overall objective of aiding the revolutionary leadership of a European working class. Eventually, the collusion of the American Communist party with racism and sexism dissuaded many blacks and women of the advantages of Soviet-oriented communist activism.

The second surge of anticapitalism was an integral part of the so-called New Left of the 1960s. Sociologist Stanley Aronowitz has described the sixties' radicalism as the movements of a generation, which were not oriented around any particular class or race issue.[58] While this might characterize certain aspects of the radical critique

[56] Davis, *Women, Race and Class*.

[57] See Vincent Harding, *The Other American Revolution* (Los Angeles and Atlanta: University of California, Los Angeles, Center for Afro-American Studies, and Institute of the Black World, 1980), for discussion of blacks and communist organizing.

[58] Stanley Aronowitz, "When the New Left Was New," in Sayres et al., eds. (n. 36 above), 11–43.

of the liberal society, his interpretation does not account for the ideological and activist history that informed both the black and women's liberation efforts of that decade. In an analysis of the contradictions and dilemmas of the New Left, Peter Clecak described the era as one that lacked a vision of a new society beyond the negation of the present ills of poverty, racism, imperialism, and hegemony. Its apocalyptic perspectives on American society and utopian images of community were founded on a fundamental acceptance of capitalist notions of individualism, personal gain, and personal liberty.[59] By implication, much of the New Left lacked a basic, critical understanding of the dynamics of oppressions as group and systemic processes.

The disillusionment that characterized the New Left movement was compounded by the frustration of its failure to organize the urban poor and racial minorities. The free speech and antiwar activists, Students for a Democratic Society and the Weather Underground (i.e., the weathermen), mistakenly attempted to organize northern urban communities using SNCC's southern mobilization model. At another level, new leftists did not understand that most members of oppressed groups desired a piece of the American Dream, not its destruction. The efforts to create coalitions with civil rights and black nationalist groups were strained and defeated because of the conflicting objectives and tactics. The aims of civil rights groups were integrationist through nonviolent means; and while black militants advocated armed defense or even revolution and adopted a Maoist, anticapitalist program, their separatist orientation made black-white alliances almost impossible. Moreover, while the Left condemned the role of U.S. imperialism in Southeast Asia, it ignored the advance of Western, capitalist interests into the continent of Africa, especially South Africa.

At the same time, women active in the New Left became increasingly frustrated with the theoretical and strategic indifference to the woman question. The sexual politics within the movement subjected women to traditional gender role assignments, sexual manipulation, male leadership and domination, plus a concentration on an essentially male issue, the draft.[60] Once again, invisibility

---

[59] Clecak.

[60] Heidi Hartmann and Zillah Eisenstein provide theoretical critiques of monist Marxism as an adequate avenue for women's liberation. Both Lydia Sargent and Sara Evans detail the sexual politics on the Left (see Heidi Hartmann, "The Unhappy Marriage of Marxism and Feminism," in Sargent, ed. [n. 44 above]; Eisenstein, "Reform and/or Revolution: Toward a Unified Women's Movement," in Sargent, ed. [n. 44 above], 339–62; Sargent, "New Left Women and Men: The Honeymoon Is Over," in Sargent, ed. [n. 44 above], xi–xxxii; and Evans [n. 9 above]).

typifies the role of black women in New Left radical politics. Black women responded by incorporating class interests into their race and gender politics. In the founding documents of various black feminist organizations, scathing critiques of the political economy are a cornerstone of the analysis of domination. For example, the *Combahee River Collective Statement* pointedly declared that "the liberation of all oppressed peoples necessitates the destruction of the political-economic systems of capitalism and imperialism, as well as partriarchy. . . . We are not convinced, however, that a socialist revolution that is not also a feminist and anti-racism revolution will guarantee our liberation."[61] This excerpt clearly articulates an understanding of multiple jeopardy and its function in the dominant society and within liberation politics. Out of necessity, black women have addressed both narrow labor and broad economic concerns.

Political theorist Manning Marable has argued that progressive forces must uproot racism and patriarchy in their quest for a socialist democracy through a dedication to equality.[62] Yet a major limitation of both unionism and radical class politics is their monist formulations, wherein economics are exaggerated at the expense of understanding and confronting other oppressions such as racism and sexism. Despite the historical examples of black women and men and white women as union activists and socialists and the examples of the sporadic concern of organized labor and leftists with race and gender politics, class politics have not provided the solution to black women's domination because they continue to privilege class issues within a white male framework. Given the inability of any single agenda to address the intricate complex of racism, sexism, and classism in black women's lives, black women must develop a political ideology capable of interpreting and resisting that multiple jeopardy.

Multiple consciousness in black feminist ideology

Gloria Joseph and Jill Lewis have suggested that black women face a dilemma analogous to that of Siamese twins, each of whom have distinct and incompatible interests.[63] Black women cannot, they argue, be wholeheartedly committed and fully active in both the black liberation struggle and the women's liberation movement,

---

[61] See Combahee River Collective, *Combahee River Collective Statement: Black Feminist Organizing in the Seventies and Eighties* (New York: Kitchen Table Press, 1986), 12–13.
[62] Marable (n. 31 above).
[63] Joseph and Lewis (n. 25 above), 38.

because of sexual and racial politics within each respectively. The authors recognize the demands of multiple jeopardy politics and the detrimental effect of neglecting these dual commitments. But what they fail to consider are the multiple and creative ways in which black women address their interdependent concerns of racism, sexism, and classism.

Black women have been feminists since the early 1800s, but our exclusion from the white women's movement and its organizations has led many incorrectly to assume that we were not present in the (white) women's movement because we were not interested in resisting sexism both within and without the black community. What appears recently to be a change in black women's position, from studied indifference to disdain and curiosity to cautious affirmation of the women's movement, may be due to structural changes in relationships between blacks and whites that have made black women "more sensitive to the obstacles of sexism and to the relevance of the women's movement."[64] Black women's apparent greater sensitivity to sexism may be merely the bolder, public articulation of black feminist concerns that have existed for well over a century. In other words, black women did not just become feminists in the 1970s. We did, however, grant more salience to those concerns and become more willing to organize primarily on that basis, creating the Combahee River Collective, the National Black Feminist Organization, and Sapphire Sapphos. Some black women chose to participate in predominantly white, women's movement activities and organizations, while others elected to develop the scholarship and curriculum that became the foundation of black women's studies, while still others founded black feminist journals, presses, and political organizations.[65]

Several studies have considered the relevance of black women's diverse characteristics in understanding our political attitudes; these

[64] Lewis (n. 25 above), 341.

[65] For information on the development of black feminist scholarship and academic programs, see Patricia Bell Scott, "Selective Bibliography on Black Feminism" in Hull et al., eds. (n. 31 above); Black Studies/Women's Studies Faculty Development Project, "Black Studies/Women's Studies: An Overdue Partnership" (Women's Studies, University of Massachusetts—Amherst, mimeograph, 1983); Nancy Conklin et al., "The Culture of Southern Black Women: Approaches and Materials" (University: University of Alabama Archives of American Minority Cultures and Women's Studies Program, Project on the Culture of Southern Black Women, 1983); the premier issue of *Sage: A Scholarly Journal on Black Women* 1, no. 1 (Spring 1984); and the establishment of Kitchen Table: A Women of Color Press, New York. The Center for Research on Women at Memphis State University, the Women's Research and Resource Center at Spelman College, and the Minority Women's Program at Wellesley College are among the academic centers.

reports seem fairly inconsistent, if not contradictory.[66] The various findings do suggest that the conditions that bring black women to feminist consciousness are specific to our social and historical experiences. For black women, the circumstances of lower socioeconomic life may encourage political, and particularly feminist, consciousness.[67] This is in contrast to feminist as well as traditional political socialization literature that suggests that more liberal, that is, feminist, attitudes are associated with higher education attainment and class standing. Many of the conditions that middle-class, white feminists have found oppressive are perceived as privileges by black women, especially those with low incomes. For instance, the option not to work outside of the home is a luxury that historically has been denied most black women. The desire to struggle for this option can, in such a context, represent a feminist position, precisely because it constitutes an instance of greater liberty for certain women. It is also important to note, however, that the class differences among black women regarding our feminist consciousness are minimal. Black women's particular history thus is an essential ingredient in shaping our feminist concerns.

Certainly the multifaceted nature of black womanhood would meld diverse ideologies, from race liberation, class liberation, and women's liberation. The basis of our feminist ideology is rooted in our reality. To the extent that the adherents of any one ideology insist on separatist organizational forms, assert the fundamental nature of any one oppression, and demand total cognitive, affective, and behavioral commitment, that ideology and its practitioners exclude black women and the realities of our lives.

[66] See Andrew Cherlin and Pamela Waters, "Trends in United States Men's and Women's Sex-Role Attitudes: 1972–1978," *American Sociological Review* 46 (1981): 453–60. See also, Janice Gump, "Comparative Analysis of Black Women's and White Women's Sex-role Attitudes," *Journal of Consulting and Clinical Psychology* 43 (1975): 858–63; and Marjorie Hershey, "Racial Difference in Sex-Role Identities and Sex Stereotyping: Evidence against a Common Assumption," *Social Science Quarterly* 58 (1978): 583–96. For various opinion polls, see "The 1972 Virginia Slims American Women's Opinion Poll" and "The 1974 Virginia Slims American Women's Opinion Poll," conducted by the Roper Organization (Williamstown, Mass.: Roper Public Opinion Research Center, 1974). See Barbara Everitt Bryant, "American Women: Today and Tomorrow," National Commission on the Observance of International Women's Year (Washington, D.C.: Government Printing Office, March 1977). Gloria Steinem, "Exclusive Louis Harris Survey: How Women Live, Vote and Think," *Ms. Magazine* 13 (July 1984): 51–54.

[67] For analyses of the influence of socioeconomic class and race on feminist attitudes, see Willa Mae Hemmons, "The Women's Liberation Movement: Understanding Black Women's Attitudes," in *The Black Woman*, ed. LaFrances Rodgers-Rose (Beverly Hills, Calif.: Sage Publications, 1980), 285–99; and Ransford and Miller (n. 16 above).

A black feminist ideology, first and foremost, thus declares the visibility of black women. It acknowledges the fact that two innate and inerasable traits, being both black and female, constitute our special status in American society. Second, black feminism asserts self-determination as essential. Black women are empowered with the right to interpret our reality and define our objectives. While drawing on a rich tradition of struggle as blacks and as women, we continually establish and reestablish our own priorities. As black women, we decide for ourselves the relative salience of any and all identities and oppressions, and how and the extent to which those features inform our politics. Third, a black feminist ideology fundamentally challenges the interstructure of the oppressions of racism, sexism, and classism both in the dominant society and within movements for liberation. It is in confrontation with multiple jeopardy that black women define and sustain a multiple consciousness essential for our liberation, of which feminist consciousness is an integral part.

Finally, a black feminist ideology presumes an image of black women as powerful, independent subjects. By concentrating on our multiple oppressions, scholarly descriptions have confounded our ability to discover and appreciate the ways in which black women are not victims. Ideological and political choices cannot be assumed to be determined solely by the historical dynamics of racism, sexism, and classism in this society. Although the complexities and ambiguities that merge a consciousness of race, class, and gender oppressions make the emergence and praxis of a multivalent ideology problematical, they also make such a task more necessary if we are to work toward our liberation as blacks, as the economically exploited, and as women.

Department of Sociology
Dartmouth College

THE SOCIAL CONSTRUCTION OF BLACK FEMINIST THOUGHT

PATRICIA HILL COLLINS

Sojourner Truth, Anna Julia Cooper, Ida Wells Barnett, and Fannie Lou Hamer are but a few names from a growing list of distinguished African-American women activists. Although their sustained resistance to Black women's victimization within interlocking systems of race, gender, and class oppression is well known, these women did not act alone.[1] Their actions were nurtured by the support of countless, ordinary African-American women who, through strategies of everyday resistance, created a powerful foundation for

Special thanks go out to the following people for reading various drafts of this manuscript: Evelyn Nakano Glenn, Lynn Weber Cannon, and participants in the 1986 Research Institute, Center for Research on Women, Memphis State University; Elsa Barkley Brown, Deborah K. King, Elizabeth V. Spelman, and Angelene Jamison-Hall; and four anonymous reviewers at *Signs*.
[1] For analyses of how interlocking systems of oppression affect Black women, see Frances Beale, "Double Jeopardy: To Be Black and Female," in *The Black Woman*, ed. Toni Cade (New York: Signet, 1970); Angela Y. Davis, *Women, Race and Class* (New York: Random House, 1981); Bonnie Thornton Dill, "Race, Class, and Gender: Prospects for an All-Inclusive Sisterhood," *Feminist Studies* 9, no. 1 (1983): 131–50; bell hooks, *Ain't I a Woman? Black Women and Feminism* (Boston: South End Press, 1981); Diane Lewis, "A Response to Inequality: Black Women, Racism, and Sexism," *Signs: Journal of Women in Culture and Society* 3, no. 2 (Winter 1977): 339–61; Pauli Murray, "The Liberation of Black Women," in *Voices of the New Feminism*, ed. Mary Lou Thompson (Boston: Beacon, 1970), 87–102; and the introduction in Filomina Chioma Steady, *The Black Woman Cross-Culturally* (Cambridge, Mass.: Schenkman, 1981), 7–41.

This essay originally appeared in *Signs*, vol. 14, no. 4, Summer 1989.

this more visible Black feminist activist tradition.[2] Such support has been essential to the shape and goals of Black feminist thought.

The long-term and widely shared resistance among African-American women can only have been sustained by an enduring and shared standpoint among Black women about the meaning of oppression and the actions that Black women can and should take to resist it. Efforts to identify the central concepts of this Black women's standpoint figure prominently in the works of contemporary Black feminist intellectuals.[3] Moreover, political and epistemological issues influence the social construction of Black feminist thought. Like other subordinate groups, African-American women not only have developed distinctive interpretations of Black women's oppression but have done so by using alternative ways of producing and validating knowledge itself.

A Black women's standpoint
The foundation of Black feminist thought

Black women's everyday acts of resistance challenge two prevailing approaches to studying the consciousness of oppressed groups.[4] One approach claims that subordinate groups identify with the powerful and have no valid independent interpretation of their own oppression.[5] The second approach assumes that the oppressed are

[2] See the introduction in Steady for an overview of Black women's strengths. This strength-resiliency perspective has greatly influenced empirical work on African-American women. See, e.g., Joyce Ladner's study of low-income Black adolescent girls, *Tomorrow's Tomorrow* (New York: Doubleday, 1971); and Lena Wright Myers's work on Black women's self-concept, *Black Women: Do They Cope Better?* (Englewood Cliffs, N.J.: Prentice-Hall, 1980). For discussions of Black women's resistance, see Elizabeth Fox-Genovese, "Strategies and Forms of Resistance: Focus on Slave Women in the United States," in *In Resistance: Studies in African, Caribbean and Afro-American History*, ed. Gary Y. Okihiro (Amherst, Mass.: University of Massachusetts Press, 1986), 143–65; and Rosalyn Terborg-Penn, "Black Women in Resistance: A Cross-Cultural Perspective," in Okihiro, ed., 188–209. For a comprehensive discussion of everyday resistance, see James C. Scott, *Weapons of the Weak: Everyday Forms of Peasant Resistance* (New Haven, Conn.: Yale University Press, 1985).

[3] See Patricia Hill Collins's analysis of the substantive content of Black feminist thought in "Learning from the Outsider Within: The Sociological Significance of Black Feminist Thought," *Social Problems* 33, no. 6 (1986): 14–32.

[4] Scott describes consciousness as the meaning that people give to their acts through the symbols, norms, and ideological forms they create.

[5] This thesis is found in scholarship of varying theoretical perspectives. For example, Marxist analyses of working-class consciousness claim that "false consciousness" makes the working class unable to penetrate the hegemony of ruling-class ideologies. See Scott's critique of this literature.

less human than their rulers and, therefore, are less capable of articulating their own standpoint.[6] Both approaches see any independent consciousness expressed by an oppressed group as being not of the group's own making and/or inferior to the perspective of the dominant group.[7] More important, both interpretations suggest that oppressed groups lack the motivation for political activism because of their flawed consciousness of their own subordination.

Yet African-American women have been neither passive victims of nor willing accomplices to their own domination. As a result, emerging work in Black women's studies contends that Black women have a self-defined standpoint on their own oppression.[8] Two interlocking components characterize this standpoint. First, Black women's political and economic status provides them with a distinctive set of experiences that offers a different view of material reality than that available to other groups. The unpaid and paid work that Black women perform, the types of communities in which they live, and the kinds of relationships they have with others suggest that African-American women, as a group, experience a different world than those who are not Black and female.[9] Second,

[6] For example, in Western societies, African-Americans have been judged as being less capable of intellectual excellence, more suited to manual labor, and therefore as less human than whites. Similarly, white women have been assigned roles as emotional, irrational creatures ruled by passions and biological urges. They too have been stigmatized as being less than fully human, as being objects. For a discussion of the importance that objectification and dehumanization play in maintaining systems of domination, see Arthur Brittan and Mary Maynard, *Sexism, Racism and Oppression* (New York: Basil Blackwell, 1984).

[7] The tendency for Western scholarship to assess Black culture as pathological and deviant illustrates this process. See Rhett S. Jones, "Proving Blacks Inferior: The Sociology of Knowledge," in *The Death of White Sociology*, ed. Joyce Ladner (New York: Vintage, 1973), 114–35.

[8] The presence of an independent standpoint does not mean that it is uniformly shared by all Black women or even that Black women fully recognize its contours. By using the concept of standpoint, I do not mean to minimize the rich diversity existing among African-American women. I use the phrase "Black women's standpoint" to emphasize the plurality of experiences within the overarching term "standpoint." For discussions of the concept of standpoint, see Nancy M. Hartsock, "The Feminist Standpoint: Developing the Ground for a Specifically Feminist Historical Materialism," in *Discovering Reality*, ed. Sandra Harding and Merrill Hintikka (Boston: D. Reidel, 1983), 283–310, and *Money, Sex, and Power* (Boston: Northeastern University Press, 1983); and Alison M. Jaggar, *Feminist Politics and Human Nature* (Totowa, N.J.: Rowman & Allanheld, 1983), 377–89. My use of the standpoint epistemologies as an organizing concept in this essay does not mean that the concept is problem-free. For a helpful critique of standpoint epistemologies, see Sandra Harding, *The Science Question in Feminism* (Ithaca, N.Y.: Cornell University Press, 1986).

[9] One contribution of contemporary Black women's studies is its documentation of how race, class, and gender have structured these differences. For representative

these experiences stimulate a distinctive Black feminist consciousness concerning that material reality.[10] In brief, a subordinate group
not only experiences a different reality than a group that rules, but
a subordinate group may interpret that reality differently than a
dominant group.

Many ordinary African-American women have grasped this
connection between what one does and how one thinks. Hannah
Nelson, an elderly Black domestic worker, discusses how work
shapes the standpoints of African-American and white women:
"Since I have to work, I don't really have to worry about most of the
things that most of the white women I have worked for are worrying
about. And if these women did their own work, they would think
just like I do—about this, anyway."[11] Ruth Shays, a Black inner city
resident, points out how variations in men's and women's experiences lead to differences in perspective: "The mind of the man and
the mind of the woman is the same. But this business of living
makes women use their minds in ways that men don't even have to
think about."[12] Finally, elderly domestic worker Rosa Wakefield
assesses how the standpoints of the powerful and those who serve
them diverge: "If you eats these dinners and don't cook 'em, if you
wears these clothes and don't buy or iron them, then you might start
thinking that the good fairy or some spirit did all that. . . . Blackfolks
don't have no time to be thinking like that. . . . But when you don't

---

works surveying African-American women's experiences, see Paula Giddings, *When
and Where I Enter: The Impact of Black Women on Race and Sex in America* (New
York: William Morrow, 1984); and Jacqueline Jones, *Labor of Love, Labor of
Sorrow: Black Women, Work, and the Family from Slavery to the Present* (New
York: Basic, 1985).

[10] For example, Judith Rollins, *Between Women: Domestics and Their Employers*
(Philadelphia: Temple University Press, 1985); and Bonnie Thornton Dill, " 'The
Means to Put My Children Through': Child-Rearing Goals and Strategies among
Black Female Domestic Servants," in *The Black Woman*, ed. LaFrances Rodgers-
Rose (Beverly Hills, Calif.: Sage Publications, 1980), 107–23, report that Black
domestic workers do not see themselves as being the devalued workers that their
employers perceive and construct their own interpretations of the meaning of their
work. For additional discussions of how Black women's consciousness is shaped by
the material conditions they encounter, see Ladner (n. 2 above); Myers (n. 2 above);
and Cheryl Townsend Gilkes, " 'Together and in Harness': Women's Traditions in
the Sanctified Church," *Signs* 10, no. 4 (Summer 1985): 678–99. See also Marcia
Westkott's discussion of consciousness as a sphere of freedom for women in
"Feminist Criticism of the Social Sciences," *Harvard Educational Review* 49, no. 4
(1979): 422–30.

[11] John Langston Gwaltney, *Drylongso: A Self-Portrait of Black America* (New
York: Vintage, 1980), 4.

[12] Ibid., 33.

have anything else to do, you can think like that. It's bad for your mind, though."[13]

While African-American women may occupy material positions that stimulate a unique standpoint, expressing an independent Black feminist consciousness is problematic precisely because more powerful groups have a vested interest in suppressing such thought. As Hannah Nelson notes, "I have grown to womanhood in a world where the saner you are, the madder you are made to appear."[14] Nelson realizes that those who control the schools, the media, and other cultural institutions are generally skilled in establishing their view of reality as superior to alternative interpretations. While an oppressed group's experiences may put them in a position to see things differently, their lack of control over the apparatuses of society that sustain ideological hegemony makes the articulation of their self-defined standpoint difficult. Groups unequal in power are correspondingly unequal in their access to the resources necessary to implement their perspectives outside their particular group.

One key reason that standpoints of oppressed groups are discredited and suppressed by the more powerful is that self-defined standpoints can stimulate oppressed groups to resist their domination. For instance, Annie Adams, a southern Black woman, describes how she became involved in civil rights activities.

> When I first went into the mill we had segregated water fountains. . . . Same thing about the toilets. I had to clean the toilets for the inspection room and then, when I got ready to go to the bathroom, I had to go all the way to the bottom of the stairs to the cellar. So I asked my boss man, "What's the difference? If I can go in there and clean them toilets, why can't I use them?" Finally, I started to use that toilet. I decided I wasn't going to walk a mile to go to the bathroom.[15]

In this case, Adams found the standpoint of the "boss man" inadequate, developed one of her own, and acted upon it. In doing so, her actions exemplify the connections between experiencing oppression, developing a self-defined standpoint on that experience, and resistance.

[13] Ibid., 88.
[14] Ibid., 7.
[15] Victoria Byerly, *Hard Times Cotton Mill Girls: Personal Histories of Womanhood and Poverty in the South* (New York: ILR Press, 1986), 134.

The significance of Black feminist thought

The existence of a distinctive Black women's standpoint does not mean that it has been adequately articulated in Black feminist thought. Peter Berger and Thomas Luckmann provide a useful approach to clarifying the relationship between a Black women's standpoint and Black feminist thought with the contention that knowledge exists on two levels.[16] The first level includes the everyday, taken-for-granted knowledge shared by members of a given group, such as the ideas expressed by Ruth Shays and Annie Adams. Black feminist thought, by extension, represents a second level of knowledge, the more specialized knowledge furnished by experts who are part of a group and who express the group's standpoint. The two levels of knowledge are interdependent; while Black feminist thought articulates the taken-for-granted knowledge of African-American women, it also encourages all Black women to create new self-definitions that validate a Black women's standpoint.

Black feminist thought's potential significance goes far beyond demonstrating that Black women can produce independent, specialized knowledge. Such thought can encourage collective identity by offering Black women a different view of themselves and their world than that offered by the established social order. This different view encourages African-American women to value their own subjective knowledge base.[17] By taking elements and themes of Black women's culture and traditions and infusing them with new meaning, Black feminist thought rearticulates a consciousness that already exists.[18] More important, this rearticulated consciousness gives African-American women another tool of resistance to all forms of their subordination.[19]

Black feminist thought, then, specializes in formulating and rearticulating the distinctive, self-defined standpoint of African-American women. One approach to learning more about a Black women's standpoint is to consult standard scholarly sources for the

[16] See Peter L. Berger and Thomas Luckmann, *The Social Construction of Reality* (New York: Doubleday, 1966), for a discussion of everyday thought and the role of experts in articulating specialized thought.

[17] See Michael Omi and Howard Winant, *Racial Formation in the United States* (New York: Routledge & Kegan Paul, 1986), esp. 93.

[18] In discussing standpoint epistemologies, Hartsock, in *Money, Sex, and Power*, notes that a standpoint is "achieved rather than obvious, a mediated rather than immediate understanding" (132).

[19] See Scott (n. 2 above); and Hartsock, *Money, Sex, and Power* (n. 8 above).

ideas of specialists on Black women's experiences.[20] But investigating a Black women's standpoint and Black feminist thought requires more ingenuity than that required in examining the standpoints and thought of white males. Rearticulating the standpoint of African-American women through Black feminist thought is much more difficult since one cannot use the same techniques to study the knowledge of the dominated as one uses to study the knowledge of the powerful. This is precisely because subordinate groups have long had to use alternative ways to create an independent consciousness and to rearticulate it through specialists validated by the oppressed themselves.

The Eurocentric masculinist knowledge-validation process[21]

All social thought, including white masculinist and Black feminist, reflects the interests and standpoint of its creators. As Karl Mannheim notes, "If one were to trace in detail . . . the origin and . . . diffusion of a certain thought-model, one would discover the . . . affinity it has to the social position of given groups and their manner of interpreting the world."[22] Scholars, publishers, and other experts represent specific interests and credentialing processes, and their knowledge claims must satisfy the epistemological and political criteria of the contexts in which they reside.[23]

[20] Some readers may question how one determines whether the ideas of any given African-American woman are "feminist" and "Afrocentric." I offer the following working definitions. I agree with the general definition of feminist consciousness provided by Black feminist sociologist Deborah K. King: "Any purposes, goals, and activities which seek to enhance the potential of women, to ensure their liberty, afford them equal opportunity, and to permit and encourage their self-determination represent a feminist consciousness, even if they occur within a racial community" (in "Race, Class and Gender Salience in Black Women's Womanist Consciousness" [Dartmouth College, Department of Sociology, Hanover, N.H., 1987, typescript], 22). To be Black or Afrocentric, such thought must not only reflect a similar concern for the self-determination of African-American people, but must in some way draw upon key elements of an Afrocentric tradition as well.

[21] The Eurocentric masculinist process is defined here as the institutions, paradigms, and any elements of the knowledge-validation procedure controlled by white males and whose purpose is to represent a white male standpoint. While this process represents the interests of powerful white males, various dimensions of the process are not necessarily managed by white males themselves.

[22] Karl Mannheim, *Ideology and Utopia: An Introduction to the Sociology of Knowledge* (New York: Harcourt, Brace, 1936, 1954), 276.

[23] The knowledge-validation model used in this essay is taken from Michael Mulkay, *Science and the Sociology of Knowledge* (Boston: Allen & Unwin, 1979). For a general discussion of the structure of knowledge, see Thomas Kuhn, *The Structure of Scientific Revolutions* (Chicago: University of Chicago Press, 1962).

Two political criteria influence the knowledge-validation process. First, knowledge claims must be evaluated by a community of experts whose members represent the standpoints of the groups from which they originate. Second, each community of experts must maintain its credibility as defined by the larger group in which it is situated and from which it draws its basic, taken-for-granted knowledge.

When white males control the knowledge-validation process, both political criteria can work to suppress Black feminist thought. Since the general culture shaping the taken-for-granted knowledge of the community of experts is one permeated by widespread notions of Black and female inferiority,[24] new knowledge claims that seem to violate these fundamental assumptions are likely to be viewed as anomalies.[25] Moreover, specialized thought challenging notions of Black and female inferiority is unlikely to be generated from within a white-male-controlled academic community because both the kinds of questions that could be asked and the explanations that would be found satisfying would necessarily reflect a basic lack of familiarity with Black women's reality.[26]

The experiences of African-American women scholars illustrate how individuals who wish to rearticulate a Black women's standpoint through Black feminist thought can be suppressed by a white-male-controlled knowledge-validation process. Exclusion from basic literacy, quality educational experiences, and faculty and administrative positions has limited Black women's access to influential academic positions.[27] Thus, while Black women can produce knowledge claims that contest those advanced by the white male community, this community does not grant that Black women scholars have competing knowledge claims based in another knowledge-validation process. As a consequence, any

[24] For analyses of the content and functions of images of Black female inferiority, see Mae King, "The Politics of Sexual Stereotypes," Black Scholar 4, nos. 6–7 (1973): 12–23; Cheryl Townsend Gilkes, "From Slavery to Social Welfare: Racism and the Control of Black Women," in Class, Race, and Sex: The Dynamics of Control, ed. Amy Smerdlow and Helen Lessinger (Boston: G. K. Hall, 1981), 288–300; and Elizabeth Higginbotham, "Two Representative Issues in Contemporary Sociological Work on Black Women," in But Some of Us Are Brave, ed. Gloria T. Hull, Patricia Bell Scott, and Barbara Smith (Old Westbury, N.Y.: Feminist Press, 1982).

[25] Kuhn.

[26] Evelyn Fox Keller, Reflections on Gender and Science (New Haven, Conn.: Yale University Press, 1985), 167.

[27] Maxine Baca Zinn, Lynn Weber Cannon, Elizabeth Higginbotham, and Bonnie Thornton Dill, "The Cost of Exclusionary Practices in Women's Studies," Signs 11, no. 2 (Winter 1986): 290–303.

credentials controlled by white male academicians can be denied to Black women producing Black feminist thought on the grounds that it is not credible research.

Those Black women with academic credentials who seek to exert the authority that their status grants them to propose new knowledge claims about African-American women face pressures to use their authority to help legitimate a system that devalues and excludes the majority of Black women.[28] One way of excluding the majority of Black women from the knowledge-validation process is to permit a few Black women to acquire positions of authority in institutions that legitimate knowledge and to encourage them to work within the taken-for-granted assumptions of Black female inferiority shared by the scholarly community and the culture at large. Those Black women who accept these assumptions are likely to be rewarded by their institutions, often at significant personal cost. Those challenging the assumptions run the risk of being ostracized.

African-American women academicians who persist in trying to rearticulate a Black women's standpoint also face potential rejection of their knowledge claims on epistemological grounds. Just as the material realities of the powerful and the dominated produce separate standpoints, each group may also have distinctive epistemologies or theories of knowledge. It is my contention that Black female scholars may know that something is true but be unwilling or unable to legitimate their claims using Eurocentric masculinist criteria for consistency with substantiated knowledge and Eurocentric masculinist criteria for methodological adequacy.

For any particular interpretive context, new knowledge claims must be consistent with an existing body of knowledge that the group controlling the interpretive context accepts as true. The methods used to validate knowledge claims must also be acceptable to the group controlling the knowledge-validation process.

The criteria for the methodological adequacy of positivism illustrate the epistemological standards that Black women scholars

[28] Berger and Luckmann (n. 16 above) note that if an outsider group, in this case African-American women, recognizes that the insider group, namely, white men, requires special privileges from the larger society, a special problem arises of keeping the outsiders out and at the same time having them acknowledge the legitimacy of this procedure. Accepting a few "safe" outsiders is one way of addressing this legitimation problem. Collins's discussion (n. 3 above) of Black women as "outsiders within" addresses this issue. Other relevant works include Franz Fanon's analysis of the role of the national middle class in maintaining colonial systems, *The Wretched of the Earth* (New York: Grove, 1963); and William Tabb's discussion of the use of "bright natives" in controlling African-American communities, *The Political Economy of the Black Ghetto* (New York: Norton, 1970).

would have to satisfy in legitimating alternative knowledge claims.[29] Positivist approaches aim to create scientific descriptions of reality by producing objective generalizations. Since researchers have widely differing values, experiences, and emotions, genuine science is thought to be unattainable unless all human characteristics except rationality are eliminated from the research process. By following strict methodological rules, scientists aim to distance themselves from the values, vested interests, and emotions generated by their class, race, sex, or unique situation and in so doing become detached observers and manipulators of nature.[30]

Several requirements typify positivist methodological approaches. First, research methods generally require a distancing of the researcher from her/his "object" of study by defining the researcher as a "subject" with full human subjectivity and objectifying the "object" of study.[31] A second requirement is the absence of emotions from the research process.[32] Third, ethics and values are deemed inappropriate in the research process, either as the reason for scientific inquiry or as part of the research process itself.[33] Finally, adversarial debates, whether written or oral, become the preferred method of ascertaining truth—the arguments that can withstand the greatest assault and survive intact become the strongest truths.[34]

Such criteria ask African-American women to objectify themselves, devalue their emotional life, displace their motivations for furthering knowledge about Black women, and confront, in an adversarial relationship, those who have more social, economic,

[29] While I have been describing Eurocentric masculinist approaches as a single process, there are many schools of thought or paradigms subsumed under this one process. Positivism represents one such paradigm. See Harding (n. 8 above) for an overview and critique of this literature. The following discussion depends heavily on Jaggar (n. 8 above), 355–58.

[30] Jaggar, 356.

[31] See Keller, especially her analysis of static autonomy and its relation to objectivity (67–126).

[32] Ironically, researchers must "objectify" themselves to achieve this lack of bias. See Arlie Russell Hochschild, "The Sociology of Feeling and Emotion: Selected Possibilities," in *Another Voice: Feminist Perspectives on Social Life and Social Science*, ed. Marcia Millman and Rosabeth Kanter (Garden City, N.Y.: Anchor, 1975), 280–307. Also, see Jaggar.

[33] See Norma Haan, Robert Bellah, Paul Rabinow, and William Sullivan, eds., *Social Science as Moral Inquiry* (New York: Columbia University Press, 1983), esp. Michelle Z. Rosaldo's "Moral/Analytic Dilemmas Posed by the Intersection of Feminism and Social Science," 76–96; and Robert Bellah's "The Ethical Aims of Social Inquiry," 360–81.

[34] Janice Moulton, "A Paradigm of Philosophy: The Adversary Method," in Harding and Hintikka, eds. (n. 8 above), 149–64.

and professional power than they. It seems unlikely, therefore, that Black women would use a positivist epistemological stance in rearticulating a Black women's standpoint. Black women are more likely to choose an alternative epistemology for assessing knowledge claims, one using standards that are consistent with Black women's criteria for substantiated knowledge and with Black women's criteria for methodological adequacy. If such an epistemology exists, what are its contours? Moreover, what is its role in the production of Black feminist thought?

The contours of an Afrocentric feminist epistemology

Africanist analyses of the Black experience generally agree on the fundamental elements of an Afrocentric standpoint. In spite of varying histories, Black societies reflect elements of a core African value system that existed prior to and independently of racial oppression.[35] Moreover, as a result of colonialism, imperialism, slavery, apartheid, and other systems of racial domination, Blacks share a common experience of oppression. These similarities in material conditions have fostered shared Afrocentric values that permeate the family structure, religious institutions, culture, and community life of Blacks in varying parts of Africa, the Caribbean, South America, and North America.[36] This Afrocentric consciousness permeates the shared history of people of African descent through the framework of a distinctive Afrocentric epistemology.[37]

[35] For detailed discussions of the Afrocentric worldview, see John S. Mbiti, *African Religions and Philosophy* (London: Heinemann, 1969); Dominique Zahan, *The Religion, Spirituality, and Thought of Traditional Africa* (Chicago: University of Chicago Press, 1979); and Mechal Sobel, *Trabelin' On: The Slave Journey to an Afro-Baptist Faith* (Westport, Conn.: Greenwood Press, 1979), 1–76.

[36] For representative works applying these concepts to African-American culture, see Niara Sudarkasa, "Interpreting the African Heritage in Afro-American Family Organization," in *Black Families*, ed. Harriette Pipes McAdoo (Beverly Hills, Calif.: Sage, 1981); Henry H. Mitchell and Nicholas Cooper Lewter, *Soul Theology: The Heart of American Black Culture* (San Francisco: Harper & Row, 1986); Robert Farris Thompson, *Flash of the Spirit: African and Afro-American Art and Philosophy* (New York: Vintage, 1983); and Ortiz M. Walton, "Comparative Analysis of the African and the Western Aesthetics," in *The Black Aesthetic*, ed. Addison Gayle (Garden City, N.Y.: Doubleday, 1971), 154–64.

[37] One of the best discussions of an Afrocentric epistemology is offered by James E. Turner, "Foreword: Africana Studies and Epistemology; a Discourse in the Sociology of Knowledge," in *The Next Decade: Theoretical and Research Issues in Africana Studies*, ed. James E. Turner (Ithaca, N.Y.: Cornell University Africana Studies and Research Center, 1984), v–xxv. See also Vernon Dixon, "World Views and Research Methodology," summarized in Harding (n. 8 above), 170.

Feminist scholars advance a similar argument. They assert that women share a history of patriarchal oppression through the political economy of the material conditions of sexuality and reproduction.[38] These shared material conditions are thought to transcend divisions among women created by race, social class, religion, sexual orientation, and ethnicity and to form the basis of a women's standpoint with its corresponding feminist consciousness and epistemology.[39]

Since Black women have access to both the Afrocentric and the feminist standpoints, an alternative epistemology used to rearticulate a Black women's standpoint reflects elements of both traditions.[40] The search for the distinguishing features of an alternative epistemology used by African-American women reveals that values and ideas that Africanist scholars identify as being characteristically "Black" often bear remarkable resemblance to similar ideas claimed by feminist scholars as being characteristically "female."[41] This similarity suggests that the material conditions of oppression can vary dramatically and yet generate some uniformity

[38] See Hester Eisenstein, *Contemporary Feminist Thought* (Boston: G. K. Hall, 1983). Nancy Hartsock's *Money, Sex, and Power* (n. 8 above), 145–209, offers a particularly insightful analysis of women's oppression.

[39] For discussions of feminist consciousness, see Dorothy Smith, "A Sociology for Women," in *The Prism of Sex: Essays in the Sociology of Knowledge*, ed. Julia A. Sherman and Evelyn T. Beck (Madison: University of Wisconsin Press, 1979); and Michelle Z. Rosaldo, "Women, Culture, and Society: A Theoretical Overview," in *Woman, Culture, and Society*, ed. Michelle Z. Rosaldo and Louise Lamphere (Stanford, Calif.: Stanford University Press, 1974), 17–42. Feminist epistemologies are surveyed by Jaggar (n. 8 above).

[40] One significant difference between Afrocentric and feminist standpoints is that much of what is termed women's culture is, unlike African-American culture, created in the context of and produced by oppression. Those who argue for a women's culture are electing to value, rather than denigrate, those traits associated with females in white patriarchal societies. While this choice is important, it is not the same as identifying an independent, historic culture associated with a society. I am indebted to Deborah K. King for this point.

[41] Critiques of the Eurocentric masculinist knowledge-validation process by both Africanist and feminist scholars illustrate this point. What one group labels "white" and "Eurocentric," the other describes as "male-dominated" and "masculinist." Although he does not emphasize its patriarchal and racist features, Morris Berman's *The Reenchantment of the World* (New York: Bantam, 1981) provides a historical discussion of Western thought. Afrocentric analyses of this same process can be found in Molefi Kete Asante, "International/Intercultural Relations," in *Contemporary Black Thought*, ed. Molefi Kete Asante and Abdulai S. Vandi (Beverly Hills, Calif.: Sage, 1980), 43–58; and Dona Richards, "European Mythology: The Ideology of 'Progress,' " in Asante and Vandi, eds., 59–79. For feminist analyses, see Hartsock, *Money, Sex, and Power*. Harding also discusses this similarity (see chap. 7, "Other 'Others' and Fractured Identities: Issues for Epistemologists," 163–96).

in the epistemologies of subordinate groups. Thus, the significance of an Afrocentric feminist epistemology may lie in its enrichment of our understanding of how subordinate groups create knowledge that enables them to resist oppression.

The parallels between the two conceptual schemes raise a question: Is the worldview of women of African descent more intensely infused with the overlapping feminine/Afrocentric standpoints than is the case for either African-American men or white women?[42] While an Afrocentric feminist epistemology reflects elements of epistemologies used by Blacks as a group and women as a group, it also paradoxically demonstrates features that may be unique to Black women. On certain dimensions, Black women may more closely resemble Black men, on others, white women, and on still others, Black women may stand apart from both groups. Black feminist sociologist Deborah K. King describes this phenomenon as a "both/or" orientation, the act of being simultaneously a member of a group and yet standing apart from it. She suggests that multiple realities among Black women yield a "multiple consciousness in Black women's politics" and that this state of belonging yet not belonging forms an integral part of Black women's oppositional consciousness.[43] Bonnie Thornton Dill's analysis of how Black women live with contradictions, a situation she labels the "dialectics of Black womanhood," parallels King's assertions that this "both/or" orientation is central to an Afrocentric feminist consciousness.[44] Rather than emphasizing how a Black women's standpoint and its accompanying epistemology are different than those in Afrocentric and feminist analyses, I use Black women's experiences as a point of contact between the two.

Viewing an Afrocentric feminist epistemology in this way challenges analyses claiming that Black women have a more accurate view of oppression than do other groups. Such approaches suggest that oppression can be quantified and compared and that adding layers of oppression produces a potentially clearer standpoint. While it is tempting to claim that Black women are more oppressed than everyone else and therefore have the best standpoint from which to understand the mechanisms, processes, and effects of oppression, this simply may not be the case.[45]

[42] Harding, 166.

[43] D. King (n. 20 above).

[44] Bonnie Thornton Dill, "The Dialectics of Black Womanhood," *Signs* 4, no. 3 (Spring 1979): 543–55.

[45] One implication of standpoint approaches is that the more subordinate the group, the purer the vision of the oppressed group. This is an outcome of the origins of standpoint approaches in Marxist social theory, itself a dualistic analysis of social

African-American women do not uniformly share an Afrocentric feminist epistemology since social class introduces variations among Black women in seeing, valuing, and using Afrocentric feminist perspectives. While a Black women's standpoint and its accompanying epistemology stem from Black women's consciousness of race and gender oppression, they are not simply the result of combining Afrocentric and female values—standpoints are rooted in real material conditions structured by social class.[46]

Concrete experience as a criterion of meaning

Carolyn Chase, a thirty-one-year-old inner city Black woman, notes, "My aunt used to say, 'A heap see, but a few know.' "[47] This saying depicts two types of knowing, knowledge and wisdom, and taps the first dimension of an Afrocentric feminist epistemology. Living life as Black women requires wisdom since knowledge about the dynamics of race, gender, and class subordination has been essential to Black women's survival. African-American women give such wisdom high credence in assessing knowledge.

Allusions to these two types of knowing pervade the words of a range of African-American women. In explaining the tenacity of racism, Zilpha Elaw, a preacher of the mid-1800s, noted: "The pride of a white skin is a bauble of great value with many in some parts of the United States, who readily sacrifice their intelligence to their prejudices, and possess more knowledge than wisdom."[48] In describing differences separating African-American and white women, Nancy White invokes a similar rule: "When you come right down to it, white women just *think* they are free. Black women

---

structure. Because such approaches rely on quantifying and ranking human oppressions—familiar tenets of positivist approaches—they are rejected by Blacks and feminists alike. See Harding (n. 8 above) for a discussion of this point. See also Elizabeth V. Spelman's discussion of the fallacy of additive oppression in "Theories of Race and Gender: The Erasure of Black Women," *Quest* 5, no. 4 (1982): 36–62.

[46] Class differences among Black women may be marked. For example, see Paula Giddings's analysis (n. 9 above) of the role of social class in shaping Black women's political activism; or Elizabeth Higginbotham's study of the effects of social class in Black women's college attendance in "Race and Class Barriers to Black Women's College Attendance," *Journal of Ethnic Studies* 13, no. 1 (1985): 89–107. Those African-American women who have experienced the greatest degree of convergence of race, class, and gender oppression may be in a better position to recognize and use an alternative epistemology.

[47] Gwaltney (n. 11 above), 83.

[48] William L. Andrews, *Sisters of the Spirit: Three Black Women's Autobiographies of the Nineteenth Century* (Bloomington: Indiana University Press, 1986), 85.

know they ain't free."[49] Geneva Smitherman, a college professor specializing in African-American linguistics, suggests that "from a black perspective, written documents are limited in what they can teach about life and survival in the world. Blacks are quick to ridicule 'educated fools,' . . . they have 'book learning' but no 'mother wit,' knowledge, but not wisdom."[50] Mabel Lincoln eloquently summarizes the distinction between knowledge and wisdom: "To black people like me, a fool is funny—you know, people who love to break bad, people you can't tell anything to, folks that would take a shotgun to a roach."[51]

Black women need wisdom to know how to deal with the "educated fools" who would "take a shotgun to a roach." As members of a subordinate group, Black women cannot afford to be fools of any type, for their devalued status denies them the protections that white skin, maleness, and wealth confer. This distinction between knowledge and wisdom, and the use of experience as the cutting edge dividing them, has been key to Black women's survival. In the context of race, gender, and class oppression, the distinction is essential since knowledge without wisdom is adequate for the powerful, but wisdom is essential to the survival of the subordinate.

For ordinary African-American women, those individuals who have lived through the experiences about which they claim to be experts are more believable and credible than those who have merely read or thought about such experiences. Thus, concrete experience as a criterion for credibility frequently is invoked by Black women when making knowledge claims. For instance, Hannah Nelson describes the importance that personal experience has for her: "Our speech is most directly personal, and every black person assumes that every other black person has a right to a personal opinion. In speaking of grave matters, your personal experience is considered very good evidence. With us, distant statistics are certainly not as important as the actual experience of a sober person."[52] Similarly, Ruth Shays uses her concrete experiences to challenge the idea that formal education is the only route to knowledge: "I am the kind of person who doesn't have a lot of education, but both my mother and my father had good common sense. Now, I think that's all you need. I might not know how to use thirty-four words where three would do, but that does not mean that

[49] Gwaltney, 147.
[50] Geneva Smitherman, *Talkin and Testifyin: The Language of Black America* (Detroit: Wayne State University Press, 1986), 76.
[51] Gwaltney, 68.
[52] Ibid., 7.

I don't know what I'm talking about . . . I know what I'm talking
about because I'm talking about myself. I'm talking about what I
have lived."[53] Implicit in Shays's self-assessment is a critique of the
type of knowledge that obscures the truth, the "thirty-four words"
that cover up a truth that can be expressed in three.

Even after substantial mastery of white masculinist epistemologies, many Black women scholars invoke their own concrete
experiences and those of other Black women in selecting topics for
investigation and methodologies used. For example, Elsa Barkley
Brown subtitles her essay on Black women's history, "how my
mother taught me to be an historian in spite of my academic
training."[54] Similarly, Joyce Ladner maintains that growing up as a
Black woman in the South gave her special insights in conducting
her study of Black adolescent women.[55]

Henry Mitchell and Nicholas Lewter claim that experience as a
criterion of meaning with practical images as its symbolic vehicles
is a fundamental epistemological tenet in African-American
thought-systems.[56] Stories, narratives, and Bible principles are
selected for their applicability to the lived experiences of African-
Americans and become symbolic representations of a whole wealth
of experience. For example, Bible tales are told for their value to
common life, so their interpretation involves no need for scientific
historical verification. The narrative method requires that the story
be "told, not torn apart in analysis, and trusted as core belief, not
admired as science."[57] Any biblical story contains more than characters and a plot—it presents key ethical issues salient in African-
American life.

June Jordan's essay about her mother's suicide exemplifies the
multiple levels of meaning that can occur when concrete experiences are used as a criterion of meaning. Jordan describes her
mother, a woman who literally died trying to stand up, and the
effect that her mother's death had on her own work:

> I think all of this is really about women and work. Certainly
> this is all about me as a woman and my life work. I mean I am

[53] Ibid., 27, 33.

[54] Elsa Barkley Brown, "Hearing Our Mothers' Lives" (paper presented at the
Fifteenth Anniversary Faculty Lecture Series, African-American and African Studies, Emory University, Atlanta, 1986).

[55] Ladner (n. 2 above).

[56] Mitchell and Lewter (n. 36 above). The use of the narrative approach in
African-American theology exemplifies an inductive system of logic alternately
called "folk wisdom" or a survival-based, need-oriented method of assessing
knowledge claims.

[57] Ibid., 8.

not sure my mother's suicide was something extraordinary. Perhaps most women must deal with a similar inheritance, the legacy of a woman whose death you cannot possibly pinpoint because she died so many, many times and because, even before she became your mother, the life of that woman was taken. . . . I came too late to help my mother to her feet. By way of everlasting thanks to all of the women who have helped me to stay alive I am working never to be late again.[58]

While Jordan has knowledge about the concrete act of her mother's death, she also strives for wisdom concerning the meaning of that death.

Some feminist scholars offer a similar claim that women, as a group, are more likely than men to use concrete knowledge in assessing knowledge claims. For example, a substantial number of the 135 women in a study of women's cognitive development were "connected knowers" and were drawn to the sort of knowledge that emerges from first-hand observation. Such women felt that since knowledge comes from experience, the best way of understanding another person's ideas was to try to share the experiences that led the person to form those ideas. At the heart of the procedures used by connected knowers is the capacity for empathy.[59]

In valuing the concrete, African-American women may be invoking not only an Afrocentric tradition, but a women's tradition as well. Some feminist theorists suggest that women are socialized in complex relational nexuses where contextual rules take priority over abstract principles in governing behavior. This socialization process is thought to stimulate characteristic ways of knowing.[60] For example, Canadian sociologist Dorothy Smith maintains that two modes of knowing exist, one located in the body and the space it occupies and the other passing beyond it. She asserts that women, through their child-rearing and nurturing activities, mediate these two modes and use the concrete experiences of their daily lives to assess more abstract knowledge claims.[61]

Amanda King, a young Black mother, describes how she used the concrete to assess the abstract and points out how difficult mediating these two modes of knowing can be:

[58] June Jordan, *On Call: Political Essays* (Boston: South End Press, 1985), 26.
[59] Mary Belenky, Blythe Clinchy, Nancy Goldberger, and Jill Tarule, *Women's Ways of Knowing* (New York: Basic, 1986), 113.
[60] Hartsock, *Money, Sex and Power* (n. 8 above), 237; and Nancy Chodorow, *The Reproduction of Mothering* (Berkeley and Los Angeles: University of California Press, 1978).
[61] Dorothy Smith, *The Everyday World as Problematic* (Boston: Northeastern University Press, 1987).

The leaders of the ROC [a labor union] lost their jobs too, but
it just seemed like they were used to losing their jobs. . . .
This was like a lifelong thing for them, to get out there and
protest. They were like, what do you call them—
intellectuals. . . . You got the ones that go to the university
that are supposed to make all the speeches, they're the ones
that are supposed to lead, you know, put this little revolution
together, and then you got the little ones . . . that go to the
factory everyday, they be the ones that have to fight. I had a
child and I thought I don't have the time to be running
around with these people. . . . I mean I understand some of
that stuff they were talking about, like the bourgeoisie, the
rich and the poor and all that, but I had surviving on my mind
for me and my kid.[62]

For King, abstract ideals of class solidarity were mediated by the
concrete experience of motherhood and the connectedness it involved.

In traditional African-American communities, Black women find
considerable institutional support for valuing concrete experience.
Black extended families and Black churches are two key institutions where Black women experts with concrete knowledge of what
it takes to be self-defined Black women share their knowledge with
their younger, less experienced sisters. This relationship of sisterhood among Black women can be seen as a model for a whole series
of relationships that African-American women have with each
other, whether it is networks among women in extended families,
among women in the Black church, or among women in the
African-American community at large.[63]

Since the Black church and the Black family are both woman-
centered and Afrocentric institutions, African-American women
traditionally have found considerable institutional support for this
dimension of an Afrocentric feminist epistemology in ways that are
unique to them. While white women may value the concrete, it is

[62] Byerly (n. 15 above), 198.

[63] For Black women's centrality in the family, see Steady (n. 1 above); Ladner (n.
2 above); Brown (n. 54 above); and McAdoo, ed. (n. 36 above). See Gilkes,
" 'Together and in Harness' " (n. 10 above), for Black women in the church; and
chap. 4 of Deborah Gray White, *Ar'n't I a Woman? Female Slaves in the Plantation
South* (New York: Norton, 1985). See also Gloria Joseph, "Black Mothers and
Daughters: Their Roles and Functions in American Society," in *Common Differences: Conflicts in Black and White Feminist Perspectives,* ed. Gloria Joseph and Jill
Lewis (Garden City, N.Y.: Anchor, 1981), 75–126. Even though Black women play
essential roles in Black families and Black churches, these institutions are not free
from sexism.

questionable whether white families, particularly middle-class nuclear ones, and white community institutions provide comparable types of support. Similarly, while Black men are supported by Afrocentric institutions, they cannot participate in Black women's sisterhood. In terms of Black women's relationships with one another then, African-American women may indeed find it easier than others to recognize connectedness as a primary way of knowing, simply because they are encouraged to do so by Black women's tradition of sisterhood.

The use of dialogue in assessing knowledge claims

For Black women, new knowledge claims are rarely worked out in isolation from other individuals and are usually developed through dialogues with other members of a community. A primary epistemological assumption underlying the use of dialogue in assessing knowledge claims is that connectedness rather than separation is an essential component of the knowledge-validation process.[64]

The use of dialogue has deep roots in an African-based oral tradition and in African-American culture.[65] Ruth Shays describes the importance of dialogue in the knowledge-validation process of enslaved African-Americans: "They would find a lie if it took them a year . . . the foreparents found the truth because they listened and they made people tell their part many times. Most often you can hear a lie. . . . Those old people was everywhere and knew the truth of many disputes. They believed that a liar should suffer the pain of his lies, and they had all kinds of ways of bringing liars to judgement."[66]

The widespread use of the call and response discourse mode among African-Americans exemplifies the importance placed on dialogue. Composed of spontaneous verbal and nonverbal interaction between speaker and listener in which all of the speaker's statements or "calls" are punctuated by expressions or "responses" from the listener, this Black discourse mode pervades African-American culture. The fundamental requirement of this interactive network is active participation of all individuals.[67] For ideas to be tested and validated, everyone in the group must participate. To

[64] As Belenky et al. note, "Unlike the eye, the ear requires closeness between subject and object. Unlike seeing, speaking and listening suggest dialogue and interaction" (18).

[65] Thomas Kochman, *Black and White: Styles in Conflict* (Chicago: University of Chicago Press, 1981); and Smitherman (n. 50 above).

[66] Gwaltney (n. 11 above), 32.

[67] Smitherman, 108.

refuse to join in, especially if one really disagrees with what has been said is seen as "cheating."[68]

June Jordan's analysis of Black English points to the significance of this dimension of an alternative epistemology.

> Our language is a system constructed by people constantly needing to insist that we exist. . . . Our language devolves from a culture that abhors all abstraction, or anything tending to obscure or delete the fact of the human being who is here and now/the truth of the person who is speaking or listening. Consequently, *there is no passive voice construction possible in Black English*. For example, you cannot say, "Black English is being eliminated." You must say, instead, "White people eliminating Black English." The assumption of the presence of life governs all of Black English . . . every sentence assumes the living and active participation of at least two human beings, the speaker and the listener.[69]

Many Black women intellectuals invoke the relationships and connectedness provided by use of dialogue. When asked why she chose the themes she did, novelist Gayle Jones replied: "I was . . . interested . . . in oral traditions of storytelling—Afro-American and others, in which there is always the consciousness and importance of the hearer."[70] In describing the difference in the way male and female writers select significant events and relationships, Jones points out that "with many women writers, relationships within family, community, between men and women, and among women— from slave narratives by black women writers on—are treated as complex and significant relationships, whereas with many men the significant relationships are those that involve confrontations— relationships outside the family and community."[71] Alice Walker's reaction to Zora Neale Hurston's book, *Mules and Men,* is another example of the use of dialogue in assessing knowlege claims. In *Mules and Men,* Hurston chose not to become a detached observer of the stories and folktales she collected but instead, through extensive dialogues with the people in the communities she studied, placed herself at the center of her analysis. Using a similar process, Walker tests the truth of Hurston's knowledge claims: "When I read *Mules and Men* I was delighted. Here was this perfect book! The 'perfection' of which I immediately tested on my

[68] Kochman, 28.
[69] Jordan (n. 58 above), 129.
[70] Claudia Tate, *Black Women Writers at Work* (New York: Continuum, 1983), 91.
[71] Ibid., 92.

relatives, who are such typical Black Americans they are useful for every sort of political, cultural, or economic survey. Very regular people from the South, rapidly forgetting their Southern cultural inheritance in the suburbs and ghettos of Boston and New York, they sat around reading the book themselves, listening to me read the book, listening to each other read the book, and a kind of paradise was regained."[72]

Their centrality in Black churches and Black extended families provides Black women with a high degree of support from Black institutions for invoking dialogue as a dimension of an Afrocentric feminist epistemology. However, when African-American women use dialogues in assessing knowledge claims, they might be invoking a particularly female way of knowing as well. Feminist scholars contend that males and females are socialized within their families to seek different types of autonomy, the former based on separation, the latter seeking connectedness, and that this variation in types of autonomy parallels the characteristic differences between male and female ways of knowing.[73] For instance, in contrast to the visual metaphors (such as equating knowledge with illumination, knowing with seeing, and truth with light) that scientists and philosophers typically use, women tend to ground their epistemological premises in metaphors suggesting speaking and listening.[74]

While there are significant differences between the roles Black women play in their families and those played by middle-class white women, Black women clearly are affected by general cultural norms prescribing certain familial roles for women. Thus, in terms of the role of dialogue in an Afrocentric feminist epistemology, Black women may again experience a convergence of the values of the African-American community and woman-centered values.

The ethic of caring

"Ole white preachers used to talk wid dey tongues widdout sayin' nothin', but Jesus told us slaves to talk wid our hearts."[75] These words of an ex-slave suggest that ideas cannot be divorced from the individuals who create and share them. This theme of "talking with the heart" taps another dimension of an alternative epistemology used by African-American women, the ethic of caring. Just as the ex-slave used the wisdom in his heart to reject the ideas of the

---

[72] Alice Walker, *In Search of Our Mothers' Gardens* (New York: Harcourt Brace Jovanovich, 1974), 84.

[73] Keller (n. 26 above); Chodorow (n. 60 above).

[74] Belenky et al. (n. 59 above), 16.

[75] Thomas Webber, *Deep Like the Rivers* (New York: Norton, 1978), 127.

preachers who talked "wid dey tongues widdout sayin' nothin'," the ethic of caring suggests that personal expressiveness, emotions, and empathy are central to the knowledge-validation process.

One of three interrelated components making up the ethic of caring is the emphasis placed on individual uniqueness. Rooted in a tradition of African humanism, each individual is thought to be a unique expression of a common spirit, power, or energy expressed by all life.[76] This belief in individual uniqueness is illustrated by the value placed on personal expressiveness in African-American communities.[77] Johnetta Ray, an inner city resident, describes this Afrocentric emphasis on individual uniqueness: "No matter how hard we try, I don't think black people will ever develop much of a herd instinct. We are profound individualists with a passion for self-expression."[78]

A second component of the ethic of caring concerns the appropriateness of emotions in dialogues. Emotion indicates that a speaker believes in the validity of an argument.[79] Consider Ntozake Shange's description of one of the goals of her work: "Our [Western] society allows people to be absolutely neurotic and totally out of touch with their feelings and everyone else's feelings, and yet be very respectable. This, to me, is a travesty. . . . I'm trying to change the idea of seeing emotions and intellect as distinct faculties."[80] Shange's words echo those of the ex-slave. Both see the denigration of emotion as problematic, and both suggest that expressiveness should be reclaimed and valued.

A third component of the ethic of caring involves developing the capacity for empathy. Harriet Jones, a sixteen-year-old Black woman, explains why she chose to open up to her interviewer: "Some things in my life are so hard for me to bear, and it makes me

---

[76] In her discussion of the West African Sacred Cosmos, Mechal Sobel (n. 35 above) notes that Nyam, a root word in many West African languages, connotes an enduring spirit, power, or energy possessed by all life. In spite of the pervasiveness of this key concept in African humanism, its definition remains elusive. She points out, "Every individual analyzing the various Sacred Cosmos of West Africa has recognized the reality of this force, but no one has yet adequately translated this concept into Western terms" (13).

[77] For discussions of personal expressiveness in African-American culture, see Smitherman (n. 50 above); Kochman (n. 65 above), esp. chap. 9; and Mitchell and Lewter (n. 36 above).

[78] Gwaltney (n. 11 above), 228.

[79] For feminist analyses of the subordination of emotion in Western culture, see Hochschild (n. 32 above); and Chodorow.

[80] Tate (n. 70 above), 156.

feel better to know that you feel sorry about those things and would change them if you could."[81]

These three components of the ethic of caring—the value placed on individual expressiveness, the appropriateness of emotions, and the capacity for empathy—pervade African-American culture. One of the best examples of the interactive nature of the importance of dialogue and the ethic of caring in assessing knowledge claims occurs in the use of the call and response discourse mode in traditional Black church services. In such services, both the minister and the congregation routinely use voice rhythm and vocal inflection to convey meaning. The sound of what is being said is just as important as the words themselves in what is, in a sense, a dialogue between reason and emotions. As a result, it is nearly impossible to filter out the strictly linguistic-cognitive abstract meaning from the sociocultural psycho-emotive meaning.[82] While the ideas presented by a speaker must have validity, that is, agree with the general body of knowledge shared by the Black congregation, the group also appraises the way knowledge claims are presented.

There is growing evidence that the ethic of caring may be part of women's experience as well. Certain dimensions of women's ways of knowing bear striking resemblance to Afrocentric expressions of the ethic of caring. Belenky, Clinchy, Goldberger, and Tarule point out that two contrasting epistemological orientations characterize knowing—one, an epistemology of separation based on impersonal procedures for establishing truth, and the other, an epistemology of connection in which truth emerges through care. While these ways of knowing are not gender specific, disproportionate numbers of women rely on connected knowing.[83]

The parallels between Afrocentric expressions of the ethic of caring and those advanced by feminist scholars are noteworthy. The emphasis placed on expressiveness and emotion in African-American communities bears marked resemblance to feminist perspectives on the importance of personality in connected knowing. Separate knowers try to subtract the personality of an individual from his or her ideas because they see personality as biasing those ideas. In contrast, connected knowers see personality as adding to an individual's ideas, and they feel that the personality of each group member enriches a group's understanding.[84] Similarly, the significance of individual uniqueness, personal expressiveness,

[81] Gwaltney, 11.
[82] Smitherman, 135 and 137.
[83] Belenky et al. (n. 59 above), 100–130.
[84] Ibid., 119.

and empathy in African-American communities resembles the importance that some feminist analyses place on women's "inner voice."[85]

The convergence of Afrocentric and feminist values in the ethic-of-care dimension of an alternative epistemology seems particularly acute. While white women may have access to a women's tradition valuing emotion and expressiveness, few white social institutions except the family validate this way of knowing. In contrast, Black women have long had the support of the Black church, an institution with deep roots in the African past and a philosophy that accepts and encourages expressiveness and an ethic of caring. While Black men share in this Afrocentric tradition, they must resolve the contradictions that distinguish abstract, unemotional Western masculinity from an Afrocentric ethic of caring. The differences among race/gender groups thus hinge on differences in their access to institutional supports valuing one type of knowing over another. Although Black women may be denigrated within white-male-controlled academic institutions, other institutions, such as Black families and churches, which encourage the expression of Black female power, seem to do so by way of their support for an Afrocentric feminist epistemology.

The ethic of personal accountability

An ethic of personal accountability is the final dimension of an alternative epistemology. Not only must individuals develop their knowledge claims through dialogue and present those knowledge claims in a style proving their concern for their ideas, people are expected to be accountable for their knowledge claims. Zilpha Elaw's description of slavery reflects this notion that every idea has an owner and that the owner's identity matters: "Oh, the abominations of slavery! . . . every case of slavery, however lenient its inflictions and mitigated its atrocities, indicates an oppressor, the oppressed, and oppression."[86] For Elaw, abstract definitions of slavery mesh with the concrete identities of its perpetrators and its victims. Blacks "consider it essential for individuals to have personal positions on issues and assume full responsibility for arguing their validity."[87]

[85] See ibid., 52–75, for a discussion of inner voice and its role in women's cognitive styles. Regarding empathy, Belenky et al. note: "Connected knowers begin with an interest in the facts of other people's lives, but they gradually shift the focus to other people's ways of thinking. . . . It is the form rather than the content of knowing that is central. . . . Connected learners learn through empathy" (115).

[86] Andrews (n. 48 above), 98.

[87] Kochman (n. 65 above), 20 and 25.

Assessments of an individual's knowledge claims simultaneously evaluate an individual's character, values, and ethics. African-Americans reject Eurocentric masculinist beliefs that probing into an individual's personal viewpoint is outside the boundaries of discussion. Rather, all views expressed and actions taken are thought to derive from a central set of core beliefs that cannot be other than personal.[88] From this perspective, knowledge claims made by individuals respected for their moral and ethical values will carry more weight than those offered by less respected figures.[89]

An example drawn from an undergraduate course composed entirely of Black women, which I taught, might help clarify the uniqueness of this portion of the knowledge-validation process. During one class discussion, I assigned the students the task of critiquing an analysis of Black feminism advanced by a prominent Black male scholar. Instead of dissecting the rationality of the author's thesis, my students demanded facts about the author's personal biography. They were especially interested in concrete details of his life such as his relationships with Black women, his marital status, and his social class background. By requesting data on dimensions of his personal life routinely excluded in positivist approaches to knowledge validation, they were invoking concrete experience as a criterion of meaning. They used this information to assess whether he really cared about his topic and invoked this ethic of caring in advancing their knowledge claims about his work. Furthermore, they refused to evaluate the rationality of his written ideas without some indication of his personal credibility as an ethical human being. The entire exchange could only have occurred as a dialogue among members of a class that had established a solid enough community to invoke an alternative epistemology in assessing knowledge claims.[90]

The ethic of personal accountability is clearly an Afrocentric value, but is it feminist as well? While limited by its attention to middle-class, white women, Carol Gilligan's work suggests that there is a female model for moral development where women are more inclined to link morality to responsibility, relationships, and the ability to maintain social ties.[91] If this is the case, then African-

[88] Ibid, 23.
[89] The sizable proportion of ministers among Black political leaders illustrates the importance of ethics in African-American communities.
[90] Belenky et al. discuss a similar situation. They note, "People could critique each other's work in this class and accept each other's criticisms because members of the group shared a similar experience. . . . Authority in connected knowing rests not on power or status or certification but on commonality of experience" (118).
[91] Carol Gilligan, *In a Different Voice* (Cambridge, Mass.: Harvard University Press, 1982). Carol Stack critiques Gilligan's model by arguing that African-Americans invoke a similar model of moral development to that used by women (see

American women again experience a convergence of values from Afrocentric and female institutions.

The use of an Afrocentric feminist epistemology in traditional Black church services illustrates the interactive nature of all four dimensions and also serves as a metaphor for the distinguishing features of an Afrocentric feminist way of knowing. The services represent more than dialogues between the rationality used in examining biblical texts/stories and the emotion inherent in the use of reason for this purpose. The rationale for such dialogues addresses the task of examining concrete experiences for the presence of an ethic of caring. Neither emotion nor ethics is subordinated to reason. Instead, emotion, ethics, and reason are used as interconnected, essential components in assessing knowledge claims. In an Afrocentric feminist epistemology, values lie at the heart of the knowledge-validation process such that inquiry always has an ethical aim.

Epistemology and Black feminist thought

Living life as an African-American woman is a necessary prerequisite for producing Black feminist thought because within Black women's communities thought is validated and produced with reference to a particular set of historical, material, and epistemological conditions.[92] African-American women who adhere to the idea that claims about Black women must be substantiated by Black women's sense of their own experiences and who anchor their knowledge claims in an Afrocentric feminist epistemology have produced a rich tradition of Black feminist thought.

Traditionally, such women were blues singers, poets, autobiographers, storytellers, and orators validated by the larger community of Black women as experts on a Black women's standpoint. Only a few unusual African-American feminist scholars have been able to defy Eurocentric masculinist epistemologies and explicitly embrace an Afrocentric feminist epistemology. Consider Alice Walker's description of Zora Neale Hurston: "In my mind, Zora Neale Hurston, Billie Holiday, and Bessie Smith form a sort of unholy trinity. Zora *belongs* in the tradition of Black women singers, rather than among 'the literati.' . . . Like Billie and Bessie she followed

---

"The Culture of Gender: Women and Men of Color," *Signs* 11, no. 2 [Winter 1986]: 321–24). Another difficulty with Gilligan's work concerns the homogeneity of the subjects whom she studied.

[92] Black men, white women, and members of other race, class, and gender groups should be encouraged to interpret, teach, and critique the Black feminist thought produced by African-American women.

her own road, believed in her own gods, pursued her own dreams, and refused to separate herself from 'common' people."[93]

Zora Neale Hurston is an exception for, prior to 1950, few Black women earned advanced degrees, and most of those who did complied with Eurocentric masculinist epistemologies. While these women worked on behalf of Black women, they did so within the confines of pervasive race and gender oppression. Black women scholars were in a position to see the exclusion of Black women from scholarly discourse, and the thematic content of their work often reflected their interest in examining a Black women's standpoint. However, their tenuous status in academic institutions led them to adhere to Eurocentric masculinist epistemologies so that their work would be accepted as scholarly. As a result, while they produced Black feminist thought, those Black women most likely to gain academic credentials were often least likely to produce Black feminist thought that used an Afrocentric feminist epistemology.

As more Black women earn advanced degrees, the range of Black feminist scholarship is expanding. Increasing numbers of African-American women scholars are explicitly choosing to ground their work in Black women's experiences, and, by doing so, many implicitly adhere to an Afrocentric feminist epistemology. Rather than being restrained by their "both/and" status of marginality, these women make creative use of their outsider-within status and produce innovative Black feminist thought. The difficulties these women face lie less in demonstrating the technical components of white male epistemologies than in resisting the hegemonic nature of these patterns of thought in order to see, value, and use existing alternative Afrocentric feminist ways of knowing.

In establishing the legitimacy of their knowledge claims, Black women scholars who want to develop Black feminist thought may encounter the often conflicting standards of three key groups. First, Black feminist thought must be validated by ordinary African-American women who grow to womanhood "in a world where the saner you are, the madder you are made to appear."[94] To be credible in the eyes of this group, scholars must be personal advocates for their material, be accountable for the consequences of their work, have lived or experienced their material in some fashion, and be willing to engage in dialogues about their findings with ordinary, everyday people. Second, if it is to establish its legitimacy, Black feminist thought also must be accepted by the community of Black women scholars. These scholars place varying amounts of importance on rearticulating a Black women's standpoint using an Afro-

[93] Walker (n. 72 above), 91.
[94] Gwaltney (n. 11 above), 7.

centric feminist epistemology. Third, Black feminist thought within academia must be prepared to confront Eurocentric masculinist political and epistemological requirements.

The dilemma facing Black women scholars engaged in creating Black feminist thought is that a knowledge claim that meets the criteria of adequacy for one group and thus is judged to be an acceptable knowledge claim may not be translatable into the terms of a different group. Using the example of Black English, June Jordan illustrates the difficulty of moving among epistemologies: "You cannot 'translate' instances of Standard English preoccupied with abstraction or with nothing/nobody evidently alive into Black English. That would warp the language into uses antithetical to the guiding perspective of its community of users. Rather you must first change those Standard English sentences, themselves, into ideas consistent with the person-centered assumptions of Black English."[95] While both worldviews share a common vocabulary, the ideas themselves defy direct translation.

Once Black feminist scholars face the notion that, on certain dimensions of a Black women's standpoint, it may be fruitless to try to translate ideas from an Afrocentric feminist epistemology into a Eurocentric masculinist epistemology, then the choices become clearer. Rather than trying to uncover universal knowledge claims that can withstand the translation from one epistemology to another, time might be better spent rearticulating a Black women's standpoint in order to give African-American women the tools to resist their own subordination. The goal here is not one of integrating Black female "folk culture" into the substantiated body of academic knowledge, for that substantiated knowledge is, in many ways, antithetical to the best interests of Black women. Rather, the process is one of rearticulating a preexisting Black women's standpoint and recentering the language of existing academic discourse to accommodate these knowledge claims. For those Black women scholars engaged in this rearticulation process, the social construction of Black feminist thought requires the skill and sophistication to decide which knowledge claims can be validated using the epistemological assumptions of one but not both frameworks, which claims can be generated in one framework and only partially accommodated by the other, and which claims can be made in both frameworks without violating the basic political and epistemological assumptions of either.

Black feminist scholars offering knowledge claims that cannot be accommodated by both frameworks face the choice between accepting the taken-for-granted assumptions that permeate white-male-controlled academic institutions or leaving academia. Those

---

[95] Jordan (n. 58 above), 130.

Black women who choose to remain in academia must accept the possibility that their knowledge claims will be limited to those claims about Black women that are consistent with a white male worldview. And yet those African-American women who leave academia may find their work is inaccessible to scholarly communities.

Black feminist scholars offering knowledge claims that can be partially accommodated by both epistemologies can create a body of thought that stands outside of either. Rather than trying to synthesize competing worldviews that, at this point in time, may defy reconciliation, their task is to point out common themes and concerns. By making creative use of their status as mediators, their thought becomes an entity unto itself that is rooted in two distinct political and epistemological contexts.[96]

Those Black feminists who develop knowledge claims that both epistemologies can accommodate may have found a route to the elusive goal of generating so-called objective generalizations that can stand as universal truths. Those ideas that are validated as true by African-American women, African-American men, white men, white women, and other groups with distinctive standpoints, with each group using the epistemological approaches growing from its unique standpoint, thus become the most objective truths.[97]

Alternative knowledge claims, in and of themselves, are rarely threatening to conventional knowledge. Such claims are routinely ignored, discredited, or simply absorbed and marginalized in existing paradigms. Much more threatening is the challenge that alternative epistemologies offer to the basic process used by the powerful to legitimate their knowledge claims. If the epistemology used to validate knowledge comes into question, then all prior knowledge claims validated under the dominant model become suspect. An alternative epistemology challenges all certified knowledge and opens up the question of whether what has been taken to be true can stand the test of alternative ways of validating truth. The existence of an independent Black women's standpoint using an Afrocentric feminist epistemology calls into question the content of what currently passes as truth and simultaneously challenges the process of arriving at that truth.

Department of Afro-American Studies
University of Cincinnati

---

[96] Collins (n. 3 above).

[97] This point addresses the question of relativity in the sociology of knowledge and offers a way of regulating competing knowledge claims.

WALTER R. ALLEN   is professor of sociology at the University of California, Los Angeles. His research focuses on inequality linked to race, gender, and class in American institutions and life. He is coeditor of *Beginnings: The Social and Affective Development of Black Children* (Hillside, N.J.: Erlbaum, 1985) with Margaret Spencer and Geraldine Brookins and the author of *The Colorline and the Quality of Life in America* (New York: Russell Sage, 1987) with Reynolds Farley. His most recent work is *College in Black and White: Black Students on Black and White Campuses* (Albany: State University of New York Press, in press), coedited with Edgar Epps and Nesha Hanif.

MAXINE BACA ZINN   is professor of sociology at the University of Michigan—Flint. She has published a variety of articles on family, race, and gender. She is coauthor with D. Stanley Eitzen of *Diversity in American Families* (New York: Harper & Row, 1987), a textbook that seeks to demythologize the family and show how public issues shape the private lives of a population varied in class, race, and gender, and of *The Reshaping of America* (Englewood Cliffs, N.J.: Prentice-Hall, 1988), a volume examining the social consequences of the changing economy. She is now working on a collection of readings about women of color.

ELSA BARKLEY BROWN   is a lecturer in history and sociology at the State University of New York at Binghamton. She is interested in the historical development of African-American communities in the southern United States, particularly the relationship between culture, class, and consciousness in the formation and maintenance of communities. She is also exploring the development of theoretical frameworks and methodological approaches that provide a holistic view of the lives of African-American peoples.

RITA CARROLL-SEGUIN   is assistant professor of sociology at the State University of New York College at Cortland. She is interested in stratification processes, in particular, the relationship between state activity, ethnicity, and household income strategies. Her recent publications include "The Proletarianization of Asian-American Women in Hawaii," in *Research in Inequality and Social Conflict*, vol. 2, ed. Michael Dobroski and Isador Williams (Greenwich, Conn.: JAI Press, in press); "Asian-American Success in Hawaii: Myth, Reality or Artifact of Women's Labor," in *Race, Sexism and the World System*, ed. Joan Smith et al. (Westport, Conn.: Greenwood Press, 1988): 187–207, coauthored with James A. Geschwender; and "The Portuguese and Haoles of Hawaii: Implications for the Origin of Ethnicity," *American Sociological Review* 53, no. 4 (August 1988): 515–27, coauthored with

James A. Geschwender and Howard Brill. Currently she is collaborating with Robert L. Bach on a book-length study of Southeast Asian refugees.

PATRICIA HILL COLLINS   is associate professor of Afro-American studies and sociology at the University of Cincinnati. She is the author of "Learning from the Outsider Within: The Sociological Significance of Black Feminist Thought," *Social Problems* 33, no. 6 (October/December 1986): S14–S32; "The Meaning of Motherhood in Black Culture and Black Mother/Daughter Relationships," *Sage* 4, no. 2 (Fall 1987): 2–9; and *Black Feminist Thought* (Winchester, Mass.: Unwin Hyman, 1990).

MARY CORCORAN   is professor of political science and social work at the University of Michigan. Her research interests include sex-based wage differences, intergenerational mobility, and poverty. She is coauthor with Christopher Jencks et al. of *Who Gets Ahead* (New York: Basic, 1979).

BONNIE THORNTON DILL   is associate professor of sociology and founding director of the Center for Research on Women at Memphis State University. She currently serves as a research professor with the center. She has published in *Feminist Studies* and the *Journal of Family History* and is currently working on an edited book on women of color in the United States as well as a research project on female-headed families in rural Southern communities.

GREG J. DUNCAN   is program director of the Institute for Social Research at the University of Michigan. Primarily interested in the dynamic aspects of poverty, welfare, and labor markets, he is author with Richard D. Coe et al. of *Years of Poverty, Years of Plenty* (Ann Arbor, Mich.: Institute for Social Research, 1984), which summarizes the findings from the Panel Study of Income Dynamics project.

JAMES A. GESCHWENDER   is chair of sociology at the State University of New York at Binghamton. He has published in the area of racial and ethnic stratification with special emphasis on Afro-Americans on the U.S. mainland and on Asian-Americans in Hawaii. He is coauthor with Rita M. Carroll-Seguin of "The Proletarianization of Asian-American Women in Hawaii," in *Research in Inequality and Social Conflict*, vol. 2, ed. Michael Dobroski and Isador Williams (Greenwich, Conn.: JAI Press, in press). At present he is exploring ethnic and gender issues through comparative Canadian–United States research projects.

CHERYL TOWNSEND GILKES   is associate professor of sociology and African-American studies at Colby College in Waterville, Maine. Her publications include articles related to black women and their community work and articles assessing the role of women in the construction of African-American religious tradition. Her current research examines the importance of the Sanctified Church in a changing African-American community. An ordained Baptist minister, she serves as an associate minister at the Union Baptist Church of Cambridge, Massachusetts.

SHARON HARLEY   is associate professor of Afro-American studies at the University of Maryland at College Park. Her published work includes "Mary Church Terrell: Genteel Militant," in *Nineteenth-Century Black Leaders*, ed. August Meier and Leon Litwack (Urbana: University of Illinois Press, 1989), 307–21; "Black

Women in a Southern City: Washington, D.C., 1890–1920," in *Sex, Race, and the Role of Women in the South*, ed. JoAnne V. Hawks and Sheila L. Skamp (Jackson: University of Mississippi, 1983): 59–74; and *Women in Africa and the African Diaspora* (Washington, D.C.: Howard University Press, 1987), coedited with Rosalyn Terborg-Penn and Andrea Benton Rushing. She is currently working on an article on the development of a working-class consciousness among Afro-American women.

MARTHA S. HILL   is associate research scientist at the Institute for Social Research at the University of Michigan. Her research focuses on dynamic analyses of behavior related to economic well-being and family structure. Her work, including "Welfare Dependence within and across Generations," *Science* 239, no. 4839 (January 29, 1988): 467–71, coauthored with Greg J. Duncan and Saul D. Hoffman, examines childhood economic experiences and influences of childhood factors on adult circumstances and various aspects of marriage, living arrangements, child support, poverty, and labor market experience.

DEBORAH K. KING   is associate professor of sociology at Dartmouth College. Her gender research primarily concerns the development of an Afrocentric perspective on race, class, and gender in black women's political consciousness and activism. Presently she is completing a book that examines the enforcement of affirmative action policies in institutions of higher education.

DIANE K. LEWIS   is professor of anthropology at the University of California, Santa Cruz. Her research on minorities and the AIDS epidemic is reflected in her published work, which includes "Human Immunodeficiency Virus Seroprevalence in Female Intravenous Drug Users: The Puzzle of Black Women's Risk," coauthored with John K. Watters, in *Social Science and Medicine* (in press); and "The Prevalence of High Risk Sexual Behavior in Male Intravenous Drug Users with Steady Female Partners," coauthored with John K. Watters and Patricia Case, *American Journal of Public Health* (in press).

MICHELINE RIDLEY MALSON   is an assistant professor in public policy at Duke University. Her interests include research on black single-parent families headed by women, black women and gender roles, and social policy and social programs. She is author·of "Black Women's Sex Roles: The Social Context for a New Ideology," *Journal of Social Issues* 39, no. 3 (1983): 101–14; and "The Social Support Systems of Black Families," *Marriage and Family Review* 5, no. 4 (1983): 37–58; and she is coeditor with Jean F. O'Barr, Sarah Westphal-Wihl, and Mary Wyer of *Feminist Theory in Practice and Process* (Chicago: University of Chicago Press, 1989).

SUSAN A. MANN   is associate professor of sociology and director of the women's studies program at the University of New Orleans. She has published a number of articles on rural development in the United States, domestic labor, abortion, and child care—most recently, "Modernization and the Family: A Theoretical Analysis," *Sociological Perspectives* 32, no. 1 (Spring 1989): 109–27, coauthored with A. V. Margavio. Her book *Capitalism and American Agriculture: Obstacles to the Use of Wage Labor* is forthcoming from the University of North Carolina Press.

ELISABETH MUDIMBE-BOYI   is associate professor in the Romance studies department at Duke University. Her most recent publications include *L'Oeuvre Romanesque de Jacque-Stephen Alexis, ecrivain Haïtien* ([1975]; rev. ed., Paris: Editions Silex, 1990); "Ken Bugul, Senegalese Writer," in *Fifty African and Caribbean Female Writers*, ed. Anne Adams (Westport, Conn.: Greenwood Press, 1990); and "Pluie et vent sur Télumée miracle de Simone Schwarz-Bart: Mémoire du temps et prise de parole," *Selected Proceedings of the Third and Fourth Annual Wichita State University Conference on Continental, Latin American, and Francophone Women Writers* (Washington, D.C.: American University Press, 1989). She is an editorial board member of *Research in African Literatures* and an associate editor of *Signs*.

JEAN F. O'BARR   is director of women's studies at Duke University, where she teaches in the political science department. Her interests focus on contemporary feminism and women in higher education. She is the editor of *Women and a New Academy: Gender and Cultural Contexts* (Madison: University of Wisconsin Press, 1989); and coeditor of *Reconstructing the Academy: Women's Education and Women's Studies* (Chicago: University of Chicago Press, 1988) with Elizabeth Minnich and Rachel Rosenfeld, *Sex and Scientific Inquiry* (Chicago: University of Chicago Press, 1987) with Sandra Harding, and *Feminist Theory in Practice and Process* (Chicago: University of Chicago Press, 1989) with Micheline R. Malson, Sarah Westphal-Wihl, and Mary Wyer. She currently serves as editor of *Signs*.

DIANNE F. SADOFF   is professor of English at Colby College in Waterville, Maine. Interested in psychoanalysis, literary theory, and nineteenth-century feminism, she has written *Monsters of Affection: Dickens, Brontë, and Eliot on Fatherhood* (Baltimore: Johns Hopkins University Press, 1982), as well as essays on Victorian and contemporary writers. She is currently working on a book on the consolidation of institutional culture in the nineteenth century and a book on teaching literary theory to undergraduates.

PATRICIA J. WILLIAMS   is a professor in the law school at the University of Wisconsin—Madison. She teaches commercial and consumer law and jurisprudence and is currently working on a book that examines the intersection of constitutional rights and commercial interests.

MARY WYER   is managing editor of *Signs*. She was associate acquisitions editor at the University of Wisconsin Press, 1980–82, and administrative coordinator of the Women's Studies Program at MIT, 1983–85. She is coeditor of *Feminist Theory in Practice and Process* (Chicago: University of Chicago Press, 1989) with Micheline R. Malson, Jean F. O'Barr, and Sarah Westphal-Wihl.

INDEX

Lightning Source UK Ltd.
Milton Keynes UK
UKHW010138300921
391396UK00004B/208